NOT ONLY THE MASTER'S TOOLS

Cultural Politics & the Promise of Democracy
A Series from Paradigm Publishers
Edited by Henry A. Giroux

NOT ONLY THE MASTER'S TOOLS
African-American Studies in Theory and Practice

EDITED WITH AN INTRODUCTION BY

LEWIS R. GORDON AND
JANE ANNA GORDON

Paradigm Publishers
Boulder • London

Copyright © 2006 by Lewis R. Gordon and Jane Anna Gordon

Published in the United States by Paradigm Publishers, 3360 Mitchell Lane Suite E, Boulder, Colorado 80301 USA.

Paradigm Publishers is the trade name of Birkenkamp & Company, LLC, Dean Birkenkamp, President and Publisher.

Library of Congress Cataloging-in-Publication Data

Not only the master's tools : African-American studies in theory and practice / edited with an introduction by Lewis R. Gordon and Jane Anna Gordon.
    p. cm.
    Includes bibliographical references and index.
    ISBN 1-59451-146-2 (hc) — ISBN 1-59451-147-0 (pbk)
    1. African Americans—Study and teaching.   2. African Americans—Intellectual life. 3. African American philosophy.   I. Gordon, Lewis R. (Lewis Ricardo), 1962–   II. Gordon, Jane Anna, 1976–

    E184.7.N68 2006
    973'.04960730071—dc22

                                                            2005030856

Printed and bound in the United States of America on acid-free paper that meets the standards of the American National Standard for Permanence of Paper for Printed Library Materials.

Designed and Typeset by Straight Creek Bookmakers.

10   09   08   07   06
1   2   3   4   5

To "Uncle Paget,"

a tireless warrior in the struggle for ideas

Contents

ᗡ

Introduction:
Not Only the Master's Tools

Lewis R. Gordon and Jane Anna Gordon

✧

"The master's tools will never dismantle the master's house." So went Audre Lorde's credo in *Sister Outsider*, which has stood as a guiding principle of subaltern studies. It has meant avoiding the trappings of Eurocentric scholarship and the disciplinary edicts encompassed by it.

The guiding principle of this collection of essays, with no disrespect to Lorde's important contributions intended, is that dismantling the master's house is a misguided project. Even if it were true that his house cannot be dismantled by his tools, slaves have historically done something more provocative with such tools than attempt to dismantle the Big House. There are those who used those tools, developed additional ones, and built houses of their own on more or less generous soil. It is our view that the proper response is to follow their lead, transcending rather than dismantling Western ideas through building our own houses of thought. When enough houses are built, the hegemony of the master's house—in fact, *mastery itself*—will cease to maintain its imperial status. Shelter needn't be the rooms offered by such domination.

The area of research that became known as Black Studies, then African-American Studies and then Africana Studies, has faced questions of how its subject matter should be approached. The dominant approach is to treat Black Studies as an area of research in which training in other disciplines is applied to the study of black people. Whether as Black Studies, African-American Studies, or Africana Studies, a peculiar feature of this area of research is its clear interdisciplinary ethos. To be in Black Studies means, always, to have more than one disciplinary identity and to face the accompanying concern of which disciplines are best suited for engagement with the African diaspora. In some programs and departments, for instance, the view was that the purpose of this area of research was to respond to the lacuna of historical and social scientific research on black folk. The result was a preference for social scientifically oriented disciplines and research studies such as those found in history, anthropology, economics, sociology, and political science departments. Moreover, the founding of Black Studies programs in the late 1960s—often through mechanisms of student protest, most of which was linked to the Black Power movement—came with the prevalent demand for knowledge that would affect national policy. Such demand was ironic since the first Black Studies program, at San Francisco State University, was founded by a group of artists, including Leroi Jones/ Amiri Barka and Sonia Sanchez, from the Black Arts Movement. A moment's look into the tenets of that movement clarifies why they decided to found programs for the academic study of black folk: Indeed, the basic argument of the Black Arts Movement was that art affects the symbols by which people appear in the world—and how people appear has great political consequence. Black Power demanded that control of the means of image production be seized, and the artist intellectuals of the Black Arts Movement attempted to do just that.

Black Studies/African-American Studies/Africana Studies was born with the express purpose of *decolonizing the minds of people, especially black people.* Although much knowledge can be produced by writing histories and social scientific studies, no amount of information could get very far in the absence of minds unable to see or understand it. Important as empirical work has been and continues to be, without interpretation, even at the level of the methods used for organizing the research and gathering data, such work would be meaningless. The power of interpretation is such, however, that it, too, is embedded in a special type of interpretation or hermeneutic without which it, as well, would be meaningless. And that interpretation we call *theory.*

Without a theoretical framework, the kind of hermeneutic that brings meaning to interpretations, most interpretations would function no better than simple hypotheses in long strings of ideas with the lukewarm designation of "maybe." Theoretical frameworks, however, also tend to be embedded in experiences germane to societies and their theorists whose creative work stimulated their birth. What this means is that the theories on which interpretations depend become that on which even our empirical work relies, and such dependency has political consequences. Should Black Studies abrogate responsibility for the theoretical frameworks that inform its production of knowledge, then the very decolonization project sought would be undermined. We call this consequence *epistemological colonization.*

Theory is not only a tool of the master. It belongs to us all since it is that without which we could not build our own thought. There is, then, an important role for theoretical work in Black Studies/African-American Studies/Africana Studies. The purpose of this collection of essays is to undertake such theoretical exploration. To achieve that task, we have organized the text in two parts. Part I explores the location of thought and the question of theoretical reason by examining the geopoliticality of reason. By this, we mean the convergence of place and power in the formation of thought. Each of the essays in that section addresses a dimension of Frantz Fanon's insight, in *Black Skin, White Masks,* that modern reason seems to exhibit an allergic reaction to black folk. They each also engage and expand upon W. E. B. Du Bois's insight into the doubled existence stimulated by such a problematic historic relationship to the norms of reason in the modern world. Part II examines the question of practical reason and what it means to be, in Fanon's terms, *actional.* In keeping with the guiding position of the essays in that section, which is that thought and action need not be separated, they explore some of the salient ways in which both affect and effect each other in pedagogy under conditions of slavery, intimate relations in a world devoid of normative approval, struggles with and for legitimacy in political life, and ethical reflection under circumstances that call for engagement with a historically rich yet hostile social world.

It is with these considerations in mind that we now begin our journey.

Acknowledgments

‌❧

We would like to thank Henry Giroux for his encouragement and support in the course of this project. "Papa John" Comaroff and "Grandma Jean" Comaroff deserve thanks, as well, for their supportive discussions while we were thinking through this project. And we here extend special thanks to Doug Ficek, our very gifted graduate research assistant at the Institute for the Study of Race and Social Thought, who carefully read through the manuscript and offered valuable suggestions for its improvement. Joyce Ann Joyce and Walter Gholson also deserve thanks for their availability during times of need as well as those of joy. Thanks as well to Susan Herbst, whose creativity and generosity continue to be inspiring. And as always, our love to our children, Mathieu, Jennifer, Sula, and Elijah; may wisdom always accompany you on life's way.

Jane Anna and Lewis R. Gordon

PART ONE
THE GEOPOLITICALITY OF AFRICAN-AMERICAN EPISTEMIC STRUGGLES

I
African-American Philosophy, Race, and the Geography of Reason

Lewis R. Gordon

✧

> Reason was confident of victory on every level. I put all the parts
> back together. But I had to change my tune. That victory played
> cat and mouse; it made a fool of me. As the other put it, when I
> was present, it was not; when it was there, I was no longer.
>
> —*Frantz Fanon*

African-American philosophy is one of the most recently developed
areas of theoretical reflection in African-American Studies. Its emergence is in many ways marked by the realization of many scholars
that philosophy offers much to the enterprise of studying the African diaspora, and that the unique categories of thought endemic to
that diaspora offer many challenges to modern and contemporary
philosophy. Central to this development has been the importance of
philosophical anthropology in the study of race and the challenges
posed by race to our understanding of philosophical anthropology.
Added to this insight is the anxiety that is a function of studying
Africana communities and the ideas they stimulate.

African-American philosophy is an area of Africana philosophy.
By "Africana philosophy" I mean the set of philosophical problems
and their critical discussion raised by the historical political situation of the African diaspora. African-American philosophy focuses
on the New World aspect of that diaspora.

Although Africans in America preceded the introduction of Europeans and even the conception of "America," "Europe," and "Africa,"

the convergence of the three is, for the most part, a modern affair. The peculiarity of that convergence has the form of what Michel Foucault, in *"Society Must Be Defended,"* calls "subjugated knowledge." It is a form of thought that relates to modernity in much the same way as does the "unconscious" in Freudian psychoanalysis—that is, as a repressed reality. But as Jean-Paul Sartre pointed out in his discussion of bad faith in the first part of *Being and Nothingness,* the "unconscious" seems to have a rather clear point of view. The African-American experience of repression has been both psychoanalytical and political. The psychoanalytical aspect pertains to psychosocial invisibility. The political aspect, which also has historical implications, concerns the set of repressive practices that mark the modern world's relation to black communities—relations of colonization and racism. The consequence is one not only of social and political invisibility but also of historical amnesia. That people have been settling in the southern hemisphere of the New World for more than 40,000 years suggests that the question of African America poses a double movement of people to the New World, whom *we,* people of today, could recognize as those we call *black people,* and then subsequently, with respect to more recent black people from Africa, whom we could call *modern black people.*[1] The tendency to locate blackness as a fundamentally modern phenomenon means, however, that those premodern, morphologically dark people who lived in the Americas for so many millennia before Columbus's 1492 expedition should properly be designated not as black people but simply as early or premodern Americans. We may ask, as well, how we should place premodern Scandinavians such as Leif Erikson and his crew of Vikings, who made it to the northern New World as early as 1001 a.c.e. By the same stroke of reasoning that would make it ridiculous for us to say that Erikson was not "white" because of the absence of the epistemic framework for such an identity until the nineteenth century, we should be able to admit, at least, that those settlers in ancient South America nearly 40,000 years ago were black simply because the only morphologically white people around at that time were the Neanderthals in Europe and Western Asia. In this sense, then, Black American history has a large premodern set of chapters to be written.

Complicating the matter, however, is that not all people who are designated African in the contemporary world are also considered black anywhere. And similarly, not all people who are considered in most places to be black are considered African anywhere. There are nonblack Africans who are descended from people living on the African continent who can be traced back more than a millennium, and there are indigenous Pacific peoples and peoples of India whose consciousness and life are marked by a black identity. One could claim that in the context of North, Central, and South America, "black" and "African" are sufficiently identical to warrant their functioning as synonyms. A problem, however, is that such a view raises important questions of what it means to study blacks and to study Africans and to study their convergence in African America. For example, black studies, although it includes much of Africa, also extends beyond its reach. To accommodate this extension, one needs to add the term "diasporic," and with that addition, one would expect some isomorphism with the term "black." But even that does not work since, as we have just seen, the *modern* African diaspora is very different from its premodern notion. The premodern or, better, *primordial* African diaspora is, after all, *humanity* itself since it refers to the initial groups of people who spread across the earth from Africa during those times. Unless it is simply by fiat, we thus cannot avoid struggling with the distinctiveness of the categories "black" and "African."

Let us, then, simply use the term *African American* to refer specifically to the convergence of African and black in the New World continents and regions of the modern world. And by African-American philosophy let us then mean the modern philosophical discourse that emerges from that diasporic community, including its Francophone, Hispanophone, and Lusophone creolizations. To articulate the central features and themes of the thought based on that intellectual heritage, I would like to begin by outlining the ideas of two men who have been the greatest influences on many (if not most) of us in the field—namely, W. E. B. Du Bois and Frantz Fanon.

W.E.B. Du Bois is important to the study of blacks and the development of black thought in the New World because he articulated most of the important themes of this area of inquiry. If there is any doubt, a consultation of nearly every text in the field would reveal his influence. Although many concepts have been generated by this great writer's work, I should like to focus on just two here, since in many ways they have proven to be the most persistent in the thought of subsequent generations of Africana thinkers.

Du Bois and the Theodicean Problematic

Du Bois recognized that the *question* of black people was of philosophical importance. He formulated it hermeneutically, in *The Souls of Black Folk,* as *the meaning* of Negro/black. He understood, from his earlier empirical work on blacks in Philadelphia, that studying black people was not like studying other peoples. In his essay "The Study of the Negro Problems," he made this clear in terms of the challenges it posed to positivistic science. In the first chapter of *The Souls of Black Folk,* he put it thus: "What does it mean to be a problem?" I have provided a detailed discussion of the implications of this question in the fourth chapter of my book *Existentia Africana.* For our purposes here, however, I should like simply to point out that the question has an implicit methodological position: People should be studied as human beings, but what do we do when the humanity of some groups is challenged? We need, in other words, to find a way to study black people without black people becoming problems-in-themselves.

The question of problem-people also raises a theodicean question. From the conjunction of the Greek words "Zdeus" (which became "deus," "theus," and then "theo") and "dike," the term "theodicy" refers to God's justice or the justice of God. It is an area of inquiry in which one attempts to find an account of the compatibility of an all-good and all-powerful God with a world marked by injustice and evil. Theodicean problems emerge, as shown in John Hick's *Evil and the God of Love* and Kwame Gyekye's *An Essay on African Philosophical Thought,* from any system of thought in which God or a perfect set of gods is the source both of being and of value. Most theodicean arguments defend God's goodness as compatible with God's omniscience and omnipotence either through an appeal to our ignorance of God's ultimate plan for us all or through an appreciation of the freedom endowed to us by God. In the first instance, the conclusion is that things only *appear* bad because serving God's purpose is ultimately good. In the second, injustice and evil are our fault because they are consequences of our free will, which is, in the end, a good thing. In either formulation, God is without culpability for evil and injustice. In the Modern Age, theodicy has paradoxically been *secularized.* Whereas God once functioned as the object, the rationalization, and the legitimation of an argument, other systems have come into play, such as systems of knowledge and political systems, and they have taken up the void left by God. The clear system of knowledge is modern science and the modes of rationalization it offers. Political systemic rationalization avers an intrinsic goodness and justice of the given political system. Thus, unlike the Foucauldian model in *Discipline and Punish* that queries the phantom head of the king in nondiscursive practices, we face here the persistent grammar of theodicy even in an avowed-secular age. In the context of modern attitudes toward and political treatment of black folks, a special kind of theodicean grammar has asserted itself. The appeal to blacks as problem-people is an assertion of their ultimate location *outside* the systems of order and rationality.[2] The logic is straightforward: A perfect system cannot have imperfections. Since blacks claim to be contradictions of a perfect system, the imperfection must either be an error in reasoning (mere "appearance") or lie in black folk themselves. Blacks become rationalized as the extraneous *evil* of a *just system.*

The formation of such systems and their theodicean rationalizations lead to the generations of new forms of life—namely, those in the system and those outside the system. The "outside" is an invisible reality generated, in its invisibility, as nonexistent. The effect, then, is that a new link with theodicy emerges and the result is *theobiodicean*—that is, characterized by the rationalization of forms of life that are inherently justified versus those that could never be justified under the principles of the systems that form both. The result is, as Du Bois famously observed, the splitting of worlds and consciousness itself into the normative and its contradictions.

Du Bois outlines the relationship of blacks to the political and epistemic order of the modern world in *The Souls of Black Folk* and in the section on white folks in *Darkwater* through the lived-reality of double consciousness. Discussion of this concept is vast in the secondary literature on Du Bois, which I will not outline here.[3] Instead, I should like simply to focus on my reading of the concept as fundamentally coextensive. It manifests itself, in other words, in several organizing motifs. The first, negative formulation is of the psychological constitution of the self. There, one is yoked to a self-image that is entirely a function of how one is seen by others. To be black, in that sense, means to be so in exclusively white terms. Another version of double consciousness emerges from the double standards of citizenship, whereby one is, say, born an American but discovers that one is not fully a citizen by virtue of being racially designated black. Why, we may ask, is being black treated as antipathetic to being an American? This leads to the notion of irreconcilable doubleness, whereby being black does not equal being an American—yet much of what is original about being an American, as Ralph Ellison showed in *Going to the Territory,* comes from blacks in America. This insight is crucial because the mainstream (i.e., white) American self-image is one of supposedly being an original site from which blacks play only the role of imitation. Think of Toni Morrison's brilliant exploration of this thesis in *The Bluest Eye,* in which, as Gary Schwartz (1997) showed, blackness suffered the plight of being a mere imitation of life. To be an imitation is to stand as secondary to another standard—namely, the original or the prototype. We see this view of blacks in popular culture, where the adjective "black" is added to things white to suggest imitation: black Jesus, black Mozart, Ms. Black America, and so on. Blacks are even treated as imitations of their own artifacts. Few today realize, for instance, that rock 'n' roll is a form of black music, and most of the people following the Jewish and Christian faiths imagine them to be European in origin instead of East African and from the *colored* Middle East.

There is also an epistemological dimension of double consciousness. The correlate of normative knowledge is the set of mainstream disciplines and their approaches to the study of black folk. The standard view is that things white represent universality and things black are locked in the web of particularity. The problem with this view from the perspective of double consciousness is that it relies on denying the contradictions of the system. Thus, only the false, self-deceiving image of a pristine, all-encompassing (white) America is offered. Blacks in America exemplify the contradictions of the political and epistemological system; they are the nation's dirty laundry. The exposure of contradictions means that whereas whiteness relies on a narcissistic self-deceptive notion of the American social and political system's completeness, blackness relies on pointing out the system's incompleteness, imperfections, and contradictions. This is the insight behind the black folk adage: "One mind for the white man to see/Another that I know is me." In short, the black world is more linked to truth than the white world because the black world realizes that the domain over which truth claims can appeal is much larger than the white world in general is willing to admit. The black world and the white world in this formulation do not refer to every individual black or white person but to those who live by the value systems of these worlds. For instance, whites who study America through the lens of Black Studies often develop the same outrage that blacks and other people of color share. Unlike the popular claim that the purpose of Black Studies is to offer the narcissism of images of the self in the form of instructor, a view totally compatible with white-centric studies but in black face, the more awkward reality is that it offers something sufficiently lacking in the (white) dominant disciplines to stimulate such ire on the part of students—namely, *truth*. It is not that there is *no* truth in most areas of the humanities and the social sciences, as well as the life sciences; rather, there is *limited* truth in these areas precisely because of the imposition of white normativity as a subtextual mode of legitimation. One could argue that pursuing truth in the way demanded by Black Studies might be too much to demand of instructors from other disciplines, but such an excuse could hardly be accepted by Black Studies scholars, all of whom have to work through the tenets of a minimum of two disciplinary perspectives—the white normative one and the contradictions they see from the standpoint of the world of color. What they take the time to learn is exactly what students think scholars and teachers committed to knowledge and learning should do: Explore the full domain of their subject matter, which includes taking its contradictions seriously. They may not be perfect in such an endeavor, but the spirit of such an approach offers a set of obligations responding to which would constitute a more rigorous pursuit of truth.

Epistemological doubling leads to axiological questions emerging from white normativity. Here the problem of value can be examined through, ironically, Friedrich Nietzsche's *Will to Power*, on the one hand, and Anna Julia Cooper's "What Are We Worth?" from *A Voice from the South*, on the other. According to Nietzsche, values suffer the symptomatic fate of nihilism when undergoing the social process of decay. When healthy, the response to the adversities of life takes the form of bringing about life-affirming values. The unhealthy response is to seek the elimination of adversity instead of issuing a constructive response to it. From a white normative perspective, white people are healthier than black people because of the absence of social pathologies associated with black people. Yet, an immediate black response is that most white people could not live in the shoes of black folk. Think, for instance, of the statistics on suicide: A mere 1 or 2 percent rise in unemployment, as Alvin Poussaint and Amy Alexander show in *Lay My Burden Down,* leads to suicide among whites, while many blacks, particularly black men, consistently experience an unemployment rate that is double that of their white counterparts. The travails faced by blacks in the modern age stimulated the leitmotif of modernity—namely, the blues. Although whites, too, suffer the blues, the fact is that the blues came out of black, not white, America. The litany of contributions—from George Washington Carver's discoveries of hundreds of things to do with a peanut to African Americans' development of unique religious institutions and innovations in mathematics and physics, despite lynchings, American Apartheid, and systematic policies of underdevelopment—suggests, from the Nietzschean perspective, a greater degree of health in black America than might be expected. Added to this observation is Cooper's efficiency thesis of health: that a system and a group within it are healthy if they are able to contribute much more to society than what is invested in them. The upshot of the matter is that while American public discourse protests against investing in black America, the amount expended on white America, especially as one climbs the economic ladder, far exceeds what those individuals are able to contribute. Many blacks with less simply produce more than many whites with more. This is not to say that the argument must be race specific. After all, there are affluent blacks in whom much has been invested without many social returns. But the numbers of such blacks are so small that the point becomes inconsequential. At the systemic level, we must ask whether the social and economic investment in white supremacy produces a healthy or sick value system. That it is increasingly very expensive "to live white" offers a negative answer.

Finally, but not exclusively so, there is the phenomenological consequence of all this. That double consciousness is a form of *consciousness* already locates it as a subject rich with phenomenological significance. Phenomenology, after all, examines meaningful reality as constituted by consciousness, wherein consciousness is understood in its intentional form as always having to be *of* something. The consciousnesses that manifest themselves in double consciousness are (1) consciousness of how mainstream America sees itself (dominant "reality") and (2) consciousness of its contradictions (black reality). Since to see both is to see the dialectical relationship constitutive of truth, then the first by itself must manifest a form of consciousness that hides itself. The first, by itself, stands as a form of bad faith. Of course, there could be a third form: consciousness of both while denying itself in a reaffirmed unity of the first. That, too, is a form of bad faith; but, as Ralph Ellison showed in the Golden Day episode in *Invisible Man*, where the protagonist encounters a group of educated blacks on a day out from the local asylum, such flight opens the door to madness. As Fanon later observed in his resignation letter from Blida-Joinville Hospital in Algiers, published in *Toward the African Revolution:* "Madness is one of the means man has of losing his freedom" (p. 53).

Although there is much more that can be said about Du Bois's thought, our main point is established in these two governing themes: Domination and oppression underlie American discursive practices of knowledge and power. Du Bois places the philosophical anthropological problem at the forefront with the normative one: We must ask what it means *not* to be a problem, and we need also to ask what it means to be so in a world in which not being so would not be tantamount to being sick.

Fanon's Sociogenic Analysis

An added feature of a phenomenological turn is not only its foundations in an intentional theory of consciousness but also the phenomenological injunction against notions of disembodied consciousness. Du Bois's reflections bring to the fore the lived reality of a problematic consciousness. Such a consciousness finds itself embroiled in a dialectic of constantly encountering an alien reflection of the self in the social world. Fanon, in *Black Skin, White Masks,* presents a powerful portrait of what it means to live ensnared by the search for the self in an antipathetic other's eyes, or *the dialectics of recognition.* He shows that colonialism created a form of phobogenic imposition that infected intersubjective relations and the methods of their understanding and evaluation. Put concretely: Reason had a tendency to exit whatever room he entered. Fanon's critique, even of methodologies offered by colonial disciplinary practices, can be characterized as the identification of *epistemological colonialism*—colonization at the level of knowledge.[4]

The alien black self is one of the products of such colonial practice. Yet, knowledge of the constructed aspects of a self fails to transform that self where the standpoint of appearance is always a colonial one. In effect, the search for recognition, of being valued as a self, of appearing to others, suffers from a psychopathological factor: Modern colonialism leaves no room for a normal black body. The basis of so-called recognition is stratified abnormality. The black is either flawed by virtue of not being white or flawed by virtue of appearing "too white," which is abnormal for a black. Further, since the Self-Other dialectic constitutes ethical relationships premised upon a hidden equality (each self is another's other and vice versa), and since antiblack racism depends on a fundamental inequality (a human-below-human relation from the standpoint of the white, a human-other-human relation from the standpoint of the black), a system of unilateral ethical relations results, wherein blacks experience ethical responsibility in relation to whites but whites do not exemplify such reciprocity. The consequence is that racism destroys the Self-Other dialectic and collapses into the doubled world identified by double consciousness: a Self-Other *and* Nonself-Nonother structure. It is, in other words, the denial of the humanity of the black as *another human being* before the white. In effect, then, the struggle against at least the antiblack racism manifested by modern colonialism entails an effort to change what Fanon calls the *sociogenic* consequences of that world, to transform the society into both formal and substantive instances of reciprocal Self-Other dialectics of ethical relations between whites and blacks. Fanon's later, well-known call, that we should change our material conditions and our *concepts* to set afoot a new humanity that manifests healthier social relations, is a consequence of this argument.

The relevance of Fanon's thought to African-American philosophy pertains to the understanding of black identity, the internal dynamics of liberation that are hallmarks of black thought, and the metacritical reflections on how one goes about such discourses. There is, as well, the question of thought itself. How much can one expect from a discursive practice when one also aspires to liberation? Fanon's thought on Nègritude is instructive here. The term itself was coined by Martiniquan poet Aimé Césaire, Fanon's *lycée* teacher and future foe. Fanon saw an exemplification of black resistance in Nègritude poetry, whose content extolled the virtues of the night against the blinding rays of the sun. Africa and, indeed, the black self were valorized by Nègritude poets such as Césaire and Léopold Senghor, the future first president of independent Senegal. Although he was woken from his poetically induced dialectical slumber by Jean-Paul Sartre, who pointed out in his essay "Black Orpheus" that Nègritude could at best be a negative moment in a revolutionary dialectic that called for a universal struggle, Fanon found solace in his later observation, in *A Dying Colonialism,* that it was *blacks* who created Nègritude. What this means is that Nègritude should not be entirely rejected as a potential revolutionary force because it brought to the fore a central theme in Fanon's fight against stratified abnormality—the importance of agency or, in his terms, becoming *actional.* One must, in Fanon's view, fight for and seize one's freedom. In Fanon's writings, it is far more humiliating to have our freedom handed to us than to have had it taken away in the first place. We must be responsible for our freedom.

Fanon thus responds to the dialectics of recognition not by asking to be seen but by seeking to go beyond the dialectic itself. Focusing on dismantling the master's home will still leave the problem of being homeless, but focusing on building another home could achieve the important task of rendering the master's home irrelevant without which his mastery loses its force. We could read this as a case for an important role for thought.

African-American Philosophies

Du Bois and Fanon have influenced the problematics of contemporary African-American philosophical thought. These include African-American analytical philosophy, prophetic pragmatism, Afrocentrism, Afro-postmodernism, Afro-poststructuralism, African-American existentialism, and phenomenology.

African-American analytical philosophy is, basically, the application of Anglo-analytical philosophy to black problems. Major proponents of this approach are Anthony K. Appiah, Bernard Boxill, Bill Lawson, Howard McGary, Charles Mills, Adrian Piper, John Pittman, Laurence Thomas, and Naomi Zack. Although very fruitful in the analysis of such terms as "race," "black," "respect," and "social justice," used in debates over these issues, this approach suffers from several criticisms already advanced by Du Bois and Fanon, the most crucial of which is the presumption of the validity of interpretation *within* the system as presently constituted. Thinking is, however, greater than the application of a precluded method. It requires dealing with the idiosyncrasies of reflection that enable method and thought itself to be subject to evaluation. This is Du Bois's and Fanon's insight into the study of what it means to be problems and the importance of taking seriously the illustrative potential of contradictions and failures. But even more damaging is the critique of continued theodicean practices. The radicality of critique demanded by thinking black in a world that treats thinking conjoined with blackness in black thought as an oxymoron means that the legitimating aspects of analytical philosophy must also be interrogated. The critique, then, is that although useful, as the important work of the aforementioned list of philosophers attests, analytical African-American philosophy is not sufficiently radical. There is, of course, some irony here, for there are black analytical philosophers who address black themes with all the resources available to them *as analytical philosophers.* To their surprise, and often chagrin, however, they discover that doing so has led to the charge that many of them are no longer doing analytical philosophy. Fanon's rejection of the dialectics of recognition would be instructive here. Analytical philosophers of African- American thought should simply not seek a recognition that has analytically defined them as standing outside its purview of what it means to be normal.

Prophetic pragmatism raises similar concerns. It was developed by Cornel West, who argued, following Richard Rorty, that philosophy is a special kind of writing and American philosophy is the set of pragmatist writings that supposedly constitute the indigenous philosophy of the United States. In *Prophesy, Deliverance!* West advocated his own brand of what he at that time called a revolutionary Afro-Christianity or prophetic pragmatism. This form of thought is a conjunction of pragmatism, Marxism, and prophetic Christianity. The argument for pragmatism is twofold. First, since African Americans are Americans, it follows that they exemplify America's indigenous philosophy. Second, since the problems faced by African Americans are social and historical, then the critical, socially engaged, and historical work of Deweyan pragmatism will be useful to African Americans. With regard to Marxism, its egalitarianism and fight against poverty and capitalist exploitation are relevant to disenfranchised black populations. Prophetic Christianity brings the critical engagement with power that marked the lives of ancient Hebrew prophets with a shared concern for egalitarian politics and the plight of the poor. Although West appealed to three influences, his thought easily reveals a fourth and a fifth addition—namely, existentialism and black radical humanism. The existential element comes to the fore in his persistent discussions of dread, despair, and disease. It is also made explicit through West's appeal to the thought of Søren Kierkegaard and Anton Chekhov. A wonderful section from *Prophesy, Deliverance!* is West's discussion, in the third chapter, of traditional black responses to racism. What that chapter reveals, especially in West's defense of the African-American humanist tradition, which he sees in jazz music and in such authors as Ralph Ellison and James Baldwin, is that there is an independent black tradition of thought on which to make his argument.

Prophetic pragmatism has had a strong influence on what could be called the "Princeton School" of African-American thought, which produced Michael Eric Dyson, Victor Anderson, William Hart, and Eddie Glaude, Jr. Central in their work is historically informed social criticism of black religious and popular culture. Along with prophetic pragmatists, there are also pragmatist philosophers, such as Leonard Harris, Judith Green, and Johnny Washington, who build their work on the thought of Alain Locke.[5] There are several primary criticisms of the prophetic pragmatist project that should be considered. The first is that it is simply incorrect to say that pragmatism is the indigenous philosophy of the United States, and it is even more incorrect to take the position that pragmatism is the earliest American philosophy. One could argue that the problems of existence and struggles over racism and philosophical anthropology began from the moment of colonization and continued through the work of abolitionists and, unfortunately, apologists for slavery and racism. But more, and this is ironically so given West's appeal to Christianity, the tendency to focus on pragmatism is connected to the prejudices of treating philosophy as antipathetic to religious thought. Josiah Royce, a contemporary of the classical pragmatists C. S. Peirce, William James, and John Dewey, handled this question well in his *Religious Aspects of Philosophy,* but we could go back a little more than a century earlier and ask, as George Cotkin has in *Existential America,* about the significance of Jonathan Edward's thought for our understanding of American philosophy. And along with Edwards, we could ask about the thought of black and brown religious thinkers on subjects ranging from metaphysics to ethics. Further, we could ask about the centering of Christianity and the model of the prophet. That approximately 30 percent of the slaves brought from Africa to the New World were Muslim, that there are Afro-Jewish communities, and that large numbers of African-Americans were mixed with Native Americans—whom they knew not only as biological kin but also culturally—raises serious questions about the Christian model.[6] This question of the identity of African Americans makes it all the more crucial to ask why the "African" in "African American" is suppressed by the triumvirate of pragmatism, Marxism, and prophetic Christianity. And more, since New World black people are, in the end, a creolized population of many groups, where even the black groups are comprised by a constant flow of people back and forth through the Caribbean and South America and Africa as well as by a constant infusion of different linguistic groups, how could a model such as West's, which is generally the one presumed by most African- American Studies programs, work without begging the question of a conception of African America that is no longer dominant and may never have actually been accurate? Oddly enough, "black" seems to encompass this diasporic group more than would the term "Afro-American" or "African American." But finally, the major feature of prophetic pragmatism that is perhaps its most limiting is its preference for criticism over theory. Prophetic pragmatism draws much from postmodern poststructural thought, in which theory is rejected as a master narrative but criticism is preferred as a proverbial speaking of truth to power. Such a turn consigns prophetic pragmatism to the fate of most postmodernist discourses: Criticizing the present and the past, important though it may be to do so, *left by itself* is not necessarily the best way to build the future. This conclusion, by the way, is one with which classical pragmatists would agree, especially since they not only did social criticism but also constructed theories of nearly everything from experience to the process of thinking.

Afro-postmodernism and Afro-postmodern poststructuralism face many of the objections just raised against prophetic pragmatism.

Important though the developments in both may be, they have also had the negative consequence of standing in the way of imaginative thought. In many ways, this is a function of the antifoundationalism they share. How can one build new ideas when such activities are ruled against in advance as constructing imperial, master narratives? The turn to postmodern criticism has produced a body of literature, which meets the condition of texts in the debate with which to constitute a philosophy. But there are times when it is difficult to go on without some coherence. For instance, postmodernism is marked by strong antihumanist sentiments. But nearly all black postmodernists advance some kind of humanism, and rightfully so since there would be something strange about people whose oppression is marked by dehumanization to then reject being human beings. The fight against racism is for the humanity of people whose humanity has been denied. The impact of postmodern criticism, wedded to at least the language of textual (the undecidability of signification) and genealogical (the discursive unfolding of power and knowledge) poststructuralism, has been such, however, that certain themes have come to dominate discussions of race, gender, sexual orientation, and class in such a way as to close off thinking. These tropes have become sedimented tools the effect of which is to shut down discussion and thinking rather than to stimulate engagement. Examples here include ascriptions of "binary analysis," "essentialism," and the noncontextual presumption of symmetry. Binaries are rejected *as binaries* in this discourse, which means, paradoxically, that there must be something *essentially* wrong with binaries and this is asserted by a critical perspective that is against making essential claims. Why *must* binaries be outlawed in an analysis? Binaries persist in many settings where they are not only accurate ascriptions but also productive. The computers on which most of us write our criticisms wouldn't function without binary operations, and even more, thought itself could not function without the ability to make distinctions at any moment of which constitutes a structure of is and is-not. But more, an *is* and *is-not* structure is not necessarily a binary structure, as Aristotle pointed out more than two millennia ago in his *Metaphysics,* since the possibilities that constitute is-not are infinite. That which is-not is not necessarily in opposition to what-is without an added value to what it means for something to be. Here we have the classic problem of the ontological argument where God supposedly must exist because of having the essential quality of being perfect. Not-to-exist means to lack perfection, which would make nonexistence supposedly an impossible attribute of God.

Anti-essentialism carries a similar fate. In most postmodern discussions, there is a slide from essence to essentialism, where it becomes the case that to appeal to essence is to be essentialist. This is, however, an error in reasoning, since one could easily articulate a theory of essence without making that theory of essence a necessity imposed on all of reality. The correlates, whether types or totalizations, could function in ways that do not eliminate contingency from the world. The conflation is a function of not distinguishing between areas of knowledge in which *generality* rules over *exactitude*. One could have the latter in mathematics and in the natural and theoretical sciences, but in the social sciences and the humanities, identification of phenomena requires working according to rules whose underlying subject matter always asserts an exception. The error is to make the exception the rule and the rule the exception. There are, as a matter of empirical fact, many aspects of social life over which we make fairly accurate predictions and assessment, but it would be irresponsible to claim that we make foolproof claims. Those general moments are not ones of collapsing into essential*ism* but simply descriptions that are communicable because thematic. Although many postmodernists, in the wake of Jacques Derrida's discussion of *différance,* seek untranslatable terms, the true logic of such a turn is that in principle incommunicability should pertain as well to the self posing the concept to the self. The structure of such a proposal should be such that the moment it is posed to another it is not communicated, which applies, as well, to the self posed to the self as other. In every moment of posing of the self as other is an implicit appeal to others through which and with which to communicate.

There is thus a problem at the heart of postmodern discourses, which is that they fold in on themselves. Here is an added paradox. To work, the arguments must not assert an *a priori* commitment for or against asymmetry or symmetry. Either must be examined as *ex post facto* descriptions in an argument. If an asymmetry is asserted prior to its concrete manifestation, the appeal would collapse into a necessary asymmetry. One could claim that it is not a necessary asymmetry but an arbitrary one; but if that is so, the modal question of whether that is a necessary arbitrariness or not would emerge. The case of symmetry is very similar. Although there is an injunction against binaries, symmetrical assertions abound in places where there is a claim of difference. This assertion usually takes the form of appealing to the social constructivity of the asymmetry to begin with. If, however, the social construction of asymmetry is to be identified in the service of delegitimating the asymmetry, does it not lead, then, to an underlying symmetry at the level of negation? That is to say, if asymmetry is only a social creation, what, then, is symmetry? If we assert, as well, the social constructivity of symmetry, then a prior neither-nor must be the case. The trade-off, then, is to make us all the same by virtue of what we are not. This reciprocal relativism of not-being functions like the empty set in formal logic: It generates validity for everything that flows from it.

The main problem with all this, in the end, is best exemplified by an insight from Karl Jaspers in *Philosophy of Existence* (p. 61): Philosophy can help no one suffering from a lack of reality. The problem with postmodernist criticism is that it has generated nothing more than a body of critical literature. Compare the consequences of that literature with those of the body of literature that constituted modern science. The defenders of modern science need simply remind us that much of reality is on their side. Equations do add up; rockets do fly; antibiotics kill most bacteria; X-rays reveal the outline of bones; computers compute; living things have microsequential structures that combine and adapt; and on and on. In short, the bodies of literature that constitute modern science extend in their impact beyond self-reference. They appeal ultimately to criteria under which and through which they can be affirmed or rejected. A similar conclusion can be ascribed to historical literary writings as well, including the poststructural genealogical ones, although they lack the exactness of the theoretical and natural sciences.[7] Wedded to archaeology and a variety of other sciences, history lends itself to confirmation and rejection in ways that *a priori* rejections of binaries and essentialism do not. For how can one reject a charge of essentialism when the basis of the charge is that one has made an essential claim? If one denies having made an essential claim, that is not necessarily the affirmation of anti-essentialism. If one admits having made an essential claim, that does not amount to an affirmation or rejection of essentialism. In short, for the criticism to have an impact, it must displace the accused from the tenets that ground his or her inquiry in the first place, including that of grounding it at all.

The question that comes to the fore in all this for African-American and indeed all Africana and black thought is this: Can its proponents afford to sacrifice reality?

It strikes me that the people who can most afford giving up reality are those who are already supported by a system that would make such a turn an inconsequential one. How can a case for social emancipation work, however, if, in the end, reality is not on the side of the people who seek liberation? As even the ancient Stoics knew: Delusional freedom is not freedom at all but another kind of bondage.

This is not to say that there is no insight in understanding the social constitutionality of meanings, as many postmodernists and postmodern poststructuralists aver, but we should bear in mind the dangers of reducing the social world to an ontology of all reality. Try as we may, none of us could proceed in our well-formed conceptual frameworks in the broad nothingness out of which we have come and the haunting realization that that nothingness *for us* is a mere relative moment of a vast, preceding reality and an even more tremendous succeeding one.

These reflections on postmodernism are akin to some of the problems raised by and addressed in the existential phenomenological approach to African-American and Africana philosophy, an approach that is sometimes called *postcolonial phenomenology*. It is a form of Africana phenomenology that comes out of the convergence of black existential thought and creolized forms of phenomenology. Let me first outline black existential thought.

Black existential thought builds upon problems of existence generated by the complex history of black peoples. The word "existence" comes from the Latin expression *ex sistere*, which means to stand out. When one "exists," one literally "emerges" from indistinction or insignificance. The word today is associated with simply *being,* but its etymology suggests *to live* and *to be.* To exist in this sense is to become fully aware of being alive and what that signifies. Although human beings evolved in Africa, as outlined above, and then spread across the globe and eventually adapted in ways that transformed us into groups from dark to light, the notion of *black people* is uniquely a function of constructions that have been premised upon how lighter-skinned peoples have looked at darker-skinned ones over, at least, the past 2,000 years. Black existential thought emerges from the lived reality of such people.

In precolonial Africa, problems of existence were struggled with, as Paget Henry has argued in "African and Afro-Caribbean Existential Philosophies" (1997a), primarily over the self that emerged from theologies, ontology, and ethics premised upon a cosmological paradox of predestination and an unfolding future. Appeals to pre-destination required individuals to seek out their unique "calling" in life, a view that located much agency or responsibility in individuals linked to a broad community of elders, ancestors, deities, and an ultimate being. A form of humanism resulted in which there was always something people could do about their situation, as Kwame Gyekye argued in his discussion of African humanism in *An Essay on African Philosophical Thought.* In most African systems, the past has greater ontological weight than the present, and the future has none since it has not yet occurred. The philosophy of history that emerges is existential since it relies on individuals to invent or make the future, but they must do so in the context of a calling that is paradoxically uniquely suited for them. It would be incorrect to call this an essentialism since such necessity would have to be imposed on the ontological status of the future, which has already been rejected by the cosmological and ontological assumptions of the argument. Added to these traditional existential beliefs were the developments of Judaism and Christianity in antiquity in the Eastern regions of Africa and the Middle East, the subsequent de-velopment of Islam in the Middle Ages, and the many mixtures of those religions and other African religions as various empires under their rubric spread across Africa. By the time of the Arabic, East In-dian, and Atlantic slave trades, the questions of existence faced by African individuals and non-Africans concerned about the lives of black people also included their relationship to the rationalizations of slavery advanced by the religions of those who enslaved them and their contrast from traditional, African views of enslavement. Since the focus of this chapter has been on New World blacks, let us devote the rest of this discussion to their thought on existence.

The problems of existence that emerged for black peoples in the New World are primarily but not exclusively racialized slavery and antiblack racism. Together these posed the problem of black suffering and the sustained black concern with freedom/liberation and what it means to be human. Such responses emerged not only in the many struggles fought by black people in the modern world but also through their thought, literature, and music.

All existentialisms negotiate the relationship of thought to experience. Experience is lived and precedes thought, but thought is what brings meaning and understanding to experience. The first, most influential wave of black existential reflection was in music and then literature. The quintessential black existential response in music is the blues. The blues focuses on life's difficulties and brings reality to the world of *feeling* or black suffering and joy. As an art form, the blues defies predictability and human closure. It welcomes improvisation, which makes it and its offspring—jazz, rhythm and blues, soul, funk, reggae, samba, salsa, and hip hop—exemplars of the existential credo of existence preceding essence and its connection to the question of freedom. What's more, the unique ways in which the blues brings to life the reality of and paradoxically joyful insight into suffering—to face it instead of avoiding it—points to an anthropology of black adulthood as a struggle against despair. This makes the blues an important adversary of antiblack racism. Racism attempts to force black people to the developmental level of animals at worst and children at best, freeze them there, and denigrate black self-value. The blues, by contrast, encourages maturation and growth, and is life affirming.

The impact of the blues is that it permeates nearly all black aesthetic productions. It can be found in paintings and sculptures, dramas and dance. I should, however, like to focus here on literary production since texts and their context have been the guiding themes of our discussion. Black existential literature constitutes a classic body of fiction and prose. Although one could find existential insights in the eighteenth-century poetry of Phillis Wheatley and the various early narratives and novels by former slaves and freed blacks in the nineteenth century, the first explicitly existential set of black literary writings are those of Richard Wright from the 1930s to the late 1950s. Wright articulates black experience at the level of what existentialists call a *situation,* where human beings' encounters with each other create meanings that they do not necessarily intend. In *Native Son,* the protagonist Bigger Thomas finds himself "in a situation" when he helps his employer's drunken white daughter to her bedroom after chauffeuring her and her boyfriend around town and realizes that they were at risk of being "discovered." Wright provides reflections on the relationship between choice and options for "the marginalized" of the modern world, who find themselves constantly thrown into "situations" they would prefer to have avoided, and he outlines many of the classic existential problems of freedom and responsibility that follow. Why is it, he asks us, that U.S. society "makes" Bigger Thomases, people who, in attempting to assert their humanity, become its troublemakers to be forced back "into their place" while being held responsible for their actions? Like all existentialists, Wright is able to criticize a system for what it does to people while at the same time recognizing the importance of responsibility, even under grave, systemic injustice, as a necessary condition for human dignity and maturation. In his last novel, *The Outsider,* he expands this question from North America to the Modern World, which, he argues, makes demonic those who live on its underside. Wright's outsider, Cross Damon, finds himself incapable of experiencing responsibility because he lives in a world that inhibits his development into a man. The paradox of the novel is that Damon's greatest fear is realized when he dies feeling "innocent" after killing several people.

Other literary examples of black existential thought can be found in the writings of Ralph Ellison and James Baldwin, both of whom explored problems of black invisibility as a function of hypervisibility. I have already mentioned how Ellison laments the madness faced by educated blacks, whose achievements they naively expected to bring about their inclusion (visibility) instead of heightened exclusion (invisibility) in U.S. society, for they live in a social world in which they exemplify the "impossible." Baldwin brings such questions to interracial and bisexual settings, as seen, for example, in *Another Country,* and he looks at the question of suffering as a struggle to defend the possibility of genuine human relationships. He also explores the question of theodicy through the lived reality of what it means to be a black child struggling to love a God that seems not to like, much less love, black people. The question of invisibility and theodicy takes on a unique form, as well, in the novels of Toni Morrison, as earlier suggested—particularly her inaugurating work, *The Bluest Eye.* There, Morrison brings out the peculiarity of notions such as "ugliness" and "beauty" that dominate women's lives in general, but black women's in a profound way through expectations of mimesis. The expectation that black women copy the appearance of white females subordinates their lives since all imitations are ultimately inauthentic. They live by a standard that they can never meet. This theme of inauthenticity is taken to another level when Morrison writes of bad "mixtures" in a world that blurs the lines between adults and children, the consequence of which is molestation and incest—mixtures that, in stream with Ellison, produce madness. More recently, in *Freedom in the Dismal,* Monifa Love brings many of these existential themes together through a provocative exploration of the meaning of freedom in the midst of very limited options. In the Caribbean, the most influential existential novel is George Lamming's *In the Castle of My Skin,* where the characters fight against the torrents of history and the congealing force of slime that leeches upon projects of humanistic struggle.

Black theoretical reflections on existence can be found in writings as early as those of Frederick Douglass, most of which constitute a constant meditation on freedom and the meaning of being human. The four most influential black existential texts are perhaps, however, W. E. B. Du Bois's *The Souls of Black Folk* and *Darkwater,* and Frantz Fanon's *Black Skin, White Masks* and *The Wretched of the Earth.* Du Bois, as we have seen, advanced the question of what it means to be a problem and the double experience of being forced to live publicly by what the white world believes is true while knowing the truth, simultaneously lived by blacks, as contradictions of white society. He raised the existential and theodicean problem of the meaning of black suffering, and we could also add here that he outlined the importance of black music as a life-affirming music.

Douglass and Du Bois converge in the reflections of Frantz Fanon. In *Black Skin, White Masks,* Fanon advanced a sociogenetic approach to the study of antiblack racism while defending human agency. He echoes Du Bois by pointing out that truly critical investigation requires identifying racism even at the level of method, which in turn requires, paradoxically, a methodology of not presuming a method. In existential language, a given method would be a presumed essence before the emerging existent. Fanon then shows how every effort to escape blackness fails because "escape" is in itself a form of failure. For instance, although we articulate meaning and identity through language, the black condition is such that change of language does not entail change of being. Choosing a white lover to help one deny one's blackness has the same consequence; denial is, in the end, a false reality, and its result would be, presaging Toni Morrison, an affirmation of whites as the standard of value.

Although in most of his writings Fanon attacks the blues in favor of written poetry, his reflections in *Black Skin, White Masks* ironically have an unmistakable blues structure. He goes through processes of repetition that lead to tears through which he is able to face the pathologies of "reality," and the truth here is that Eurocentric society cannot see black *adults* and does not know what it means for black people to be "normal." Blacks seek to become men and women, but they find themselves locked at a level below that status in the white world. In his final work, *The Wretched of the Earth,* he explores what it means to be "the damned" (*les damnés*), what it means for every generation to find its mission, and what it means for us to be responsible for humanity's future.

More recently, black existential thought has taken a turn toward pragmatism and existential phenomenology. Although best known as the leading proponent of prophetic pragmatism, Cornel West is also without question the leading exemplar of existential pragmatism. His focus on dread, despair, death, disease, and, in his most popular work, nihilism in black communities reveals, as I have earlier argued, a profoundly existential dimension of his thought.

All this brings us now to the phenomenological approaches to black existential thought.

The best-known black existential phenomenologists are William R. Jones, Lucius T. Outlaw, Paget Henry, and the author of this chapter, although there is now a new multiracial generation of scholars that includes James Bryant, David Ross Fryer, Jane Anna Gordon, Stephen Haymes, Patricia Huntington, Kenneth Knies, Renee Eugenia McKenzie, and Nelson Maldonado-Torres, all of whom are engaging this area of thought in productive ways. In *Is God a White Racist?* Jones argues that black suffering cannot be addressed theologically without collapsing into a theodicy (thought on God's ultimate justness) that rationalizes antiblack racism. He advances a humanistic appeal in which people are responsible for history. The influence of Jones's thought can be attested to by the continued fruitful critique of theodicy offered not only by my work but also by those of the other authors in the present volume. In *On Race and Philosophy*, as well as in his lectures on Alfred Schutz's phenomenology, Outlaw focuses on struggles against racism, the need for black-affirming environments, and the development of an antiracist philosophy. And Paget Henry, in his book *Caliban's Reason*, looks at consciousness of the Afro-Caribbean self and the poetic and historical responses developed for its emancipation.

My own work is perhaps the most explicitly phenomenological of the wave of black existential writings over the past decade, and along with Lucius T. Outlaw and Paget Henry, I have defended the value of Africana thought as an antidote to epistemological colonialism where blacks are expected to depend exclusively on white thinkers for philosophical reflection on black experience. Africana phenomenological work examines the relationship between consciousness and the world of meaning and, following Fanon, argues that colonizing processes must be fought against also at the level of method. The result is an Africana postcolonial existential phenomenology linked to the lived-experience of black folk in the modern age. This existential philosophy leads to a variety of explorations of the contemporary human condition, such as (a) oppression as an attempt to eliminate a genuinely human world and (b) the need for values premised upon ancestral obligation as a fight against nihilism—that is, against human denigration through understanding how the ancestors struggled against worse odds.

Other themes are the importance of black existential thought in the effort to articulate the humanity of dominated people, especially in race theory and theories of oppression; the importance of developing a livable mode of everyday existence; the power of black music as a life-affirming music; the articulation of rigorous ways of studying and understanding black people; the symbiotic relationship of identity and liberation; and crises of knowledge and their impact on the formation of people in each epoch. Like Cornel West, I see nihilism as a fundamental problem of our time, but, I should like to add, I argue that it is symptomatic of a process of social decay. It strikes me as incorrect to say that many blacks are nihilists because they lack faith in the United States. It is, after all, healthier to suspend serious attachment to a decaying society and transcend it through what I call "teleological suspensions," where liberation requires a constant commitment to freedom and humanity and the virtues required for such devotion.[8]

Today there is a rich array of intellectuals who can be called black existentialists. One set consists of some of the contributors to my edited volume *Existence in Black: An Anthology of Black Existential Philosophy* (1997a); and others—such as the philosopher of education Stephen Haymes, who has built upon black existential phenomenology in his study of the pedagogical practices of slaves (an example of which appears in the present volume), the philosopher Clevis Headley, who has produced an impressive array of essays on black aesthetics and race theory, and the Eritrean philosopher Tsenay Serequeberhan, who is perhaps the chief proponent of black hermeneutical existential philosophy—are developing new areas of existential reflection.

Returning, then, to the problems outlined by Du Bois and Fanon, Africana existential phenomenology addressed the problematic of problem-people and the demand of a decolonized methodology in several ways. First, for such an approach to function as properly phenomenological, it must commit an act of ontological suspension, or suspension of the natural attitude. This means that it is able to look at what it *means* to be a problem instead of simply what it *is* to be a problem. The separation of meaning from being here enables one to suspend the seriousness of the value-category of blackness and, in that stroke, take seriously the distinction of having problems versus being them. But more salient is the immediate connection to the "consciousness" aspect of double consciousness. The concept is already phenomenological in its structure and content. Next, the question of decolonizing method comes to the fore in our understanding of the redundancy of the term "postcolonial phenomenology." For phenomenology requires not only suspension of ontological commitments but also those commitments connected to the evaluation and means of going about making commitments. Such a move pushes the inquirer up against whatever limits it may exemplify, which means that the movement was not presumed but encountered in the moment of investigation. In short, even the method is being subject to a suspension that outlaws the movement of a colonizing episteme as a legitimating process. The point is perhaps most stark in the case of logic. A proper self-critical phenomenological investigation requires suspending the legitimating and ontological force of logic itself, because even logic must be subjected to a process of legitimation if it is to be accepted; the very notion of "evidence," in other words, must be made *evidential.* Ironically, this means taking reality seriously without placing a false domain or circle around it. The Fanonian demand of not assuming one's method is, then, in this sense, also a phenomenological one.

Perhaps the most fruitful aspect of Africana phenomenology is that it supports examining the lived-reality of black folk and the imaginative interplay of engagements with the social world. What this means is that there is room for recognizing both the impositions of reality and the creative potentials of thought. Since an underlying theme of the present engagement with African-American Studies is the question of thought itself as a tool of building alternative houses, I should like to turn to one of the most claustrophobic yet paradoxically generative rooms of the master's house—namely, race.

Although African-American Studies need not be race studies, the peculiar anxiety over African America is the *African* element in the equation in terms of its genealogical link with blackness. Much was to be done in Black Studies, but dominant America does not really want *black* studies because, as we have seen in our discussion of Du Boisian double consciousness, neither America in the north nor America in the south really wants to look into the mirror and find a truthful reflection of itself. Evasion is thus the primary *modus operandi* of this terrain of thought, and we find it in many forms. Think, for instance, of the ongoing discussions of the relationship between race and class. The error here is the failure to appreciate what Oliver Cox called the proletarianization of blacks.[9] Why must they be seen as categories over and against each other? Although not all such blacks were slaves (Pedro Alonso Niño, for example, was a navigator on Columbus's first voyage), the reality of slavery in the economies and political institutions that followed has been so pervasive that all New World blacks are yoked to it. Thus, much of the understanding of blacks in the Americas is the constant problem and problematic of labor, dehumanization, and resistance to exploitation. These considerations have a profound impact on the study of such blacks. Fanon's quip from *Black Skin, White Masks* is illuminating in this regard:

One day St. Peter saw three men arrive at the gate of heaven: a white man, a mulatto, and a Negro.

"What do you want most?" he asked the white man.
"Money."
"And you?" He asked the mulatto.
"Fame."
St. Peter turned then to the Negro, who said with a wide smile:
"I'm just carrying these gentlemen's bags." (p. 49)

One could easily add the gender dimension to labor along with this point. The existence of middle-class black men and women doesn't negate the modern history that has linked blacks not only to labor but also to *slave labor.* The distinction between labor and slave labor is located at the point of entitlement. Slave labor is denied *any* entitlement whatsoever, and thus it makes any effort toward recompense appear to be a crossing of sacred borderlines. The slaves and slave descendants who seek more for their labor—in fact, seek *anything* for their labor—encounter a world that treats them as transgressors.[10] Thus, calling, say, the Irish "the blacks of Europe" in the European context fails to address the fact that there are blacks in Europe and in Ireland who turn out to be black in North America, South America, Asia, and Australia, and those blacks, often designated by the term "Negroes," carry the weight of a history of being expected to carry bags for the whites and the many shades beyond which blacks represent the nether zone. The modern world hates to see black folks resting.

Black reality is not faring well in the third millennium of the common era. To understand the situation, we could go back to W. E. B. Du Bois's much criticized speech "On the Conservation of Races," which he presented in front of the Negro Academy in 1897. Beyond its many famous insights, ranging from the observation of two-ness and double consciousness to the sloppiness of race discourses, is its peculiar policy query. It can be summarized thus: What should the world look like at the end of the twentieth century? After having seen what European conquest and colonization did to the indigenous people of North America, Du Bois was in fact imploring his fellow black intellectuals to take seriously what the European nations were doing to Africa. If the American project were effected in Africa, then the indigenous population faced the possibility of being reduced, as in the case of the indigenous Americans, to 4 percent of their original numbers. Du Bois and his fellow Pan-Africanists, in spite of their arrogance and at times racism (many considered indigenous Africans "savages"), managed to fight an important war against genocide. Although Du Bois argued, for instance, that race was social and historical, he also had to find a way to link black culture to black bodies to avoid genocide in a world that enjoyed, perhaps even loved, black culture but hated black people. He thus advanced the contradictory argument that race was contingent but that its cultural markers were necessarily linked to the bodies with which we associate it. Black people, from that point of view, were thus both contingently and necessarily black.

We today face the mixed assessment of the efforts of Du Bois and his fellow Pan-Africanists at the dawn of the twentieth century. The African continent is now the habitat of only 8 percent of the human species, and the neoliberal and global policies of Europe and North America have placed upon contemporary generations of humanistic intellectuals an obligation similar to the one experienced by those more than a century ago: How do we respond to policies whose consequence is a new form of colonization of Africa and an expedited demise of its indigenous peoples?

The question of the relation of blacks, both qualitatively and quantitatively, to the rest of the human species brings the human question to the fore. For blacks in Africa are not like indigenous peoples elsewhere. Some indigenous peoples in Africa represent, in many ways, the indigeneity of the human species itself. They are, literally, in their extraordinarily diverse combinations of genetic material, all of "us." And the same applies to the mythic life embedded in the ancient archaeological and paleolithic remains scattered about the continent of Africa.

The rest of this discussion will take place in three parts: First, an exploration of the problem of reductionistic experience; second, an advancement and critique of disciplinary decadence and race; and third, an outline of theoretical themes offered by what I call a teleological suspension of Western thought, or shifting the geography of reason.

Experiencing Experience

Let us now go further into the problem of experience only summarized earlier. Experience is something uniquely offered by the members of cultural groups under study here. Acting under the dictates of standpoint epistemological approaches, one could take the position that one has limited knowledge of any group of which one is not a member. This leads to two approaches. The first is the undesirable approach, given our anticolonial concerns: Use informants (members of the group) and acknowledge one's limitations as an outsider. The second, often desirable approach: Be the informant and the theorist by studying one's own group. On both counts, experience is a key factor.

Experience is, however, a sacred cow. Everyone, for instance, has had the experience of trying to figure out his or her experience. When this happens, the self becomes untrustworthy. One seeks a trusted confidant for assistance. What this tells us is that the figuring out of experience brings something to experience that goes beyond the self as the source of legitimation. The interpretation of experience is not, that is, a private affair. It is part of the complex world of communication and sociality. This dimension of experience raises some problems of its own. First, it is very important what both the one who experiences and those who interpret the experience draw on for the development of their interpretation. If the one with experience plays no role in the interpretation of the experience, then a form of epistemic colonization emerges, as we have seen, where there is dependence on the interpretations from another's or others' experience as *the* condition of interpreting experience.[11] The more concrete manifestation of this relationship is familiar to many black intellectuals. In most academic institutions, including some, unfortunately, in regions dominated by people of color, the following formula holds: Colored folks offer experience that white folks interpret. In other words, formulating theory is a white affair. Paraphrasing Arthur de Gobineau, theory is white as experience is black. We see this from even colored theorists who prefer to examine the world of color through Martin Heidegger, Jacques Lacan, Jacques Derrida, or Michel Foucault instead of through the resources of thought offered by Anna Julia Cooper, W. E. B. Du Bois, C. L. R. James, Richard Wright, Ralph Ellison, Frantz Fanon, V. Y. Mudimbe, James Cone, Sylvia Wynter, George Lamming, Elsa Goveia, Angela Y. Davis, and Paget Henry, to name but several, in addition to the resources of thought offered by the full spectrum of the human species.

This is not to say that experience should be rejected in the theoretical work of people of color. The impetus behind the appeal to experience is after all the terrible history of the human sciences, in which European theorists acted as though people of color had no inner or subjective life. To appeal to colored experience was also an effort at asserting the reality of one's inner life. This is why Du Bois wrote of "souls" and "consciousness" and Fanon wrote of "lived experience."

The task, then, is to avoid *reductionistic* experience—that is, to avoid reducing people of color *only* to their experiences and, worse, to the epitome of experience itself. There is, by the way, an ironic, performative contradiction to such efforts beyond the reality of epistemic colonization: To lock oneself at the level of experience is a theoretical move *beyond* experience. In effect, then, the abrogation of theory to whites is a form of *bad* theory. This form of bad appeal leads to a peculiarly existential failure—the failure to appreciate ourselves as *thinking* beings. Such a lack of appreciation blinds us to a precious dimension of the human condition. No one incapable of thinking can be expected to be taken seriously as a human being.

Disciplinary Decadence, Race, and Racism

Any African-American thought that does not address race and racism would be severely limited. It is not that every instance must address these issues, but that the overall project must have such an encounter as part of its program. All discussions of race and racism rest on their discussant's conception of human studies. Human studies has been, and in many instances continues to be, dominated by two kinds of disciplinary fallacies. The first is methodological with two dimensions of its own. The first dimension was pointed out by W. E. B. Du Bois a century ago. It is, as we have seen, the social scientific tendency to make colored people into problems themselves instead of studying them as people who face problems. We have already devoted much of this chapter to discussing that fallacy. The second dimension emerges in Fanon's *Black Skin, White Masks,* where he declares: "It is good form to introduce a work in psychology with a statement of its methodological point of view. I shall be derelict. I leave methods to the botanists and the mathematicians. There is a point at which methods devour themselves" (p. 12). We have already offered some discussion of this claim. Let us here elaborate what Fanon means by this assessment. It is easier to study what does not think and cannot return the look and study *you*. It is like looking at a pointing finger instead of that at which the finger points. As signifying beings, the action by human beings always points beyond the human. The human being is always involved in future-oriented activity that always tests the scope of law-like generalizations.[12] This is why human studies at best derives principles and is an interpretive affair. The best "laws" of human nature we could find or develop are simply those that we share with animals but which, by virtue of speech and culture, we have already gone beyond. As Fanon puts it in *Black Skin, White Masks:*

> The only possibility of regaining one's balance is to face the whole problem, for all these discoveries, all these inquiries lead only in one direction: to make man admit that he is nothing, absolutely nothing—and that he must put an end to the narcissism on which he relies in order to imagine that he is different from the other "animals."
>
> This amounts to nothing more nor less than *man's surrender.* (p. 22)

The second disciplinary fallacy is what I call *disciplinary decadence.*[13] This phenomenon is the error of disciplinary reductionism. It involves ontologizing one's discipline—literally, collapsing "the world" into one's disciplinary perspective. Many scholars have witnessed its various incarnations: Literary scholars who attack social scientists for not being literary; social scientists who attack literary scholars for not being social scientific; natural scientists who reject the humanities on the basis of their lack of "scientific rigor"; historians who reject everyone else for not being historical; and philosophers who reject everyone else for not being philosophical—and especially historians for being historical. The specifics, according to each discipline, take on a variety of "isms."

In race theory, for instance, there is *biologism,* where the biologist presumes the meaning of concepts to be embedded in the organism without an account of the social processes that make those meanings normative. There is *psychologism,* which presumes, for example, that race and racism are dimensions of an individual perspective. There is social psychology, true, but in the end, psychologism is about the dispositions or cognitive states of individuals. Thus, a radical relativism is difficult to avoid in psychologistic appeals. Worse, a form of metaphysical nominalism emerges in which institutions and language structures become fictional. Here, sociology could serve as a corrective, except in cases where it collapses into *sociologism,* which presumes (1) either the quantitative or demographic character of race and racism or (2) the reduction of all race and racist phenomena to the social world. Here, there is a failure to address the natural *and* psychological dimensions of the human condition: We are simply not only social beings. The *literary textualist* approach commits the fallacy of presuming that the answers to race questions are intratextual and intertextual. In effect, it is as if the answers are already there and we need only decode them. In the cases in which the texts are literally published or unpublished written manuscripts, there are so-called race theorists, for example, who think that specializing in race theory is a matter of simply figuring out the position of a particular race theorist. It collapses theoretical work simply into, at best, the function of an interpretive critic. And finally, though not exhaustively, there is *historicism,* which treats race as a function of the historical determination of social forces. Here, we have a mixture of sociologism and textualism, for in the end, the answers are embedded in forces that simply have to be tabulated or decoded. There are other philosophical problems with this approach. For one thing, there are clear transhistorical dimensions of human differentiation, which even an appeal to the "epoch" cannot ignore. In the United States, for instance, there is a debate about the moral turpitude of the "founding fathers," a group of white propertied individuals who, in effect, hijacked the ideals of the American Revolution. In their defense, some scholars have argued that we should not judge people of the past by values of the present.[14] The reply, however, is that such critics want to eat their cake and have it too. For how radically different are values over a period of ten generations of people in the same country? Do not both the eighteenth century bourgeoisie and "we" share the same valuative epoch? Is not calling us members of "Western civilization" a way of articulating that shared value? Since the argument requires shared values, and since such critics already take the position that Western civilization is "our" value base, there is something contradictory at work in their objection. If the response requires a greater gap in time, how great should it be? A thousand years? Ten thousand? A hundred thousand? Finally, there is nearly no historic moment in which there is unanimity over values. There are always dissenters; in the case of the United States, there were blacks, indigenous people, white women, and many others who protested as their revolution was sold out from under them.[15]

A viable response to disciplinary decadence is what I call *teleological suspensions of disciplinarity*. The concept of teleological suspension first emerged in the thought of Søren Kierkegaard in *Fear and Trembling* as a critique of Hegel's system. Hegel had advanced his system of the dialectical unfolding of Absolute knowledge, of the domestication of all reality by the historically marching force of reason understood as an isomorphism of rationality and reality.[16] Such an unfolding culminates in a theology or systematizing of God. Kierkegaard's objections were on many levels. He agreed that morality, rules, and systems are located at the level of what he called "the universal" but pointed out that faith transcends the universal. In other words, God cannot be domesticated by universal categories, even of morality, but is instead the teleological foundations of them. God is, in other words, "right" even when God goes beyond the universal. A paradox thus emerges. The individual of faith suspends the universal in the spirit of God, a teleological pursuit, which requires the emergence of an ethics, religious ethics, which is itself always subject to its own suspension by virtue of its teleological source of valuation.[17] I have argued in "Introduction: The Call in Africana Religion and Philosophy" (2001a) that this approach need not be limited to discussions of ethics. It can serve as a metatheoretical assessment of theory and disciplinarity as well. In philosophy, for instance, professionalism has created a near-deontological conception of philosophical work as the quest for intrasystemic consistency.[18] Most "great" philosophers, however, emerged either from the periphery of the discipline or through a commitment to questions that, in their time, appeared beyond the scope of the discipline itself. In effect, then, "great" philosophy emerged from thinkers who were not worried about whether they were philosophers. Such suspension could be performed in many other disciplines; it involves taking the risk of suspending the ontological priority of one's field or discipline for the sake of a greater purpose or cause. For black peoples in the modern world, this cause or purpose has often taken two forms: survival and freedom.

The concerns of survival and freedom stimulated two correlative, philosophical concerns of being and liberation. The former pertains to questions of who or what we are, of identity and its ontological dimensions. The latter emerges through the historical reality of colonialism and racism. Beyond the question of the meaning of liberation, the struggle against colonialism and racism is primarily a matter of the relation of theory to practice. The identity question, however, takes concrete form in the social identities of race and ethnicity. Today, such matters of identity and liberation are complicated by two extremes that dominate academic theoretical reflection: neopositivism and postmodern hermeneuticism. In philosophical terms, neopositivism, as in earlier instances of positivism, aims for a form of exactness, as in the exact sciences, that renders "meaning" and "interpretation" suspect. Postmodern hermeneutics has the advantage of looking at the world of interpretation, but it does so at the expense, as we saw in the previous section, of truth and objectivity—in fact, of reality itself. In many respects, both converge in that they collapse into obsession over methodology at the expense of truth. The neopositivist believes that all truth beyond what is gained by the methods of the exact sciences is trivial and therefore inconsequentially dropped. The postmodern hermeneuticist takes the position that truth can never meet tests of permanence and exactitude, which means that it should be subordinated to processes of interpretation. A question that is raised in response to both, however, is that of the dynamism of truth. Why can't truth be dynamic?

The neopositive and postmodern hermeneutical limitations play themselves out in contemporary race theory (perhaps the most recurring focus of the identity question). These limitations are guided by several of the postmodern clichés of binarism, anti-essentialism, and presumed symmetry discussed earlier. In race theory, they are advanced against race by the antirace wing as follows. Natural scientists reject race; therefore, so should the rest of us. This position is held by such theorists as K. Anthony Appiah and Naomi Zack. Natural science is treated as the proper ontology with which to deal with reality, and all that is not grounded in such is often referred to, by these theorists, as "fictions." These theorists also argue that the best way to get rid of racism is to get rid of race. Paul Gilroy's *Against Race* brings him into this camp. And then there is a third wing: The concept of race lacks rigor when dealing with racial mixture. There are several camps here.[19] Some, like Naomi Zack, argue that "mixed race" is a nonracial category, literally "racelessness." Others, especially those involved in Latin-American cultural studies and philosophical thought, argue, through such notions as *mestizo* identity, that mixtures are *unique* racial categories.

In response to the claim of the scientific invalidity of race, we may wonder why the natural sciences should be treated as the *final* arbiter of everything. Wouldn't that be a case of disciplinary decadence? When I defended natural science against postmodern discourses in the previous section, my point was that natural science stays attuned to the governing force of reality, but it does not follow that the only form of systematic inquiry in which to do so is natural science. Why, then, couldn't the following argument hold: Race proves the limitations of the natural sciences, if by natural sciences are meant such disciplines as physics, chemistry, and biology. There are many things that cannot be explained in terms of these disciplines. Take, for example, the concept of "meaning." Or, for that matter, these disciplines themselves—the concepts of "physics," "chemistry," and "biology." There are many concepts the treatment of which exemplifies the limitations of science. Karl Jaspers, in *Philosophy of Existence,* and the Japanese philosopher Keiji Nishitani, in *Religion and Nothingness,* have shown, for instance, that *religion* is a limit not only for science but also for philosophy. This limit means that the areas of inquiry under discussion must be attuned to the uniqueness of their domain of thought.

The argument against race on the basis of the natural sciences suffers, then, also from the fallacy of authority. Why are natural scientists more authoritative than scholars in other areas of inquiry? The appeal to researchers in the natural sciences as final arbiters on race begs the question of the type of phenomenon race must be. But worse, even internal to the natural and life sciences, there are scientists who believe in races—researchers for whom a difference of .0002 or .0001 is as wide as the Grand Canyon—and not all of them are nutty eugenicists such as those at the Charles Darwin Institute in Ontario, Canada, or the Straussians from the University of Chicago who have set the tone for contemporary neoconservative racist appeals to the impact of climate on intelligence.[20] One encounters race in typical consultations with physicians worldwide;

and in the fields of obstetrics, pediatrics, and hematology, failure to take race seriously can have severe consequences. In such cases, there is a familiar Anglo-Caribbean expression known as *breeding*. In truth, the term *race*, whose etymology extends to the Italian *raza*, was originally used in the early modern period (circa sixteenth century) to refer to the reproduction of selected traits in plants and animals. Today, science—namely, genetics—is in fact showing that we are all variations of a small group of dark-skinned peoples from the Southeastern region of Africa, in spite of popular artistic efforts to present these people as very hairy and very dirty white men. Put differently, every one of us on the earth today is simply a variation of what we now call "black people." If we look at race as a manifestation of the selection of traits to be carried on—selection, in the case of human beings, mediated by culture—then it should be clear that what much of humanity has been aiming for is to split off into different *species* of hominids, or new species of people. This is a biological aim that is socially mediated.

The aim for a separate species of hominids raises a question that challenges the argument that advances the rejection of race as the basis of rejecting racism. There are existential and material responses. The existential response is that one could be committed to antiracism while believing in race. In other words, even if different species of hominids were to emerge, we would still face similar existential, ethical, and political questions of how to act on such difference. This was *in fact* the reality of people in Europe and the Americas in the nineteenth century, since they *believed* in such difference. For them, a black and a white might as well have been a donkey and a horse, the combination of which would be a sterile mule from which they acquired the term "mulatto." In many respects, every fertile mulatto challenges racial ideology, so, in a way, Naomi Zack is right in saying that mixed-race people offer a special challenge.[21] The problem, however, is whether anyone really takes seriously that such reproduction is not possible. The term *mulatto* also alludes to another process of race and racism: naming.

The argument that racism depends on race raises the question of whether a phenomenon must have a "name" or a "conceptual" apparatus for its existence. That there are many instances in which we respond to things whose names we do not know, or that stand outside of our understanding or range of familiar objects, is the counterargument to required-naming—provided we reject linguistic idealism. By linguistic idealism, I mean the view that nothing can exist without a name. I doubt, in the end, that most neopositivists and postmodern hermeneuticists would like to maintain this position. There is, however, an insight raised by the question of naming if we ground it in the process of language as a communicated reality. Communication, at least at the level of *human communication,* requires social and cultural dimensions. These dimensions, as Frantz Fanon has argued in *Black Skin, White Masks,* are reservoirs of creativity, and the things they create are, in his words, *sociogenic*—that is, social in their origins. What this means is that the social world can create and eliminate *kinds* of people. Once created, the claim that their identities themselves are the problems is a failure to address the social dynamics of their creation; it makes them the problems instead of the society that created them. But more, although society creates identities, popularly known, redundantly, as "social constructions," there is an error in condemning such constructions as fictions. Social walls function as impasses just as well as those made of bricks and stones. The mechanisms of dismantling them and building new structures are what is different. The social ones are dependent on human reality for every moment of their maintenance but not for the entirety of their being. What is *understood,* for example, if another species one day decodes our world will be the world we have created, a world that might outlive us, albeit fragmented, as do ancient ruins across the contemporary landscape.

There is much more that I can say on race—for instance, on the asymmetry inherent in semiotic relations from black to brown to white; on genealogical dynamics of how power/knowledge relate to the social world of race; on the complexity of creolization and racial thought—but I should like to move toward concluding here since those discussions are available elsewhere.[22]

Power, Choice, and Shifting the Geography of Reason

I see African-American thought as a species of, although not exclusive to, Africana thought. By this, I mean African-influenced thought. It is not exclusively so because the New World is a convergence of many cultures, but a problem with many of those other cultures, save many of the Native American ones, is often their resistance to mixture. The European elements see themselves as properly European to the extent that they exclude the others. It undergirds the racial notion of whiteness as "pure." A similar reality applies to Asian elements, although there are, in fact, many mixtures internal to Asian communities *in Asia*. The African and the Native American elements are, however, those that most seem to accommodate mixture. Not only was there creolization of African languages in pre-colonial Africa and the same creolization processes among Native New World populations, but one finds that those are the communities that most manifest creolization in the New World, and they do so for obvious reasons: They have the least resources with which to dictate the limits of their identities. For them, survival requires mediation that leads to creolization. The political reality, which in turn has epistemological consequences, is that European ordering of these populations under the category of "primitive" over the past 500 years has led to a negative zone with regard to studying what they offer the world of *ideas*. The fact that the African-descended and the Native-descended comprise a large combined population in North America, the African-descended now comprise the majority of people in the Caribbean, and the African- and Native American-descended comprise the majority in Central and South America means, as Paget Henry has shown in *Caliban's Reason,* that a vast reservoir of epistemic contributions has been left by the wayside.

If these elements of the creolized societies of the New World were taken into account, a vast array of research would open up. It would be necessary to revisit and address, for instance, questions of myth. Myths are more complicated than simply the Greco-Roman and Mesopotamian ones that dominate our Western education and psychic life, as expressed in orthodox and semiotic-psychoanalysis. Asian myths are older, and we often forget that since we are all descended from a species that evolved in Africa, then so, too, did the prototypes for all our myths. These African myths undergird our understanding of basic reality. For example, much is discussed today about how the lives of women are changing without an analysis of the organizing myths that situate our understanding of women and men, females and males, and feminine and masculine and the other possible organizations of sex and gender-related ways of living. Women did not always live as the subordinates of men, and in the past, there were peculiar conditions under which men emerged in leadership over women and vice versa. Nomadic, pastoral, and hunting societies lived differently from settler societies, and societies with a mixture of these elements faced complex questions on the distribution of labor. The Mediterranean, for example, is a place where northern hunters and southern agrarian communities met, and their organizing myths reveal much anxiety over the relation of the feminine to the masculine. Our world is structured by bureaucratic and market forces that provide new outlets for such myths. Today, one "hunts" for a job and, if successful, gains tools of "currency." Those tools are used to "gather" needs or amusements for the family or other basic unit. All of this is familiar to anthropologists and students of antiquity and paleolithic periods. That most of the world today functions according to the rules of settler societies renders the maintenance of patriarchy absurd, and it is no wonder that there is heightened gender conflict worldwide as some societies attempt to hold on to the permanence of values that were a function of a particular period of, say, masculine ascent.

What all this means is that theories that simply attempt to subordinate one category to another—for example, gender over all others, race over all others, class over all others, sexual orientation over all others—suffer from the fallacy of treating social realities as deontological—that is, as having absolute, duty-bound values and meanings.[23] Shifts occur in societies that affect, among other things, power dynamics, and power dynamics affect social meaning. "Power" is a term that is not often clarified these days in the academy, and since the most influential kind of American political thought—namely, liberal political theory—seems to have completely ignored power while earning its bread and butter, the decline of reflection on power in the academic mainstream appears to be a function of a conviction of its seeming irrelevance. Most often, in other corridors of the academy, it is Foucault's use of the term that is presumed, as if his formulations were the be-all and end-all of discourses on power. We should, however, remember that power emerges in the thought of such thinkers as Hegel as a function of dialectical opposition of consciousness and recognition; Marx, as ownership over the means of production; Gramsci, as hegemony; Hannah Arendt, as uncoerced exchange in a public sphere the emergence of which are deeds worthy of glory; Thomas Hobbes and Carl Schmitt, as legitimate force, which is issued only by the sovereign or the state; and Elias Canetti, as the godlike range of actions that transcend those locked under its grip as mere mortals, and these are but a few instances. The way in which I am using "power" is a phenomenological revision of Canetti's view with some compatibility with Foucault's and Fanon's. Power, from this perspective, begins where force ends. Think of the game of cat and mouse. When the cat catches the mouse, force is the reality of tooth and claw. But cats sometimes let their prey go, and the mouse attempts to run away. The problem is that the cat's reach extends to the area over which it can move faster than the mouse; thus, run though the mouse may try with all its might, the cat will seem to pop up everywhere as if out of thin air. That "everywhere" is the sphere of influence. Everyone has a sphere of influence over his or her body and what he or she can immediately hold. That sphere is "force." Other people, however, have a sphere of influence that go well beyond their immediate spatial-temporal coordinates. Thus, they could be at one point of the world while influencing the activities of people at another point. They could have died many years ago, while conditioning many people in the present and the future. And, as Foucault showed in *Discipline and Punish*, they could even be inside one's head. This is power. In government jurisdiction terms, a mayor's power has range over a city; a governor's, over a state or island; a president or prime minister's, over a country; and the president or prime minister of an imperial nation has power over its colonies. Since today the U.S.A. is the main empire (China not withstanding and Britain delusionally so), one sees the validity of this point on the level of countries. But it holds, too, on the level of institutions such as corporations and nonprofit organizations, and groups of people such as Europeans and Africans, or women and men. Whether they admit it or not, rich people are more powerful by virtue of the range of their influence always transcending their immediate selves or bodies. They could be in one part of the world vacationing while making money through someone else's labor in another part of the world. Shifts in recognition under the laws and decline in interests for certain types of activities traditionally attributed to men have led to a restructuring of the range of women's influence. What women can *do* in many contemporary societies, albeit not ideal for many women, transcends the immediacy of force. As these forces are transcended, the organizing power of different myths should come into play.[24]

All this said, here are some considerations to ponder by way of concluding.

First, thought must address its epoch, which paradoxically requires being a little bit ahead of itself, as I pointed out earlier with the argument about teleological suspensions. Genuine twentieth-century thinkers posed problems, for instance, that genuine twenty-first-century thinkers must both engage and go beyond. Late nineteenth- and twentieth-century examples of such thinkers include Max Weber (with his treatment of bureaucracies and secularization), W. E. B. Du Bois (with his treatment of problematic people and double consciousness), Anna Julia Cooper (with her efficiency theory of human contribution and worth), Antonio Gramsci (with his theories of cultural capital, hegemony, and critique of common sense), along with such twentieth-century luminaries as C. L. R. James (with his theory of state capitalism and creative universality), Hannah Arendt (with her discussion of the relation of power to labor, work, and action, and the negative effects consumption has on the political), Frantz Fanon (with his argument for the semiotic and material transformation of social reality in the constitution of human reality), and Sylvia Wynter (with her persistent inquiries into what she calls the "science of the word" and her quest for what she calls "the human after man"). We could add to this list the tasks outlined by Nelson Maldonado Torres of post-continental thinking and by Kenneth Knies of constructing post-European sciences.[25]

Such thinking does not mean that we should avoid "grand theory." Opposing grand theory is a level of caution reminiscent of traps set by Zeno in Greek antiquity. Zeno demonstrated that motion isn't possible because one would have to traverse an infinitesimal number of half-steps before completing a first step. The same argument was placed upon time: an infinitesimal number of halves to each unit of time. Or, for that matter, one could think of the old story of bumblebees. Bumblebees should not be able to fly. But they do. In similar kind, one's best response to Zeno is simply to take a step and check the change of time. There are many things that we should not be able to do *in theory*. It is a fool who clings to any validity that defies existence or, for that matter, reality. It has been a mission of thinking that humanity tries to reach beyond the limits imposed upon us. The failure of grand theories carries the paradox of their success: They enabled, even in their failure, a transformation of the human condition.

African-American thought should take seriously the critique of the rural-urban divide in Africana thought. We should recognize that thought is affected by the exigencies of space. For example, much political thought is prejudiced by its etymological foundations— namely, in the Greek polîs, or city-state. Barbarians stood outside such walls. Cities, however, required ways of organizing people that increasingly created distances between them. For matters of exigency, numbers and measurement facilitated such organization, and owing to the large number of people who occupied cities, representation proved more efficient in their administration. Moreover, the walls of ancient cities enclosed the people in a way that made the necessity of their interaction an *externally imposed* condition instead of an internal one. That meant that they were bound without necessarily an *internal identity of membership*. The implication here is that we should not presume a symmetric understanding of political life when we move from urban to rural, because the values of politics are more conducive to the former than to the latter. The historic relation of the world outside the city to those inside was one of war. The rural aim is the elimination of politics. This doesn't mean that the political cannot emerge outside the city walls, but it often does so through self- or group encirclement to create an internal dialectic of oppositional claims—in short, the duplication of the city structure. I bring this up because of the ongoing problem in black politics of black nationhood. In many ways, white supremacy and antiblack racism function as those encircling walls that necessitate an internal political relationship to those inside the city. What this means, then, is that the search for an *internal necessity* in black politics and black life is a mistaken understanding of what such relationships are. The internal opposition is a fundamentally *political one* because of that external necessity, which means, then, that dissent and opposition versus unanimity are, in the end, primary features of black life.

The earlier discussion of power returns in the form of the question of oppression. For it should be clear that the sphere of influence, the social reach of an individual by virtue of his or her social role or social identity, affects the life opportunities of people in each region. It affects them not only on the level of the rural in relation to the urban but also on that of countries in relation to other countries. The political reach of each community is not equal, and none of them is equal to the political reach of the dominating groups of North American, European, and Northern Asian nations. On the level of groups, there are groups that face oppression by virtue of the reach of their actions that transcend force. When people lack power, their spheres of influence move inward to the self to the point of *implosion.* Thus, oppression is a function of the range of "normal" actions available before the process of implosion begins. An oppressing people have options available to them to avoid implosion; oppressed people do not. That is why oppressed people are always trying to "fix" themselves. They live in a world where, as Foucault observed, their bodies are forced to become prisoners of their souls. It is the only sphere over which they have effective reach. One can readily see that this observation suggests that notions such as "victim" and "innocence" have nothing to do with oppression. Oppression is about imposed limitations; victimization is about being both innocent and harmed. An oppressed person needn't be innocent. What is crucial is that the options in a society be such that the sphere of normative action is accessible. Normative action is the set of activities expected for a human being to live with dignity among his or her fellow human beings.

This point about dignity and living among one's fellow human beings raises the question of freedom. Freedom, as opposed to mere liberty, is a meaning-constituting activity. Oppression is experienced in a situation of limited liberty because one's freedom is always faced as a possibility of action. The fact that one can live through oppression in many ways—albeit not the most desirable way to live—poses freedom as a constant demand on human existence.

The question of freedom also raises the question of the philosophical anthropology that it demands. The complexity of the human being as both the impediment to and the source of freedom is a case in point. Human beings both create the world we live in and are conditioned by that world. To take on such a complex dynamic, we must, then, take on the question of "reality" in our thought. That question pertains to the relationship between our embodiment and the social world, and it relates to the question of the ontology necessitated by the emergence of social *reality.*

Looking into the reality of the social world means, as well, challenging the sacred-secular divide. Consider Edward Blyden's observation in *African Life and Customs* (1908) that it is much easier to change the theology of a people than their religion. The normative underpinnings are the religious reality. Returning to Cornel West, although there are many black Christians in the New World, it is incorrect to say that that is all they are. One learns a lot about people's beliefs during times of birth, puberty, marriage, and death. A mere glance at many New World black people's rituals around these phenomena reveal the continued normative force of Yoruba, Akan, and other African religious influences. Nor are the East African and Middle Eastern influences limited to Christianity. The Islamic and Judaic dimensions of New World black normative life should be taken seriously, especially among such groups as Rastafarians and, given the increased influence of Asia in the New World, Hindus, Buddhists, and Taoists. In the end, New World *thought* requires an engagement with these resources for the understanding of the self and community in an increasingly global context.

The counsel on religion applies as well to aesthetic productions. What is New World black thought without its variety of music, dances, plastic arts, foods and drinks, clothing? And in all this are varieties of expression that contribute to the discourse on New World black ideas. Many New World black people use song lyrics as they do proverbs, and while these may not be the be-all and end-all of thought (which they need not and shouldn't be), they are at least a contribution. An insight from such production is the call to be epistemologically imaginative. By resisting in-advance rejections of such terms as "binaries" and "dualism," New World black thought can work through such categories when they are most relevant. We should bear in mind, as we think through subverting Shakespeare's *Tempest,* that whereas Prospero Studies dominated the "modern world," Caliban Studies might be the future so long as we continue to fight for our freedom, so long as both such studies are teleologically suspended for the sake of freedom.

All this brings us finally to the transformation of the geography of reason. We must ask whether the Reason that runs out of the room that the Black walks into is being reasonable at all. We may also wonder whether that house itself may be one that stands on a foundation that is too shaky for our occupation. Perhaps what we are asking for requires building a new house on a different foundation, which amounts to a shift or expansion in the scope of reason. The geography of reason has been yoked to the path of European and

American development. This development has been a familiar trope in various periods of history. Egyptians, for instance, expanded to the limits of their environment, and in their wake emerged Greece and subsequently Rome in the north. In Rome's wake stood its aqueducts and highways, which netted an entire area in the Holy Roman Empire. And in that empire's fall emerged a series of consolidations that became Europe in the north and the Islamic world in the south and east, and in their fall came Europe's offspring, America, and its two rivals—first the former Soviet Union (the East) and an unbalanced Islamic world (the Middle East) conditioned by reactions to American policies. But empires do not exist forever. The resources required to maintain them are often more than the rest of humanity can bear. In the emergence of the American and lesser eastern empires were the various slave trades—Atlantic and East Indian and Mediterranean (Arabic). These trades, and many of their fallen empires, have left tracks that stand as highways across oceans and sky, through which the geography of reason can be renegotiated. The question of thought as we face the nihilistic forces of the twilight of rapacious imperialism is whether to step toward this new possibility of reason, which, in the end, is the beginning of an effort toward a genuinely *new* world.

Notes

1. Paleoarchaeologist Walter Neves of the University of São Paolo has uncovered 50,000-year-old human artifacts as well as 9,000- to 12,000-year-old skulls in Brazil that, after forensic reconstruction, reveal that their owners were "negroid" in appearance. Neves and his colleagues argue that these people were part of the Australian Aboriginal groups who migrated to Australia 60,000 years ago; their descendants were conquered by northern groups of Asiatic peoples between 7,000 and 9,000 years ago, during which they suffered near extinction save for the few hybrid descendants who survived over the millennia in such places as Terra del Fuego on the southern coast of South America. This research suggests a challenging consideration for African-American Studies. Although the notion of "America" or "the Americas" is meaningless in the context of those paleolithic times, it raises questions about the impact of early African and African-descended cultures on the geographical terrain that has come to be known as such. Whether they came to South America by way of the Pacific Ocean or directly from the southern regions of Africa into the Atlantic Ocean, the reality of the matter is that the people who remained on the African continent underwent nearly 40,000 years of transformation, subsequently including processes of creolization involving changed human populations who returned to Africa before meeting up with their ancestors in South America in the fifteenth century. The story of ancient peoples from Africa inhabiting South America also raises

profound questions about the subsequent histories of conquest in the Americas, making the tragedies of the New World more old than new. See Neves and his colleagues' groundbreaking work in the following articles: "The Zhoukoudian Upper Cave Skull 101 as Seen from the Americas" (Neves and Pucciarelli 1998), "Modern Human Origins as Seen from the Peripheries" (Neves, Powell, and Ozolins 1999), and "Early Holocene Human Skeletal Remains from Santa do Riacho, Brazil: Implications for the Settlement of the New World" (Neves, Prous, Gonzàlez-José, Kipnis, and Powell 2003).

2. Jane Anna Gordon offers development of this insight in her book *Why They Couldn't Wait* (2001) and chapter 3 of her dissertation "The General Will and Political Legitimacy: Secularization, Double Consciousness, and Force in Modern Democratic Theory" (2005). See also her chapter in Part II of this volume.

3. For a survey of some of this discussion, see Ernest Allen's "On the Reading of Riddles: Rethinking Du Boisian 'Double Consciousness'" (1997), Sandra Adell's *Double Consciousness/Double Bind* (1994), and Tukufu Zuberi and Elijah Anderson's commemoration issue of the *Annals of the American Academy of Social and Political Science* (2000).

4. The ideas that my colleagues Paget Henry, Nelson Maldonado-Torres, Claudia Milian Arias, Rowan Ricardo Phillips, Kenneth Knies, Jane Anna Gordon, and I have been working on over the past decade come out of Du Bois's and Fanon's insight on the colonization of knowledge and the need to construct new kinds of human study. See the References for some of our relevant work.

5. A variety of scholars working on and through the thought of Alain Locke appears in *Critical Pragmatism of Alain Locke* (1999), edited by Leonard Harris.

6. For demographics on antebellum black Muslims in America, see Allan Austin's *African Muslims in Antebellum America* (1997); for discussion of African-American Jews and the diversity of American Jews, see Diane Kaufman Tobin et al., *In Every Tongue* (2005); and for discussion of Afro-Native Americans, see William Katz, *Black Indians* (1986).

7. Let me take the opportunity to note here the difference between postmodern poststructuralism and poststructuralism. The former deploys poststructural analysis in the service of an ideological framework against certain narratives, whereas the latter has no preconceived position regarding narratives. Thus, there can be poststructuralists who are not postmodernists. Such scholars could conclude, for example, that postmodernism is peculiarly Eurocentric and that their work simply attempts to unveil the structural process or unfolding of power and its relationship to knowledge in given moments, or perhaps they would be interested in the relationship between knowledge and the constitution of different forms of life. Poststructuralism has been particularly useful, for instance, in the body of literature on the concept of "invention" in much of contemporary African philosophy. For a discussion of the impact of V. Y. Mudimbe, K. Anthony Appiah, Kwame Gyekye, Oyèrónké Oyewùmí, Elias Bongmba, Kwasi Wiredu, Nkiru Nzegwu, and Tsenay Serequeberhan, see the fourth chapter of my book *Disciplinary Decadence* (2006). Sylvia Wynter's work is also an example of a poststructuralism that could be mischaracterized as postmodernism. See, for example, her chapter in this volume. For discussion of her work, see Paget Henry's chapter on her thought in *Caliban's Reason* (2000a) and *After Man, the Human: Critical Essays on the Thought of Sylvia Wynter* (2005), edited by Anthony Bogues et al.

8. These themes of decay I explore in more detail in *Disciplinary Decadence*.

9. Oliver Cromwell Cox, *Race: A Study in Social Dynamics* (2000). For recent discussion of the proletarianization of blacks, see Joe R. Feagin, *Racist America* (2000).

10. Studies abound. For examples, see Elsa V. Goveia, *Slave Society in the British Leeward Islands at the End of the Eighteenth Century* (1965) and *Historiography of the British West Indies* (1980); Joan Dayan, *Haiti, History, and the Gods* (1998); Sibylle Fischer, *Modernity Disavowed* (2004); *Caribbean Slavery in the Atlantic World: A Student Reader,* revised and expanded edition, edited by Verene A. Shepherd and Hilary Beckles (2000); and, of course, C.L.R. James, *The Black Jacobins: Toussaint L'Ouverture and the San Domingo Revolution,* 2nd ed., rev. (1938/1989). In the North American context, see Rogers M. Smith, *Civic Ideals: Conflicting Visions of Citizenship in U.S. History* (1997); Herbert G. Gutman, *The Black Family in Slavery and Freedom: 1850-1925* (1976); Angela Y. Davis, *Women, Race, and Class* (1983); and Herbert Aptheker, *American Negro Slave Revolts* (1963).

11. For more discussion, see Lewis R. Gordon, *Existentia Africana* (2000: ch. 2).

12. For discussion, see, for example, the fourth chapter of *Existentia Africana* (2000b) as well as Peter Caws, *Ethics from Experience* (1996). Some earlier efforts by Caws include *The Philosophy of Science* (1965) and *Science and the Theory of Value* (1967). See also his recent *Yorick's World: Science and the Knowing Subject* (1993).

13. See Lewis R. Gordon, *Fanon and the Crisis of European Man* (1995b: ch. 5).

14. See, for example, Shelby Steele, *The Content of Our Character* (1990), and John McWhorter, *Losing the Race* (2001).

15. See the following two excellent studies: Rogers M. Smith's *Civic Ideals* and Joe Feagin's *Racist America.*

16. This dialectic of an unfolding Absolute is in most of Hegel's writings, but see especially his *Science of Logic* (1989).

17. For discussion of there not being the elimination of ethics but its paradoxically ethical suspension, see Calvin O. Schrag, *Betwixt and Between* (1994: 27-32).

18. For an account of the political dynamics of such professionalization, see John McCumber's *Time in the Ditch* (2001) as well as Nelson Maldonado-Torres's discussion in Chapter 2 of this volume.

19. All of these emerge in Naomi Zack's *American Mixed Race* (1995). Two other recent anthologies are David Parker and Miri Song's *Rethinking Mixed Race* (2001) and Jayne O. Ifekwunigwe's *"Mixed Race" Studies: A Reader* (2004).

20. The work of J. P. Rushton represents the Charles Darwin Institute. For a critique and discussion of the Straussian neoconservatives, see Anne Norton's *Leo Strauss and the Politics of Empire* (2004).

21. Yet here we find problems with the mixed-race theorists who argue for the uniqueness of biraciality. In effect, this construction functions like the "mule" construction since they cannot reproduce their identity. Two "biracial" partners would not produce a "biracial" child. They would have to find a white partner with whom to produce a "biracial" offspring. Oddly, the same logic doesn't apply to finding a black partner. At most, one would say that the offspring has some mixture. For more discussion, see Lewis R. Gordon, *Her Majesty's Other Children* (1997b: ch. 3). See also Helena Jia Hershel, "Therapeutic Perspectives on Biracial Identity Formation and Internalized Oppression" (1995: 169-181).

22. I have written on these matters in my books *Bad Faith and Antiblack Racism* (1995a/1999), *Fanon and the Crisis of European Man* (1995b), and *Her Majesty's Other Children* (1997b).

23. For a similar critique, see John L. and Jean Comaroff, *Of Revelation and Revolution,* Vol. 2 (1997: 18).

24. In American popular culture, this has been happening on the level of animal totems. The male lion and bulls with flaring nostrils have been replaced by lionesses and cows. The popularity of the cow should not be underestimated. Think of how many Hollywood films with cow totems have popped up over the past decade (e.g., *Brother Where Art Thou* [2000] and *Me, Myself, and Irene* [2000]); and in Chicago, Illinois, there was a cow exhibit throughout the city in the mid-1990s. Cow iconography is everywhere as well: cow pillows, stuffed cows, and so forth.

25. Maldonado-Torres and Knies offer discussions of their positions in Chapters 2 and 3, respectively.

2
Toward a Critique of Continental Reason

Africana Studies and the Decolonization of Imperial Cartographies in the Americas

Nelson Maldonado-Torres

✦

What does it mean to say, as Ebrahim Moosa (2001) recently put it, that "[w]e are compelled by the lessons of history to understand that humanity is global and not continental"? What lessons are these? In what way do we still persist in being continental? And what is at stake in our alleged fixation with continentality? Moosa, a native of South Africa, himself performed an act of trans-continentality as he delivered these words in an address to a U.S. audience just a few months before the tragic events of September 11th.[1] "Americans," to be sure, have heard similar calls from different groups of peoples on this side of the Atlantic Ocean long before that tragic date and its aftermath. Paradigms of migration and diaspora, along with the defiant claims of nonassimilationist politics, put into question the very meanings of American and Latin American identity.[2] While these paradigms and forms of politics have elicited important work in cultural studies, they have not been equally influential in philosophy.[3] And philosophy undoubtedly remains one of the disciplines in which the continental spirit is most active and seductive.

I would like to thank Eduardo Mendieta for his comments on earlier versions of this chapter. I also wish to thank the recently inaugurated Caribbean Philosophical Association for giving me the hope that, together, we will be able to move beyond the illusions and problematic dimensions of continental thought toward a postcontinental and nonimperial geography of reason.

The aim of this chapter is to articulate some of the challenges posed by Africana Studies to the discipline of philosophy and, more particularly, to the articulation of the analytic/continental divide. In the search for a postcontinental philosophical way of thinking, I consider the efforts of Cornel West, whose appraisal of American pragmatism explicitly involves a claim to supersede the limits of analytic and continental philosophy. After reflecting on the virtues and limitations of West's project, I will attempt to clarify the specific challenges of Africana Studies to continental thought. Beyond the particularity typically allotted to ethnicity, and different from both nationalism and cosmopolitanism, Africana Studies, along with other Ethnic Studies departments and programs that emerged in the wake of the 1960s, promotes the decolonization of knowledge and identities and opens up a horizon of reflection that allows a conception of the *humanum* as global without being continental.[4]

On the Difference Between Analytic and Continental Philosophy

A few years ago, an editorial of the *American Philosophical Quarterly* formulated the difference between so-called analytic and continental philosophical trends in terms of focus and originality ("A Case" 1996). The editorial points out what has already become common parlance in philosophical circles: While analytic philosophers are concerned with problems, continental philosophers deal with historical figures. Since an idea is true or not independent of who formulated it or when it was uttered, one is tempted to conclude that analytic philosophy is more strictly philosophical than its epic contender. The editorial suggests, however, that analytic philosophy's reliance on the problem-solving approach does not sufficiently take into account the extent to which problem solving is constrained by the ways in which problems are formulated in the first place. Continental philosophy's preference for the study of historical figures responds precisely to the awareness that a problem is defined by a perspective, tradition, or vocabulary. In this perspective, great thinkers are not so much those who solve a problem as those who shift the grounds of traditional ways of thinking and provide new horizons for the exploration of old and new problems. Thus, what continental philosophy loses in respect to uniformity of vocabulary and perspective, it gains in freshness and originality. However, this advantage can turn into a capital problem inasmuch as the creation of universes of meaning, to put it in the editorial's terms, "can easily descend into pretentious gibberish" ("A Case" 1996: 131).

"Analytic" and "continental" are not terms that define philosophical movements or that necessarily delimit the activity of any single philosopher. Philosophers who are associated with any of these terms may not themselves use such terms as a form of self-description. Yet, as the above-quoted editorial makes evident, this situation has not much changed the continued use of the terms or the reference to certain kinds of philosophical expressions typically linked to them.[5] According to Jonathan Rée, the difference between analytic and continental may be traced back to John Stuart Mill's distinction between Bentham and Coleridge (see Critchley 1998: 15). Mill speaks of "Continental philosophy" to denote the particular German influence on the latter author. For Mill, the difference between Bentham and Coleridge is best articulated in terms of the difference between the questions "Is it true?" and "What is the meaning of it?" (*ibid.*). One question leads to a quasi-scientific approach to reality, while the other invokes the examination and elaboration of multiple horizons of meaning for the investigation of any given phenomenon. While Mill could not have anticipated the ways in which what is known today as continental philosophy has evolved, he surely was right in pointing to two dominant approaches or tendencies in modern Western philosophy. While influential figures like Gottlob Frege, Bertrand Russell, and Rudolf Carnap gave to philosophy a more scientific outlook, the work of the later Edmund Husserl, Martin Heidegger, and Hans-Georg Gadamer, to name a few, questioned the dominant epistemic status of the sciences and offered new bases from which to pursue philosophical explorations that received their inspiration in fields in the humanities such as history and literature. From here some have spelled out the contrast between analytic and continental philosophy in terms of the divide between the sciences and the humanities in the modern university (e.g., Putnam 1997; Rorty 2002).

The link between analytical philosophy and science partly explains the reason for the prominence of analytic philosophy, particularly in capitalist countries (see Rajchman and West 1985: x). Yet, this tie by itself does not explain why analytic philosophy has come to overshadow so radically alternative philosophical productions in the

United States, including its main contemporary contender, continental philosophy. As with all institutional matters, the reasons for this hegemony are not purely intellectual but political as well. Although its dominance began to be visible in the 1950s, the context that facilitated the hegemony of analytic philosophy may be traced back to the 1920s. It was then that a reaction against progressivism began to erode the basis of a way of thinking that went back to the writings of Emerson and Whitman in the nineteenth century. As Morris Dickstein puts it, both Emerson and Whitman proposed a "genuinely fresh start" for the New American nation, "an escape from the heavy hand of European tradition, an emancipation by self-definition" (Dickstein 1998: 5). These ideals became part of the emerging pragmatism, which was challenged by psychoanalysis and crisis theology, among other movements whose less optimistic tone fit better with the times in Europe during the 1920s. A few decades later, gradually, but systematically, both pragmatism and its temporary contenders were displaced by analytic philosophy. The context of World War II and its aftermath had much to do with this. As John McCumber documents in his partial history of the discipline, the gradual ascendance of analytic philosophers in the 1950s is intimately connected to the Cold War and, more particularly, to McCarthyism. "The McCarthy era," McCumber explains, "imposed an important restriction on just what kind of goal philosophers can pursue. It limited them to the pursuit of true sentences (or propositions, or statements)" (McCumber 2001: xix). The search for truth was posited as an antidote to presumably ideological expressions and controversial positions in a time of strong repression of public discourse and intellectual agendas. McCarthyism made clear that "scholars must avoid not only conspiracies but even open commitment to positions on controversial questions, except where they can take such positions on the basis of dispassionate objectivity. The possession of objective, scientific knowledge, and that alone, entitles them to a hearing—or a job. The *raison d'être* of the university is not open discussion but the timeless, selfless quest of truth" (*ibid.:* 40).

When the wave of phenomenology and existentialism arrived in the United States in the late 1950s and early 1960s, analytic philosophy was already in a position of dominance. As McCumber notes, the particularly introspective and individualistic imported versions of these philosophical approaches helped them to supplant metaphysics and pragmatism and to become the privileged others of analytic philosophy (McCumber 2001: 83). This shift was confirmed when European contenders such as deconstructionists, psychoanalysts, and genealogists were added to the list of European cohorts in the late 1960s. It is in relation to this unexpected growth that the concept of "continental" emerged in the United States. The term aimed to distinguish the dominant analytic from other philosophical expressions that were recently imported from Europe, particularly from France and Germany. The difference between the tendencies was clear at both the intellectual and the political levels. While analytic philosophy reflected a certain commitment to the Enlightenment's vision of universality, continental philosophy adopted a more skeptical stance in respect to the Enlightenment's epistemological ambitions and historical promises. And while there were some exceptions to the rule, analytic philosophy remained in close proximity to the institutional framework that contributed to its dominance, whereas the new wave of continental philosophy was intimately tied to some of the protest movements in Europe and the United States. These affiliations surely affected style and focus as well. While analytic philosophers have tended to maintain a formal style and a uniform vocabulary, continental philosophers are sometimes prone to explore original forms of expression and vocabulary. It is precisely these two elements, the stylistic and the political, that a group of scholars chose to highlight in their public statement against one of the dominant voices in continental philosophy, Jacques Derrida:

> M. Derrida's career had its roots in the heady days of the 1960's and his writings continue to reveal their origins in that period. Many of them seem to consist in no small part of elaborate jokes and puns ("logical phallusies" and the like) and M. Derrida seems to us to have come close to making a career out of what we regard as translating into the academic sphere tricks and gimmicks similar to those of the Dadaists or of the concrete poets.[6]

Although one would have expected a more careful and balanced judgment from those who often pride themselves in deciphering the mysteries of the principles of knowledge, this statement clearly points to the cultural backlash that separates many contemporary analytic from continental philosophers. Analytic philosophers tend to guard jealously the gates of professional philosophical exploration from those figures whose style tends to be more esoteric and experimental. Ralph Humphries is surely right when he states: "The institutional division between continental and analytic is a fact, and this is evidenced by the predominance of analytically trained philosophers in Anglophone departments of philosophy, an ascendancy which has sought over time to determine unequivocally what it is to do philosophy" (Humphries 1999). In short, if, on the one hand, the vocabulary of continental philosophy "can easily descend into pretentious gibberish," on the other, the serious analytic philosopher often falls victim to the "philosopher king" complex.

The analytic philosopher's claim to epistemic clarity and unequal logical skills is often countered by the continental philosopher's pride in criticism and originality. However revolutionary the thinkers who form part of continental philosophy's canon may be, this characterization tends to elide the persistence of a strongly self-referential attitude in continental philosophy. Originality hardly flourishes in an area increasingly marked by the requirements of expertise and submission to the authority of a thinker. Continental philosophy is also for the most part limited by a strong Eurocentric perspective. McCumber notes, for instance, how those American continental philosophers with something original to say had to fight not only against the dismissal of their analytic counterparts but also against the "Eurocentric prejudice of their own confreres" (McCumber 2001: 85–86). It is ironic that McCumber himself attempts to bridge the gap between analytic and continental philosophy by introducing stronger doses of Hegel and Heidegger, two of the most influential and original but also most Eurocentric thinkers in the modern West. The point is not that the philosophical production of Eurocentric thinkers could not somehow be redeemed, or that their Eurocentric perspective vitiates their entire work. The point is rather that McCumber seems to be much more sensitive to the Eurocentric perspectives of students of continental philosophy than to the Eurocentrism of the figures that he invokes. McCumber fails to examine carefully the extent to which continental philosophy's typical critiques of the Enlightenment and the scientific pathos that accompanies analytic philosophy typically assume a Eurocentric vision. What is usually identified as continental philosophy does not oppose history, tradition, or power to the more ahistorical and abstract conceptions of subjectivity and knowledge that emerged from the Enlightenment. It has always been a certain kind of European history, tradition, and conception of power that they have come to highlight. In this respect, continental philosophy has shown itself to be not only *from* the continent but also *of* the continent. As it takes a universalistic approach, referring to the human being in general when it rather examines the particular historical formation of European subjectivity, it becomes a most influential designer of academic global designs out of the particular historical experience of Europe and European Man.[7] Eurocentrism and a certain continentalist vision rather than "pretentious gibberish" may very well represent the most fundamental challenge for followers of the continental tradition.

One may argue that continental philosophers would betray the turn to history, tradition, and power if they did not rely precisely on a particular history, tradition, or context in which power unfolds. The contrary would be precisely to *de*-historicize history. The reply to this objection is that for the most part continental philosophers have invested the particular with the force of the universal, and that they have hardly recognized the provinciality of their views. If this is the case, one might be led to think that it suffices if continental thinkers simply modify their claims by avoiding the mistake of taking them as a model to measure or evaluate other histories and cultures. Unfortunately, things are not so easy. The problem is that in its commitment to the continental perspective, the continental approach does not adequately portray the formation of communities and human interaction. Is there such a thing as the European spirit or European Man?[8] Continental philosophy loses from view the extent to which the very idea of the European has a darker side that it has not been able to spell out or uncover completely.[9] Insofar as this darker side is constitutive of the European's very identity, philosophical formulations uncritically centered on Europeanity tend to be rather limited and quite problematic perspectives.

The intense skepticism that found expression in the varieties of continental philosophy in the late 1960s has hardly led to a radical questioning of its Eurocentric tendencies and its commitment to a continental vision of space. Indeed, if continental and analytic philosophy part ways in their relation to the Enlightenment and the heritage of the Parisian uprisings of 1968, they both meet once more and reinforce their common ground in their respective indifference and lack of engagement with theoretical elaborations that have emerged in the south—and the south, to be sure, is meant here not literally but as a metaphor for social and geopolitical subalterity and liminality. That is, the analytic philosophers who depicted and condemned Derridean deconstruction in relation to the upheavals of the 1960s, and the continental philosophers who were marked by the wake of deconstruction, hardly pay attention, among other important ways of thinking, to the challenges posed by the expressions of the 1960s in the south—including marginalized ethnicities in the north. The debate between analytic and continental philosophers is a family quarrel, and both benefit from the game.[10] They both tend to be equally dismissive of the struggles from racialized and subaltern peoples and their efforts to establish institutional structures that create a space for alternative theoretical projects. From this perspective it appears that if Derrida's project is problematic, as analytic philosophers have not ceased to insist, it may not be because of its close links with the 1960s but because of its selective attachment to the 1960s as they took place in the north, and particularly in Paris with the provincial debate between Marxists and Heideggerians.[11] Derrida presupposes a horizon of investigation that is European. I do not mean to deny that his philosophical perspective may be partly indebted to ideas and concerns that emerged out of Europe. But, to the extent that they are, they are not properly acknowledged and tend to be neutralized by his own Eurocentrism. This posture is by no means unique to Derrida. It is perpetuated in the work of philosophers who cannot perceive relevant epistemic perspectives and questions outside the figures in the well-established canon of continental or analytic philosophy.

One of the legacies of the struggle of minorities during the 1960s in the United States is the formation of Ethnic Studies programs and departments throughout the nation.[12] These include Black Studies, African-American Studies, Ethnic Studies, Chicano Studies, and Native American Studies, among several others. These programs and departments have tended to focus on the revisionist project of correcting problematic historical, cultural, and literary analyses that either downplay or exaggerate the role of the different ethnic populations that they study. In short, they have come to address the problem of the invisibility and distorted visibility of ethnic minorities in scholarship. Gradually, they have also become an umbrella for the development of social scientific approaches that bring into focus problems confronted by these different populations. Theorists in Ethnic Studies departments, like scholars in other areas in the humanities and social sciences, frequently borrow ideas from continental philosophers in order to pursue this task. The reason is that, similar to continental philosophers, theorists in Ethnic Studies are deeply interested in reflecting critically about history, tradition, and power. Scholars interested in the predicament of ethnic populations are sometimes critical of diverse philosophical positions. But their theoretical contributions have not been mobilized in the direction of dislocating the analytic/continental divide in an explicit manner.[13] I have in mind here not so much the study of ethnic philosophies as the challenge posed by the epistemological framework introduced by Ethnic Studies approaches.[14] I would like in what follows to spell out some ideas about the character of this epistemological framework and to explore an alternative way of overcoming the analytic/continental divide. I will do this by critically engaging the thought of Cornel West. I focus on West because, more than any other philosopher of his generation, he has questioned the definition of philosophical visions limited by the analytic/continental divide. He has also offered a progressive, postsecular, and geopolitically distinct form of philosophical discourse: American prophetic pragmatism. West's genius takes us a long way into the project of effectively overcoming the limitations that are often associated with analytic and continental philosophy, yet his discourse stops short of achieving a postcontinental vision. A critical examination of his efforts will show how the rejection of "European hero worshipping" hardly eradicates by itself the problematic tendencies related to the privileged role of continentality in philosophical expressions.

Ethnos, Ethos, and Ethics: American Pragmatism and the Crucible of Time

The main opposition to the analytic/continental divide in the United States has come from sectors interested in spelling out the particularity of U.S. American philosophy, which is typically understood as American pragmatism. It is arguably none other than the most celebrated living African-American philosopher and religious thinker, Cornel West, who has articulated this view most cogently and elegantly. His most comprehensive elaboration of it appears in his renowned *The American Evasion of Philosophy* (1989a). In this work, West traces the complex path of pragmatism, which is presented as the native philosophy of the United States. West's *American Evasion* was published in 1989, a crucial moment for the redefinition of the self-conception and foreign policy of the United States. Indeed, this date is important to an understanding of the significant structural changes of the economic, military, and political order in the entire globe. The destiny of the opposition to totalitarian and capitalist regimes that 1968 made so apparent became clear in 1989. Where totalitarian socialism ended, capitalism reigned all the more, or at least that is the tendency we have observed since 1989. While in 1968 the imperial tendencies of the United States were unmasked, 1989 testified to the emergence of a new form of patriotism that even thinkers of the left have come to embrace (see particularly Rorty 1998).

American Evasion is very significant because it interrupts a tendency that had remained dominant since the early 1970s. After 1968, an impetuous new generation of scholars in the United States found in the French intellectual production many of the critical tools that they thought they needed to give expression to their post-1968 sensibility. There was an atmosphere of intoxication that did not fail to give rise to a furious reaction against the new offenders. Scholars like Cornel West were convinced that analytic philosophy could continue its dominant course, but only at the price of irrelevance or dogmatism.[15] West was receptive, but by no means satisfied by the continental tradition of critique. In pragmatism, West found a tradition of enquiry that appeared to be as different from analytic philosophy as it was from the most recent continental philosophical production. In *American Evasion,* West makes a decisive nationalist turn and depicts pragmatism as a particularly American form of reflection that celebrates much of what continental philosophy had made so unpopular, including the emancipatory commitment to democracy and freedom, which West perceived as paradigmatically American.[16]

The interest in articulating a particularly American philosophy raises interesting questions. For although we are said to have French, German, and British philosophies we hardly see these differences played out in the name of the right for particularity, at least in a way that breaks the horizons of the analytic/continental divide.[17] The case of the United States is peculiar since its present role of leadership in the economy and military management of the world-system does not hide the fact that it was once a colonial territory. The United States is something like the Cinderella of nation-states. The most remarkable difference from the original story is that once the United States escaped the bondage of its mother and sisters, it turned as tyrannical as they were. Tyrannical power, however, does not compensate for cultural sophistication. And, although the United States may currently be the locus of financial prosperity and military might, it has not been considered—at least until relatively recently—to be, like other powers in the past, the locus of culture or civilization. The United States has clearly attempted to compensate for this. And perhaps its more successful effort is being carried out today in the war against terror. Samuel Huntington's idea of the clash of civilizations announced the radical turn (Huntington 1996). For, first of all, it elevated the principle of American politics to the level of a civilization, and, second, it translated power differentials into cultural conflicts. After Huntington, military aggressions tend to be interpreted as inevitable civilizational conflicts.

In a sense, Huntington radicalized the patriotic turn announced in West's *Genealogy* (1989b) and gave it a strongly conservative direction. But, however successful attempts at presenting the United States as the locus of Western culture or civilization in mass media may have been, the academy forgets less easily. And among the different disciplines that bring out the "civilizational complex," philosophy may well stand at the very top. However secure and self-confident a particular group may be, philosophy can easily provoke the most long-standing and dangerous inferiority complexes. The dreams of reaching equality are shattered by the discriminating philosophical gaze that points to the absence of philosophy and thus of reason in the "cultural" or "religious" group in question.[18] Human groups may possess the most beautiful literature, religion, and arts, while at the same time losing the essential and, according to traditional philosophical views, that which is most characteristically human, the power of reason. The medication is well known: Go to the Greeks. But drinking from the Greeks' philosophical well is hardly enough. You must follow the European path. And nobody will be closer to this path than the Europeans themselves.[19] Thus, the trace of a difference always remains and one's psychotic delusions can only grow. Unless. . . . Yes, unless one can demonstrate that reason has not necessarily followed the path drawn by imperial cartographies and that it has also visited other lands. West's *American Evasion* is clearly an effort in this direction. Yet, its nationalist spirit limits the possibilities of his project and puts him in line with the detractors of the heritage of the 1960s. Ironically, if it were not for this heritage, interest in African-American contributions to philosophy and religious thought, including West's own work, would probably be much lower than it is today.

Consistent with his critical view of the heritage of the 1960s, West's contribution to the heated debates over the philosophical import of French theory did not involve a systematic exploration of the possible contributions of Africana thought.[20] In his formulation, African-American philosophers can challenge the analytic/continental divide in philosophy only by highlighting the American side in the hyphenated formula of their ethnic identity. It is fundamentally as Americans that they would have to enter the philosophical wars.[21] West does not pursue the path of trying to explore the epistemic potential of a dead or ignored African-American philosophy because, presumably different from African or Jewish philosophers, African Americans cannot pinpoint an ancient tradition that would give expression to their own particular wisdom. In addition, West does not believe that African Americans have produced a first-rate theoretical work.[22] As a result, he suggests, African Americans lack the resources to question the analytic/continental divide by drawing on their own peculiar sources. However, as Americans, African Americans share, if not a particular tradition, at least a peculiar *ethos* with the American people. Both the American Revolution and the slaves' struggle for freedom, along with the immigrant investment in the American Dream, reflect a particular appreciation of freedom and possibility. It is precisely this cultural ethos that inspires and nourishes American pragmatism. As West makes clear in his introduction to *The American Evasion of Philosophy:*

> American pragmatism is a diverse and heterogeneous tradition. But its common denominator consists of a future-oriented instrumentalism that tries to deploy thought as a weapon to enable more effective action. Its basic impulse is a plebeian radicalism that fuels an antipatrician rebelliousness for the moral aim of enriching individuals and expanding democracy. (West 1989a: 5)

American pragmatism appears to be the distinctive American response to the approach taken and the problems confronted by epistemology-centered philosophy and foundationalism. Against continental philosophy with its overly skeptical tones, its antipatriotic tendencies, and its Europeanizing gaze, American pragmatism reveals, as it were, the universal significance of the American ethos, allegedly reflected in its commitment to a postfoundational search for truth that is guided by the pragmatic ideals of democracy and freedom.

In the Introduction to *The Cornel West Reader,* West asserts that "[t]o be American is to give ethical significance to the future by viewing the present as a terrain capable of transcending any past and thereby arriving at a new identity and community" (West 1999: xix). West is well aware that this "futuristic orientation often degenerates into an infantile, sentimental or melodramatic propensity toward happy endings, so that dreams of betterment downplay the dark realities of suffering in our midst"; yet one wonders to what extent the very shift from ethnos or ethnicity to ethos, and the exploration of cultural ethos in terms of temporality, has dangerous consequences or implications (*ibid.*). Consider that Hegel, long before West, had conceived of America in terms of futurity.[23] West's view on this matter is not by any means identical with that of Hegel. While the former observed America from the perspective of imperial Europe, without being able to break the logic that sustained that vision, the latter rather seems to articulate a postcolonial nationalism of sorts. This nationalism becomes most evident when West, very much in line with the ethos of his culture, conceives of America as a *people,* and not as a conglomerate of cultures and peoples who inhabit two continents. In this respect, Hegel may have had a more correct vision of things than West. For he thought about America in more encompassing terms. While the differences between Hegel and West are very important, it is nonetheless clear that implicit in their conceptions of "America" is the idea that if America represents the future, continental Europe may very well be interpreted in light of a particular affinity with the past.[24] It is not accidental that continental philosophy, as it appears in the writings of Hegel, Marx, Dilthey, Heidegger, and Gadamer, among other prominent figures in the field, bring up the question of history and historicity in a prominent form. Even deconstruction and genealogical poststructuralism rely precisely on the notion of a past that perpetually haunts the present and that makes it necessary for the philosopher, as it were, to exorcize it.

It is evident that if American philosophy does not reflect the same concern with the past, this is largely the case because, leaving aside indigenous communities, for U.S. Americans the past is too short and a large part of it is tied to a history of colonization. The drive to the future is clearly facilitated by the absence of the weight of a millenary tradition and history. Indeed, the futuristic orientation represents, in a way, the only recourse for Americans to achieve a sense of self-realization and maturity. Without this fixation with the past, the claims of Western philosophy and its tradition, to be sure, weigh much less, and the efforts at imposition can be more easily *evaded*. This explains to some extent why analytic philosophy has been so dominant in the United States. Its dominance in philosophy departments may not have only to do with its homogeneous style, its alleged quasi-scientific rigor, and its easy conciliation with the demands of departmentalization and the corporate structure of the university.[25] Analytic philosophy, as it has been defined and practiced by many in the United States, facilitates the erasure of the question of history and historicity, focusing more instead on the question of abstract foundations for knowledge. Ironic as it may sound, in a way at least, the dominance of analytic philosophy in the United States may partly respond to the postcolonial need of freezing history, when history tends to give *a priori* advantage to the old imperial continent where true culture and civilization are allegedly located. In the United States, analytic philosophy is, to some extent, philosophy with a vengeance. Few have perceived the pathos behind this philosophical trend. But those who see American pragmatism as their salvation make it all clear. As the pathos of this vengeance proves unsavory and its thirst for epistemic foundations problematic, pragmatism turns the tables by recovering the relevance of history—but, as it were, in reverse, by privileging futurity over the past and the present. Thus, while continental philosophy emphasizes history and power (the past), analytic philosophy focuses on an always permanent present, and pragmatism centers more on the future.

The exploration of cultural ethos, tendencies in philosophical production, temporal dynamics, and geopolitical considerations would hardly be complete without considering the role of the gradually forgotten participant in the civilizational encounter between Europe and the "new" world: Latin America. Although Latin America is part of the putatively New World, the impetus for innovation and drive for the future there are clearly not as distinct as in the United States. It is as if only one country in the two American continents fulfilled the promise of the "discovered" lands. That is why it is so unproblematic for Americans to identify America with their own country. As we have seen, West is not an exception to this rule. But if Latin America does not share with the United States its drive for the future, what, then, is the dominant temporal dynamic in the region? Latin America has been characterized as a highly politicized context damaged by continuous upheavals. Since the independence of most Latin American countries, there has been an urgent need to create democratic institutions and a state of right.[26] There has been a need, but hardly a fulfillment or an accomplishment. As Anibal Quijano makes clear:

> The problem with Latin America ... was that just when its modernity seemed to enter the phase of demarcation of its specificity and maturity with respect to Europe, when it began to define itself as a new social and cultural possibility, it fell victim to its colonial relationship with Europe and was subjected to a literally Kafkaesque "metamorphosis." ... So, while in Europe modernity was part of a radical mutation of society, feeding off the changes prepared by the emergence of capitalism, in Latin America, from the end of the eighteenth century on, modernity was linked to an adverse social context, in which the decline of the economy and the breakdown of the mercantilist system permitted the social sectors most antagonistic to it to occupy the leading positions in the elaboration of Latin America's independence from Europe. (Quijano 1995: 205)

Although Latin America's connection with the past is complex and hardly follows the logic of linear temporality, it is still possible to say that the region seems to remain always in the past, trying to reach not some kind of future but simply that which for "developed" countries exists as the present. The history of Latin America may be seen as a constant effort to keep in touch with the present—that is, to be real in some way or to keep with how things go. To be sure, this ethos and this temporal mode do not emanate from some mysterious Latin American essence. They point rather to the legacy of imperial designs. The past of Latin America, is, like that of the United States, both recent and seriously dislocated by the colonial period. Latin America cannot take refuge in the past. But neither can it take refuge in the future, since relations of power have led it to remain in the shadows of other nations. Latin America tends toward the present, but not toward its own present. It tends toward the present of other nations without ever fully accomplishing this act. Thus, while the United States aims to escape from a colonial past, Latin America remains in constant crisis (or between crisis and damnation) since it cannot but aim toward a present that can never be and cannot project itself adequately toward the future. We can therefore say that if Europe's ethos gives expression to a temporality of *past*-present-future, and the United States' ethos to that of past-present-*future,* Latin America lives, for the most, under the mode of past-*present*-future. Besides the obvious difference in emphasis, Latin America differs from the other two in that while Europe's past and the United States' future are theirs, Latin America's present is not its own present but the present of Europe and the United States—that is, of "developed" countries. If the region has learned something from the tragedies of the last century, it should be aware by now that it will not be able to escape this circle by further attempts at incorporation or by Heideggerian-like acts of solitude that promise authenticity but only end up invoking authoritarian regimes or Führer principles.[27]

It is important to recognize that although no territory simply shares homogeneously the ethos and temporal modalities that I point out here, this exploration sheds some light into the ethos that finds expression in state politics and in the attitudes of many subjects in those regions.[28] Indeed, the ethos of a region is tied as much to an international dimension of power dynamics as to the sustenance of an internal political and social order with unequal relations of power. The look toward the future is convenient, particularly with such a problematic recent past as that of the United States. The difficulty of coming to terms with slavery and to consider seriously the question of reparations is connected to the fundamental incapacity to give due ontological weight to the past. Liberalism in the United States has no historical depth.[29] Also important is the way in which migrant populations are treated. "The future of our Nation" is constantly used against the menacing presence of border subjects and of southern migrants who make it to the north. It is as if the temporal vortices of the nation would be distorted by the *presence* of subjects who come from a different space and time zone. Otherwise put, the future of the United States makes their present/presence untenable. A clear example of this is Samuel Huntington's hysterical response to what he deems the "Hispanic challenge."[30] A similar equation of past, present, and future occurs in Europe and Latin America. Europe recognizes the past, but it is also a convenient past—that is, an imaginatively reconstructed past with a glorious continuity that justifies the perception that Europe represents the climax of humanity. Latin America, on the other hand, always with its crises and revolutions, tries to enter into the present, but since its presence is molded in the image of someone else's present, more often than not it takes the form of repetition (via "development"), which involves the eradication of whatever *in us* is clearly different *from them*. Latin America, therefore, aims toward a present, but one, as it were, without the presence of Indians and Blacks.[31] This tendency is also followed in the United States and arguably characterizes a fundamental dimension of our modern experience.[32]

However strongly the politics of every region responds to a particular ethos, it is clear that the internal temporal dynamics in Europe and the Americas can hardly be accounted for solely in terms of differences in national culture. Indeed, if something should be clear by now, it is the idea that differences in temporal modes do not obey solely the logic of cultural differences. What we have here instead is power differentials that sediment themselves and promote distinct attitudes and behaviors that are taken as natural expressions of the way things supposedly are. Whatever culture may be, as Walter Mignolo has suggested, it can hardly escape the power dynamics that derive from geopolitical relations. Indeed, one cannot but wonder, as Mignolo does, about the extent to which "the very concept of 'culture' is a colonial construction" (Mignolo 1995/1999: 41). From this perspective, to affirm, for instance, that "culture matters," as Huntington and others do, is not so different from disguising power relations and their effects as cultural differences.[33] Alternatively, to affirm, for instance, as José David Saldívar (1997) does, that "border matters" is to take the nexus between space, culture, and power as the point of departure. Saldívar's explorations of theory and insurgent forms of life in the U.S. Southwest borderlands can be seen as the postcolonial response to the more simplistic mainstream liberal conception articulated by Huntington. A related position is that of Cornel West in *Democracy Matters* (2004). West's Americanism puts him somewhere between Huntington's culturalist nativism and Saldívar's progressive postcolonial vision. As much as he criticizes U.S. imperialism in *Democracy Matters,* West's vision of America leads him to disregard indigenous subjectivities and border realities. West's brave and eloquent critiques of empire are important and timely, yet critiques of empire alone do not amount to decolonization. Neither left Eurocentrism Žižek nor (left) Americanism (West) can do that. The sources and orientation for decolonial perspectives are found elsewhere.[34] Africana Studies provides a most important space for this form of reflection.

The main point that I want to make here is simple: The role of geopolitical power dynamics in the formation of identities and cultures is such that no ethos can be elucidated only with reference to internal cultural virtues or alleged potentialities. Moreover, the temporal modes that characterize each region are deeply interrelated. The dominant patterns behave as if there were some age-old inherited order of things that produces these temporal fluctuations among different cultural expressions. But how to characterize this order? Are analytic, continental, and West's own American pragmatism aware of it? Or are they rather inserted in this order and unknowingly providing ideological support? It is in response to these questions that we may find the basis for a definition of the current role of Africana Studies in particular and of Ethnic Studies in general. In a way, the challenge is, as Sylvia Wynter (1995) has so aptly articulated it, to radicalize, instead of refraining from, the critical import and epistemic challenge of the social movements and academic programs that were founded after the upheavals of the 1960s.

The Significance of TimeSpace Realities

Europe and the Americas share long ties that go back more than five hundred years now. According to Immanuel Wallerstein, they were the locus in the "long sixteenth century" of the emergence of what is clearly one of the more, if not the most, powerful historical systems in world history: the capitalist world-economy (see, among others, Wallerstein 1979). A historical system, for Wallerstein, has not only a temporal dimension but a spatial one as well. He introduces the term "TimeSpace" in order to convey the idea that time and space cannot be conceived as disconnected wholes (Wallerstein 1991). Following Fernand Braudel's typology of temporality, Wallerstein outlines different forms of TimeSpace. The capitalist world-economy, for instance, is a category that pertains to the analysis of structural TimeSpace realities. Structural TimeSpace refers to the coordination between long-term historical systems and large- scale spatial configurations. It makes reference not to events but to structural patterns, which alone make it possible to interpret the meaning and function of events. Contrary to Claude Levy-Strauss's structuralist anthropology, history is fundamental here to a proper identification and understanding of the complex patterns of any given structure. In short, structure, temporality, and spatiality work together as a single analytical category. Although this is arguably the fundamental category of world-system analysis, Wallerstein numbers and describes other forms of TimeSpace. These include episodic geopolitical TimeSpace, cyclico-ideological TimeSpace, and eternal TimeSpace (Wallerstein 1991: 139–145).

In contrast to Wallerstein's approach to the study of historical systems, dominant views in the social sciences tend to ignore both the intricate connection between space and time and the need for differentiating between different forms of TimeSpace. Analytic and continental philosophy stand in a similar relation to Wallerstein's conceptual contribution. Analytic philosophy, with its peculiar suspension of temporality, is not so distant from the nomothetic social sciences and their fixation in eternal TimeSpace. Eternal TimeSpace is found precisely in the "universally true scientific theorems" of the social sciences that can be validated irrespective of particularities in time and space (Wallerstein 1991: 144–145). It is not so easy to find a parallel to continental philosophy in the social sciences. Because of their propensity to idealism, one is tempted to refer to the temporality that is usually presupposed by continental philosophers as *spiritual time.* Spiritual time would be a sort of active temporality or set of epistemes that animates the historical process. Following Wallerstein, one can conceive of a sort of spiritual TimeSpace that combines spiritual time with the typical continental Eurocentrism. That is, the space of spiritual time would no doubt be the continent of Europe. If one were to extend these reflections to American pragmatism, it is possible to say that the kind of temporality advocated by West could be rendered as pragmatic time. This is a temporality oriented by a particular accent on action and its fruits. The spatial component of pragmatic TimeSpace would be precisely what we are used to calling "America"—that is, the continentalized (not merely continental) United States.

As different as they may seem at first sight, it is clear that these three philosophical expressions have in common, along with dominant views in the social sciences, a dismissal of structural TimeSpace. Structural TimeSpace is fundamental here because it helps us to understand the synchronization of the temporal dynamics that transpire in the dominant ethos of Europe and the Americas. In their respective investment in different dimensions of temporality, figures from Europe, the United States, and Latin America do not pay attention to, or are unable even to take cognizance, of the "larger picture."[35] This larger picture shows the interrelation between temporal accents in places where the dominant historical system saw its birth. But temporal dynamics cannot be accounted for completely in terms of the exploitation of human labor, which is what capitalism usually stands for. The interrelational temporal dynamics in Europe and the Americas are first and foremost an effect of colonial relations and, more particularly, of the coloniality of power and the idea of race. Quijano explains:

> America was constituted as the first space/time of a new model of power of global vocation, and both in this way and by it became the first identity of modernity. Two historical processes associated in the production of that space/time converged and established the two fundamental axes of the new model of power. One was the codification of the differences between conquerors and conquered in the idea of "race," a supposedly different biological structure that placed some in a natural situation of inferiority to the others. The conquistadors assumed this idea as the constitutive, founding element of the relations of domination that the conquest imposed. On this basis, the population of America, and later the world, was classified within the new model of power. The other process was the constitution of a new structure of control of labor and its resources and products. (Quijano 2000: 533–534)

The articulation of these two processes is what Quijano refers to as the coloniality of power. This concept is critical since it makes clear that it is racial domination, and not only exploitation, that is at work in the temporal and spatial configuration of modernity.[36] This form of domination—based on the division of territories and the categorization of peoples according to the logics dictated by the imperial upsurge of a rising Christian and, subsequently, secular Europe—marks subjects, territories, languages, and cultures and overdetermines them from without, thus radically modifying their horizon of possibilities. It becomes clear, then, that differences in space make a difference in respect to experiences of time. *Trying to subvert imperial dynamics by reaffirming the particularity of the temporal mode of any particular region is bound to repeat that which is aimed to be vanquished. Losing from view how spatial relations that are shaped by the coloniality of power are constitutive of experiences of time can only lead to one-sided responses to the imperial gesture.*

What is the lesson, then? That any significant transgression of the forms of power that have been dominant in the West for more than five centuries now should involve a questioning of both time dynamics and spatial relations. Both philosophical reflection and the study of the African diaspora demand an analysis of what Eduardo Mendieta has called *chronotopology* (Mendieta 2001a). Chronotopology is "the science of macromapping time and space" (Mendieta and Lange-Churión 2001: 19). It studies "how space and time are produced by society, and how society, in turn, is enabled to produce and reproduce itself through the binding of space and time" (Mendieta 2001a: 180). Now, for Mendieta, "if space and time are produced, there is not just a science of their production, but also a history of different spatiotemporal regimes" (*ibid.:* 182). To chronotopology Mendieta adds the concept of heterochronotopology—namely, "the idea that the study of the production of space and time must also be the study of the different forms of their production, the different regions within specific spatiotemporal regimes" (*ibid.*). My previous reflections on the dominant spatiotemporal regimes in the Americas can be seen as a preliminary exercise into heterochronotopology. In the form that it appears here, heterochronotopology aims to clarify how space and time are mobilized into the qualification of Otherness. In this context, heterochronotopology may be referred to as a science, but only in a very loose sense. Science has some vices—among them, the idea that it can know or, in this case, map the world from a position of neutrality. This vice may be traced back to the sixteenth century when imperial cartographers mapped for the first time the contours of the globe.[37] In order to guarantee the expression of different voices and ways of mapping the world, one would have to refer to something like "hetero-heterochronoto-pologies," or simply to a transdisciplinary form of knowledge that aims to liberate peoples, to decolonize knowledges, and to change the world to the measure of nonracist and nonsexist interhuman relations. The crucial aim here is to indicate a transformation from the natural imperial and colonial attitudes to a *decolonial attitude.* It is the decolonial attitude that is at the heart of a consistent postcontinental philosophy.[38] Whatever it may be called, though, it is clear that this is the only way in which heterochronotopology becomes useful for Africana Studies. Africana Studies could remap spatiotemporal regimes in light of the movements, experiences, and problems confronted by African peoples and peoples of the African diaspora throughout the world.

Whereas Africana Studies aims to collaborate in the decolonization of spatiotemporal regimes, analytic and continental philosophies have typically satisfied themselves with fulfilling functions as priests and guardians of the spatiotemporal gates of modernity. Among other ways, they do this either by trying to ignore or by formulating one-sided dimensions of TimeSpace. Analytic philosophy, for instance, is typically dismissive of both time and space. Continental philosophy, by contrast, tends to reify the historical experience and legitimate the geopolitical order that begot the centrality of Europe in the capitalist world-economy. West's pragmatism opens a new possibility in the debate between analytic and continental philosophers. His exploration, however, is doubly limited: first, because it does not pay attention to the philosophical relevance of temporal dynamics in other parts of the Americas and, second, because it aims to vanquish imperial dynamics by focusing on (national) time alone. The critique of the imperial order that was born in the conquest of the Americas, and that was later rearticulated in different moments as former colonies gained independence and as the United States came to occupy a more central position in the world system, cannot dispense with a critique of spatial relations and an investigation into structural TimeSpace realities. The reconfiguration of power relations in 1848 and 1898 in the Americas, for instance, had a double effect: On the one hand, as Walter Mignolo points out, power relations transformed Spanish America from the western margin of Europe into the southern margin of the United States, and, on the other, they certified the temporal dimension of the Spanish American ethos; stuck in the past, they would always strive to arrive at an always evanescent present (Mignolo 2000a: 108–109). Although West justly condemns American imperialism, he fails to consider the way in which the articulation and affirmation of his American identity itself confirms the horizon of meaning opened up by the reconfiguration of imperial relations. Pledging allegiance to the idea of America implies both a validation of the spatial constitution of the nation and an endorsement of the national aspiration to represent, by itself, a whole continent. Criticizing "estadounidense" imperialism and pledging allegiance to America is a contradiction in terms.[39]

One of the challenges and promises of Ethnic Studies departments in the United States is precisely the pursuit of an analysis and a critical revision of the constitution of TimeSpace realities. To be sure, this involves a suspension of the commitment to national conceptions of space and time and national ontology.[40] Feminists of color have made exemplary moves in this direction. Take, for instance, Norma Alarcón, Caren Kaplan, and Minoo Moallen's idea that "[w]omen are both of and not of the nation. Between woman and nation is, perhaps, the space or zone where we can deconstruct these monoliths and render them more historically nuanced and accountable to politics" (Alarcón, Kaplan, and Moallem 1999: 12). "Nationalism," they add, "or even ... 'denationalization,' cannot bring us to this site of betweenness that allows us to query those productions of modernity. How to imagine or retheorize this space of betweenness or relationality that structures the sexual politics of postmodernity?" (*ibid.:* 14). This is, to be sure, one of the more serious questions and challenges confronted by African-American Studies specifically and Ethnic Studies in general. African-American Studies confronts the challenge of imagining not only alternative expressions of temporality but also new cartographies and new sexual politics. This involves a drastic change in the geographical unit of analysis as well as an intrepid examination of the lived experiences of peoples that uncovers their more or less articulated new spatial imaginaries and the significance of transnational interactions in the constitution of that experience. The contribution of African-American Studies and

Ethnic Studies in general to philosophy is equally important, since they defy the premises of the triangular and intra-imperial debate among analytic philosophers, continental philosophers, and American pragmatists.[41] While these philosophies privilege either eternal or continental rationality (either European or American), Ethnic Studies opens up the possibility of developing a postcontinental, postimperial, and truly postcolonial form of rationality. Nothing less than the suspension of imperial continental ontology is at stake here. We are called to think beyond the boundaries of the nation-state as a unit, as well as beyond the imperial conception of continental unity, which erases heterogeneity and relationships of power in nations and more ample spaces. Postcontinental philosophy refers to a form of thinking that is simultaneously post-Eurocentric, post-American, and post-Latin American and which refuses to find an anchor in any nation or continent.[42] This is both the promise that it makes and the challenge that it poses to other philosophical expressions.

Another promise of Africana Studies is to defy the imperial horizon of eternal, European-idealistic, and American pragmatic TimeSpace by opening up what Wallerstein has referred to as transformational TimeSpace, which in this context may be better formulated as a transmodern, antiracist, and postcolonial transformational TimeSpace.[43] Transformational TimeSpace is, to quote Wallerstein, "the time of which the theologians speak, *kairos* as opposed to *chronos,* the 'right time' as opposed to 'formal time'" (Wallerstein 1991: 146). Wallerstein believes that *kairos* has a secular translation in the concepts of "crisis" and "transition." Fundamental to the three ideas is the supposition that the time is right for change and that people need to make a moral choice. The challenge posed by Africana Studies has not only an epistemological but also an ethical dimension.[44] The lines between human sciences and ethical human transformation take a particular form here as they are bridged by the questioning of imperial TimeSpace realities. Suddenly we have the possibility of accessing an enchanted realm where fact and value, scientific investigation and ethics, and even philosophical reflection and religious thought cannot be radically divorced from one another.[45] They rather find new forms of articulating themselves in relation to the ethical task of transforming the world to the measure of nonimperial forms of human interrelationality.

The forms of critique and radical social action that became particularly pronounced in the 1960s hardly concluded in that era. While some groups are attached to the value of abstract universality, the arguments by ethnic groups that defy the logic of such claims have become more pronounced. Mistaken perceptions of these demands have led both rightist and leftist figures to affirm problematic notions of patriotism and to make "pleas" for Eurocentrism.[46] Liberals, in turn, have generally opted for an allegedly more benign universal cosmopolitanism (e.g., Nussbaum 1996: 2-17). It is fair to ask how Africana Studies should position itself in this debate. Here, again, Wallerstein provides a useful reflection:

> Within the United States the voice of oppressed groups has become more stridently "ethnic," relying far less on appeals to universal values than it previously did. In response to both geopolitical decline and the more ethnocentric style of oppressed groups in the United States, the defenders of privilege have resorted to demands for an "integrating" patriotism.

> But the response to a self-interested patriotism is not a self-congratulatory cosmopolitanism. The appropriate response is to support forces that will break down existing inequalities and help create a more democratic, egalitarian world. ...

> What is needed educationally is not to learn that we are citizens of the world, but that we occupy particular niches in an unequal world. (Wallerstein 1996: 123-124)

Africana Studies could become the locus for the articulation of a critical consciousness that not only creates innovative ways to describe and defy the structures of power that dominate peoples of African descent but also develops a position different from patriotism, ethnocentrism, Eurocentrism, and universal cosmopolitanism. Africana Studies would tend, in this sense, to side with proposals like those of Saldívar and Mignolo, who call for a critical cosmopolitanism (Mignolo 2000c; Saldívar 1991). Far from the sometimes justly criticized limitations and excesses of identity politics, Saldívar proposes

> a new American literary, cultural, and critical cosmopolitanism that fully questions as much as it acknowledges the Other, thereby serving as a more adequate and chastening form of self-knowledge. This

new critical cosmopolitanism neither reduces the Americas to some homogeneous Other of the West, nor does it fashionably celebrate the rich pluralism of the hemisphere. Rather, by mapping out the common situation shared by different cultures, it allows their differences to be measured against each other as well as against the (North) American grain. (Saldívar 1991: 4)

Saldívar not only anticipates here the chronotopological science articulated later by Mendieta but also provides a good example of how chronotopology can be of significant value for cultural studies. His sophisticated study of Chicana/o, Latin American, Caribbean, and African-American literary productions surpasses the limits of simple-minded comparativism, and elevates the study of culture to the articulation of new spatiotemporal imaginaries. Saldívar's analysis of Américo Paredes, Gloria Anzaldúa, Jose Martí, and Ntozake Shange is complemented by the works of Chicana authors, such as Emma Pérez (1999), who explicitly problematize the linear model of time in traditional historical accounts. Saldívar's "critical cosmopolitanism" and Pérez's "decolonial imaginary" offer powerful resources with which to develop a critical thinking with alternative conceptions of space and time. These conceptions aim to do justice to the experience of migration, the confrontation with racism, and the struggle for justice. They make clear that not much will be done in the direction of liberation without shifting our epistemic and spatiotemporal horizons. In this, Chicana/os and African-Americans share a similar project. They both further a critical chronotopological vision.

Africana Studies could therefore become the source of alternative ideals that show not only the limits of Western conceptions of cosmopolitanism but also problems with dominant notions of democracy and equality.[47] This task leads us away from both Cornel West and Immanuel Wallerstein: While the former remains within the limits of patriotism, the latter supposes a standard vocabulary that articulates the demands and ideals that orient the aspirations of diverse groups of people.[48] I would argue that what is needed is a form of transgresstopic hermeneutical critique—that is, a form of interpretation and critical analysis that takes the particularity of spatial location into account, but that, at the same time, invites a transgression of any claim for new grounds.[49] Instead of the universal cosmopolitan, what we find here is the possibility of a transversal critical consciousness, one in which the impetus for the critique of structures of domination and exploitation is matched only by the awareness of the fragility of one's critical endeavor and by the openness to different voices, vocabularies, and concerns.[50] For Africana Studies to achieve this, it would clearly have to enter into a more dynamic relationship with other forms of Ethnic Studies, in addition to engaging critically dominant forms of understanding ethics, justice, and critical rationality, including those proposed by defenders of an analytic, a continental, and a pragmatic approach. This also applies the other way around; that is, Ethnic Studies programs need to strengthen each other and not forget the vital contributions to theory and critique that have emerged and continue to be produced in African-American and Africana Studies. Together, the different approaches and methodological orientations currently associated with Ethnic Studies could also provide the theoretical articulation of spatiotemporal changes that break the horizon of continentality. In this way, Ethnic Studies has much to contribute to the transformation, not only of philosophy, but to the humanities and the social sciences.[51] Africana Studies, like other forms of Ethnic Studies in academia, is called on to contribute to the task of providing a consistent picture of the globality, not the continentality, of the human.

Coda: Critical Thinking Out of the Ditch

I provided here a succinct articulation of the distinction between analytic and continental philosophy. I discussed some of the problematic tendencies in each approach and pointed to limitations in several attempts to overcome them. I focused on Cornel West's answer to the problems, not only because his response is marked by the epistemological configuration that I am trying to elucidate here—that is, Africana Studies—but also because his version of pragmatism stands as one of the most sophisticated and rich philosophical expressions of the times. My critique of his answer to the limits of the analytic/continental divide points to ways in which West sustains a continental way of thinking. When it comes to philosophy, West maintains a problematic vision that extends the rights of continentality to the United States and juxtaposes it to Europe. Although West opposes imperialism, he does not examine the extent to which the continental vision of the United States carries the traces of it. And, while he is interested in promoting transformation, his dominant focus on temporality does not allow him to observe the extent to which the unity between time and space renders problematic his project of redeeming "America."

West is not alone in trying to overcome the limits of the analytic/continental divide by privileging temporality over spatiality. John McCumber joins him in his dismissal of spatiality as a fundamental axis in the production of critical thinking. McCumber finds in continental philosophy, and more particularly in the work of Hegel and Heidegger, the possibilities of properly thematizing the philosophical import of the past and the future. He differs from West in that he does not believe that pragmatism represents a privileged expression of the orientation toward the future. On the surface at least, McCumber has a more ambitious project in mind. As Mc-Cumber himself puts it, he believes that he has found "a paradigm that would relate philosophical thought to the past and future just as rigorously as analytical philosophy relates it to the present" (Mc-Cumber 2001: 163). McCumber believes that this paradigm offers a viable and more comprehensive path to the search for the truth. As the three modes of time—past, present, and future—are tied together in the articulation of an allegedly viable epistemological paradigm, the combination of analytic and continental philosophies seems to correct their respective deficiencies and to guarantee the future of philosophy.

Although I celebrate McCumber's originality, I am, at the same time, deeply concerned by the lack of awareness about the limitations of his project. The most obvious limits are, indeed, connected to a most patent "forgetfulness" of spatiality in his reflections. First of all, in *Time in the Ditch* McCumber seems to assume that the only legitimate philosophical expressions that have emerged or that can take place in "America" are analytic and continental. He believes that by bringing them together in a new paradigm he offers a viable path to "American" philosophers. To be sure, this statement is true, but only if by "Americans" he means citizens of the United States who are satisfied with conceiving their country as a continent and who believe that the nation-state/continent can become a legitimate locus for thinking. McCumber does not consider the extent to which indigenous conceptions of land, migratory movements, border culture, and double-consciousness, among an extended variety of cultural elements and concepts tied to the historical experience of diverse ethnic groups in the United States, strongly puts into question the dominant and hegemonic conception of "America" and offer resources to rescue the relevance of nonimperial and postcontinental conceptions of time and space in philosophical reflection. McCumber's dismissal of spatiality makes him unable to uncover the ways in which the general framework of his work reproduces features that pertain to an imperialistic epistemological formation.

At its best, Africana Studies offers a cure for the different species of amnesia of spatiality and the related satisfactions with the blessings of imperial spatial formations. Africana Studies demands a decolonization of philosophy and its transformation into a critical thinking that clarifies and offers solutions to persistent problems confronted by the African diaspora in its passage through many oceans and territories in the globe. In Africana Studies, philosophy becomes a tool, and not an end in itself. The end, rather, is posited by the need for liberation, which is closely linked to the struggle for nonsexist and nonracist forms of human sociality. Africana Studies also invites academics to examine the contributions to philosophy and critical thinking by Africans and peoples of the African diaspora. Subalternity, forced exile, slavery, systematic exclusion, social invisibility, migration, and double-consciousness are not only conditions to be analyzed but also loci from which thought emerges. The voices that erupt there may very well challenge our typical conceptions of spatiality and, with that, help us in rescuing critical thinking from the analytic and continental ditches.

Notes

1. The date is significant because in the address Moosa highlights the need for a global movement for justice beyond the unilateral demands of any single nation-state.

2. To be sure, Africana Studies is anchored in a diasporic vision. A good reference to understand the history and some of the important issues in the field is Conyers (1997). For a more recent and equally insightful discussion, see the special issue on diaspora in *The Black Scholar* 30, nos. 3 and 4 (2000). A good example of the literary and academic expressions of nonassimilationist movements that took place in the 1960s and '70s is found in the writings of Chicana feminists like Cherríe Moraga, Gloria Anzaldúa, Norma Alarcón, and others. They bring migration, sexuality, gender oppression, and resistance to assimilation in the "American melting pot"

into focus. For a recent anthology, see García (1997). For a more classic statement from women of color, see Moraga and Anzaldúa (1983). Also relevant in this context is the work of José David Saldívar, who has brought studies on migrant culture in contact with the theorization of black British diaspora culture by scholars in the Birmingham Center for Contemporary Cultural Studies (see, among others, Saldívar 1997).

3. There are certainly first-rate works in philosophy that go in this direction. Valuable contributions in philosophy include Harris (1983), Outlaw (1996), Gordon (2000b), and Henry (2000). In this chapter I try to make explicit some of the intellectual moves and challenges raised in these and other texts of similar note.

4. In this line, Moosa points out in his address: "Therefore, as we enter the 21st century, we have a collective responsibility as an international community not as a single nation or a regional power but as a collective of human societies to consciously commit ourselves to pursue the trajectory of advancing the *humanum* and to resist the culture of barbarity. We have the choice as to which legacy we are going to bequeath to the unborn and born. Together we also have the responsibility to contest the legacy of the 20th century" (Moosa 2001). To think the human, beyond the shadows of Man, is also central to the work of Sylvia Wynter. See especially Wynter (1984: 19-65, 1989: 637-647, 1990: 432-469, 2000: 25-76).

5. Consider the amount of volumes that focus on the elucidation of the epistemological bases and history of each philosophical style. On the analytic side, see, among others, French, Uehling, and Wettstein (1981); Munitz (1981); Martinich and Sosa (2001); and Stroll (2000). The continental side counts an equally copious number of works: Solomon (1988); Kearny (1994); Silverman, Sallis, and Seebohm (1983); Watson (1999); Critchley and Schroeder (1998).

6. This public letter appeared in the *New York Times* on May 9, 1992. The cited passage is quoted in Humphries (1999).

7. For a critical analysis of the elaboration and imposition of global designs, see Mignolo (2000b).

8. For a more detailed critical account on the idea of European Man, see Maldonado-Torres (2002).

9. For an analysis of the "darker side" of Europe in the Renaissance, see Mignolo (1995/1999).

10. I owe this formulation to Wahneema Lubiano.

11. For a critical reconstruction of this debate and the resulting poststructuralist takeover, see Ferry and Renaut (1990).

12. For a discussion of the specific case of Black Studies, see Hine (1997) and Turner (1997).

13. In different degrees and forms, Jorge Garcia, Eduardo Mendieta, and Walter Mignolo point to some important features in the task of dislocating the analytic/continental divide in their contributions to a supplement of *Philosophy Today* entitled *Extending the Horizons of Continental Philosophy*. See Garcia (1999), Mendieta (1999), and Mignolo (1995/1999).

14. For rich and informative discussions of the methodological and epistemological issues raised by the emergence of Black or Africana Studies, see James L. Conyers, Jr., ed., *Africana Studies,* especially the chapters by Asante (1997), Turner (1997), and Stewart (1997). Walter Mignolo offers a concise but powerful formulation of similar issues from the perspective of Latino Studies (see Mignolo 2000a).

15. This concern is made clear in Rajchman and West (1985).

16. For a detailed critical study of West's nationalist shift, see Wood (2000).

17. For a discussion of the complex character of so-called national and ethnic philosophies of this kind, see Garcia (1999). My point here is that the complexity of nationalist or ethnic European philosophies have not led them to break with the analytic/continental divide.

18. I put "cultural" and "religious" in parentheses because the meaning of these terms is partly established by the colonial history that I critically analyze here. For an insightful analysis of the formative dimension of imperial designs in the study of religion, see, among others, McCutcheon (2000). I will comment below on the colonial dimension of "culture."

19. For a lucid articulation of this point, see Outlaw (1996: 34-35).

20. West points out that the '60s led to a disorientation of intellectual polemics, to inescapable ideological polarization, and to an abandonment of the national traditions of thought (see West 1989: 238-239). For an instructive critique of the lack of serious recognition of the achievements of Africana thought in West's work, see Gordon (2001b: 38-58).

21. This statement applies strictly to philosophy and not to other areas such as the arts or religion. For West's invaluable contribution to those areas, see, among others, West (1982) and Gates, Jr., and West (2000).

22. West himself has alluded to his "tendency to downplay the achievements of Black scholars and writers when compared with canonical European ones or Black musicians" (West 2001: 349).

23. For an exposition and critical commentary of Hegel's reflections on the Americas, see Marquínez-Argote, González Alvarez, and Beltrán Peña (1979). Also pertinent in this respect are Antonello (1944) and O'Gorman (1941). For more recent elaborations on the same theme, see Casalla (1992) and Chavolla (1993).

24. If one follows Anibal Quijano's ideas on the role of America in the European utopian imaginary, it is possible to say that whatever there is of an orientation to futurity in modern Europe is, in great part, indebted to its relationship with the Americas (see Quijano 1995: 203).

25. For an insightful critical view of the position of the humanities in the corporate university, see Mignolo (2000d).

26. For a concise and clear account of the similarities and differences in the emergence and constitution of the nation-state in Europe, the United States, and the Southern Cone, see Quijano (2000: 556-570).

27. Attempts at incorporation have only brought about financial and political tragedies in Latin American nation-states. The case of Argentina is just the last in a history of failures and crises in the region. For a sober analysis of alternatives emerging in Latin America today, see Quijano (1995: 2001).

28. Variations in forms of production, social organization, and colonial history make a difference in respect to temporal modes. And since there is no fully homogeneous nation-state or territory, it is clear that we will find different modalities of time within any single nation-state, continent, or subcontinent. Yet, at the same time, it is possible to identify dominant socioeconomic systems with pretensions to hegemony. As Quijano notes, with modernity there was a change in the social image of time: "The past is replaced by the future as the privileged seat of the hopes of humanity" (Quijano 1995: 203). Clearly enough, my argument here is that the privilege of the past in Europe was not totally eradicated, at least in its philosophical expressions. This is made clear, or so I have argued, when one compares continental philosophy with American pragmatism.

29. The withdrawal of the U.S. delegation to the World Conference against Racism, Racial Discrimination, Xenophobia and Related Intolerance held in Durban, South Africa, from August 31 to September 7, 2001, testifies in great part to this characteristic feature of U.S. liberalism. This is not to deny that the withdrawal was also largely motivated by conflicts of interests in regard to the allegedly negative depiction of Israel in documents of the conference.

30. In this connection, see Huntington (2004). For a critical commentary on Huntington's main theses, see Maldonado-Torres (forthcoming [b]).

31. For a more detailed account of how this process took place in different parts of Latin America from the perspective of the coloniality of power, see Quijano (2000: 562-569).

32. For a work that elucidates the links between anti-indigenous and antiblack racism, on the one hand, and the formations of modern identity, on the other, see Wynter (1995) and Maldonado-Torres (forthcoming [d]). For a philosophical elaboration of antiblack racism in the modern world, see Gordon (1995/1999).

33. I refer to Harrison and Huntington (2000).

34. For a critique of Eurocentrism and Americanism and the articulation of a decolonial perspective based on the works of Fanon and Anzaldúa, see Maldonado-Torres (forthcoming [b]). For a more complete articulation of these points, see Maldonado-Torres (forthcoming [a]).

35. I owe my use of this term to Mignolo (2000a). The "larger picture" is another way of referring to structural TimeSpace.

36. According to Quijano, while capitalism refers to the structural articulation of all the historically known forms of exploitation (i.e., control of work) around the salarial form known as capital, coloniality of power refers more precisely to the pattern of domination that involved the racist classification of peoples around the globe. For Quijano, "*El eurocentramiento del patrón colonial/capitalista de poder no se debió sólo, menos principalmente, a la posición dominante en la nueva geografía del mercado mundial, sino sobre todo a la clasificación social básica de la población mundial en torno a la idea de raza. La concentración del proceso de formación y consolidación del moderno estado-nación en Europa Occidental, no podría ser explicado, ni entendido, fuera de dicho proceso*" (quoted from his manuscript "Globalización, colonialidad y democracia," later published with the same title in Quijano 2001).

37. For a thorough examination of the problematic cognitive vision that shaped the cartography of the sixteenth century, see Mignolo (1995/1999). I owe to Santiago Castro-Gómez the link I have drawn between sixteenth-century cartography and the later dominance of what he calls "*la hybris del punto cero*" [the hybris of point zero], or the belief in the idea of complete objectivity and neutrality in nineteenth- and twentieth-century social sciences.

38. For an articulation of the decolonial attitude, see Maldonado-Torres (forthcoming [a] and [c]).

39. For lack of a better adjective in the English language to refer to the particularity of the United States, I suggest that the Spanish "estadounidense" be adopted. Through the use of this term, the most recent contributions of Spanish to English may prove productive beyond the world of the Simpsons and other such sitcom characters. See on this point Maldonado-Torres, "Decolonization and the New Identitarian Logics after September 11: Eurocentrism and Americanism against the Barbarian Threats" (2005: 35-67).

40. For a critique of the commitment of areas of study with U.S. national ontology see Lisa Lowe, "Epistemological Shifts: National Ontology and the New Asian Immigrant." In *Orientations: Mapping Studies in the Asian Diaspora,* edited by Kandice Chuh and Karen Shimakawa, 267–76. Durham: Duke University Press, 2001.].

41. It is important to recognize the efforts of Gregory Pappas, who has attempted to highlight the "Latin" traits of thinkers like John Dewey and William James. He comments: "It is almost as if the aim of these philosophers was to *balance* America. It is almost as if they thought that something may be learned from the culture that originated south of the Rio Grande" (Pappas 1998: 105). Although I do not necessarily share Pappas's celebratory spirit, and although I remain concerned about the possible risk of cultural essentialism in his analysis, I nonetheless think that he goes a step beyond West in the decontinentalization of pragmatism.

42. For examples of this form of theorizing see Lewis R. Gordon, *Existentia Africana: Understanding Africana Existential Thought* (2000); Walter Mignolo, "(Post)Occidentalism, (Post)Coloniality, and (Post)Subaltern Rationality" (2000: 86–118); Mignolo, *The Idea of Latin America* (2005); Maldonado-Torres, "Decolonization and the New Identitarian Logics after September 11: Eurocentrism and Americanism against the Barbarian Threats" (2005: 35–67); Maldonado-Torres, "Post- imperial Reflections on Crisis, Knowledge, and Utopia: Transgresstopic Critical Hermeneutics and the 'Death of European Man'" (2002: 277–315); "Searching for Caliban in the Hispanic Caribbean" (2004b: 106–22). For a postcontinental intervention in Husserlian phenomenology that targets the idea of Europe see the essay by Knies in this volume. See also the dossiers on Caribbean Philosophy in the web journal *Worlds and Knowledges Otherwise* (http://www.jhfc.duke.edu/wko/about.php (forthcoming)].

43. *Transmodernity* is one of Enrique Dussel's felicitous terms. For a discussion of transmodernity and a comparison with postmodernity, see Dussel (1999).

44. The links among crisis, epistemological change, ethical choice, and the Africana experience are masterfully articulated in Gordon (1995b).

45. With enchantment, I refer to Sylvia Wynter's and not to Max Weber's reflections on this theme. Wynter calls attention to the need for both disenchantment with our present ontology of Man and a subsequent re-enchanted science of the human (see Wynter 1990).

46. Rightist affirmations of patriotism and Eurocentrism are prevalent these days in speeches by most politicians in the United States, particularly President Bush. For leftist affirmations of these two themes, see Rorty (1998) and Žižek (1998). One cannot cease to be amazed at this end-of-the-century/beginning-of-the-new-millennium alignment between the right and the left.

47. For a superb example of these combined activities, see Coles (2003). Coles brilliantly articulates what he sees as the advantages of a radically democratic and cosmopolitical "nepantlist generosity" in respect to a political liberalism of the Rawlsian kind. For a more classical perspective on the differences between liberalism and liberation, see Eddins and Eddins (1983).

48. While Eduardo Mendieta made an extraordinary effort to present West as a postuniversal cosmopolitan, I tend to agree on this point with Mark David Wood's description of the unsurpassable limits of West's prophetic pragmatism. See Mendieta (2001b) and Wood (2000). Interestingly enough, as Mendieta's labor as an editor and commentator makes clear, he himself seems to be more aware of the need for something like a critical cosmopolitanism than either West or Wood, the latter of

whom relies on a quite traditional leftist grammar. See, among others, David Batstone et al. (1997) and Mendieta (1999).

49. For a more comprehensive articulation of the concept of transgresstopic critical hermeneutics, see Maldonado-Torres (2002).

50. The universal is to the modern as the transversal is to the transmodern. As I use it here, transversality refers to the ways in which discourses break the imaginaries that pretend to make them fit the mold of a ground or foundation. In short, it pertains to the transaction among discourses, and to the many trangressions that occur in the process. Transversality thus joins Dussel's transmodernity and Mignolo's notion of pluriversality in a family of concepts. For expositions of these themes, see Dussel (1999) and Mignolo (2000c: 743ff). It is pertinent to note here that transmodernity, pluriversality, and transversality represent ethical responses to the limits of modernity, postmodernity, Eurocentrism, and abstract universality. This ethical dimension, along with the notion of fragility and instability, is central to more recent "cosmopolitical" proposals. I have in mind here Romand Coles's (2003) exploration of "nepantlist generosity" in the writings of Gloria Anzaldúa and other feminists of color in his "Contesting Cosmopolitan Currencies."

51. This point goes along with Johnnella Butler's proposal of Ethnic Studies as a matrix that advances the transformation of the humanities and the social sciences. Such transformation, to be sure, can be linked to efforts to build alternative institutions of higher learning and new programs within the university. See Johnnella E. Butler, "Ethnic Studies as a Matrix for the Humanities, the Social Sciences, and the Common Good," in *Color-Line to Borderlands: The Matrix of American Ethnic Studies*, edited by Johnnella E. Butler (2001: 18-41). See also Mignolo, "Globalization and the Geopolitics of Knowledge: The Role of the Humanities in the Corporate University" (2003: 97-119); Mignolo, "Las humanidades y los estudios culturales: proyectos intelectuales y exigencias institucionales" (2003: 31-57); Mignolo, "Os esplendores e as misérias da sciência: colonialidade, geopolítica do conhecimento e pluri-versalidade epistémica" (2003: 631-71); and Linda Tuhiwai Smith, *Decolonizing Methodologies: Research and Indigenous Peoples* (1999).

3
The Idea of Post-European Science

An Essay on Phenomenology and Africana Studies

Kenneth Danziger Knies

❧

This chapter sketches a direction of research that has preoccupied me ever since I began to study Africana thought and Husserlian phenomenology.[1] My guiding thesis is that the attempt to think beyond the imperial reach of Europe has generated new forms of systematic inquiry that signal the effort toward a new epoch of science. The genuine significance of this effort becomes clear only when we understand how these new fields bear an internal relationship to transcendental phenomenology—a relationship radically different from those "European sciences" whose crisis so concerned Edmund Husserl.[2] I call these new inquiries "post-European sciences."[3] With this term I refer to actual disciplines and ways of thinking that have recently achieved institutionalization within the U.S. academy, such as Africana Studies, Ethnic Studies, Latin American Studies, and postcolonial theory. But I do not think that these fields are post-European *in fact*, as if their subject matter or historical origin could designate them as such. I single out these inquiries because they contain an animating *telos* that points toward a radical rethinking of theory itself, a rethinking capable of drawing science beyond a myopic closure that we will call "European." If I am right, then we do not get at the ultimate significance of Africana Studies when we view it as an "interdisciplinary" expansion of the traditional disciplinary matrix, a provisional corrective to exclusionary academic practice, or an aspect of the struggle for black liberation. These accounts of the field certainly have their validity. But as post-European science, Africana Studies is bound up with a turning point in the life of Reason, a turning point that concerns the very possibility of achieving rigorous theory.

To understand what is at stake here, we must not think of Europe as a place on the map. Considered as an epochal phenomenon, Europe belongs to the domain of *spiritual shapes,* which do not figure in the physical geography of the globe. We get a sense of them when we reflect on our original experience of those human contexts that afford our purposefully living its at-homeness and supplying it with its imperatives. One lives "in" a particular spiritual shape not as a consequence of one's location with respect to geopolitical borders but because the questions or problems one encounters in everyday life are tacitly referred to as a particular kind of understanding that would function as an ultimate court of appeal. Following Edmund Husserl, we provisionally define the spiritual shape of Europe as a supranational unity characterized by its having the theoretical attitude as its governing norm-style. This means that Europe is essentially oriented by the Idea of philosophical reason and expresses itself in the sciences that Western humanity accepts as well-founded and traditional. We will have to understand why this unlikely definition must take precedence over all other historical, political, or anthropological ways of understanding "Europe." Only then can we appreciate the immense difficulty, the decisive importance, of thinking in a truly post-European manner. Only then can we see that post-European science is *not* a particular project that may or may not succeed while science and philosophy "proper" continue onward. It bears upon the very possibility of rigorous philosophical inquiry.

But aren't these claims fantastic? Given the natural and human sciences, with their established methods and practical successes, how can one bind the fate of philosophy to these newborn fields, which often seem to be struggling for their roots? We may reply by asking about the presumption on the part of the European sciences that they constitute branches of a unified and rationally ordered inquiry. Does this confidence stem from having clarified the ultimate meaning of concepts foundational to their areas of study? Or does it rather stem from a conviction that the *telos* of Reason is bound to the development of European cultural forms as if by some sacred covenant? What if this unfounded confidence is part and parcel of the crisis of European science that Husserl began to diagnose a century ago? What if this myth of European humanity as the sole crucible for theoretical reason is so powerful that it has infiltrated even the most sophisticated attempts to found philosophy on the successes, failures, and crises of European science?

Tying the fate of philosophy to the Idea of post-European science will also provoke skepticism from another quarter. Post-European science itself often concurs with European science on its hidden but most essential thesis. Namely: *that philosophy as rigorous science is impossible upon the demise of European spirit.* The post-European sciences have exposed a prejudice at the heart of Western reason that consists in the *a priori* decision to promote all things European to the rank of universally valid norms. And it is tempting to pass from this discovery to the conviction that the very project of aiming at truths that hold good for everyone and for always is some kind of ideological mirage. Here, I can only offer the assertion that this conviction is bound to end in absurdities. The quest for universal, all-temporal truths is not the symptom of a uniquely European hubris. Rather than repeating the idea that rigorous philosophy is a specifically European pastime, our direction of research aims to show why transcendental phenomenology, as a method of rigorous thinking, can come into its own only upon the maturation of the post-European sciences.

The present chapter announces this research in two parts: (1) With Africana Studies in mind, I will sketch the movement by which post-European science transcends the pathological restriction of subjectivity it discovers at the heart of European Reason and encounters imperatives that lead it to phenomenology. (2) I will outline how Husserl's thought clarifies the proper goal of post-European science, while exhibiting shortcomings that only the development of post-European science can solve. I will also suggest that a phenomenological understanding of how "myth," "nation," and "travel" function in the origination of philosophical thinking is crucial to the project of achieving a global philosophy for the post-European epoch.

I

My experience with Africana Studies has convinced me that this area of inquiry cannot be looked at as an interdisciplinary meeting place for disciplinary specialists who happen to gather information pertaining to a specific domain. The Idea animating this field is far more epistemologically revolutionary. My claim is that there are essential reasons why one cannot simply be an anthropologist, historian, or philosopher and really contribute to advancing the project of Africana Studies. The movement by which post-European science becomes conscious of this extradisciplinary location, suspends the authority of the constituted disciplines, and aims to secure its own truthfulness forces it to seek a radical beginning for itself where theoretical self-responsibility is at issue. As we will see, this movement will bring it into dialogue with phenomenology at the very moment that Husserl makes the goal of rigorous thinking synonymous with an overcoming of the crisis of European science.

As I see it, there are two leading directions for thinking that open up with the Idea of post-European science. The first direction can originate from the disciplinary study of any community functioning non-normatively within the context of "Europe," first understood simply as a place, culture, or history. These investigations begin as straightforward disciplinary understandings of their subject matter, or may traverse disciplines if the object of study requires a confluence of perspectives. At this level, a center of post-European science is conceived of as a meeting place where disciplinary specialists bring their expertise to bear upon a specific object: the human realities of the African diaspora, for instance. The fierce opposition to the establishment of such centers of study on the part of institutions of higher learning is already indicative of a serious problem, not only on the level of politics but on the level of the life of reason itself. It suggests that the continuous exclusion from serious study of the topics around which the post-European sciences would propose to unite disciplinary expertise is no coincidence. It indicates that "the human realities of the African diaspora" is not just another subject about which learned people may speak truthfully. Speaking truthfully about such matters triggers anxieties that lie at the heart of Euro-reason.

But this is just why the conception of post-European science as a site of convergence for the traditional disciplines is inadequate.

New objects of theory need not alter the constitution of theory itself, and research projects that demand a cross-disciplinary communication can still betray a naïve acceptance of knowledge-claims made in accordance with disciplinary conventions. The beginning of a genuinely post-European reorientation occurs when this traditional interdisciplinarity is replaced by an extradisciplinarity that renders problematic the constituted forms of knowing. Often this reorientation begins with the realization that the evidential and methodological criteria operative in the governing mode or modes of inquiry collapse in the study of people less than other in the eyes of European Man. Or else it is motivated by the realization that the very upholding of these criteria serves to constitute these populations as subaltern. In either case, this reorientation does more than simply expand the field of realities open to serious study. It generates new conceptual resources, calls into question methodological imperatives, and makes impossible a reliance on disciplinary conventions that decide what counts or does not count as a legitimate problem for knowledge.

Let's consider two brief examples. The case of W. E. B. Du Bois is well known in this regard (see, for example, Gordon 2000b: ch. 4). When Du Bois writes, in *The Souls of Black Folk,* that "most Americans answer all questions regarding the Negro *a priori*" and insists that "the least that human courtesy can do is listen to evidence," he is appealing not only to American society at large but also to the disciplinary establishment on whose authority such evidence is presented (Du Bois 1969: 69). The sociological studies undertaken by Du Bois follow from the recognition that "we seldom study the condition of the Negro to-day honestly and carefully. It is so much easier to assume that we know it all. Or perhaps having already reached conclusions in our own minds, we are loath to have them disturbed by facts"(Du Bois 1969: 95). In other words, when it comes to the study of black populations, the measured accumulation and evaluation of data, so prized in social science, is too often "falsified and colored by our wishes or our fears"(Du Bois 1969: 115). Du Bois thus turns back upon social science, confronts it with its own criteria, and finds it incapable of sustaining its professed rationality in its treatment of the cluster of problems concerning the "color-line." As is often the case with this turn toward post-European science, the imperative to assert the humanity of a dehumanized group leads to a larger confrontation with the mode of rationality operative in the guiding discipline, which cannot come to grips with the rigorous study of uniquely human phenomena. Beginning from a description of the lived realities of black folk, Du Bois thus initiates a radical reflection on the possibility of human science, leading to what Lewis Gordon has termed his "existential sociology."

We might also consider an example from the field of linguistics. In "The Negro's Dialect," Anna Julia Cooper exposes the endemic failure to understand the black person as a speaking, expressive subject. It is presumed that a black person's words are the mere interpretation of a racial identity, rather than of musical, literary, or theoretical meanings. She shows how a simple extension of principles already operative in contemporary linguistics to the study of "Negro folk speech" reveals the naïveté with which vocalizations that are linguistically impossible have been accepted as authentically black. The occasion for her reflection is a controversy surrounding Paul Robeson's performance in *Othello*. Theater critics are concerned to evaluate the artistic implications of Robeson's "slipping" into the "soft slur of the Southern Negro"(Cooper 1998a: 238). According to Cooper, there is specific focus on one particular line attributed to Robeson, who, "at the tragic moment of Othello's sublime fury demands 'Where am dat handkerchief, Desdemona?'" (Cooper 1998a: 238). Through a consideration of how language transformation takes place within a largely illiterate community (here black slaves in the American South), Cooper shows the absurdity of "am dat" as an utterance organically born from *any* folk dialect. "It is a principle of grammar ... that irregularities are accepted last and that in verbs the third singular is made to serve for the irregular first and second ... 'am dat' does not bear the hallmark" (Cooper 1998a: 242). Through similar procedures, Cooper goes on to show how one could establish standards by which to evaluate the legitimacy of several speech forms attributed to "Negro folk speech." And yet, Robeson, according to several sources, *did* say "am dat," no doubt at the behest of artistic instruction to provide a "racial touch" and "original flavor"(Cooper 1998a: 239). In fact, notes Cooper, one cannot be surprised at such phenomena in a culture where "a black man is not a true black unless he says 'am dat'" (Cooper 1998a: 238). It is in exploring the implications of this staged folk-speech that Cooper raises a number of fresh problems for the study of linguistic alienation and the role of artistic and literary expression in its exacerbation or amelioration.

This essential development of post-European science, for which we could find hundreds of striking examples in the history of Africana Studies, entails an awareness that the constituted disciplines fail to be rigorous because they encounter subjectivity only within the confines of a socially dominating group. A social setting whose very functioning depends upon evading the humanity of human beings tends to institutionalize ways of knowing that further and legitimate this evasion. In short, there are certain things about which European science does not want to know, and in order to know them truthfully, it is not enough to plead for the admission of new facts and figures. One must bracket the established frameworks that prefigure how one should conceptualize one's object of study, and attend directly to matters about which standard knowledge practices seem hell-bent on remaining naïve. Simply by taking the position that it has to do with human beings and human realities, a form of properly post-European science thus emerges at the moment that it calls into question the rigor of the traditional discipline or disciplines to which it belonged. What is most common here is an effort to push beneath constituted concepts and achieve a reflective elucidation of the lived experiences that first pose problems for knowledge. As Frantz Fanon well knew, this means being "derelict" with respect to method, not in order to eschew intellectual thoroughness but in order to develop a manner of thinking appropriate to the phenomena at hand.

Thus, it would no longer make sense to conceive of an institution of post-European science as a meeting place for disciplinary specialists who happen to focus on facts pertaining to a specific domain. Rather, one would have to imagine a community of trained scholars ever willing to interrogate the fundamental presumptions of their disciplines, and to suspend the authority of convention in the face of phenomena that require the formation of new concepts and methods of analysis.

This encounter with the peculiarly "European" limits of disciplinary knowledge opens a second trajectory along which post-European science becomes cognizant of its exilic location. But rather than pressing toward a direct treatment of phenomena, this trajectory recoils into a stance of epistemic critique. Here, the established mode or modes of European science become the explicit object rather than the guide of thought, and are henceforth accompanied by a meta-disciplinary understanding of the relationship between knowledge production and processes of oppression. The European sciences are subjected to a critique that debunks their status as uninterested models for rational thinking and situates them in a context of power relations. Suddenly, the "underside" of modernity is not a mere factual occurrence that provides the ugly material basis for the achievement of lofty thoughts. The highest scientific and philosophic insights themselves appear to be constituted through an order of knowledge that cannot think philosophy or science otherwise than European. And this project of realizing truth through the maintenance of European tradition seems inseparable from the creation of the subaltern against whom Europe understands itself and the height of its thought.

The critical-theoretical approaches that here join the post-European problematic (whether "postcolonial," "Marxist," or "poststructural") are not simply historical, politico-economic, or anthropological insofar as they include, as an essential possibility, a reflection upon these disciplines that exposes their being premised upon a false universality rooted in Western chauvinism. "Europe" or "The West" is now understood, not as a particular history or culture, but as a history and a culture that mistakes itself for *the* history and culture, and aims to become, through its self-understanding, the vehicle for demonstrating the superiority of European Man. From the standpoint of post-European science, to situate a science or discourse as "Western" means to draw its production of purportedly universal and uninterested truths within a particular historical, cultural, or epistemic frame, and to gesture toward a space of knowing beyond its bounds. "The West," then, appears as an ultimate horizon within which a specific tradition of thought gains undue authority through its incorporation into an imperial design. For the legend of an immanently reasonable European Man, the post-European sciences substitute this real-life leviathan, which thinks the thoughts that sustain its existence as much as it plunders the world for its sustenance.

Let's briefly consider V. Y. Mudimbe's *The Invention of Africa* as exemplary of this direction since it will aid us in our encounter with Husserl. The text evaluates Western social sciences, particularly modern anthropology, as "constrained discourses" that "develop within the general system of knowledge which is in an interdependent relationship with systems of power and social control" (Mudimbe 1988: 28). The discursive production of "Africa" within Western anthropology cannot be divorced from the overarching milieu of European conquest within which it develops. "The anthropologist did not seem to respect the immanence of human experience and went on to organize, at scientific expense, methods and ways of ideological reduction: Concrete social experiences were looked at and interpreted from the normativity of a political discourse and its initiatives"(Mudimbe 1988: 89). The thought-objects of anthropology are thus stripped of their pristine status and integrated into a complex network of power/knowledge in which the figures of Africa and the African "become not only the Other who is everyone else except me, but rather the key which, in its abnormal differences, specifies the identity of the Same"(Mudimbe 1988: 12). A chief accomplishment of Mudimbe's is to formulate, alongside a notion of ideological or individual-behavioral ethnocentrism, an ethnocentrism of "epistemological filiation." This latter is what gives to anthropology "its significance as a discipline, and its credibility as a science"(Mudimbe 1988: 19), despite its ritual function in effecting the self-identification of European Man as the standard of humanity. In theorizing a dependent relation to The West by way of "epistemological filiation," Mudimbe shows how a straightforward appropriation of concepts and categories binds several avowedly Afrocentric or post-Western discourses to the very thing they hope to negate (Mudimbe 1988: 85). The archaeological research into the construction and transmutation of imperial discourse on Africa and Africans thus becomes a necessary preparation for research that would make contact with African realities beyond the boundaries of this closure, where an "absolute discourse" might begin from the starting point of African subjectivity itself (Mudimbe 1988: 200).

Along this critical trajectory, post-European science seems obliged to assume philosophical self-responsibility. If the European sciences include the mythical glorification of European Man as an inner-determination of their sense, then the philosophy of which these sciences are branches must be interrogated as well. Thus, post-European science thinks itself into a situation where it cannot assume the validity of any established European philosophy, and is drawn to a critical encounter with this philosophy by its own momentum. In fact, by holding a sidelight to the sociopolitical contexts that cradle European philosophical thought, the post-European sciences have successfully drawn out its particularity and shown up its comfort in an imperial order. But if it is to establish definitively the problem-horizons it unfolds, post-European science must seek an ultimate grounding of its own scientificity. So if it follows up its implications, post-European science arrives at the question of the relation between the scientificity of its science and the speaking, thinking behemoth called "Europe" or "The West." This question will throw it open to the problem of its own rigor and its needing to secure a basis in an as yet undisclosed post-European philosophy.

There is an obvious institutional implication to this epistemological movement. A center of post-European science cannot distinguish itself properly through an emphasis on a particular area or mode of disciplinary inquiry, nor can it rest content with the critical iterations brought about in these disciplines by theoretical self-reference[4] or interdisciplinary cross-fertilization. Philosophy is necessary. Of course, this does not mean that the standard questions normally associated with philosophy departments must take center stage if post-European science is to verify itself. It means that the nature of post-European scientific work entails a rethinking of constituted forms of knowledge that cannot proceed from within their own matrices. The need for philosophy does not entail a dependence upon extant philosophy departments; it requires that post-European science assume responsibility for philosophical questioning on its own.

II

Let's retrace the path we have just described. In "Europe," the fields animated by the Idea of post-European science have discovered a pathological restriction of subjectivity that cripples the advance of theoretical knowledge, inhibits its proper aims, and encourages a naïve provincialism. This discovery has led to a radical suspension of disciplinary knowing and has posed two distinct but intimately related imperatives for thought: (1) the need to bracket the authority of the extant disciplines in order to build new concepts from a reflection on the experiences in which problems for knowledge are first encountered and (2) the demand for an explicit critique of "Europe," not solely as an anthropological or historical formation, but as a myopic tradition of thinking in which the sciences of anthropology and history, for instance, may participate.

When we let the idea of post-European science guide us to an encounter with phenomenology, we approach it not as a topic in intellectual history but as a way to think. For it is in the thought of Edmund Husserl that a rigorous reflection on the meaning of experience and a critique of European reason become synonymous. For Husserl, in order to achieve a philosophical reflection that returns "to the things themselves" it is necessary to free thinking from its entanglement in a uniquely European crisis. The European epoch, in its ultimate philosophical sense, is defined by a thinking that presupposes the power to theorize and then proceeds to do theory in such a way as to deny, deify, or forget this power. It is the failure of human beings to take responsibility for the theoretical subjectivity that it claims for itself. This failure, for Husserl, manifests itself in a history of epistemic crises that stem from the effort to explain consciousness as a being or relation belonging to the positive-scientific domains of objects. Thinking itself thus becomes reducible to a historical, psychical, or natural *fact*, and the ultimate reality of any phenomenon comes to depend upon its place in the psychophysical nexus of nature or in an empirical development of social and cultural formations. *Sociology, history, and physics are European sciences because they participate in this reductive movement, not because the study of social, historical, or physical phenomena is somehow European by right.* For us, what is important here is that to think according to naturalism or historicism is to participate in a uniquely European movement of intellectual irresponsibility that continues to plague disciplinary understanding. Post-European science, if it understands its goal, cannot repeat these mistakes, and cannot understand the ultimate sense of the European crisis or its own situation with recourse to such procedures.

But phenomenology is not just an essential possibility open to thought. Its systematic self-understanding originates in the philosophical and scientific life of Continental Europe. Indeed, it is essential to our proposed direction of research to recognize that "Europe" is not just one question among others for phenomenology. Whatever investigations phenomenology might undertake into the nature of lived-experience, it cannot understand its own genesis without reflecting on the debt it owes to the specific tradition of thinking that it simultaneously belongs to and transcends. This is why, in his later writings, Husserl begins referring to a crisis not simply of the sciences but of the *European* sciences (Merleau-Ponty 1964a/1989: 89). Husserl is not asserting that phenomenology is somehow the expression of a uniquely European worldview or disposition. He is saying that at the height of phenomenological reflection, in an effort to begin thinking radically for himself, the phenomenologist does not experience himself as a bare cogito but as open to "living motivations"(Husserl 1965: 146) that inspire his thinking. In the very act of suspending all traditional validities, the philosopher opens himself to the influence of the tradition of *theory*, which consists precisely in the effort to suspend traditional validities. He thus feels his thinking motivated by a movement of thought that it simultaneously inherits and transforms. In Husserl's case, this movement of thought is the crisis-ridden development of European science to which his own phenomenology owes its genesis. So following up the path of these motivations by investigating the meaning of "Europe" is not an incidental task for phenomenology. It is a primary and ultimate question, crucial to its self-understanding.

This notion that a critical reflection on the meaning of "Europe" is necessary to the very possibility of genuine philosophy is a dynamic point of contact between the development of Husserlian phenomenology and the idea of post-European science. And yet, it is significant that even as Husserl situates his diagnosis of modern epistemic crises within an overall account of European "sickness," he never mentions the European provincialism that post-European science discovers at the heart of Euro-reason. So how can we be sure that phenomenology is not "European" in the sense that it partakes of the superstition that holds Europe to be the sole spiritual homeland of rigorous theory? One look at Husserl's 1935 *Vienna Lecture* shows us that we cannot be sure. In fact, at the most mature stage of his thinking, Husserl seeks to ground the very possibility of phenomenology with reference to "a remarkable teleology inborn ... *only* in our Europe" (Husserl 1999: 273). It is true that if philosophy is to understand itself fully, and thus become genuine philosophy, it must reflect on the tradition of thought from which it originates, and it must do so in such a way that it does not compromise the theoretical purity of its orientation toward truth-in-itself. Thus, if Husserl had in fact established rigorous philosophy on the basis of African or Asian traditions, one could equally expect a rumination on the "remarkable teleology" inborn in African or Asian humanity. But what do we make of this "only"? How does phenomenology know that there is no *telos* of Reason animating non-European humanity? Is this a question of fact? Or is this sense of exclusivity somehow transmitted along with the "living motivations" that philosophical thought inherits at the height of the European crisis?

If this *"only* in Europe" were simply a matter of Husserl's falling prey to the European chauvinism characteristic of his place and time, there would be nothing here of note. We would simply reprimand Husserl for not being sharp enough in his reductions, and take over the phenomenological method as the ultimate basis for post-European thinking. But I want to suggest that there are motivations to this "only" that have methodological import and that reveal the necessity of an internal communication between phenomenology and the idea of post-European science. The *Vienna Lecture* is not just a text; it is the place where the tradition of European philosophy tries to get clear about the meaning of its Europeanness, enacts the prejudice of its epoch with remarkable self-awareness, and gives us resources for thinking beyond the European closure.

The lecture is based on an account of the maturation of human-kind according to its progression through three stages in the life of Reason. This is worked out in terms of the doctrine of spiritual shapes that I mentioned at the beginning of these remarks. As everyday purposeful living increasingly calls its own grounds into question, it traditionalizes itself within community horizons where the natural, mythico-practical, and finally theoretical attitudes function as governing norm-styles. The natural attitude is the attitude of everyday living and of the knowing that takes advantage of accumulated experience in order to address problematic things, contexts, and situations in the world. The mythico-practical attitude breaks from the natural attitude in that it aims at a systematic knowledge of the world that would have validity for everyone. But, unlike the theoretical attitude, it takes "the world" as a domain of unquestionable powers bound up with the fate of human beings, and so seeks its knowledge for the purpose of co-existing with these powers in the happiest possible manner (Husserl 1997: 284).

Further, it understands "everyone," not in the sense of any rational being, but in the sense of anyone living within the encompassing community horizon. The theoretical attitude aims at a decisive suspension of all traditional validities, and undertakes a practically disinterested investigation for which nothing is beyond question, and which pursues truth-in-itself for its own sake, as an absolute value for humanity (Husserl 1997: 278).

Since the lecture is *organized around* the idea that the *telos* of Reason is inborn only in Europe, these attitudes are assigned to humanity such that Europe just *is* the only spiritual shape governed by the theoretical norm-style whereas non-Europe just *is* the spiritual shape limited by the mythico-practical orientation, despite its "so-called" philosophies.[5] This means that the European crisis necessarily appears as a crisis of science, and as Europe's betrayal of its own-most mission. Furthermore, it means that the phenomenological understanding that reflects on and transcends this crisis can only appear as the fulfillment of a uniquely European promise. As a consequence, *we* cannot truly understand phenomenology without reactivating this entire tradition. When we do our own phenomenology, we belong to it and carry it forward. To be blunt, according to Husserl, no matter who or where we are, the moment we begin reflecting radically, we become "good Europeans." We accrue a transcendental debt to the Europeanized ancient Greeks, whom the European Renaissance invented as its benefactor.

Europe thus comes to understand itself as a self-contained spiritual shape that does not participate in the same development that governs the rest of humanity as historically determined *anthropos*. Naturally, every spiritual shape exists in a finite historical space-time wherein we can mark its boundaries. And if we trace the development of spiritual shapes geographically and historically we will find that they pass one into the next through relations of influence or conflict. The accomplishments and failures of various "peoples" thus appear as episodes within a "single life" of spirit, and the task of a universal history would simply be to trace the spiritual relations that bind them one to the other. From this perspective, humanity "is like a sea, in which men and peoples are the fleetingly formed, changing, and then disappearing waves" (Husserl 1997: 274). But Europe does not belong to this ever-changing sea; it is a *continental shape* that emerges from its depths. Its unique solidity as a spiritual unity results from the fact that Europe's actual-historical orientation toward the infinite tasks of Reason makes it the sole embodiment of the teleological idea that just so happens to coincide with what is essential to humanity as such. Europe is the solid ground where Reason gets its footing in history. This is why, for Husserl, Europeans' consciousness of Europe as spiritual homeland cannot be accounted for with reference to the relative differences between confrere and alien, or the familiar and the strange: "[T]his essential difference between familiarity and strangeness, a fundamental category of all historicity which relativizes itself in many strata, cannot suffice.... [T]here is something unique here [in Europe] that is recognized in us by all human groups, something that becomes a motive for them to Europeanize themselves, whereas we, if we understand ourselves correctly, would never Indianize ourselves for example" (Husserl 1999: 275). In other words, if *we Europeans* understand that our Europe is not "merely an empirical anthropological type like 'China' or 'India'" but, in its teleological sense, coincides with what defines the essence of humanity, we will see that "the Europeanization of all other civilizations bears witness to the rule of an absolute meaning" (Husserl 1999: 16). Such is Europe's self-understanding at the height of its philosophical awareness.

Ironically, it is in describing the emergence of Greco-European philosophy against the backdrop of the mythico-practically oriented ancient Greek nation that Husserl provides us with resources that help clarify the myopia of the European epoch, as well as aid us in thinking beyond it. What Husserl discovers is that philosophical questioning cannot even become a goal without a variation on my national or supranational mythos. This variation takes place in the attitude of curiosity, a playful attentiveness within the natural attitude, unique in that it has let all pressing life interests drop:

> In this attitude [of curiosity], man views first of all the multiplicity of nations, his own and others, each with its own surrounding world which is valid for it, is taken for granted, with its traditions, its gods, its demons, its mythical powers, simply as actual world. Through this astonishing contrast there appears the distinction between world-representation and actual world, and the new question of truth arises: not tradition-bound, everyday truth, but an identical truth which is valid for all who are no longer blinded by traditions, a truth-in-itself. (Husserl 1999: 285–286)

Husserl is not doing history here. He is describing what is necessary to any origination of philosophy as such. *So what is such a politically over-determined entity as a "nation" doing in a phenomenological account of the genesis of philosophical questioning?* Why do dwelling in a "nation" and then curiously encountering the surrounding worlds of one's own and other nations constitute essential moments in emergence of philosophy?

Things become clearer if we remember that we are working at a very basic level of meaning-formation. We are experiencing the "nation" before it has become the object of political-scientific understanding or the theme of a political reason that submits power and authority to a rational economy of distribution. Such knowledge presupposes the breakthrough of the theoretical orientation, whereas the problem confronting us is to account for the very emergence of theory. Here, "nation" means precisely the home of specific mythical powers, gods, demons, and traditions. It is home to these powers in the sense that it is the dwelling wherein they need not account for themselves, where they are accepted without judgment, and are ultimately beyond question. However far this abode stretches, however long its structures can be held together, so far and long is the reach of the "pre-European" nation.

This reach is not geographical in the sense of objective space. It is determined by the scope of the mythico-practical norm-style. At the most primordial level, the nation is the spiritual place wherein the powers that govern my fate are at home. It is a "community-horizon" within which ultimate questions about who I am and what the world is are referred to a coherent matrix of myths. The reason philosophy cannot emerge from a fascination about the nature of the heavens, or what lies beyond the ocean, or even what constitutes the good life is that, within the unbroken bonds of the nation, curiosity has myth as its final horizon. There is no room for a questioning that declares itself insubordinate to every practical, mythical, and religious motivation or consequence. For this, a curious encounter with the facticity of foreign nations is necessary, an encounter that transpires under a suspension of all life-interests that draw the thought of other nations under practical and diplomatic imperatives. Only this kind of encounter can motivate an insight into the contingent and arbitrary nature of one's own national mythos, and set philosophy on its course. Only then does the ideal of a global philosophical community whose members struggle to see by their traditions, rather than be blinded by them, come into view.

This encounter can be described as a discipline of *travel*. In the sense I am using the term here, one can travel without going anywhere, or go to the farthest reaches without traveling at all. What is essential to travel is that an encounter with the facticity of the foreign opens my understanding to a visitation whereby my own zone of familiarity stands out in its character of being unthinkingly accepted. It is on the basis of this discipline that the idea of philosophy first comes into being. Now once the goal of philosophical research has become established, and philosophical communities begin to form, philosophy cannot abandon the discipline of travel to which it owes its origination. It must subsume the productive force of travel under a theoretical interest, reflect upon its methodological significance, and incorporate it into its methodical advance. This is because as soon as philosophy begins, it already dwells in the life of nations, and speaks forth from mythological commitments that threaten to obscure its theme.

Husserl's changing views on the phenomenological method of "free variation"[6] demonstrate an increasing awareness of how philosophy can reactivate the discipline of travel that first gave life to its task. By the time of the *Vienna Lecture,* Husserl believed that a variation taking place solely in the imagination of the investigator is not adequate to the goal of intuiting essences. The phenomenologist's situation in a specific history and tradition requires that his philosophical imagination be *spurred* by contact with unfamiliar facts concerning the essence in question (Merleau-Ponty 1964a/1989: 90–91). His mind must *travel,* not in the sense of an actual "going," but in the sense of an encounter with the facticity of the foreign that shows up his own traditional involvement as one possible involvement among many. In a letter to Lucien Levy-Bruhl praising his *Primitive Mythology,* Husserl admits that this position entails that empirical ethnographic research have a positive methodological significance for phenomenology. The phenomenologist has no right to declare the *a priori* irrelevance of such facts since they aid the variation on which his eidetic intuition will found itself. He wrote this letter roughly two months before penning "only in our Europe" into the *Vienna Lecture.*

Now it is no use speculating on Husserl's psychological motivations. It is, however, a matter of principle that phenomenology leans upon *travel* in order to orient its theoretical gaze. But does the supranational unity of Europe know how to travel? Do European anthropology and ethnography motivate the kind of variation on Europe's supranational validities necessary to spur the phenomenological imagination? Or are they precisely a ritual enactment of European Man's self-identification as standard of humanity? Mudimbe has shown how the anthropological figure of non-European difference has served as "the key, which, in its abnormal differences, specifies the identity of the same." A reflection on the spiritual shape of European Man shows that, even at the highest levels of his philosophical life, he does not encounter what is not himself as "foreign" or "other." Rather, Europe *constitutes* its peripheries through a self-centering that measures European Man against subaltern variants of itself. The European spirit, perhaps, has never known how to travel, no matter how far it goes, no matter the reach of its conquest and its commerce. Perhaps what is essential to it is that it never encounters itself *qua* variant, but only as *a priori* standard. This is certainly a problem for ethical and political life, but it is also a problem for theory. We have seen how this myopia can obscure phenomenology's understanding of its innermost meaning, leading it to reenact the European superstition on a transcendental level.

If anthropological understanding, broadly conceived, is a necessary aid to philosophical reason, then the radical reconstitution of the human sciences beyond the bounds of the European mythos is crucial to the fate of knowledge. Our reflections on the relationship between national mythoi and the philosophical orientation have shown us that the global and transcendental perspectives approach one another, and that it is in this approach that the transition from the mythico-practical to the theoretical norm-style is achieved. But insofar as humanity's self-understanding is governed by the development of European anthropological sciences, this approach may not be possible. The achievement of philosophy as rigorous science requires the redrawing of the human sciences from a post-European perspective. In their effort to transcend European provincialism, the post-European fields have already begun to achieve this task, and are thus clearing the way for a genuine philosophy. This is not a matter of fulfilling a uniquely European promise but one of making a promise Europe could never properly make. As we aim at this global-transcendental philosophy, we must make the phenomenologically clarified notions of nation and travel *methodological* problems. An existential *a priori* to the human sciences cannot secure its concepts without a cross-traditional encounter as spur to its philosophical imagination.

Does all this amount to an espousal of "lateral universalism"? Am I just saying that the working out of concepts is founded upon the achievement of an "international philosophical community"? Recall that the phenomenon of Europe already comes to self-understanding as a *supranational* unity. Europe is precisely that system of nations in which the breakthrough of the theoretical attitude as the governing norm-style has caused an upheaval in cultural existence such that all traditional life-ways are potentially brought before the bar of reason. For Husserl, humanity Europeanizes itself by passing from nation-shapes still governed by the mythico-practical orientation into nation-shapes where national myths, powers, and gods have become problems for a critical reflection that gears itself toward radical evidence and truth. In this sense, there are no non-European nations insofar as they are capable of entering into conflict and cooperation with other nations under the guidance of universal norms. But I have suggested the possibility that this supranational unity called Europe *constitutes itself* against a non-European periphery that it cannot encounter as foreign or alien, but only as an *a priori* subaltern against which it measures itself as *a priori* standard. We have even witnessed this constitution at the height of European philosophical reflection on the meaning of Europe. No, post-European philosophy does not come about through a lateral exchange between national philosophical traditions. I have in mind something far more "vertical."

So where, then, is the spiritual birthplace of post-European theory? We have seen that philosophy does not come from nowhere. It is necessarily born from a "nation" insofar as this term signifies a community horizon wherein purposeful life is encompassed by a historically profound matrix of traditions and myths. *Post-European philosophy can be born from only the spiritual shape that forms at the periphery of Europe.* But we must pause again to fend off our natural tendency toward the geography of the globe. The periphery of Europe, like Europe itself, is primarily a spiritual shape, not a region one could localize on a map. It is a periphery that cuts right through Europe's geographical center. It encompasses all humanity that stands at the edge of European Man's self-centering as *a priori* standard. This periphery is thus an under-periphery, the counterpart to Europe's understanding of its own height. To give a historical coherence to this spiritual shape, to cultivate its traditions and practices, to construct a home for its gods and its mythical powers: All of these are essential tasks that follow in the wake of the idea of post-European science. This obviously has absolutely nothing to do with "nationalism" in the conventional sense of the term, especially insofar as it connotes an uncritical valorization of customary life-ways or the goal of participating in the European system of nations. Frantz Fanon, the foremost theorist of the spiritual shape that wells up at the under-periphery of Europe, has already described its complex re-constitution of traditional practices as well as its necessarily ambivalent relationship to European nationhood. No nationalism. It is simply a question of creating for human accomplishments a spiritual infrastructure within which they can appear as what they are, rather than as pale imitations, exotic curiosities, or cheap tokens. The spiritual unity in which global-transcendental philosophy has its birthplace is not a European dependency, nor is it another continental shape that one might oppose to Europe. It is Diasporic, a going out from Europe into the world.

Notes

1. The ideas outlined here were originally presented at the Caribbean Philosophical Association meeting on "Shifting the Geography of Reason," which took place in Barbados in May 2004. There was, unfortunately, not enough space available in the present volume for the editors to provide a longer, more detailed version of this research, which I hope will come to print soon in a suitable forum.

2. Husserl's primary philosophical concern at the end of his life was to develop a way into phenomenology through the historical crisis of the "European sciences." See his *The Crisis of European Sciences and Transcendental Phenomenology: An Introduction to Phenomenological Philosophy.* I cannot integrate an introduction to phenomenology into this outline, but an excellent place for the interested reader to begin is Maurice Natanson's *Edmund Husserl: Philosopher of Infinite Tasks.*

3. The term "science" will surely seem out of place in this context. It seems odd to speak of science in connection with matters concerning the world in which we actually live out our lives. We prefer to speak of interpretation, criticism, and so on. But this is because we operate under a reductive understanding of science that restricts it to the technical application of formulae to an "external" world. We then face the problem of whether human reality can be explained through such exacting procedures, or whether it constitutes a separate "internal" sphere to be investigated by the humanities, which appreciate the world of history, culture, and ethics, *but*

which can definitively establish nothing. This is the false dilemma that makes us feel as if our souls are being sent to the laboratory when we hear the phrase "human science" or "philosophy as rigorous science." But if we understand science from the perspective of its vital accomplishment, rather than its technical application, we will see things differently. Following Husserl, we understand the goal of science as a rationally ordered, methodologically transparent, and essentially unfinished inquiry that aims at the acquisition of truths that hold good for everyone, now and always. As such, sciences can be exact or inexact, descriptive or explanatory, depending upon the nature of their object. From this vantage, the possibility of a science of the accomplishments of human spirit, including science itself, comes into view. This is what I take "philosophy" to mean.

4. Theoretical self-reference refers to a technical problem in the phenomenology of the special sciences. It is outlined in Eugen Fink's *Sixth Cartesian Meditation* (1988: 13-19). When a specialized science turns back on itself and places its own thinking within its object domain, it immediately confronts the danger of relativism. According to Fink, there are at least three emblematic modes of theoretical self-reference in the mundane sciences: epistemic self-relativization, self-exemplification, and infinite regress. What holds constant in all modes of mundane self-reference is that the natural attitude remains unbroken through all its reflective iterations, and that the objects of reflection are placed squarely in the existing world. Mundane self-reference, then, does not represent a genuine heightening of reflection (despite its apparent profundity). It merely expands the field of objects of study to encompass one more object, the thinking of the theorist himself.

5. For a further discussion of the importance of the mythico-practical/theoretical distinction, see pages 167-194 of Paget Henry's *Caliban's Reason: Introducing Afro-Caribbean Philosophy* (2000a). Although Henry's focus is on Habermas, this chapter opens up the question of what is mythical about myth far more than Husserl's *Vienna Lecture.* It also questions the role of the myth/theory dichotomy in the constitution of Euro-Reason.

6. There is no space in which to explain the place of free variation in phenomenological method. For a brief but thorough account, see pages 321-354 of Edmund Husserl's *Experience and Judgment* (1997), especially section 87.

4

On How We Mistook the Map for the Territory, and Re-Imprisoned Ourselves in Our Unbearable Wrongness of Being, of *Désêtre*

Black Studies Toward the Human Project

Sylvia Wynter

‑๑

I

An Argument

> [T]he idea that Western thought might be exotic if viewed from another landscape never presents itself to most Westerners.

> *—Amiri Baraka (1963)*

> It is the opinion of many Black writers, I among them, that the Western aesthetic has run its course.... We advocate a cultural revolution in art and ideas.... In fact, what is needed is a whole new system of ideas.

> *—Larry Neal (1971)*

> I would like to refer you to an essay by the late Dr. Du Bois where he ... says that, up until the point that he really came to terms with Marx and Freud, he thought "truth wins." But when he came to reflect on the set of lived experiences that he had, and the notions of these two men, he saw ... that if one was concerned about surviving ... about ... "the good life" and moving any society

toward that, then you had to include a little something other than
an interesting appeal to "truth" in some abstract, universal sense.
—*Gerald McWhorter (1969)*

The emergence of the Black Studies Movement in its original thrust,
before its later cooption into the mainstream of the very order of
knowledge whose "truth" in "some abstract universal sense" it had
arisen to contest, was inseparable from the parallel emergence of
the Black Aesthetic and Black Arts Movements and the central rein-
forcing relationship that had come to exist between them.* As with
the latter two movements, the struggle to institute Black Studies
programs and departments in mainstream academia had also owed
its momentum to the eruption of the separatist "Black Power" thrust
of the Civil Rights Movement. It, too, had had its precursor stage in
the intellectual ferment to which the first southern integrationist
phase of the Civil Rights Movement had given rise, as well as in the
network of extracurricular institutions that had begun to call for the
establishment of a black university, including, *inter alia,* institutions
such as the National Association for African-American Research, the
Black Academy of Arts and Letters, the Institute of the Black World,
the New School of Afro-American Thought, the Institute of Black
Studies in Los Angeles, and Forum 66 in Detroit. The struggle for
what was to become the institutionalization of Black Studies was
to be spearheaded, however, by a recently enlarged cadre of black
student activists at what had been, hitherto, almost purely white
mainstream universities, all of whose members had been galvanized
by Stokely Carmichael's call, made in Greenwood, Mississippi, for a
turning of the back on the earlier integrationist, "We shall overcome"
goal of the first phase of the Civil Rights Movement, and for the
adoption, instead, of the new separatist goal of Black Power.

All three movements had been moved to action by the 1968 murder
of Martin Luther King, Jr., and by the toll of burning inner cities and
angry riots that followed in its wake. These events were particularly
decisive for the Black Studies Movement. The new willingness of
mainstream university administrators to accede to the student activists'

---

*This chapter is the original, full-length version of an essay bearing the same name
that appears, in significantly shortened and revised form, in *A Companion to African-American Studies* (2006). (It appears with apologies to June Jordan, riffing on
Milan Kundera, and to Aimé Césaire for the term *désêtre* [translated as *dysbeing* on
the model of *dysgenic*]).

demands for the setting up of Black Studies programs and departments was made possible by the trauma that gripped the nation. Once established, these new programs and departments functioned to enable some of the major figures of the then far more powerful and dynamic Black Arts and Black Aesthetic Movements to carry some of their work into the academic mainstream, even where they, too, like Black Studies as a whole, were to find their original transgressive intentions defused, their energies rechanneled as they came to be defined (and in many cases, actively to define themselves so) in new "multicultural terms" as African-American Studies; as such, this field appeared as but one of the many diverse "Ethnic Studies" that now served to re-verify the very thesis of Liberal universalism against which the challenges of all three movements had been directed in the first place.

The destinies of the three movements would, in the end, differ sharply. The apogee years for all three movements (1961–1971) were to see the publication of a wide range of anthologies of poetry, theater, fiction, and critical writings, but also the publication of three scriptural texts specific to each. Whereas 1968 saw the publication of *Black Fire: An Anthology of Afro-American Writings,* edited by Leroi Jones and Larry Neal, as *the* definitive anthology that crystallized the theoretical discourse and practice of the Black Arts Movement, the year 1969, which saw the publication of *Black Fire* in the paperback version, marked the publication of the proceedings of a 1968 symposium, "Black Studies in the University," which had been organized by the Black Student Alliance at Yale University. The conference was financed by the Yale administration. In 1971, the edited collection of essays by Addison Gayle, Jr., *The Black Aesthetic,* as *the* definitive text of what was to become the dominant tendency of that movement, was also published.

The paradox here, however, was that despite the widespread popular dynamic of the Black Arts and Black Aesthetic Movements, they disappeared as if they had never been. They were done in by several major developments. One was a tapering off of the movement of social uprising that had been the Black Civil Rights Movement, in the context of affirmative action programs that enabled the incorporation of the black middle and socially mobile lower-middle classes into the horizons of expectation of the generic white middle classes (if still at a secondary level), ending with the separation of their integrationist goals from the still ongoing struggles of the black lower and under classes. This separation had itself begun to be effected in the wider national context, both by the subsiding of radical new-left politics subsequent to the ending of the Vietnam War and by the rightward swing taken by the society as a whole in reaction against the tumultuous years of the 1960s.

Second, their demise was hastened by the defection of the most creatively original practitioner of the Black Arts Movement, Leroi Jones/Amiri Baraka, and his conversion from Black Power nationalism (of which the Black Arts and Black Aesthetic Movements had been the "spiritual arm") to the Maoist wing of Marxism-Leninism as a universalist counter to the universalism of Liberalism. The Black Nationalist Movement had arisen to contest the latter, which he hoped would avoid the trap of the cognitive and psycho-affective closure into which the Black Arts and Black Aesthetic Movements seemed to have fallen.

A third development—the rise of black feminist thought and fiction, which took as one of their major targets the male and macho hegemonic aspect of the black nationalist aesthetic and its correlated Black Arts Movement, even where black women had played as creative a role as the men—also took its toll.[1]

Jones/Baraka's Maoist-Leninist defection as well as the feminist defection by black women were serious blows. The *coup de grace* to both the Black Arts and the Black Aesthetic Movements, however, was to be given by the hegemonic rise of a black (soon to be "African- American") poststructuralist and "multicultural" literary theory and criticism spearheaded by Henry Louis Gates, Jr. It was this thrust that would displace and replace the centrality of the Black Aesthetic Movement, redefining the latter's Reformation call for an alternative aesthetic able to contest what Pierre Bourdieu (1984) was later to identify as the "monopoly of humanity" of our present mainstream bourgeois aesthetics, with the reformist call for an alternative "African-American" literary canon ostensibly able to complement the Euro-American literary one and, therefore, to do for the now newly incorporated black middle classes what the Euro-American literary canon did and continues to do for the generic, because white, and hegemonically Euroamerican middle classes.

In her book entitled *Black Women Novelists and the Nationalist Aesthestic* (1994), Madhu Dubey perceptively summarizes Gates's critique of the two movements whose disappearance he was instrumental in effecting. While not refuting this critique—which argued, *inter alia,* that the black aestheticians had been duped by the tropes of figuration of the "text of blackness"—Dubey nevertheless poses a fundamental question, one that gave rise to both the title of this chapter and the thrust of my Argument. While she first notes that both the Black Aesthetic and Black Arts Movements had sought to "unfix the notion of Blackness from the traditional color symbology of the West" and to challenge the "Western equation" of blackness "with ugliness, evil, corruption, and death," Gates's poststructuralist critique had now come to accuse practitioners of Black Aesthetics and Black Arts, in Derridian terms, of putting forward a "metaphysical concept" of blackness as presence and, thereby, instead of displacing an essentialist notion of identity, of having merely installed blackness as "another transcendent signified." This had then caused them to become entrapped by "racial essentialism," which by its "reversal of the Western definition of blackness," had come to depend "on the absent presence of the Western framework it sets out to subvert" (Dubey 1994: 28–29). The fact that Gates's poststructuralist activity itself depends on the "absent presence" of the very same Western framework that it was also ostensibly contesting did not detract from the success of his ongoing attacks on the Black Arts/Black Aesthetic notion of identity in terms of poststructuralism's "critique of the humanist subject."

However, while admitting the effectiveness of Gates's counter-discourse in putting the seal on the demise of these two earlier movements (as well as of Black Studies in its original 1960s conception rather than in the pacified, ethnically re-christened *African-American* Studies that it has now become), Dubey then poses the following question: Why, she asks, had it been that with all its undoubted "theoretical limitations," the Black Aesthetic "rhetoric of blackness" should so powerfully have "exerted an immense emotional and ideological influence, transforming an entire generation's perception of its racial identity"? What had lain behind the "remarkable imaginative power" of the nationalist "will to Blackness," "bristling with a sense of the possibility of blackness" that had characterized the writings of political activists like Stokely Carmichael and Eldridge Cleaver; writer activists like Leroi Jones/Amiri Baraka, Don L. Lee, Sonia Sanchez, Jayne Cortez, and Nikki Giovanni; cultural nationalists like Maulana Karenga; and literary critics and theoreticians like Carolyn Gerald, Hoyt Fuller, Addison Gayle, Jr., and Stephen Henderson? What had been the unique dynamic that had enabled the rhetorical energy of the black nationalist discourse so powerfully "to mobilize the sign of blackness"?

If Dubey's question can be answered only by making visible what Gates terms the absent presence of the very Western framework in whose terms *blackness,* like its dialectical antithesis *whiteness,* must be fitted onto a symbology of good and evil—"The white man," Fanon writes, "is sealed in his whiteness, the black man in his blackness.... How do we extricate ourselves?" (Fanon 1967b: 9-10)—and, therefore, with any attempt to unfix the sign of blackness from the sign of evil, ugliness, or negation, leading to an emancipatory explosion at the level of the black psyche, then Leroi Jones/Amiri Baraka's implicit proposal that Western thought (and therefore the cultural framework of this thought) needs to be exoticized—that is, viewed "from another landscape" by its Western, and indeed in our case, Westernized, bearer subjects—can provide us with the explanatory key to the answering of Dubey's question.

In addition, recall that the Black Arts and Black Aesthetic Movements were themselves historically linked to a series of other earlier such movements across the range of the Black African Diaspora: not only the United States' own Harlem Renaissance Movement but also the Negritude Movement of Francophone West Africa and the Caribbean, the Afro-Cuban and Afro-Antillean Movements of the Hispanic Caribbean, and the ongoing Rastafari-Reggae religiocultural movement—an invention of the endemically jobless underclass of Jamaica, which explosively flowered at the same time as the Black Arts and Black Aesthetic Movements, musically interacting (by means of the transistor radio) with the "Black Power" musical popular expressions of the 1960s and '70s as iconized in the archetypal figure of James Brown. They were also linked synchronically to the global field of the anticolonial movements as well as to the anti-apartheid movement in South Africa. Any attempt to "exoticize" Western thought by making visible its "framework" from "another landscape" links us, then, to a related paradox defining all three movements. This paradox was that of their initially penetrating insights gained by the very nature of a wide range of globally subordinated peoples moving out of their Western assigned places and calling into question what was, in effect, the structures of a global world system, as well as the multiple social movements of other groups internal to the West, such as feminists, gay activists, Native Americans, Chicanos, Asian-Americans, and students, all mounting similar challenges—insights, therefore, into the nature of that absently present framework which mandated all their/our respective subjections.

All this led, for a brief hiatus, to the explosive psychic *cum* political emancipation not only of blacks but of many other non-white peoples and other groups suffering from discrimination, yet also, on the other hand, to their ultimate failure, in the wake of their politically activist phase, to complete intellectually that emancipation.

The literary scholar Wlad Godzich (1986) perceptively identifies the nature of this paradox when he notes that although it should have been obvious at the time that the great sociopolitical upheavals of the late 1950s and '60s, especially those grouped under the names of decolonization and liberation movements, would have had a major impact on our ways of knowledge, this recognition has not occurred for two reasons. The first is due to the "imperviousness of our present disciplines, to phenomena that fall outside their pre-defined scope"; the second, to "our reluctance to see a relationship so global in reach—*between the epistemology of knowledge and the liberation of people*—a relationship that we are not properly able to theorize." This reluctance was, therefore, not an arbitrary one, as proved in the case of the Civil Rights Movement in the United States. For while the earlier goals of the movement as it began in the South, because directed against segregation and therefore couched in terms of the universalist premises of mainstream Liberal discourse, could be supported (once the move to include the North and the West and therefore the economic apartheid issue of an institutionalized jobless and impoverished underclass, all interned in the inner-city ghettoes and their prison extensions, had led in the direction of the call for Black Power), the situation had abruptly changed. Godzich suggests that an epistemological failure emerged with respect to the relation between the claim to a black particularism over against Liberalism's counter-universalism, on the one hand, and over against that of Marxism as a universalism, on the other. Since in the case of the latter, because based on the primacy of the issues confronting the Western working classes postulated as the globally generic working class, this in the same way as their issue, postulated as that of the struggle of labor against capital, had also logically come to be postulated as *the* generic human issue. While given that Liberal humanism is itself based on the primacy of the issue of the Rights of Man as *the* defining premise that underlies both our present order of knowledge and its correlated mainstream aesthetics, the claims to the particularism of a Black Arts and a Black Aesthetic as well as to

Black Studies in its original conception—these are the correlates of the claim to Black Power, which had itself been based on a return to the earlier recognition made in the 1920s by Marcus Garvey that, in the later words of the Barbadian novelist George Lamming, "'the Rights of Man' cannot include the 'Rights of the Negro' who had been institutionalized discursively and empirically, as a different kind o' creature to 'Man'" (Lamming 1970 [1953]: 297)—were to find themselves met with outright hostility on the part of mainstream intellectuals/academics and aestheticians.

The implacability of this hostility was to lead swiftly, as Godzich further notes, to a "reterritorialization," whose goal was to reincorporate these movements, sanitized of their original heretical dynamic, into the Liberal-universalist mainstream. However, while this reincorporation was effected, in the case of Black Studies, by its re-invention as "African-American Studies," and as only one "Ethnic" Studies variant among a diverse range of others, all contrasted with, at the same time as they were integrated into, the ostensible universalism of Euro-American-centered mainstream scholarship, the other two movements—by the very nature of their self-definition as a black particularism, which called into question the mainstream art and aesthetics together with their "monopoly of humanity"—were not amenable to such pacification and reincorporation. As a result, their rapid disappearance, their extinction even, hastened along by Gates's neo-universalist, poststructuralist critique, logically followed. For it had been precisely their original claim, as Godzich notes, to a black particularism over against the universalist premises of our present mainstream aesthetics and order of knowledge—their claim, in Gerald McWhorter's terms, to "something other than 'truth' in an abstract universal sense," or, in Neal's terms, to a post-Western aesthetics based on a new system of ideas, with these claims, linked to their insistent revalorizing of the negative-value connotations that both the mainstream order of knowledge and the mainstream aesthetics placed upon all peoples of Black African descent, thereby imposing upon us "an unbearable wrongness of being"—that can be identified, from hindsight, as *the* dynamic that was to exert what Dubey defines as the immense emotional influence on an entire generation's self-conception (including the kind of intellectual self-confidence that a Gates, for example, as a member of the beneficiary generation, would now come to possess).

Nevertheless, the eventual defeat both of the Black Aesthetic and Black Arts Movements as well as of Black Studies in its original conception resulted from the very process that had occasioned their initial triumph—that is, from their revalorization of their "racial blackness" as systemically devalorized by the logic of our present mainstream order of knowledge, its art, and its aesthetic. For while this strategic inversion had functioned for a brief hiatus as a psychically emancipatory movement, by its calling into question of the systemic devalorization of our physiognomic and original ethno-cultural being as a population group, its eventual failure can be seen not only in the psychic mutilation of the tragic figure of Michael Jackson, as expressed in his physically mutilated face, but also in the widespread use of plastic surgery not only by blacks but also by a wide range of other non-white groups, as well as by white non-Nordic groups themselves.[2] This latter instance provided a clue to the fact that the systemic devalorization of racial blackness was, in itself, *only* a function of another and more deeply rooted phenomenon—in effect, only the map of the real territory, the symptom of the real cause, the real issue. This was the territory that, for example, Eldridge Cleaver had glimpsed when, in his book of essays *Soul on Ice* (1968), he tried to account for the almost reflex-instinctual nature of his attraction to white women as contrasted with his lukewarm response to, for him, the always already devalorized black woman; that Gwendolyn Brooks had charted, in trying during an interview to account for the reason that successful black men also seemed instinctively to prefer lighter-skinned black women (Tate 1983); that over half a century earlier W. E. B. Du Bois, in trying to come to grips with his own double consciousness that made it difficult for him to be an American without being anti-Negro, had recognized as a new frontier with respect to the study of the still-unresolved issue of what determines—indeed, what structures—the nature of human consciousness; that Larry Neal had identified in agonistic terms as "the white thing within us." Yet, and this is *the* dilemma, all this is so as a territory or issue that cannot be conceptualized to exist in terms of the *vrai* or "regime of truth" of our present order of knowledge. Any more than—as Foucault also pointed out in the case of the eighteenth-century Classical episteme or order of knowledge that preceded our contemporary one, which was to displace/replace it during the nineteenth century—the conception of biological life could have been imagined to exist in terms of its *vrai* or "regime of truth" (Foucault 1980: 78; see also pp. 109–133). Nevertheless, as a territory, an issue—to whose empirical existence the particularity of the black experience, and therefore of our necessarily conflictual and contradictory consciousness, together with the occasional emotional release from such a consciousness—attests, as definitively as a Geiger counter attests to the empirical presence of radioactive material. This, therefore, as a hitherto unknown territory, the territory of human consciousness and of the hybrid nature-culture laws by which it is structured, was only to be identified, in the context both of the global anti-colonial struggles and of the social movements internal to the West itself, by the political activist and psychiatrist Frantz Fanon in his book *Black Skin, White Masks,* doing so from the ground of the particularity of the black experience. "Reacting against the constitutionalist tendency of the late nineteenth century," he wrote, "Freud insisted that the individual factor be taken into account through psychoanalysis. He substituted for a phylogenetic theory the ontogenetic perspective. It will be seen that the black man's alienation is not an individual question. Beside phylogeny and ontogeny stands sociogeny" (Fanon 1967b: 11).

Fanon's book was published in its original French version in 1952, one year before the publication of the Watson/Crick paper cracking the DNA code specific to the genomes of all species, including the human being. This therefore helped to emphasize that, given the genetically determined narcissism that would be endemic to all living beings in their species-specific modality, the fact that a black person can experience his or her physiognomic being in anti-narcissistic and self-alienating terms (as iconized in the tragic figure of Michael Jackson) means that human beings *cannot* be defined in purely biogenetic terms—that is, from a purely phylogenetic *cum* ontogenetic perspective, or, in other words, from the perspective of the purely physiological *conditions* of being human (i.e., phylogeny and ontogeny), as we are now defined to be in terms of our present liberal or bio-humanist order of knowledge. Indeed, as we are induced, as contemporary subjects, to psycho-affectively experience ourselves to *be,* in terms of our also bio-humanist mainstream aesthetics.

However, if, in Fanon's terms, the prognosis for black self-alienation is to be favorable, the human must be redefined in terms of the hybrid phylogony-ontogeny *cum* sociogeny mode of being that it empirically is, which is composed of descriptive statements or modes of sociogeny—in effect, of *genres* or *kinds* of being human, in whose always auto-instituted and origin-narratively inscribed terms we can alone experience ourselves *as* human. Let us note here, in passing, that the term "genre," meaning *kind* of human (as in the case of our present *kind* of human, *Man,* which *sociogenically* defines itself, in biocentric terms, on the model of a natural organism), as the model that aprioristically underlies all our present disciplines (Foucault 1970 [1973]), stems from the same etymological roots as the word "gender." This, given that from our origins on the continent of Africa until today, gender role allocations mapped onto the biologically determined anatomical differences between male and female have been an indispensable function of the instituting of our *genres* or sociogenic *kinds* of being human. This latter is so as a process for which our species-specific genome as uniquely defined by the co-evolution of language and the brain has bioevolutionarily preprogrammed us.

In effect, because the systematically induced nature of black self-alienation is itself (like that, correlatively, of homosexual self-alienation) only a function (a map), if an indispensable one, of the enacted institutionalization of our present genre of the human, *Man* and its governing sociogenic code (the *territory*), as defined in the ethno-class or Western bourgeois biocentric descriptive statement of the human on the model of a natural organism (a model that enables it to over-represent its ethnic and class-specific descriptive statement of the human *as if* it were that of the human itself), then, in order to contest one's function in the enacting of this specific genre of the human, one is confronted with a dilemma. As a dilemma, therefore, it is a question not of the essentializing or non-essentializing of one's racial blackness, as Gates argues, but rather of the fact that one *cannot* revalorize oneself in terms of one's racial blackness and therefore of one's biological characteristics, however inversely so, given that it is precisely the biocentric nature of the sociogenic code of our present genre of being human that imperatively calls for the devalorization of the characteristic of blackness as well as of the Bantu-type physiognomy—in the same way as it calls, dialectically, for the over-valorization of the characteristic of whiteness and of the Indo-European physiognomy. This encoded value-difference then came to play the same role, in the enactment of our now purely secular genre of the human *Man,* as the gendered anatomical difference between men and women had played over millennia, if in then supernaturally mandated terms, in the enactment of all the genres of being human that had been defining of traditional, stateless orders. This therefore led, in our contemporary case, to the same asymmetric disparities of power, as well as of wealth, education, life opportunities, even mortality rates, and so on, between whites and blacks that—as the feminist Sherry Ortner has pointed out in her essay "Is Female to Male as Nature Is to Culture?"—were defining of the relations between men and women common to all such orders (Ortner 1974).[3]

If, therefore, it is the very institutionalized production and repro-duction of our present hegemonic sociogenic code—as generated from its Darwinian origin-narratively inscribed biocentric descriptive statement of the human on the model of a natural organism—that calls, as the indispensable condition of its enactment, for the sys-temic inducing of black self-alienation, together with the securing of the correlated powerlessness of its African-descended population group at all levels of our contemporary global order or system-en-semble, then the explosive, psychic emancipation experienced by black peoples in the United States and elsewhere—as in the case of the indigenous "black fellas" people of Australia and Melonesia, as well as the black peoples of the Caribbean and of the then still apartheid South Africa—can now be seen in terms that explain the powerful emotional influence of the three movements that arose out of the sociopolitical black movements of the 1960s (i.e., the Black Aesthetic, Black Arts, and Black Studies Movements in their original conception), with this experience coming to an end only with their subsequent erasure and displacement. And this logically so, given that while the psychic emancipation that these movements' revalorization of the characteristics of blackness had effected was an emancipation from the psychic dictates of our present sociogenic code or genre of being human and therefore from "the unbearable wrongness of being," of *désêtre,* which it imposes upon all black peoples and, to a somewhat lesser degree, on all non-white peoples, as an imperative function of its enactment as such a mode of being, this emancipation had been effected at the level of the map rather than at the level of the territory. That is, therefore, at the level of the systemic de-valorization of blackness and correlated over-valorization of whiteness, which are themselves only proximate *functions* of the overall devalorization of the human species that is indispensable to the encoding of our present hegemonic Western-bourgeois biocentric descriptive statement of the human, of its mode of sociogeny. In other words, because the negative connotations placed upon the black population group are a function of the de-valorization of the human, the systemic revalorization of black peoples can be fundamentally effected only by means of the no less systemic revalorization of the human being itself, *outside* the necessarily devalorizing terms of the biocentric descriptive statement of *Man,* over represented as if it were by that of the human. This, therefore, as the territory of which the negative connotations imposed upon all black peoples and which serve to induce our self-alienation as well as our related institutionalized powerlessness as a population group are a function, and as such, a map. As, correlatively, are all the other "ism" issues that spontaneously erupted in the United States in the wake of the black social liberation movement, all themselves, like the major "ism" of class also, specific maps to a single territory—that of the instituting of our present ethno-class or Western-bourgeois genre of the human.

Nevertheless, because it is this territory, that of the instituting of our present biocentric descriptive statement of the human on the model of a natural organism that is elaborated by our present order of knowledge and its macro-discourse of Liberal humanism, as well as enacted by our present mainstream aesthetic, together with the latter's "monopoly of humanity" (Bourdieu 1984), with our present order of knowledge being one in whose foundational "regime of truth," objects of knowledge such as Fanon's auto-instituted modes of sociogeny or Bateson's "descriptive statements" at the level of the psyche (Bateson 1968), in effect, our *genres* or *kinds* of being human, cannot be imagined to exist, neither McWhorter's call for another "truth" able to secure the good life for black and all other peoples, nor, indeed, Larry Neal's call for a post-Western aesthetic, could have been incorporable, as they themselves had hoped, in terms of our present order of knowledge and its biologically absolute conception of the human. That is, in the way in which a later re-territorialized and ethnicized "African-American Studies," as exemplarily elaborated and brilliantly put into place by Harvard's Henry Louis Gates, Jr., would prove to be.

In this context, Jones/Baraka's implied call for the exoticization of Western thought, in order to make this thought itself, its presuppositions, together with, in Gates' terms, the "absent presence" of its framework, into new objects of knowledge, to be examined from the landscape or perspective of the *blues* people—and therefore from the perspective, not of the-people-as-*Volk* as in the cultural nationalist aspects of the Black Aesthetic and Black Arts Movements, but, as in the *popular* aspect of these movements, of the people as the movements of people who are logically excluded, as "the waste products of all modern political practice whether capitalist or Marxist" (Lyotard 1990, citing Grand 1990: 93), with their exclusion being indispensable to the reproduction of our present order—links up with Fanon's recognition that "black self-alienation" cannot be detached from the de-valorized conception of the human on the purely phylogenic/ontogenetic model of a natural organism, that is as defining of this thought as, indeed, of its correlated aesthetics. In the case of the former, as an episteme, one whose biocentric order of truth calls for the human to be seen as a "mere mechanism," and as such, one whose members are all ostensibly naturally dyselected by Evolution until proven otherwise by his/her or that of his/her population group's success in the bourgeois order of being and of things: "The advancement of the welfare of mankind," Darwin wrote at the end of *The Descent of Man* (1981 [1871]: 403), "is a most intricate problem: all ought to refrain from marriage who cannot avoid abject poverty for their children.... [A]s Mr. Galton has remarked, if the prudent avoid marriage, whilst the reckless marry, the inferior members of society will tend to supplant the better members of society." Against this biocentric, eugenist thought, and the "absent presence" of its bio-evolutionary framework or conception of the human, Fanon wrote:

> What are by common consent called the human sciences have their own drama. *Should one postulate a type for human reality and describe its psychic modalities only through deviations from it,* or should one not rather strive unremittingly for a concrete and ever new understanding of man? ... [A]ll these inquiries lead only in one direction: to make man admit that he is nothing, absolutely nothing—*and that he must put an end to the narcissism on which he relies in order to imagine that he is different from the other "animals."* ... Having reflected on that, I grasp my narcissism with both hands and I turn my back on the degradation of those who would make man a mere mechanism. (Fanon 1967b: 22–23)

II

On Exoticizing Western Thought, Visibilizing Its Framework(s), Its Invention of Man, and Thereby Also of Our "Unbearable Wrongness of Being," of Désêtre: Modernity, Secularism, and Its Epochal Transformation of the "Supreme Source of Legitimacy"

The modern collapse of "Reason" and "History" into all things European represented a failure of Reason and History that required a self-deception regarding Europe's scope. Put differently: Europe sought to become ontological; it sought to become what dialecticians call "Absolute Being." Such Being stood in the way of human being or a human way of being. It thus presented itself as a theodicy ... : If God has the power to do something about injustice and evil, why doesn't He? ... Theodicy does not disappear with modern secularism. Whatever is advanced as a Supreme Being or Supreme Source of Legitimacy faces a similar critical challenge.

—Lewis Gordon

Man: A human being (irrespective of sex or age).... An adult male person.... The male human being.... To be at one's own disposal, to be one's own master.

—Oxford English Dictionary

Native: One of the original or usual inhabitants of a country as distinguished from strangers or foreigners: now especially one belonging to a non-European and imperfectly civilized or savage race.... A coloured person or Black.... Born in a particular place or country: belonging to a particular race, distinct etc. by birth. In mod. use espec. with connotation of non-European.

—Oxford English Dictionary

Negro: an individual (esp. a male) belonging to the African race of mankind which is distinguished by a black skin, black woolly hair, flat nose and thick protruding lips.... Negress ... A female negro ... negro dog. A dog used in hunting negro slaves.... Nigger ... A negro (coll. and usu. contemptuous ... loosely incorrectly applied to members of other dark-skinned races).

—Oxford English Dictionary

121

Miranda: Abhorr'd slave,
Which any print of goodness wilt not take,
Being capable of all ill! I pitied thee,
Took pains to make thee speak, taught thee each hour
One thing or another. When thou didst not, savage,
Know thine own meaning, but wouldst gabble like
A thing most brutish, I endowed thy purposes
With words that made them known. But thy vile race,
Though thou didst learn, had that in't which good natures
Could not aside to be with. Therefore wast thou
Deservedly confined into this rock, who hadst
Deserved more than a prison.

—*Shakespeare's* The Tempest

The argument proposed in this section is that if post-medieval Renaissance Europe was to usher in the world of contemporary modernity on the basis of the epochal secularization of human identity, which it effected by means of the intellectual revolution of lay humanism, this as a revolution that, by taking to its logical conclusion St. Thomas Aquinas's medieval Christian-Aristotelian thrust toward the making of *Christian* and *Man* into conceptually different notions, was thereby to initiate, together with the religious movement of Reformation, the gradual privatization of its formerly Judaeo-Christian identity. This privatization was also of the identity that, because then functioning as the *public* identity of medieval Latin Christian Europe, had underpinned and legitimated the ostensibly supernaturally guaranteed hegemony of the institution of the Church and its celibate Clergy over the institutions, the non-celibate laity, including those of commerce and of the political state. Nevertheless, the thinkers of Renaissance Europe were to effect this secularization of its public identity in terms that were themselves generated from the monotheistic framework of Judaeo-Christianity. In consequence, if, as Jean-François Lyotard (1990: 81) has noted, the "Greco-Christian Occident" could not, and cannot, conceive of an Other to what it calls God, this characteristic was to be carried over in secular terms as the humanist intellectuals of Renaissance Europe replaced the earlier public identity *Christian* with that of their newly invented *Man* defined as *homo politicus,* and, as such, primarily the political subject of the state. It was therefore to effect this secularization of its public identity by over-representing both its first variant of *Man,* defined as political citizen and/or subject of the state, and, from the end of the eighteenth century onward, its second variant of *Man*—defined in now purely secular, because biocentric, terms as *homo oeconomicus,* and, as such, primarily as the Breadwinner/Investor subject of the nation-state—*as if* each such definition of *Man* were at the same time definitions of the human itself. In consequence, the intellectuals and creative artists of Western Europe were able to bring together their hitherto theocentric notion of *Christian* and that of their now-secular notion of *Man* (in its two variants) into conceptually different notions into the contemporary world of modernity, both in its dazzling triumphs and achievements and in its negative underside. But they were able to do so only on one condition: that they would make their culture-specific notions of *Man*—both in its first still partly secular and partly religious form, and in its now purely secular, because biocentric, form (i.e., one whose origin was now narrated as being in Evolution rather than as before, in Divine Creation)—into notions that were and are ostensibly conceptually homogenous with the reality of being human in all its multiple manifestations. With this, they were thereby making it impossible for themselves to conceive of an Other to what they called and continue to call *human.*

This central over-representation was to be effected by means of two foundational strategies, both of which function to reinforce each other, and a challenging third. The first is that of a sustained rhetorical strategy, which enables the similarity of sound between the words *Man* and the *human* to suggest the empirical existence of a parallel similarity between, on the one hand, the West's definitions or descriptive statements (Bateson 1968) of the human—i.e., *Man^1* and *Man^2*—and, on the other, what the descriptive statement of the human, as one able to incorporate both of these definitions as members of its class of all possible such definitions/descriptive statements, would have to be. Second, as if a parallel similarity also existed between the real-life referent categories of each such descriptive statement and their Fanonian modes of sociogeny (i.e., as in the case of the referent category of contemporary *Man,* who comprise, at the global level, the wealthy, developed countries of the North, or of the First World), and the real-life referent categories of that descriptive statement's Human Other: those of the Third World/Underdeveloped nations and the jobless underclasses whose members are made to function as the "waste products" of their respective nation-state's order. Third, the imperative of securing the interests and well-being of contemporary Man and its real-life referent categories need to be the same as securing the interests of the human species as a whole.

It is, however, the second foundational strategy to which the title of my argument directly refers. What is this strategy? At the end of *The Order of Things,* Foucault makes the point that *Man* is an invention not only of a recent date but one that had been specific to a "restricted geographical area"—namely, that of "European culture since the sixteenth century." As the anthropologist Jacob Pandian (1985) has also pointed out, however, this invention of *Man* had been made possible only by means of a parallel invention. And it is this invention that would define the second foundational strategy by means of which the over-representation of *Man* as if it were the human was to be institutionalized in the wake of Western Europe's expansion from the early decades of the fifteenth century onward, together with its post-1492 putting in place of the structures of what was to become our contemporary world system, the first truly global system in human history.

This second strategy, as Pandian defined it, was one by means of which Western intellectuals were to be enabled to reinvent the terms—as well as the real-life referent categories that had functioned for medieval Latin-Christian Europe as *its* theocentric metaphysical category of Otherness and, therefore, of symbolic death,[4] to the symbolic life embodied in their Judaeo-Christian matrix as the *True Christian* Self, and as a category of Otherness whose real-life referent categories were those groups classifiable as being, *inter alia, heretics, infidels, pagan, idolators,* or *Enemies of Christ* (i.e., those who having been preached the Christian word had refused it)—into new, and now secularizing, terms. That is, as a category of Otherness or of symbolic death, now defined as that of *Human* Others to the True *Human* Self of Western Europe's self-conception as *Man,* and, as such Others, logically classifiable and thereby only seeable and behavable toward as the Lack of this ostensibly only possible conception of what it is to be human.

The real-life referent categories of the discursively and institutionally invented Human Others to Man in its first *homo politicus* conception as the rational citizen or subject of the now-hegemonic

monarchical European state system (which had come to reoccupy
the earlier hegemonic place of the pre-Reformation Church) were
to be two peoples, forcibly uprooted from their own indigenous
genres of being human and, therefore, from their once-autocentric
self-conception and classified instead, as now subordinated groups,
in Western Europe's new secularizing classificatory terminology, as
Indians and *Negroes* (i.e., in the original Spanish as *indios,* men,
and *indias,* women; and as *negros,* men, and *negras,* women).[5] It
was therefore to be the peoples of the Americas and the Caribbean
who—after being conquered, Christianized, and enserfed in the imposed *encomienda* labor system, with their lands and sovereignty
forcibly expropriated—were now to be made discursively and
institutionally into, as Pandian points out, the embodiment of an
ostensibly "savage and irrational humanity," and, as such, the Human
Other to *Man,* defined as the rational political subject or citizen of
the state. Nowhere was the dialectic of this epochally new, Western-
imposed identity system to be more dramatically configured and
enacted than in Shakespeare's play *The Tempest,* as expressed in
the plotline dynamics of the relation between the "reasons of state"
hero character Prospero and his daughter Miranda, on the one hand,
and the expropriated and enslaved Caliban, on the other. With the
latter, therefore, having logically to be seen by the former *not* as the
alternative, because a geographically, ecologically, and geopolitically
different genre or mode of the human than he empirically embodied, but rather as the Lack of what they themselves were; as such,
as the "vile Race" Other to *their* "true" humanness, the evil nature
as opposed to their "good natures."[6]

This was also to be the case, even more extremely so, with
the population group of blacks of African descent transported in
chains as slaves across the Atlantic and made to provide the fixed
and coerced labor for the large-scale export plantations owned by
Western-European settlers. In that these latter were once classified
not only as Negroes but as trade goods denominated as piezas[7]
or pieces, they were, as Pandian points out, to be also assimilated
to the category of Human Otherness embodied in the "Indians,"
as, however, the latter's most extreme form; as, ostensibly, the furthest boundary limits of irrational humanity, and the "missing link"
between humans defined by their rationality and apes defined by
their Lack of it, in what was then defined, in Western classificatory

logic as "the Great Chain of Being" that supposedly reached from the highest forms to the lowest (Mosse 1985); and with the Western European population's ruling class being placed at the apex of the Chain. Toward the end of the eighteenth century and during the nineteenth, however, as Pandian also points out, a mutation in terms of Human Otherness was to occur. This, not only in the empirical context of the abolition of African slavery in the Caribbean and the Americas linked to the second wave of Western imperial expansion, but also and, centrally so, in the wake of the Western intellectual's reinvention of *Man,* in now purely secular because biocentric, *homo oeconomicus,* and therefore specifically bourgeois-capitalist terms, as distinct from the earlier landed-gentry mercantilist ones, which had come to underpin the eighteenth-century variant of the first civic humanist *homo politicus* conception of *Man.* As Pandian further notes, while the real-life referents of the Human Other to *Man* in its new conception were to be all non-Western population groups, once colonized and discursively and institutionally classified (outside the terms of their own once-autocentric self-conceptions and kinds of being human), as "Natives," it was to be the population groups of sub-Saharan Black African descent (including the now-free New World descendants of the former Middle Passage slaves) who would now be made discursively, as well as institutionally, into the primary referent of racially inferior humanity.

In consequence, our imposed and experienced "wrongness of being" and of *désêtre* (i.e., dys-being), together with its systematically induced self-alienation, would directly result from our Human Other role in the identity apparatus of the Western bourgeoisie in terms of its then new biocentric and *homo oeconomicus* descriptive statement of the human. In our role, therefore, as the primary empirical referent category of the idea, central to the now purely secular, half-scientific, half-mythic Origin Narrative as elaborated in Darwin's *The Descent of Man* (1981 [1871]), that some human beings can be, as ostensibly naturally dysselected by the processes of Evolution, in the same way as other human beings can ostensibly be naturally selected. It was therefore to be as a function of the materialization of this idea that, as Fanon points out, two population groups, one classified as white, the other as Negro and/or black, were to find themselves, the one locked into their whiteness, the other into their blackness. In that, in the same way as in the allegedly "proven case" of the "backward," primitive, and atavistic population groups of Black African descent, all therefore now held "to be a mere stage" in the slow process of evolution from monkey into man, and, as such, totally dysselected, so all members of the population group of European descent, classified as the white race, allegedly proven by the very nature of their dominant position in the global order over all other groups, now classified as non-white "native" races, that they had been, as a "race," optimally selected by evolution to embody ostensibly the biological *norm* of being human. With, therefore, this institutionalized dialectic between the two groups, each discursively and institutionally represented, one as the norm, the other as the anti-norm, now made indispensable to the enactment of the new *eugenic/dysgenic* sociogenic code, as the code in whose terms the Western bourgeoisie, unable hitherto to legitimate its role as a ruling class on the basis of the noble blood and birth model of the landed aristocracy, was now to legitimate itself as a *naturally selected* ruling class, because the bearers and transmitters of an alleged eugenic line of descent. Hence the logic of the bourgeois male titles—so and so the first (I), so and so the second (II), so and so the third (III), and so on, or, alternatively, as Senior and Junior.

Hence, also, the power and force of negation of the term "nigger" as ostensibly the dysgenic negation of what it is to be an autonomous, fully evolved human being in the ethno-class terms of Darwinian *Man* over-represented as the human. Hence, too, the logical correlation between blackness and poverty, given that, as Darwin reveals in *The Descent of Man,* the ostensibly selected most "able," who were economically successful, should be encouraged to bear many children, whereas the "poor," as a dysselected, inferior kind of human, should be discouraged from giving birth to many children, thereby reducing the transmission of their alleged biologically determined inferiority and/or dysgenicity (Darwin 1981 [1871]: 403). This is so at the same time as, at the global level, the discursive representing, as well as the empirical instituting, of all the then-colonized non-white categories of peoples, classified as *Indians, Negroes, Natives, Niggers,* as well as the "underdeveloped" Third World, the South, and, therefore, as such, made into the embodiment of the ostensible Lack of Man's True Human Self, itself represented as optimally embodied, no longer in the "reasons of state" landholder figure of Shakespeare's Prospero, but instead in the no less imperative "reasons—of the economy" figure of the global capital-accumulating Stockholder. This latter, as the new hero-figure who, by providing capital as the means of production of the then-new techno-Industrial system thereby serving to enable the mastering of the threat of the ostensibly empirical threat of "Natural Scarcity," as put forward in the Malthusian-*cum*-Ricardo economic discourse, was now made to embody iconically the new bread-winning criterion of being that is indispensable to the class supremacy of the Western, as well as the globally westernized, bourgeoisie. While if it were by their represented successful "mastering" of such scarcity (as a condition now attached, as Hans Blumenberg perceptively notes, for the first time in human history to reality as a whole)—"Mankind has always known want and the distress of being hard-pressed by nature, but the generalization of such experiences to the evaluation of reality as a whole" is linked to "a motif of modern intellectual history unknown in previous epochs[:] ... the [Malthusian] idea of *overpopulation*, of growth of a number of men beyond a natural living space (considered to be constant), and beyond the quantity of food (considered to be growing at a rate less than proportional to that of the population)" (Blumenberg 1983: 221)—that the bourgeoisie legitimated the economic projection of capitalism, a logical corollary had also followed. This was that it was precisely by such mastering that the wealthier members were/are held to have "proved," retroactively, the fact of their having been "naturally selected" by evolution to belong to the no less represented to be, in terms of the then new Darwinian Origin Narrative complex, "naturally scarce" category of fully evolved and, thereby, eugenic or "able" human beings. With the upper-class, because wealthier, members of the bourgeoisie thereby being logically represented as having been extra-humanly, because bio-evolutionarily, mandated to be the ruling class, parallel to the way in which the rule of the Emperor of Imperial China had been represented as having been as extra-humanly, if then supernaturally, ordained to be by the Mandate of Heaven (Krupp 1992).[8]

In this context, the invention of the global category of Human Others on the basis of the institutionalized inferiorization and subjugation of those human beings classified as *Indians, Natives, Negroes, Niggers* was indispensable not only to the enactment of the new sociogenic code and its dialectic of evolved/selected "symbolic life" and non-evolved dysselected "symbolic death" but also to the over-representation of this ethno-class or Western bourgeois genre or mode of being human, *as if* it were that of the human itself. An over-representation, which therefore had to repress the reality of the quite different self-conceptions and sociogenic codes of the multiple groups now subordinated and classified as *natives,* in order to enable their multiple societal orders to be studied by anthropologists, *not* as the institutions of the alternative genres of the human that they were (as studies that would have called for the relativization of the perspective of the biocentric *homo oeconomicus* genre of the human as the perspective that alone makes the discipline of anthropology itself possible) but, rather, in Western classificatory terms, as "cultures." The latter as a term taken from the agrarian, agricultural era of history of the West itself, and generalized to apply to all humans, even though not applicable, as a term, to the hunter-gatherer societies that had instituted themselves as such for the earliest and longest period of human history (Waswo 1987: 547–564).

Further, given that it was not only anthropology but also all the disciplinary discourses of our present order of knowledge, as put in place from the nineteenth century onward, that had to be elaborated on the *a priori* basis of this biocentric, *homo oeconomicus* descriptive statement and its over-representation as if it were that of the human, what McWhorter challenged as their "truth" in "some universal abstract sense," necessarily functioned and functions to effect the retroactive conflation of *Man* and the *Human,* as if they were conceptually one and the same notion; as if, therefore, Western Man's Project—one put in place in the wake of the epochal revolution of Renaissance humanism based on its separation of *Christian* and *Man* into conceptually different notions, as a separation that was to fuel both its global conquests and expansion and its invention of an entirely new mode of cognition, that of the natural sciences—was and is what a truly, and therefore inclusively, Human Project would have to be.[9]

If the use by academic scholarship of the pronoun "he" as if it were a *generic* term, which suggests that its real-life referent categories were both male and female scholars, can only be empirically validated, as Jane Gallop—coming from the perspective of Feminist Studies, which arose in the wake of multiple social movements of the 1960s—pointed out, by "veiling" the male attributes of the perspective that makes it possible for this "he" to be seen as an ostensibly neutral term as inclusive of female scholars as they were/are of the male ones, a parallel strategy with respect to the term "Man" can be seen to be at work here. If, as Gallop further proposes, this "veiling of the male attributes" had only been made possible by women scholars' acceptance of their non-generic assigned roles, until the rise of the feminist movement put an end to this acceptance, nevertheless, that earlier acceptance itself been enabled only because of the acceptance by middle-class women, both Western and westernized, of their pre-assigned role as homemakers, one complementary to their male peers' acceptance of *their* pre-assigned roles as breadwinners. This therefore meant that the attributes of the perspective that would have to be veiled in order to enable the pronoun "he" to be used as a neutral term—ostensibly inclusive of men and women scholars, at the same time as it ensured the male's superior status as the generic sex—were not only *male* (the issue of gender) but also *bourgeois* (the issue of class) and *ethnic,* and/or "local cultural," that is, the issue of *genre* classified in *Man's* terms, as that of *race.*

Hence the fact that when Western feminist scholars came to use the pronoun "she" as an ostensibly neutral term inclusive of both Western and non-Western feminist scholars, of both Western and westernized women, of both middle-class and lower/underclass women, some feminists, such as, for example, Carole Boyce Davis and Elaine Savory-Fido (1990: vii–xix), in their collection of essays *Out of Kumbla: Caribbean Women and Literature,* challenged the neutrality of that "she" by insisting on correlating, and thereby unveiling, the attributes of "race" and "class" alongside of gender: since gender, when taken by itself, at once transformed Western middle-class feminists, for whom gender is the *only* issue that blocks their full incorporation into the Western-bourgeois global structures of power, into generic feminists—indeed, into generic women.

If we see our present noun "Man" as playing a parallel role at the level of genre—and, here, the shared etymological roots of both terms, *genre* and *gender,* need to be recognized as the non-arbitrary ones that they are, given that in all human orders the narratively mandated gender roles are everywhere a central function of the enacting of our no less narratively instituted genres or modes of being human—a logical corollary follows. That is, the noun "Man" now also functions as an ostensibly neutral and universal term, whose real-life referent categories are imagined to include, at the level of gender, all women as well as all men (thereby transforming the latter into the *generic sex*); at the level of class, all classes (thereby making the Western and westernized members of the bourgeoisie into the *generic class*); at the level of sexual preferences, all sexual preferences (thereby making heterosexual preference into the *generic* preference); and, at the level of "race" or human hereditary variations, together with their genres of being human classified as "cultures" and "religions," all such "races," their hereditary variation and genres or "cultures"/religions, thereby making the Indo-European race or hereditary variation into the generic "race," at the same time as it makes its contemporary Western civilization, and/or its culture and now-privatized Christian religion, into the *generic* civilization, culture, religion. With these altogether, making its globally instituted ethno-class, or biocentric *homo oeconomicus* genre of being human, into the ostensibly *generic* or "true" human.

At the same time, it is a given that our present techno-industrial capitalist mode of economic production, as the mode of material provisioning indispensable to the continued processes of auto-institution of our present hegemonic biocentric, *homo oeconomicus Man,* over-represented as if it were the human, is thereby also represented as an economic system that is ostensibly inclusive of the interests of the "developed" and wealthy countries of the North, together with those of the Western and westernized middle classes—as interests specific to the real-life referent categories of *Man*—as well as the interests of the impoverished "underdeveloped" countries of the South/the Third World, together with the interests of the global category of the jobless Poor both North and South, who are the real-life referent categories, in *economic* terms of *Man*'s ostensible non-breadwinning Human Others, subordinated to Natural Scarcity, and, as such, imperfectly evolved. In the same way, therefore, as Jane Gallop's observation with respect to the pronoun "he," and of its over-representation as a neutral term able to include both male and female scholars, had been made believable only by the veiling of its male attributes, so in the case of the noun "Man," and its over-representation as a neutral term able to include all of the categories cited, and as an inclusion that then enables it to represent the imperative securing of *its* interests, the imperative that now governs our collective behaviors, as if it were the same as that of the securing of the interests of the human species itself, continues to be made believable only by means of a parallel systemic "veiling." By the veiling, that is, of *Man*'s specific ethno-class attributes, a veiling effected by the projected truth, "in a universal abstract sense," of our present order of knowledge, as well as by the psycho-affective closure effected by our present mainstream aesthetics. And, therefore, with both our present epistemological order and mainstream aesthetic now coming to function, in Lewis Gordon's terms, as a purely secular form of theodicy. More precisely, perhaps, as a *biodicy*, which, by replacing *Evolution and Natural Selection* in the re-occupied locus of Christian theodicy's Divine Creator, enables these bio-agencies to serve as the now de-supernaturalized Source of Legitimacy that serves to validate the functioning of our contemporary order, thereby enabling the injustice and evil of the large-scale costs to which its functioning leads—as costs that are the negative underside of the dazzling triumphs and achievements of its now purely biologized order of being and of things—to be explained *away* rather than to be explained, recognized, and confronted.

These costs have been summed up by Gerald Barney, as cited by Loyal La Rue in his book *Everybody's Story: Wising Up to the Epic of Evolution.* Calling these overall costs "the global problematique," Barney had defined it in these terms: "As we humans have begun to think globally, it has become clear that we do not have a poverty problem, or a hunger problem, or a habitat problem, or an energy problem.... What we really have is a poverty-hunger-habitat-energy-trade-population-atmosphere-waste-resource problem" (La Rue 2000: 3). "We humans," however, have not created this "problematique." Nor indeed, have we humans created the brilliant achievements and triumphs of which the global problematique is the negative underside. Rather, as Gordon's seminal insight here suggests, both are the creations of a Western Europe that sought to become *ontological*—to become, for both good and ill, what dialecticians call "Absolute Being" (Gordon 2002c: 10).

III

Unveiling the Ethno-Class Attributes of Man's "Inner Eyes" for Which Alone Other Humans Can Exist as "Natives," "Negroes," and "Niggers" Rather Than as Other Humans: On De-Universalizing Its Project, Its Genre, Its Aesthetics, Its Truth

> I am an invisible man. No, I am not a spook like those who haunted Edgar Allan Poe; nor am I one of your Hollywood-movie ectoplasms. I am a man of substance, of flesh and bone, fiber and

liquids, and I might even be said to possess a mind. I am invisible, understand, simply because people refuse to see me.

—*Ralph Ellison,* The Invisible Man

I think that tastes, odours, colours and so on are no more than mere names so far as the object in which we place them is concerned, and that they reside only in the consciousness. Hence if the living creature were removed, all these qualities would be wiped away and annihilated.

—*Galileo, Il Saggiatore, cited in Anthony Gottlieb's* The Dream of Reason: A History of Western Philosophy from the Greeks to the Renaissance (2000)

Sephocle: When one leaves home, one approaches and appreciates things in a different way.

Césaire: In the African case, it is even clearer. I realized that there were many things that astonished me in Martinique. I understood afterwards that they puzzled me because we did not have the keys and that those keys were elsewhere. They were in Africa. Let us take the case of the Martiniquan carnival: it is beautiful, it is intriguing. After visiting Africa, one realizes that so many of these masks that intrigue us in the Martiniquan carnival are simply of African origin.
Extraordinary! That mask became here in Martinique the devil because we are a Catholic country, and as we say here: the god of the vanquished became the devil of the vanquisher.

—*Aimé Césaire, "Interview" (1992)*

To the real question, How does it feel to be a problem? I answer seldom a word.
And yet, being a problem is a strange experience,—peculiar even for one who has never been anything else, save perhaps in babyhood and in Europe.

—*W. E. B. Du Bois, "On Our Spiritual Strivings," in* The Souls of Black Folk (1903)

In *The Enigma of the Gift,* the anthropologist Maurice Godelier makes a seminal breakthrough point by placing his focus on the institutional practices of traditional societies: While as human beings we can live only in societies, what tends to be ignored is the fact that we must first produce societies in order to live. *The* central task of all human social orders is that of their production and stable reproduction. Nevertheless, our oversight of the imperative central-ity of this process is itself due to the fact that, as Godelier points out, while it is we ourselves who are the individual and collective agents and authors of all such societies, from our origin as human beings, we have consistently and systemically made this fact opaque to ourselves by means of a central mechanism. This mechanism is the projection of our own agency and authorship onto extra-human agencies, with the first of those being the millennially supernatural (Godelier 1999)—that is, whether those of the deified Ancestors, nature spirits, gods, or those of the later monotheistic variants, the respective single God (all of the three Abrahamic religions, Judaism, Judaeo-Christianity, and Islam). Frantz Fanon also makes the point that it is "the human who brings societies into being" (Fanon 1967b: introduction); at the same time, his new definition of the human being as a hybrid mode of, so to speak, "nature-culture" or "ontogeny sociogeny," implies that the processes by which we produce our societies in order to live are the same auto-instituting processes by which we at the same time produce ourselves as this or that modality of an always already socialized, and therefore sociogenic, *kind/genre* of being human; and, as such, an always already inter-altruistically bonded and thereby kin-recognizing mode of the *I* and the *we*. That, in other words, is so in the same way as the projection of our own agency and authorship, with respect to the production and reproduction of our societal orders onto supernatural agencies, had enabled us to keep opaque to ourselves the fact of our own agency and authorship with respect to the putting in place of the role of allocations, divisions of labor, and structuring hierarchies specific to each such order, thereby stabilizing them, so the same projection would have enabled us, and still does, to keep opaque from ourselves our own agency with respect to the auto-instituting, autopoetic processes by means of which we produce ourselves as this or that modality of the human, or kind of an *I* and a *we*.[10]

The literary scholar Wlad Godzich also identified the fact of this projection of agency, in somewhat different terms, when he put forward the idea of the parallel projection of "spaces of Otherness," as, in effect, the also supernatural or extra-human abode of all such non-human agencies—"spaces of Otherness" that are therefore indispensable, he argues, to the instituting and legitimating of all human societies. Pointing out that because "for a society to know itself" it "must have a sense that its order is neither anarchic nor nonsensical but must be ... the realization of a true order," Godzich proposes that for this to be realized, "the foundational principles" on which the societal order is formed "cannot be found in the society itself but must be located in a space of otherness that ensures that they remain beyond the reach of human desire or temptation" (Godzich 1987: 161).

From time immemorial, in consequence, because these "foundational principles" had been attributed to varying supernatural entities, the "space of Otherness" where they and the principles they had allegedly mandated existed, had been mapped upon the physical cosmos, whether in spaces beneath the earth or, even more centrally, upon the celestial heavens. Hence, as E. C. Krupp has shown in his study of the ethno-astronomies of a wide range of human societies from the smallest hunter-gatherer groups, such as the San of the Kalahari, to large-scale ancient empires such as those of Egypt and China, in all such cases, and whatever their differential degrees of complexity, all of their respective ethno-astronomies reveal the ways in which, in each case, knowledge of the physical cosmos had been used adaptively, to map and anchor the foundational principles and, with it, the always already-legitimated status-ordering and role-allocating principles about which each such societal order self-organized itself (Krupp 1997).[11] While given that in each such society the foundational status-ordering and role-allocating principles were themselves generated from the always origin-narratively-inscribed sociogenic principle or code—as in the case of the theocentric order of Latin Christian Europe, where the *Redeemed Spirit/Fallen Flesh* sociogenic code as actualized in the categories of the celibate Clergy and the institution of the Church (the *Redeemed Spirit*), on the one hand, and of the Laity, the non-celibate married and marriageable lay men and women, together with the lay institutions such as of the state and commerce (the *Fallen Flesh*), on the other, functioned to institutionalize the primacy of the religious identity *Christian* over all others—one can generalize Gordon's insightful concept of a *theodicy* to all such supernaturally legitimated and guaranteed human societal orders. Doing this by extending the traditional meaning of *theodicy*—that is, as an order that functions to justify the ways of God to mankind—to one in which all supernaturally guaranteed orders must function in a cognitively closed manner, in order to justify the order and its everyday functioning, to its subjects, as the realization of a true, because ostensibly supernaturally mandated, order.

The historical uniqueness of Western Europe was to derive from the epochal rupture that the lay-humanist intellectuals of late medieval Latin Christian Europe had found themselves compelled to effect, if only in its then initial form, with the millennial projection of human agency onto supernatural entities that had been defining of all human societal orders and their genres of being human from our hybridly autopoetic origin on the continent of Africa[12] until the era of pre-Renaissance, late-medieval Latin Christian Europe. Why did they find themselves so compelled? In *The Medieval Imagination*, Jacques Le Goff shows the way in which, in the wake of the Gregorian Reform movement of the Church—which, having taken place between 1050 to 1215 had mandated, *inter alia*, the celibacy of the Clergy—the lay or secular world, including the institution of the political state, as well as of commerce, had became subordinated to the decision-making processes and behavior-prescribing hegemony of the Church. This hegemony had been legitimated not only by the foundational Judaeo-Christian Origin Narrative but also by means of the projected "space of Otherness" mapped upon the heavens by the Christian-Ptolemaic astronomy of the times—mapped, as well, upon the geography of the earth by the sacred Christian geography of the medieval order of knowledge.

With respect to the formulation of a general order of existence created by Judaeo-Christianity, the postulate of a "significant ill," while common to all such formulations, was uniquely represented as that of mankind's enslavement to Original Sin, at the same time as *its* prescribed cure or plan of salvation was that of redemption through Christ, by means of His Church and, therefore, of Christian baptism followed by the new converts' adherence to the prescriptive behavioral pathways laid down by the Church and Clergy. This therefore meant that the sociogenic code of *Redeemed Spirit* (as actualized in the celibate Clergy, who by their celibacy were assumed to have escaped the negative legacy of Adamic enslavement to Original Sin, itself held to be transmitted through the processes of sexual procreation), as contrasted with the *Fallen Flesh* (as actualized in the category of the married and marriageable lay men and women, as well as in all lay institutions), had functioned, as Le Goff shows, as the status-organizing principle of the social order; with the social category of, for example, the peasantry, who were allocated the manual labor role, held to have been mandated to be placed at the bottom of the social scale because of their alleged wicked indulgence in the carnal lusts of the flesh, while women's subordinate roles were held to be due to the fact that they were more given, like Eve, to sin and temptation than were men. At the same time, this code, and its status-ordering principle, had also been mapped upon the projected "space of Otherness" of the heavens, as well as upon that of the sacred geography of the Earth.[13]

The cognitively closed order of knowledge of late medieval Europe (i.e., that of High Scholasticism whose master discipline was theology) had therefore functioned to ensure that the then-emergent political states of Europe, as well as the ongoing commercial revolution, were subordinated to the hegemony of the Church in the context of the then-absolute primacy of the religious identity, *Christian.* With the result that it was through the symbolically coded "inner eyes" of that specific genre of being human that both the physical cosmos and the social order had been orthodoxly known in the specific terms of Christian-Ptolemaic astronomy and of the sacred geography of the earth, as terms that enabled the stable production and reproduction of the order. It is in the context, therefore, of the Renaissance humanists' revalorization of the "natural fallen man" of the Christian schema, and its invention of *Man* as *homo politicus,* thereby enabling the division of *Christian* and *Man* into two conceptually and institutionally separable notions, and with the latter identity, that of *Man,* coming to take primacy as the political subject of the modern European state that was itself in the process of initiating what was to be its successful challenge to, and displacement/replacement of, the hegemony of the Church, that both the new Copernican astronomy as well as the fifteenth-century voyages of the Portuguese followed by that of Columbus were to be made thinkable, imaginable. This at the same time as the state's new political public identity would come, in the wake of the religious movement of the Reformation, gradually to effect the transformation of the religious identity and practices of the Church, into a function of securing the new supra-ordinate *this-worldly* goal of securing the order and stability of the state, as well as of legitimating its global imperial expansion of conquest and expropriation of the lands of non-Christian, non-European peoples, as lands classified in Christian theological terms as *terra nullius* (i.e. nobody's land);[14] with the new *this-worldly* goal itself coming to reoccupy as the primary goal, the earlier, then primary, other-worldly goal of the Church—that of Eternal Salvation in the Augustinian "City of God" (Pocock 1975).

Now while in Christian theological terms such "justly" expropriated peoples had been classified as *Enemies of Christ,* and their lands, as such, legitimately classified as expropriable by Christian kings, this as a legitimation that had been used by the expanding European states in the first stage of their global expansion, as the Spanish state sought, in the wake of 1492, and of its invasion and conquest of the New World peoples, to legitimate its expropriation *outside* the theological terms that would have forced it to continue accepting the Papacy's claim to temporal as well as spiritual sovereignty, it set out to transform the ground on which its expropriation of the New World peoples, from Christian to Aristotelian ones, had been legitimated; and it did so on the basis of the premise, adapted from Aristotle's *Politics,* that the New World's peoples, having been intended by nature, because of their extreme irrationality, to be *natural slaves,* in the same way that the Spaniards and other Europeans had been intended by nature to be, because of their ostensible high degrees of rationality, natural masters, had been legitimately expropriated by the latter; given that it was fitting that the more rational should govern the less rational, in effect, that *Man,* the Spaniards, should govern its *Human Others,* the "Indians," until they had been taught to become *more human,* as the Spanish humanist ideologue, Ginés de Sepúlveda, argued.[15]

It is, therefore, in the context of the rise to hegemony of the modern European state over the Church, allied to the lay intellectuals' correlated civic humanist invention of *Man* as political subject of the state and, as such, as a separate notion from the then–matrix identity *Christian* as the religious subject of the Church, that what Lewis Gordon identifies as the West's quest to embody and incorporate in itself and its peoples the concept of Absolute Being would take its point of departure. With this quest then determining what would come to be the Janus-face of the West's epochal rupture with the millennial projection of agency onto the supernatural entities that had been defining hitherto, of all human kinds or genres of being human, together with their respective creeds, formulations of a general order of existence or behavior-motivational schemas. For the profound implication here was that while Christianity had seen and, indeed, continues to see itself as the only true religion, and its God as the only true God, it nevertheless has always had to acknowledge the existence of other creeds, accepting therefore its own objective relativity even while subjectively seeing itself as the only true path to salvation. This was not to be so, however, in the case of the humanists' invention of *Man* together with their classical civic humanist formulation of a "general order of existence" in whose terms Christianity's postulate of a "significant ill," as that of all mankind's enslavement to Original Sin, would be transformed into that of mankind's enslavement to the irrational aspects of its human nature. Therefore, with the new plan of redemption or salvation, now no longer based on mankind's quest for redemption from Original Sin, by primarily adhering to the prescriptive behavioral pathways laid down by the Church and its Clergy, as the only means of attaining the *other-worldly* goal of Eternal Salvation in the City of God, but one redefined in new terms. That is, by the political subjects' adhering to the prescriptive behavioral pathways laid down by the State as a function of attaining its *this-worldly* goal of ensuring its order, stability, and territorial expansion as the now-terrestrial embodiment of the "common good," in the re-occupied place of the Church.

Yet *homo politicus,* the Political citizen or subject *Man*—no longer seen at the public level as the "fallen" natural man of the Christian schema but, rather, as a "reasons of state" figure, able, like Prospero in Shakespeare's play *The Tempest,* to repress the irrational aspects of his own nature—was now Absolute *Man.* The secularizing formulation of a general order of existence now inscribed his identity, while a transformed version of the Judaeo-Christian matrix, unlike the latter, no longer had to contend with any other possible schema, any other possible variant of *Man,* given that the latter was now over-represented, in terms of its formulation, as *the* human itself. As a result, all other human beings who did not look, think, and act as the peoples of Western Europe did were now to be classified not as *Enemies-of-Christ* but, rather, as the Lack of "true humanness," allegedly because of their lack of the Western European order of rationality (over-represented as rationality in general); this, as a Lack that determined that they should be discursively and institutionally classified as *Man*'s Human Others—that is, as Caliban to Prospero—and, as such, held to be as justly expropriated of their lands and allocated to their labor roles as serfs and racialized slaves, as the peasants in the medieval order had been held to be justly condemned to their manual labor role, given their imputed wicked indulgence in the carnal lusts of the flesh.

As a result, the empirical differences between *Man*'s population groups and those of its Human Others, rather than being seeable as the differences between ecologically, geopolitically, and geographically adaptive forms of life, together with their institutionalized genres or kinds of being human that they empirically were—since such a perception would have called for the relativization of *Man*'s newly invented self-conception as Absolute Man—had instead to be seen in terms of *Man*'s newly constructed "inner eyes" or order of consciousness as less, not-quite humans, and, as such, logically classifiable, and institutionalized, as "Indians" and "Negroes." It is here that what I have referred to as the Janus-face of the epochal rupture effected by the West with its invention of *Man* and its initiation of the secularization of human existence based upon its gradual de-supernaturalization of projected agency is to be sited. In that, for the subjects of the late-medieval Christian Europe, and in terms of the "inner eyes" with which they looked with their physical eyes upon reality, the Earth had to be seen as fixed and motionless at the center of the universe as its dregs, because, ostensibly, the degraded abode of fallen mankind, and therefore of its negative "fallen flesh," its Adamic legacy of enslavement to Original Sin, as contrasted with the perfection and incorruptibility of the allegedly quite different ontological substance of the harmoniously moving heavens, and with the medieval subjects' everyday experience of this indeed for them, as for all human beings, motionless, reality of the Earth, ostensibly verifying this conception, a scientific astronomy, unlike their Christian Ptolemaic ethno-astronomy, would have been logically unimaginable, and inconceivable. While, as both Kurt Hübner and Fernand Hallyn have pointed out, it was only to be on the basis of the Renaissance humanists' re-valorized conception of the human as *homo politicus*—in effect, on the basis of their new lay or secularizing redefinition of the human at the public level of existence and, as such, outside the terms of the Spirit/Flesh code of the medieval order, and therefore, outside the terms of that new conception's "inner eyes"—that the breakthrough of a Copernicus to a scientific astronomy, based on the counter-premise that the earth also moved and was of the same substance of the heavens, was made possible. With this breakthrough, the first stage of what was to become, over the centuries, the new order of non-adaptive cognition known as the natural sciences—whose domains of knowledge are the physical cosmos, together with, after Darwin, that of the cosmos of purely organic forms of life, including the physiological conditions of our genres or sociogenic kinds of being human—was put in place.

The other side of the Janus-face was to return to Gordon's thesis, that as in the wake of its expansion the West came to conceive of itself and its peoples (especially its ruling groups) in terms of Absolute Being on the model of Shakespeare's Prospero, thereby coming to see all other population groups and their kinds of being human, not only as the Lack of the only possible mode of being human defined in non-supernatural terms, which it itself incarnated. As such, as peoples whose self-realization could only exist as a function of securing its own (i.e. the West's) and that of its own people's self-realization, while it had, indeed, de-supernaturalized the projection of agency, together with the "supreme source of legitimacy," it had also done so only by re-projecting its own agency and authorship onto entities that, while no longer supernatural, were no less extra-human. In consequence, from the sixteenth century onward, the West had begun to substitute the idea of Nature (still conceived of as the agent of the Christian God on earth), as the agent that had, in its own terms, extra-humanly mandated an alleged "by nature difference" in rationality between Western Europeans, on the one hand, and "Indians" and "Negroes," on the other; this as an ostensibly greater/lesser difference in degrees of humanity, which had legitimated the European states' respective expropriations of the New World land from their indigenous owners, the "Indians," followed by their reduction to neo-serf status, and as well, the commercialization and reduction of the other category of the "Negroes" into outright slave status, with both conjoined processes thereby setting in motion a large-scale and ongoing transfer of resources from the two latter population groups, to the peoples of Western Europe.

From the beginning of the nineteenth century onward, however, the West would shift the supreme source of legitimacy from the halfway religio-secular entity of Nature to the purely de-supernatural-ized entity of Evolution, together with its so-called mechanisms of Natural Selection and dysselection. In the former case, the West had mapped its new *Rational/Irrational* human nature code, primarily upon the empirical system of differences that existed between its own societal form of life and mode of being human, and those of the African and New World peoples, thereby replacing the "space of Otherness" of the celestial/terrestrial or Heaven/Earth line, on which the *Spirit/Flesh* code of the medieval order had been mapped, with the new "space of Otherness" of the ostensible by-nature-difference-in-rationality line drawn between its own group, and the two groups that it had subordinated, on the other, with the emergence of Darwin's theory of Evolution, and in its wake the rise of the biological sciences, a far-reaching mutation would now take place. In that, in terms of the "half-scientific, half-mythic" Darwinian Origin Narrative and its implied "formulation of a general order of existence," as put forward in *The Descent of Man,* Gordon's thesis that with "modern secularism" theodicy does not disappear but is merely replaced by whatever "is advanced as a Supreme Being or Supreme Source of legitimacy" is verified; with the exception only that given that the "Supreme Being and Supreme Source of Legitimacy" is now to be the processes of biological Evolution and its represented agent, Natural Selection/Dysselection, theodicy metamorphosizes into biodicy.

In that, whereas before, in terms of the Judaeo-Christian "for-mulation of a general order of existence," evil in the world was attributed to, in St. Augustine's fateful terms, mankind's own inher-ent failing, the result of its negative legacy of Original Sin inherited from Adam and Eve, both of whom had been given the freedom by their loving Divine Creator to sin or not to sin, evil was now to be explained, in terms of the Darwinian-Malthusian formulation of a general order of existence, in terms of a biodicy.[16] Evil in the world was now projected as being due, not to mankind's inherited negative Adamic legacy, but rather to extra-humanly determined conditions. That is, to the postulated "significant ill" of *Natural Scar-*

city correlated with the no-less postulated random bio-evolutionary processes of natural selection and dysselection, in terms of whose overall explanatory and, indeed, behavior-motivating schema, those relatively few selected were now to be seen as being as *naturally scarce* as the resources for which they all had to compete (cf. Gutting 1989: 188–189). With the further, humanly de-valorizing proviso that all human beings had now to consider themselves dysselected until each individual had proven by his/her success in the bourgeois order of things that he/she had been selected. This at the same time as the many, the lower-classes and the non-successful poor, as well as, globally, the lower because "native" races, all pre-categorized as not favored by Evolution, were now represented as only confirming their own original non-selection and, thereby, as having to accept their dysgenicity as the ostensibly unquestionable cause of their poverty.

In this context, the new post-eighteenth-century bourgeois order of things, whose capitalist economic system would put an end to the Agrarian era of mankind, thereby initiating the techno-industrial era, can now be seen as doing so on the only basis that would make it possible. That is, on the basis of the global large-scale accumulation of wealth in the hands of the few, at the cost of the impoverishment of the many, yet as a process being enabled to function within the logic of an order whose new bio-humanist formulation of a general order of existence, and its postulate of a "significant ill," would reliably serve to legitimate this dialectic of enrichment of the relatively few and the correlated systemic impoverishment of the many. Given that in terms of the new conception of Man as *homo oeconomicus* and, thereby, of its correlated formulation of a general order of existence, the postulate of a "significant ill" was now that of the threat of mankind's subordination to Natural Scarcity, with its plan of redemption/salvation, thereby calling for the human subject's imperative mastering, or at the very least, its keeping at bay, of Natural Scarcity by means of an ever-increasing process of economic growth. While the latter as a process is alone made possible by the acceleration of the profit-driven accumulation of capital called for in order to provide the means for the expanding dynamic of both large-scale techno-industrial and agricultural mass production. While because this dynamic was now represented as the only one able to keep at bay mankind's threatened subordination to

Natural Scarcity, the overall explanatory behavior-motivating schema of which it is the expression, now served to legitimate the ways of functioning of our ostensible extra-humanly mandated, global economic global-order based on free-market capitalism, to its subjects, whatever the grave social injustices and flagrant ills that continue to be generated as the logical costs of its functioning. With this being no less so than it had been in the case of the behavior-motivating schema of the medieval Latin Christian world, whose discourses of the theodicy had in a parallel way served to legitimate the functioning of that vertically hierarchical social order to its subjects, doing so in the same terms in which they had legitimated the ways of God to mankind.

Nevertheless, where in the latter order it had only been the specifically Latin Christian order of being and things, and its ethno-religious theodicy that had justified the ways of the Christian God, and, therefore, the functioning of its Latin Christian medieval order to that order's specifically *Christian* subjects, with the second post-eighteenth-century invention of *Man* in biocentric and *homo oeconomicus* terms, a mutation would be effected. Seeing that the terms of this second invention, ones that fully enabled its projection as Absolute Being because allegedly selected to be so by the bio-evolutionary processes of Evolution and Natural Selection, and which were now to serve as the justification of the processes of functioning of our present order's biodicy, this justification was now one made to all human subjects, all of whom were now imagined to have had their origin in the half-mythic, half-scientific Origin Narrative as formulated in Darwin's *The Descent of Man;* to have their origin as such, in terms of the Western bourgeoisie's *homo oeconomicus* conception of the human, *Man,* over-represented as if it were that of the human itself. While given that the empirical human species' physiological conditions of existence, whose origins were indeed in Evolution, were now conflated with those of the mode of sociogeny instituted by ethno-class *Man*'s self-conception, together with its over-representation of this conception as if it were that of the human, it was at this conjuncture that the "space of Otherness" phenomenon, first identified by W. E. B. Du Bois, as the *Color Line,* was to come centrally into existence. That is, as a line ostensibly mandated by Evolution between the "favored race"[17] or human hereditary variation as expressed in the ecologically and climatically adaptive albinism (i.e., white skin) and physiognomy of Western European peoples and their descendants, on the one hand, and on all the other darker skinned, or non-white, peoples of the earth, on the other.

As a result, whereas the *celestial/terrestrial, heaven/earth* line of the medieval order of things had been made to function as the clearly extra-humanly mandated "space of Otherness" on which to map and anchor the *Spirit/Flesh* sociogenic code about which the medieval order had self-organized its structuring hierarchies, with, however, the rise of the movement toward a scientific astronomy in the wake of Renaissance humanists' invention of political *Man* as a conceptually and institutionally separate notion from the religious identity *Christian,* thereby enabling the initiation of what would come to be the emancipation of the physical cosmos from having to be known in adaptive and therefore ethno-religious terms as it had to be known in terms of the medieval order and its theodicy, with the transformation of that order's foundational narrative and, therefore, of its formulation of a general order of existence into the now purely de-supernaturalized Origin Narrative of Evolution and Natural Selection, together with *its* biologized formulation of a general order of existence, it was to be the *Color Line* that would now function as an allegedly no less extra-humanly mandated "space of Otherness," in the re-occupied earlier place of the physical cosmos. So that, as the new "space of Otherness" divide that was now to reoccupy the order-legitimating place that had been taken by the matrix Heaven/Earth divide of medieval Europe, as well as by that of the Rational/Irrational divide of the later statist and *homo politicus* order of being and of things that had remained intact until the end of the eighteenth century, the Color or Evolved/Non-evolved line was now to be mapped upon the skin color and physiognomic differences between white and non-white. While, at its most extreme form, it was now to be mapped on the difference between, on the one hand, the skin color and "Caucasian" physiognomy of the Indo-European population group (projected *not as the climatically adaptive variation that it was* and is but, rather, as the ostensibly naturally selected biological, and therefore eugenic, norm of being human), and on the other, the skin color and physiognomy, most distant from its own, that of the Bantu peoples of Black African descent, represented *not* as the *climatically adaptive variant that it was and is,* when seen from a natural scientific perspective, but in *Man*-centric terms, which represented it as being the ostensibly most naturally dysselected and, therefore, dysgenic Other, or anti-norm, to the ostensibly eugenic norm of the Caucasian hereditary variation, of its "favored race."

It was to be as a function of the West's institutionalization of itself in terms of its then epochally new self-conception or socio-genic code as Absolute Being (whether in its first form as *homo politicus* or, from the nineteenth century onward, in its purely de-supernaturalized form as biocentric *homo oeconomicus,* with both variants over-represented as if they were the human), thereby, that the majority of the darker-skinned peoples of the earth (all of whom were now to be incorporated, willy nilly into the West's epochally new conception of the human and its correlated formulation of a general order of existence) would come to be seen, known, and classified, as we also came to see, know, and classify ourselves, not as *other* human beings but, instead, as "Native," "Negro," "Blackfel-las," and, ultimately, "Nigger" Others to the True Human Self of the West's Man. This at the same time as the mode of perception or "inner eyes" to which the ethno-class *Man*'s sociogenic code gave rise, functioned to legitimate to the West itself, its conquest and systemic expropriation of the resources as well as of the lives, "la-bor," and, thereby, sovereignty and self-conception of the majority of the non-European peoples of the planet.

Consequently, given that it would be only for the sake of, and therefore in terms of, the West's epochal enacting of its now secular self-conception as Man-as-Absolute Being, entirely new categories of people, racialized as *Indians, Negroes, Natives, Coolies, Chinks, Spics,* and so on, would be brought into existence as *Man*'s Human Others, if, to paraphrase Galileo's *Il Saggiatore,* we were to take away the West's modes or genres of being human, Man^1 and Man^2, and therefore, in Ralph Ellison's terms from *Invisible Man,* their respective symbolically coded "inner eyes" (as eyes through which, as westernized scholars, we also now look with our physical eyes upon reality), all such qualitatively pre-described categories such as *Indians, Negroes, Natives, Coolies, Chinks, Spics, Kikes,* and so on, would cease to exist. This, in the same way that, as Aimé Césaire discovered on a visit to Africa, it was only for his Christianized and westernized "inner eyes" (his order of consciousness as that of contemporary *Man's*) that the oxhead mask, as he had seen it in Martinique, had signified negatively as Christianity's "devil" (and, by implication, in correlatedly secular terms, as "savage," "uncivilized"). So that, if we were to take away those "inner eyes" and order of consciousness specific to our present genre or mode of being human and then replace them with the "inner eyes" of the traditional pre-Western, pre-Christian, and thereby once-autocentric traditional Senegalese genre of being human, the same oxhead mask would now come to signify, in canonized valedictory terms, what it meant to be initiated into adulthood, in terms of what would have to be a quite different, and still Agrarian, genre of being human, of human-hood. What it would have meant, also, for the oxhead mask to have been quite another object of knowledge, one whose role had been central to the instituting technologies by means of which the once genre-centric traditional peoples of Senegal had produced and repro-duced themselves as human. In the post–Middle Passage Caribbean, however, because, for Césaire as an educated middle-class colonial "native" subject, those "traditional inner eyes" had been taken away, obliterated, the oxhead mask as the canonized valedictory signifier of the initiated adult had ceased to exist as such an object. Only its stigmatized reality as the Western object-signifier of the Christian "devil" or of the "uncivilized" savage had remained.

If Aimé Césaire's encounter in Africa has therefore functioned to relativize the "inner eyes" of the West's Man as Absolute Being, this relativization (one that proves Fanon's thesis both with respect to the hybrid physiognomy/ontogeny *cum* sociogeny nature of our modes of being human and with respect to the fact that black self-alienation is itself systematically produced by our present mode of sociogeny, as a function of *Man's* enactment) was a later form of one that had been made clear and evident, if only for a brief interregnum, by the first encounter that had taken place between Europeans and the Bantu Congolese, in the wake of the state-dispatched Portuguese voyage that arrived at the Congo River in 1482. With this arrival, followed by the putting in place from 1484 onward of the first stage of the slave trade out of Africa, which, limited at first, would become a large-scale one in the wake of Columbus's arrival in the Caribbean, together with the subsequent expropriation of the vast territories of the Caribbean and Americas from their indigenous owners to the ownership and sovereignty of the Crown of Spain and Portugal. In that first encounter, however, if, as Ralph Ellison noted in *Invisible Man,* the invisibility of the black person as simply another human individual is an invisibility that has nothing to do with the person in question but, rather, with one prescribed by "the inner eyes with which we look with our physical eyes upon reality," with the further implication here that Du Bois's (1903) systematic experience of being "a problem" has nothing to do with *himself* but, rather, has to do with the specific construction of an order of consciousness or "inner eyes" in which he must always already be classified as a problem.

Sigbert Axelson, in his book *Culture Confrontation in the Lower Congo, Etc.* (1970), enables us to see the way in which, from the perspective of the "inner eyes" of the Bantu Congolese, it was the white skin—that is, its albinism—as well as the physiognomy of the incoming Europeans that posed a formidable problem.

As Axelson recounts, from their first sight of the Europeans and of the anomaly that their appearance represented, this problem for the Congolese was posed as a question: "Are these creatures really men (humans)? How could they be, normally human, if they were not black? Not physiognomically Bantu?" This problem was partly solved, at first, by the Congolese. When, in coming to terms with the anomaly that the Europeans represented, they had co-classified the latter (given their obvious power, as proved by their arrival on the water, on the one hand, and by their deathly pallor, their skins drained of color, on the other) with the deceased and deified ancestors whose "space of Otherness" abode was projected as existing under the water as well as underground. They had therefore seen them, at first, as messengers sent by the Ancestors—that is, as supernatural entities—and thus as abnormal with respect to being normally human. Nevertheless, in spite of this provisional classification, which would itself be later discarded, another problem remained—the aesthetic problem. For as the Spanish Catholic missionary Antonio de Teruel pointed out, in his seventeenth-century description of the inhabitants of the Congo, for the then (still genre-centric) Congolese, "only those who were of the deepest black in color were held by them to be the most beautiful" (Teruel 1663-1664).

While, because the colors of the Congolese people ranged from chestnut to deepest olive, to black, anxious mothers made use of an ointment, rubbing it on the skin of the lighter-colored infants, then exposing them to the sun in an attempt to get them to attain to the preferred deep blackness of skin color that was, for the Congolese, the mark of true beauty. Because of this criterion, albinos amongst them were held to be sacred monsters. The white skin of the Europeans, therefore, as the expression of the same, if more thoroughgoing because climatically adaptive, mutation toward albinism had caused them to be seen, by the Congolese, as Father Teruel tells us, as extremely ugly. Indeed, as one European priest's interpreter told him pityingly, his ugliness was due to his non-blackness, to his whiteness of skin. Here Teruel concludes with a trans-cultural, trans-variation comment. In the same way, he notes, as in the areas of the Congo where whites had never been seen, children ran away in horror from them, so in the remote areas of Portugal where blacks had never been seen, the children ran away in horror at the sight of black skin. In effect, because each variation had been adaptive to the climatic conditions of its origin, with its subjects thereby coming to experience themselves, through their symbolically coded "inner eyes" in which their own variation was projected as the norm of being human, a different variation had logically to be seen by the subjects of a specific variation as a "problem." While, because for both variations, the *a priori* of their own physiognomy and skin color as the norm of being human had been coded in symbolic terms by their respective foundational origin narratives and correlated formulations of a general order of existence, the "inner eyes" or orders of consciousness through which the subjects of each variation would have seen those of the other would have reinforced the reflex-instinctual aversion that each variation's subjects would have felt toward the other variation's subject's seeming abnormality.

Nevertheless, while in the wake of the 1480s encounter of Portuguese and Congolese the latter would have been seeing the white-skinned newcomers for the first time, thereby having to struggle to find a way in which they could fit the latter's anomalous appearance in terms of their traditional classificatory logic, this was not the case with respect to the Portuguese. For black-skinned, Bantu-type people had arrived in the Iberian Peninsula for several centuries before the Portuguese expeditions to Black Africa, some as Islamic converts who had come in the train of the Islamic Arab conquest of large areas of the peninsula, or as occasional slaves from pagan

Africa who had been transported across the Sahara for sale by Islamic traders. These latter, classified as *negros* and *negras,* had therefore become a constant and were made to function as the markers of extreme Otherness to the projected normality of the white-skinned Christian. In addition, in terms of the latter's Judaeo-Christian Origin Narrative, its formulation of a general order of existence—postulate of a significant ill and plan of redemption, the sharp difference in appearance of the *negros and negras* added to their slave and/or Islamic infidel status—had led to their being classified as the signifiers of the human so degraded by Original Sin as to have "fallen to the status of the apes" (Fernández-Armesto 1987)—that is, as a signifier that had marked them to be the furthest limit of being human, in terms of the Spaniards and Portuguese indigenous self-conception, as the Portuguese strangers had also marked the furthest limits of being normally human for the Bantu-Congolese, in terms of *their* indigenous self-conception.

Like the degraded fallen Earth placed at the center of the universe as its dregs, as well as like the leper proscribed outside the gates of the medieval town—this given that the cause of leprosy was attributed as God's punishment for the leper's parents having overindulged in the carnal lust of the flesh—the "Negro" had functioned as part of the signifying complex, whose function had been to induce the Christian subjects of the order to accept the reality of their own represented enslavement to Original Sin, and to be thereby strongly motivated to adhere to the behavioral pathways prescribed by the Church, ones put forward as the only possible path of redemption from that sin, of "cure" from that "ill." In addition, because the *Spirit/Flesh* code had also been mapped, not only upon the astronomy of the heavens, but also upon the "sacred geography" of the earth—that is, on a line drawn, in the case of geography, between the temperate zone with Jerusalem as its center—as a zone that, within the medieval order's Judaeo-Christian behavior-motivational schema, was held to be habitable by human beings because sited within the Christian God's providential Grace, as contrasted with places like the Torrid Zone, which, supposed to exist beyond Cape Bojador on the bulge of West Africa, was classified as being too hot for human habitation, because outside this Grace, when the Portuguese monarchs dispatched several expeditions in the early decades of the fifteenth century to attempt to sail beyond

Cape Bojador in order to reach to the source of Black Africa's gold, which Islamic traders had also brought for sale across the Sahara, the first expeditions had turned back. They had done so because of the sailors' fears not only that they would plunge into boiling waters without any hope of return but also that, in going beyond Cape Bojador, they would be turned black by God as punishment for transgressing the limits of Christian habitation prescribed by Him (Turner 1980: 120).

What therefore encountered each other in the wake of 1482 in the Congo were two quite different genres of being human, together with their respective Origin Narratives, "formulations of a general order of existence," and, thereby, two specific orders of consciousness or "inner eyes," each convinced that theirs were the only possible mode or genre of being human, their respective "regimes of truth" the only truth. Hence when, as Father Teruel also tells us, the Congolese warned the Portuguese, "Do not call us Negros, Negros are slaves, Call us Black (*Prieto*)," their warning referred to a central distinction made by their foundational Origin Narrative between black-skinned people who were free men and women of the lineage and, as such, the socially normal subjects of their order, and black-skinned people who were either Congolese who had fallen out of their lineage status and, as such, legitimately classifiable as *negros*—that is, as slaves—and so justly saleable, or other tribal peoples who had been conquered in war, and were therefore also classified as being justly saleable as *negros,* or slaves. For the Portuguese, however, in terms of their Biblical Origin Narrative (in which all black people as the descendants of Noah's cursed son, Ham, who had been condemned to be a servant to his brothers Shem and Japhet, had inherited the negative legacy of his father's curse), as well as in terms of the Bulls that the Papacy had granted the Portuguese kings in order to legitimate their right to conquer and expropriate the African territories and enslave their peoples as Enemies-of-Christ (i.e., the people who, having heard Christ's word preached to them, had refused to accept it), all black-skinned peoples were potentially classifiable, and therefore treatable, as *negros* and *negras.* In neither of these cases, therefore, could the fundamental Congolese distinction have been *meaningful.* That is, the distinction between the norm of the order, the free-born subjects who were men and women of the lineage, and as such classifiable for the

Congolese as *prietos,* blacks, and their Other, the lineageless men and women, as well as other conquered ethno-tribal groups who were legitimately slaves within the overall terms of the formulation of a general order of existence, structuring of the then still autocentric traditional order of the kingdom of the Congo: and, as such, alone classifiable as *negros.* For the Portuguese, instead, all black-skinned peoples were *negros* and potentially enslavable.

The anguished letters written in the early decades of the sixteenth century by the Christianized Mani-Congo, of the Congo King Affonso, to the Portuguese king, imploring him to help put an end to the slave trade that was breaching the fundamental distinction charting of his traditional societal order—with Portuguese slave traders and their Congolese partners, not only beginning to sell free-born men and women of the lineage (*prietos*) as slaves (*negros*) but going so far as to sell members of his, the Mani-Congo's, own royal family—would have been incomprehensible to the Portuguese king. Since the classificatory logic of the latter, both as a Christian, in terms of whose religion all black-skinned peoples, because classifiable as pagan idolaters, were seen as potential slaves who would even benefit from Christian salvation as the price of their enslavement, as well as a Renaissance European monarch, in terms of whose reasons of state ideology, all black-skinned people, whether as slaves or free men and women, were there to be exploited for the benefit of his own territorial imperial expansion as well as of his country's enrichment, based on the commercial benefits that the expanding trade in slaves, gold, as well as in the spices of the East, was then making possible (Axelson 1970).

I use the term "Ideology" in the above context as a generalized term able to include not only the theodicy of medieval Christianity but also the supernaturally guaranteed order of the Congolese based on the deified figures of the ancestors as well as of the gods, both of which had functioned to justify the functioning of that order to itself. Hence the fact, for example, that the Congolese could *not* have seen the enslavement of the category of Congolese men and women, classified as lineageless men and women, as wrong, any more than the Christians could have normally seen enslaving Ham's descendants and/or Enemies-of-Christ as wrong. This was so in general, even though some missionary priests would, indeed, so see it, while King Affonso of the Congo would attempt, if in vain, to abolish the slave trade altogether (Hochschild 1998). In addition, the term "Ideology" also enables us to include the then-secularizing, because political, "reasons of state" formulations, in whose terms the king of Portugal, like Shakespeare's Prospero, would have seen the colonizing vassalization of the kingdom of the Congo, as well as the enslavement of as many Congolese as possible, as being in both the Christian and the natural order of things. This in the same way as during the second wave of European imperialism, when the Belgian king Leopold would have seen his own even more thorough labor exploitation of the Congolese people, together with their brutally ruthless subjugation, as having been mandated by the manifest destiny of Europeans, as the ostensible embodiment of human beings who were highly evolved and civilized, because naturally selected, to subordinate and subjugate those who had been bio-evolutionarily dysselected to be "lesser breeds" without the law (Hochschild 1998).

Paul Ricoeur's redefinition of Marx's seminal conception of ideology enables us to understand, in this context, the "why" of the Janus-face of the history of Western expansion over the past 500 years, together with the relation of our "imposed wrongness" of being, or of *désêtre*/dysbeing, to the nature of this history. This as a relation that in turn enables us to grasp the large-scale implications of the initial challenge made to the negative effects of this Janus-face, in the context of the uprisings of the late 1950s, 1960s, and 1970s, by the black peoples of the United States (as members of the only race, as Césaire points out, whose humanity has been totally denied), by means of, *inter alia,* the Black Aesthetic, Black Arts, and Black Studies Movements. To understand, also, the logic of the eventual failure of these movements, given that the new truth, the new aesthetic, which they struggled, however contradictorily, to articulate, could not have been audible in terms of our present order of truth and of aesthetics, as the order of truth and aesthetics specific to our present biodicy: to its Ideology, in terms of Ricoeur's redefinition of that term.

In his 1979 essay entitled "Ideology and Utopia as Cultural Imagination," Paul Ricoeur makes use of Karl Mannheim's dialectical yoking of the terms *ideology* and *utopia*, doing so, first of all, in order to detach them from the pejorative meanings that have been placed on them. In that, if the term *ideology*, since Marx, has come to be stigmatized as "false consciousness," the term "utopia" has been no less negatively stigmatized as meaning escapist, unreal. Ricoeur's new thesis, instead, links both terms to the central point made by Marx when he proposed that the function of ideology everywhere, and in all contexts, is to over-represent a partial group interest (i.e., a special group interest) as if it were "the common interest of all the members of society" and, by doing so, to give the ideas that are generated from the perspective of this "special or partial group interest" the form of universality, representing them "as the only rational, universally valid ones." Nevertheless, Ricoeur continues, rather than seeing what is, in effect, a surplus representation as "false" and therefore as an aberration, we should instead place it in the context of the hypothesis put forward by the anthropologist Clifford Geertz in his essay "Ideology as a Cultural System." Since such a hypothesis will enable us to propose that all such surplus representations, as well as the cognitive distortions to which they necessarily lead, can be recognized as serving a basic, and indispensable, because normalizing and order-integrating, function. In that if this function, as Geertz argues, is that of "mediating and integrating human action at its public level," the criterion for the functioning of all ideologies, rather than being defined by their truth or falsity, should instead be defined by the fact as to whether or not they successfully serve to orient human social behaviors in such a way as to enable the "integrating of human action at the public level" and, thereby, to enable the stable reproduction of the specific societal order that is the condition of our existence as humans. The criterion for the functioning of all ideologies cannot therefore be that of their truth or falsity, but rather must be that of the empirical fact as to whether or not they successfully serve to integrate "human action at the public level," as the indispensable means of enabling the dynamic production and stable reproduction of the specific societal orders that, then reciprocally, make their own articulation as such Ideologies possible.

In this context, to return to Ricoeur's illuminating use of Geertz's thesis, the cognitive distortions effected by Ideologies' acts of surplus representation (as in our case where the Western bourgeois or ethno-class conception of the human, *Man,* together with the "partial interests" of its referent categories, are over-represented as those of the human) can be seen as functioning to "unify and integrate human orders by transforming sentiment into significance," thereby making it "socially available." As such, Ideology should be seen and analyzed "as a kind of figurative language" that serves to "cast personal attitudes into public form."

Here, if we see "sentiment" and "personal attitudes" cast into public form as being inseparable from Ellison's "inner eyes" and, therefore, from the always already socialized orders of consciousness through which we "look with our physical eyes upon reality," then Ideology and its processes of surplus—representation—can be recognized as being everywhere generated from those foundational "formulations of a general order of existence," which serve as the narratively, and thereby non-biogenetically, ordered programs by means of which human orders are held together; this analogically to the way in which the colony of a beehive is integrated on the basis of its species-specific biogenetic behavioral program.

In this context, Ricoeur makes use of Max Weber's insights, with respect to the role played by the legitimization of authority in all human orders, to propose that the main function of a system of Ideology is to reinforce belief in the legitimacy of each society's given system of authority in such a way that it meets the claim to legitimacy. While this claim to legitimacy can be met only "by the acts of surplus representation," which enables the interest of the beneficiary groups of the order to be seen as the interests of all, even by those who most lose out, Ideology can be seen to provide "the general horizon of understanding and mutual recognition before being unduly diverted for the sake of a ruling group, be it a class or any other dominant group" (Ricoeur 1979). That is, to enable the general order of consciousness and its "horizon of understanding" to induce the subjects of the order, to see and experience the general interests of the order as being inextricably linked to the interests of the ruling group. While, Ricoeur continues, it is precisely the attempt to link the interests of a dominant group with "the general horizon of understanding" that unifies the order, which necessarily leads to cognitive distortions.

This therefore means that the empirically unified existence of any hierarchically structured order, as in the case of our contemporary Western-bourgeois and Westernized global own, must, at the same time, attest to the functioning of a specific Ideology, its modes of surplus representation, and attendant cognitive distortions. Given that in the absence of a genuine egalitarianism, the hierarchies specific to each order, as in the case of our own, can be sustained and reproduced only by means of such Ideologies, all of which function to provide the template in whose terms such hierarchies can continue to be *experienced* by all, including the most dispossessed, as being legitimate: as the realization of a true order (because ostensibly extra-humanly mandated, rather than the humanly constructed order that it empirically is). From hence, the paradox of Ricoeur's conclusion that "even under the layer of distorting representations and its system of legitimization, the symbolic systems which orient behaviors" function, as Geertz proposes, to "provide a template or blueprint for the organization of social and psychological processes, as genetic systems provide such a template or blueprint for the organization of organic processes" (Ricoeur 1979).

This would therefore mean that in the same way as, at the purely organic level, a bee, for example, must in a law-like way know the reality of its environment in the species-specific terms that are adaptively advantageous to the reproduction of the beehive, and cannot, therefore, be expected to know its reality *outside* the terms of that species-specific standpoint (as a standpoint mandated by its genetic system, which provides the template for the beehive's overall organizational processes); so, analogically, at the hybrid organic and meta-organic level of human life, the genre-specific subject of any order, including the intellectuals of that order, whether religious or secular, must also, in a lawlike manner, know their social "reality" of which they/we are always already socialized subjects, in terms that are adaptively advantageous to the production and reproduction of that reality; and cannot, therefore, be expected normally to know its reality outside the terms of that genre-specific standpoint, as a standpoint mandated by the Ideology whose cognitive distortions function to provide a template or blueprint for the organization of social and psychological processes, indispensable to the production and reproduction of each societal order.

There is a major difference here, however, since, as shown in the specific case of the history of Western Europe, human beings differ from purely organic species in their ability, without any change in their physiology, to transform their behaviors, their social realities, and their genre-specific Ideologies, doing so by reinventing their genres or kinds of being human and, therefore, their modes of knowing, feeling, behaving in new modalities. Since, as seen in the case of the West's re-invention of its public identity from its matrix identity *Christian,* first, to that of *Man* as *homo politicus,* then again, in the nineteenth century, from that of political *Man* to that of *Man,* now biocentrically defined as *homo oeconomicus.* In both cases, however, with *Man* coming to be over-represented as if it were the human, and thereby instituted as Absolute Being—with all the rest of humankind thereby logically classified as *Man*'s Human Others (i.e., as *Indian, Native, Negroes, coolies, kikes, chinks, spics, niggers, sand-niggers,* etc.). With, in consequence, the "truth in an abstract universal sense" of our present order of knowledge, as challenged by Gerald McWhorter, lawlikely functioning as Ideology in Ricoeur's redefined sense of the term; and therefore as an order of truth indispensable to the continued production and reproduction of our present contemporary Western and Westernized order, doing so by providing its bio-humanist or liberal democratic "general horizon of understanding" incorporating of all its subjects, together with its always already legitimated system of authority.

Here Ricoeur's parally redefined concept of "utopia" in terms of its dialectic functioning with "ideology" identifies it as being, in all human orders, the liminal site or perspective that must be systemically excluded from the normal functioning of each specific order, as the condition of that order's stable production and reproduction. As such, therefore, the only perspective that carries within it the possibility of an escape from the prescriptive categories of each order's "general horizon of understanding" as well as of its legitimated system of authority.[18] Hence, Ricoeur continues, each order's mode of public knowledge or Ideology—whose function is to enable the subject of the order to know the order in terms that are adaptively advantageous to its own reproduction, and thereby to behave in ways oriented by that knowledge, and as a function that therefore calls for its intellectuals, religious or secular, to ensure the rigorous production of such knowledge—must, given its order-integrating, indeed order-producing and reproducing function, remain "impervious to philosophical attack"; it is everywhere the "systemic function of utopian modes of thought to challenge these modes of public and order-integrating thought from a place *outside* the order's mode of rationality—from *utopia,* that is nowhere" (Ricoeur 1979). From the perspective, therefore, of those whose exclusion—or systemic subordination as in the case of the laity and lay intellectuals of late medieval Europe—is the indispensable condition of the order's truth, and therefore of its existence. Or as in the case of our own "imposed wrongness of being," or *désêtre,* as experienced through the Fanonian type of black self-alienation, W. E. B. Du Bois's "double consciousness," or, in George Lamming's terms, our systemically induced self-amputation (Lamming 1984), as the ultimate Human Other to *Man* over-represented as if it were the human.

In consequence, if, as Ricoeur concludes, at conjunctural times of change, utopian or alternative modes of thought arise to "shatter a given order" by the proposal of an alternative order, and that therefore it is the role of the bearers of such alternative utopian thought "to give the force of discourse to this possibility," the original call by the three movements to center and elaborate the black perspective (as *the* perspective of the ultimate Human Other to the West's *Man,* over-represented as if it were the human and, therefore, as Legesse's liminal perspective) owe their vital emotional power and force, as well as their psychically emancipatory thrust as noted by Madhu Dubey, precisely to this attempt, however conflictually and inchoately, "to give the force of discourse to the possibility" of a new Human Project after *Man*'s. Hence the logic by which, with the reterritorialization of *Man*'s Ideology and its order-integrating program of truth (Veyne 1988), the Black Aesthetic and Black Arts Movements were to disappear as if they had never been, while Black Studies was to be incorporated into the mainstream only at the cost of the pacification of its original thrust, by means of its redefinition in *Man*'s normative terminology, no longer as a Black utopian alternative mode of thought but, rather, as Ethnic sub-text of the Ideologies of *Man*'s Word—that is, as African-American Studies.

This was to be a high price to pay at several levels. In the case of the post-1960s United States, the price paid for the incorporation of the black middle class into the consumer horizon of expectation of the generic class (the white middle class), even if, admittedly, at a still secondary level, since a middle class now re-defined in ethnic terms as *African-American* ensured that the skill-less, jobless, and therefore now increasingly criminalized underclasses were to be even more rigorously interned in "the hood" (i.e., the jobless inner-city ghettoes and their prison-system extension) as the group now sacrificially excluded from the order as the cost of the order's reproduction; and made institutionally to reoccupy the role, and *nigger* place, of the formerly, no less institutionally segregated black U.S. population group as a whole. Further, this price was itself, like many similar "local" ones, correlated with a universally applicable, species-specific one. When Einstein warned, in the wake of the splitting of the atom and the dropping of the first atomic bomb, that everything in the world had changed except the way we think about it, and that, as a result, unless mankind could come up with a new mode of thinking we would "drift towards unparalleled catastrophe," what he put his finger on was what we earlier defined as the Janus-face of the West's epochal historical rupture effected from the Renaissance onward. The rupture, that is, that had been effected by its de-supernaturalization of the projection of our agency and authorship of ourselves and our orders, onto extra-human entities, as a rupture that had enabled not only the secularization of human existence at the public level but also the correlated de-supernaturalization of the physical cosmos; with this thereby leading to the latter's processes of functioning to be freed from having to be known in terms of the specific Ideology adaptively advantageous to the instituting of each human order. To be epochally known, instead, in natural-scientific terms, as the autonomously regulated processes of functioning that they empirically are.

However, while both the physical sciences and, after Darwin, the biological sciences, were to place unparalleled power in the hands of human subjects, we would nevertheless continue to know Self, Other, and World, and therefore the hybridly sociohuman, nature-culture or phylogeny/ontogeny/sociogeny hybrid level of reality, specific to our societal orders in the same terms of Ideology that we have always memorially known it. With the result that once we had replaced the projection of our human agency and authorship onto the millennially supernatural, with that of the projection of our own agency and authorship onto the no less extra-human entities, firstly, of "nature" and then secondly, and biocentrically so, of Evolution and Natural Selection/Dys-selection, our drift as a species toward unparalleled catastrophe has only continued to increase the dynamic of its momentum.

Conclusion

Black is beautiful!

—*Black slogan chanted during the '60s*

Not so very long ago, the earth numbered two thousand million inhabitants: five million men, and one thousand five hundred million natives. The former had the Word; the other had the use of it.... The European elite undertook to manufacture a native elite. They picked out promising adolescents; they branded them, as with a red-hot iron, with the principles of Western culture.... From Paris, from London, from Amsterdam we would utter the words "Parthenon! Brotherhood!" and somewhere in Africa or Asia lips would open "... then on! ... therhood!" It was the golden age. It came to an end; the mouths opened by themselves.

—*Jean-Paul Sartre, Preface to Frantz Fanon,* Les Damnés de La Terre/The Wretched of the Earth

The peculiarity of "our place in the world" which isn't to be confused with anybody else's. The peculiarity of our problems which aren't to be reduced to subordinate forms of any other problem. The peculiarity of our history, laced with terrible misfortunes which belong to no other history.

—*Aimé Césaire, Letter to Maurice Thorez/Lettre à Maurice Thorez*

In this overall context, the major proposal here is that the calls for Black Studies, as well as for a Black Aesthetic and a Black Art, as they originally erupted in the context of the black and many other such ethno-racial social movements of the 1960s—such as those of Native Americans (Indians), Chicanos, and Asian-Americans, as well as the global anti-colonial struggles of "native" colonized peoples, together with other struggles against racial apartheid, as in South Africa and Australia—were all, fundamentally, struggles against their respective subjects' discursively and institutionally classified Human Other status. With our collectively induced experience of an imposed "wrongness of being" or of *désêtre*/dysbeing, therefore, being recognizable as an indispensable function of the instituting and enacting of our present genre of being human *Man,* and of its governing principle or sociogenic code; this at the same time as such a phenomenon cannot be seen to exist as an object of knowledge in terms of our present order of knowledge, its objective "program of Truth," and, therefore, of Ideology, in Ricoeur's redefinition of the term. As one, in other words, that provides the template or blueprint indispensable to the hierarchical integration and reproduction of our present neo-Liberal order of being and of things, which is represented as one to whose universalism there is no outside, to which there can be no alternative.

It is in this context that both McWhorter's utopian call for a "little something other than truth in an abstract universal sense," like Jones/Baraka's call to exoticize Western thought and Larry Neal's call for a post-Western aesthetic, with these calls allied to the popular slogan "Black Is Beautiful," as well as to the dynamic of black popular music, à la James Brown, of the time, can be recognized as all functioning together to *relativize Man,* together with its ethno-class system of thought, and aesthetics, its over-representation as if it were the human and therefore Absolute Being; as "the Man," in black popular slang. It is therefore in the context of their challenge to this over-representation that not only the texts cited earlier but also the range of essays, poetry, fiction, and creative writing produced by black writers in the 1960s and early 1970s must now be returned to, re-examined, and reclaimed, as the first stage, however then incomplete, of our coming to grips with the *real issue* (the territory rather than its maps) with which we are now urgently confronted. *The* issue of being now compelled—as "black" and "native" intellectuals who have hitherto only been permitted to *use* the Word of *Man,* thereby, willy nilly, serving to willingly further Man's Project, over-represented as if it were that of the Human—to create now our own Word, by separating discursively as well as institutionally, the notion of the *human* from the notion of *Man.* And to do so analogically to the way in which the lay humanist intellectuals of medieval Europe, who had hitherto only been permitted to *use* the word of God—a Word owned by the Clergy/theologians—had, by their discursive and institutional separation of the notion of *Man* from that of *Christian,* created their Word, the Word of *Man*; thereby initiating the bringing in of what is today our contemporary Western and Westernized world system.

With this new Word, however, then serving as the Word implementing of Man's Project, as a project, the range of whose dazzling triumphs and achievements is matched only by the dimensions of the costs of its negative underside—the costs of the *global problematique,* on the one hand, and, on the other, of the profound nature of black and other non-white forms (and also some white forms, as in the case of "white trash," the white lower classes, etc.)

of self-alienation, self-amputation. With all such forms being compre-hensively induced by the systemic de-valorization, as Fanon points out, of what it is to be human, in terms of our now biocentric *homo oeconomicus* descriptive statement of the human. Within, therefore, the terms of our Darwinian-Malthusian Origin Narrative, which inscribed and inscribes this descriptive statement or sociogenic code of symbolic life and death, together with its formulation of a "general order of existence" and postulate of "significant ill" as that of mankind's enslavement to dysgenicity and Natural Scarcity. This as the now purely secular and transumed variant of Christianity's *matrix Judaeo-Christian* Origin Narrative and its postulate of a "significant ill" as that of mankind's enslavement to Original Sin.[19]

Lewis Gordon identifies the specific challenge that we who now necessarily experience ourselves in terms of our ostensibly bio-evolutionarily imposed "wrongness of being," or of *désêtre*/dysbeing, in terms of the West's Absolute Man, and of its Project, must neces-sarily confront. "Rationalizations of Western thought," he writes,

> often led to a theodicy of Western civilization, ... as a system that was complete on all levels of human life, on levels of description (what is) and prescription (what ought to be), of being and value, while its incompleteness, its failure to be so, lived by those con-stantly being crushed under its heels, remained a constant source of anxiety often in the form of social denial. People of colour, par-ticularly black people, lived the contradictions of this self-decep-tion *continually through attempting to live this theodicy in good faith.* This lived contradiction emerged because a demand often imposed upon people of colour is that they accept the tenets of Western civilization without being *critical* beings.... An explosion [therefore] erupts in the soul of a black person, an explosion that splits the black person into two souls, as W.E.B. Du Bois observed in *The Souls of Black Folk* and the earlier *Conservation of the Races,* with a consciousness of a frozen "outside," of a being who is able to see *that he or she is seen as a being without a point of view, which amounts to not being seen as a human being.* (Gordon, 2002b: 10–11, emphasis added)[20]

It was precisely the eruption of this "point of view" in the texts of all three movements, in the overall context of the social movements of the 1960s, as a point of view alternative to the "rationalizations of Western thought" as well as to the "monopoly of humanity" of its aesthetics, that led, as Madhu Dubey notes, to the psychic emancipatory explosion of emotional release triggered by their revalorization of the sign of blackness—in effect, of non-being. While despite the fact that its also powerful cultural nationalist tendencies threatened to draw it back inside the orbit of Western rationalization and therefore of Man and his Project, its also no less powerful popular tendency (popular in the sense of the term applied to those whose stigmatized exclusion from the normalcy of the order is the condition of the order's functioning—in effect, a tendency based on the point of view of its irredeemable Otherness or liminality in terms of the order) would, for a brief hiatus, make visible a utopian point of view, inextricably linked to the emergent Human Project. One for which Man's Project has provided the global conditions of existence, without being able to realize a universality able to go beyond the limits of its own ethno-class, biohumanist, and therefore Liberal modality of universalism. It was, however, therefore also logical that such a point of view could have been no more containable in terms of our present Western bourgeois and, therefore biocentric, order of being, aesthetic, knowledge, and correlated program of truth, than the lay humanist point of view of late medieval Latin Christian Europe could have been containable within the latter's theodicy, its theocentric order of being knowledge, aesthetics, and thereby its theocentric "program of truth."

Nevertheless, in the same way as the lay humanists' then-utopian point of view, and its reinvention of *Man,* laid the basis for the new order that was to displace and replace that of Latin Christian medieval Europe, so the new utopian point of view, which takes the reality of our present "wrongness of being" as the point of departure for the reinvention of the human in new revalorizing Fanonian terms, is the point of view that, erupting in its first phase in the texts of the 1960s, thereby laid the groundwork, however incompletely and conflictually so, for the realization of the Human Project, and, thereby, of the new order that is imperatively to come. As one, necessarily based on the recognition, for the first time in human history, of our collective agency and authorship of our genres of being human, and, therefore, of the production of all our societies, their role allocation's and structuring's hierarchies, together with the modes of material or economic provisioning, as well as of the order of knowledge, of truth, and of the aesthetic, each of which are as indispensable as the other to the autopoeisis or instituting of each such genre of the human, of their *I*'s and their *We*'s; in effect, of ourselves, by ourselves. The Human Project, therefore, as one inseparable from the recognition of our individual and collective responsibility for the societal effects to which each such process of genre-instituting leads, as in the contemporary case of the *global problematique* identified by Gerald Barney; inseparable, thereby, from the fullest possible realization of our autonomy as humans, beyond the limits of Man's Project and, therefore, of our still ongoing "wrongness of being," of *désêtre*.

Notes

1. See Jones (Baraka) 1975. See also the following for some of the differing aspects of the Black Arts and Black Aesthetic Movements in terms of their original dynamic: Gerald 1971, Fuller 1971, Gayle 1971, Karenga 1968, de Costa 1977, Neal 1971: 370-378, Martin 1988, Jones (Baraka) 1963, Jones (Baraka) and Neal 1968, Van Deburg 1992, and Taylor 1988.

2. Recently, as China has become integrated into the Western economic system of capitalism and therefore into the absolute single criterion or standard of being and of beauty of ethno-class (Western-bourgeois) *Man,* young Chinese middle-class women, in addition to resorting to plastic surgery to change the shape of their eyes to a Western European model, are also enduring great agony in order to get their legs stretched so that they will become longer, assimilating them into the impossible ideal of thin, long-legged, white Western bourgeois models.

3. Ortner argued that the functioning of a code specific to human beings—that of symbolic life and death, as a code from our origins as a language-capacitied species—was mapped onto the anatomical differences between the male and female sexes, thereby transforming the *male/female* categories into *linguistic* ones (i.e. *man/woman, wife/husband, mother/son, brother/sister,* etc.). In consequence, if we redefine the Western cultural conception of *nature/culture* into the transculturally applicable conception of the code of symbolic life and death (Fanon's modes of sociogeny), one that enacts a value-differential between, on the one hand, the purely biological life to which women give birth, represented as symbolic death, and, on the other, that of symbolic (or "true") life to which the category of men analogically, and therefore symbolically, "give birth," then Ornter's conception can be seen as a member of the universal class. What, therefore, were and are the central functions of this code? Given the imperative function of each such code in the instituting and reproduction of human societal orders, the connoted value differential between (in traditional orders) the category of women and biological life, on the one hand, and that of men and symbolic life, on the other, would have to be systematically produced and reproduced. This, in parallel to the way in which, in our contemporary order, the code of ethno-class *Man* has been mapped onto the physiognomic and skin-color differences between peoples of Black African descent, on the one hand (as the ostensible embodiment of symbolic *death* defined as that of barely evolved, biological life), and, on the other, the peoples of Indo-European

descent (as the ostensible embodiment of fully evolved and thereby symbolic life). Hence the way in which the positive/negative value connotations/*cum* differential between "whites" and "non-whites," and, most totally, between "whites" and "blacks," must be rigorously maintained in our present order of being and of things, as the condition of the instituting of our ethno-class, or Western-bourgeois conception of the human *Man,* over-represented as if it were the human; as, in Lewis Gordon's term, *Absolute Being* (Gordon, 2002c).

4. I adapt the category of "symbolic death" from Peter Winch (1964: 307–324), who argued that the only life that human beings live is the life they represent as "symbolic life."

5. Consider the distinction that the Spanish language makes between European and native women, and that the English language erases with the use of the term "woman." While Spanish classifies the women of the two subordinated groups as *indias* (Indian women) and *Negras* (*negresses* in the older English usage), thereby making clear that the only category that is classifiable as *Woman* is a member of the dominant European group and, therefore, that it is only for the latter that the issue of gender can be *the* primary, indeed the *only,* issue, the Spanish usage makes it clear that for the descendants of the other two population groups, the issue of gender is itself only *one* aspect of the issue of the *genre of the human of Man,* in whose terms not only were their populations made into the Other to the genre of human but as woman (*indias, negras*) they were as necessarily the Other to the generic woman as in our present order of things. That is, in the same way as before the rise of feminism, the category of *Woman* was necessarily the Other to the generic sex—that is, the male sex. For insight into the functioning of generic categories and their lack, see Gallop (1985).

6. Anthony Pagden (1982) gives an excellent overview of the struggle waged by the evangelizing missionary Bartolomé de Las Casas against the arguments of royal official ideologues such as Ginés de Sepúlveda, who based the rights of the Spanish Crown to expropriate the lands of the indigenous peoples of the Caribbean and the Americas on their ostensible lack of Natural Reason, proposing, instead, that the New World Peoples, especially the Aztecs, thought and acted in terms of a quite different order of natural reason, one in which, for example, ritual human sacrifice seemed to them a rational, even a pious and virtuous act, since taken for the "good" of their "commonwealth."

7. The African slave, after being transported across the Middle Passage, was sold in the New World as a *pieza.* A *pieza*-piece was the equivalent, for example, of a "count" bunch of bananas—a stem equivalent to the length nine hands or more, which is the norm. A stem of six hands, for example, would count as a quarter bunch. The length of stems is therefore more important than the amount of bunches. So with the African, the *pieza* was the norm. The norm was a man who represented the largest possible amount of labor power. He had to have good teeth and be above average in height, free of physical defects, and between thirty to thirty-five, the years in which he had the most labor to give. (One authority, however, claims that the vintage years were from twenty-five to thirty-five.) In any case, the *pieza* was the norm. Others who did not attain these qualifications had to be added together to make up a *pieza.* Three boys or girls between eight and fifteen would make up two pieces. Two males or females between four and eight—or between thirty-five and forty, when physical powers were waning—made up one. *Piezas* over forty were sold as "refuse" at cut-rate prices. These were the "unskilled slaves," the raw labor

power. After they had been trained in the special skills required for sugar making, their skill would increase their value.

8. Lewis Gordon's (2002c) concept of mutation from the millennially supernatural "supreme source of legitimacy" to a now purely de-supernaturalized one is illustrated here by the switch from Heaven's to Evolution's mandate.

9. Both Kurt Hübner (1983) and Fernand Hallyn (1990) make the central point that the Copernican Revolution, which would eventually lead to the development of a scientific astronomy as well as to the new order of cognition that is the natural sciences, cannot be seen, as most historians of science have tended to see it, as a revolution purely internal to the development of the sciences. Rather, it must be seen in the context of the overall revolution of Renaissance humanism, and, therefore, in that of the overall instituting of what I define as the West's Project of Man.

10. Sir Stafford Beer explains Maturana and Varela's main underlying concept of "autopoesis" as homeostatic—that is, involving "a device for holding a critical system variable within physiological limits"; and in the case of autopoetic homeostasis, the "critical variable *is the system's own organization.*" Thus, even if every "measurable property of that organizational structure changes utterly in the system's process of continuing adaptation," *it* survives; that is, *the mode of organization* is its identity. Implicit in this context is the fact that the living's imperative *is its realization* rather than its mere self-preservation.

11. As Krupp points out in the case of China, "the best astronomy in the world" in the "last quarter of the thirteenth century" was "carried on at Guo Shoujing's Beijing observatory and at the 26 other field stations then established from Mongolia to the island of Hainan. Guo Shoujing used engraved metal instruments to measure the lengths of shadows and the positions of the stars and planets. Both he and the Tongtian calendar makers of 1199 a.d. measured the length of the solar year as 365.2425 days, only 26 seconds longer than it actually is."

12. In *The Mind in the Cave: Consciousness and the Origins of Art* (2002), David Lewis-Williams points out that although the Eurocentric bias in scholarship has placed the origin of human behaviors in Europe at 40,000 to 50,000 years ago, when such behaviors were said to have appeared all at once as a "package deal," recent evidence from Africa challenges this thesis. Arguing that this later evidence shows us that we need to speak of "modern human behaviors" rather than merely of "behavior," Lewis-Williams documents the origin of all such behaviors as having taken place on the continent of Africa, together with what would also have been, in Fanon's terms, the origins of the sociogenic or socializing processes by which we institute ourselves as human, thereby orienting our *eusocial* behaviors by what Ernesto Grassi (1980) defines as a new human code, that of the Sacred Word of religion.

13. The state-dispatched voyages of the Portuguese about Cape Bojador on the bulge of West Africa in search of the source of West African gold, and their landing on the shores of Senegal in the 1440s, were the first challenge to medieval Europe's sacred geography of the earth. In the logic of the latter, the area of the earth beyond Cape Bojador, which was classified as the Torrid Zone, *had to be* uninhabitable because it was projected as being outside God's providential Grace. On landing in Senegal, however, the Portuguese found it to be populated. Columbus would later use this fact to support his own claim that the Ocean Sea beyond the straits of Gibraltar was indeed navigable, thereby enabling a sea route to the spice trade of the East Indies, to be opened up by sailing West. Yet according to the sacred geography of

Latin Christian medieval Europe, the Ocean Sea *should not have been navigable,* given that the lands of the Western Hemisphere also had to be in their Aristotelian natural place under water—again because imagined to be also condemned to be uninhabitable, because also outside God's Grace. See, for this, Sylvia Wynter, "Columbus and the Poetics of the *Propter Nos*" (1991: 251þ286).

14. Valentin Mudimbe (1988: 45) documents the way in which the first phases of the European states' expansion in the fifteenth and sixteenth centuries were legitimated by the Papacy in religious and evangelizing terms, which made the Church and its missionaries co-actors with the States, their military, and their bureaucrats.

15. Ginés de Sepúlveda was the official historian of the Spanish monarch as well as his official chaplin. A humanist scholar who had translated Aristotle, Sepúlveda became in his writings the ideologue of the expansionist goals of the Spanish state. As such, he was the major antagonist of the Christian evangelizing missionary Bartolomé de Las Casas, for whom the only right that the Spanish state had to be in the Caribbean and the Americas was the right given to it and its functionaries in exchange for their helping to facilitate the Christian evangelization of the New World peoples. Against Las Casas's thesis, Sepúlveda sought to argue the case for the legitimate right of the Spanish monarchical state to the expropriated lands and sovereignty of the indigenous peoples of the New Worlds, doing so on the basis of terms that moved *outside* the religio-theological grounds on which the Papacy had granted these rights to Spain. Sepúlveda would also develop a line of argument that, basing itself on the *natural slaves/natural masters* thesis of Aristotle's *Politics,* had been put forward from the earliest decades of Spain's conquest and expropriation of New World lands, in order to establish the rights of the Spanish Crown to their possession in new juridicial terms—terms that would not have had to accept the dual spiritual and temporal claim to sovereignty by the Papacy that had been implicit in the Bulls by means of which the Pope had granted to Spain and Portugal their respective rights of possession. With this being so given, the Spanish Crown now sought to claim temporal sovereignty for itself, restricting the Papacy's sovereignty to the realm of the purely spiritual. It is on the basis of this kind of rhetorical-juridical legitimating discourse put forward by Sepúlveda, primarily from the humanist perspective of *Man* as political subject of the state even where partly couched in Christian theological terms, that what Lewis Gordon (2002b) identified as the process by means of which the West invented itself and its peoples in the terms of Absolute Being can be most clearly recognized. See also the excellent study by Anthony Pagden (1982).

16. See, for this, Hans Blumenberg (1983: 224–225). Blumenberg links the implications of Malthus's alleged "law of population" (i.e., that human populations increase at a faster rate than does their food supply) to Darwin's theory of Natural Selection as applied to the hierarchies of human societies. Thus, social hindrances such as the poor and jobless, who because ostensibly condemned to their situation by the "laws of nature," should not be relieved by the state of their poverty or joblessness.

17. Although Darwin's *The Origin of the Species* mentions the human only in passing, the second part of the book's title—*By Means of Natural Selection or the Preservation of Favoured Races in the Struggle for Life,* through its use of the term "favored races"—reveals a conflation between the term "species" and the term "races" that will enable the hereditary variations of the human species to be responded to as if these variation-differences were of the same order as the differences between species.

18. Anthony Legesse, taking his point of departure from Victor Turner's analysis of "liminal groups, liminal persons, and liminal states," further develops Turner's thesis that the liminal belongs to a "betwixt and between" social category and, as such, is a sociological non-entity. The liminal may also be an individual whose attributes violate the common categories of social classification. An example of such an individual would be a man with feminine characteristics. Another, less obvious example would be a woman who gives birth to twins. Such a mother and her children are feared and respected—indeed, elevated to the realm of the supernatural. Only animals have multiple births. The human female who shares the same attribute falls into that ambiguous category which straddles secular categories and is for that very reason elevated to the domain of the supernatural. That is the reason why, in so many African cultures, twins and their mothers are treated as anomalous sociological phenomena. They are frequently lifted out of the social system and treated symbolically and behaviorally as if they were outside the society. In that strange position they make up an important part of the sacred force that stands in conceptual opposition to the secular community. "The liminal person is not irrelevant to the structured community surrounding him. On the contrary, he is the conceptual antithesis and therefore very relevant to its continued existence. It is by reference to him that the structured community defines and understands itself" (Legesse 1973: 114–115). As such a category, Legesse then argues, the liminal person provides a perspective able to break free from the normative perspective of the community, for whose normalcy its exclusion is indispensable. "Out of this field of interaction," Legesse continues, "emerges the liminal person to remind us that we need not forever remain prisoners of our prescriptions. He generates conscious change by exposing all the injustice inherent in structure, by creating a real contradiction between structure and anti-structure, social order and man-made anarchy. This is a type of dialectic that is very different from the nonconscious phenomena which we are after" (Legesse 1973: 271).

19. Harold Bloom (1982) puts forward the rhetorical figure of transumption as the American answer to the "imported mode of deconstruction." He notes that "transumption or metalepsis" is the legitimate and traditional name in rhetoric for what John Hollander calls the "figure of interpretive allusion." Transumptive changes point toward the "diachronic concept of rhetoric, in which the irony of one age can become the ennobled synecdoche of another." While transumptive chains abound, certain "central linkages ... vital to tradition, and the crossing over in and between traditions keep the continuity going by means of its retroping of earlier tropes."

20. Gordon's thesis with respect to the imperative necessity of a black point of view enables us to see the way in which—while the original struggle for Black Studies and a Black Arts/Aesthetic had glimpsed, however still confusedly so, the imperative need for a *perspective* based on a new order of truth beyond the limits of our present concept of truth in an abstract universal sense (McWhorter 1969), as well as the need for a new aesthetics beyond the limits of our present Western bourgeois, and therefore, necessarily, an ethno- and class-centric mainstream one, because such a perspective can be realizable only by means of the institutional, and intellectual, elaboration of such a perspective based on a new Fanonian-type poetics of the human beyond the limits of contemporary *Man*'s—the defeat of any possibility of the instituting of such a counter-perspective spelled the outright defeat both of the Black Arts and Black Aesthetic Movements, as well as the defeat, by incorporation into the mainstream, of Black Studies. In that the latter, whether incorporated into the mainstream order of knowledge on the orthodox basis of the

ethnicization of the perspective of Black Studies reclassified as African-American studies, as most comprehensively and creatively effected by Henry Louis Gates, or indeed on the basis of the cultural nationalist, "Kwanza"-type tendency of a Karenga, which unlike the liminalist tendency, would also be incorporated into mainstream academia, was to find its original contestatory and transformative dynamic truncated and defeated.

A consequence of this defeat is that whereas the original call had been a call for, so to speak, affirmative action to enable the institution of a black counter-perspective and point of view, the strategy of containment would instead substitute affirmative action aimed at the incorporation of both black students and faculty into the normative point of view of our present mainstream order of knowledge and aesthetics.

For its contemporary implications, see Gans (1999: 371–390). See also Hacker (1992) and Wills (2003: 74). While written from a right-wing conservative perspective, the latter commentary nevertheless focuses on the way in which, if not precisely in these terms, the attempt of mainstream academia to deflect the original Black Studies call for a new order of truth and of knowledge by means of an affirmative action program based on obtaining "diversity" in the student body and faculty, again *uses* blacks to serve the purposes of the very mainstream and biological absolute order of knowledge, in whose prescriptive logic the black population group is already locked into its subordinated liminal role, much as the subordination of the lay world to the world of the Church and the Clergy in Latin Christian medieval and, therefore, pre-Renaissance Europe had been prescribed by that order's then theologically absolute order of knowledge and correlated conception of the human.

PART TWO
TRANSFIGURATIONS OF AFRICAN-AMERICAN BEING AND DOING

5
Pedagogy and the Philosophical Anthropology of African-American Slave Culture

Stephen Nathan Haymes

✧

In Lewis Gordon's analysis of Frederick Douglass's existential situation as a black slave, he remarks that "American slavery was a concerted dehumanizing project" (Gordon 1999: 222). He goes on further to say, "It is this dimension that garnered its peculiarly anti-black racist characteristic" (*ibid.*). Properly understood, "racism is a denial of the humanity of another human being by virtue of his or her racial membership" (*ibid.*). Such relations deny the presence of another human being because the Other is made "a form of presence that is an absence of human presence" (*ibid.:* 223). Gordon writes: "Forced into the realm of property, even linguistic appeals—cries of recognition—are muffled, unheard, waving hands, gestures for acknowledgment are invisible. It is not that they do not trigger impulses between the eyes and the brain. It is that there has been a carefully crafted discipline of unseeing. The black slave is thus a paradoxically seen invisibility in this regard; seeing him or her as a black slave triggers not seeing him or her as a human being" (*ibid.*).

Gordon's insights into the existential reality of the black slave provides a theoretical framework for understanding that the formation of slave pedagogy is connected to African-American slaves' daily confrontations of situations where their existence as human beings were constantly called into question. The result of this is that slaves gave full attention to the ontological content of antiblack racist beliefs. This meant a pedagogical orientation within African-American slave culture in which the aim of slave pedagogy was directed at not only defending but also articulating an ethical expectation or vision of the slave's humanity as a "black" person.[1] Hence, the pedagogical aim of slave culture was bound up with addressing the problem of black suffering, which in turn was linked with the slave's consciousness of his or her worth as a human being. And it is in the redressing of suffering that slave culture raises ontological and teleological questions about what a human being is and should become. Paulo Freire points out that the philosophical anthropological assumptions of pedagogy implies a "[philosophical] stance ... and that stance implies—sometimes more, sometimes less explicitly—an interpretation of man and the world" (Freire 1970a[1988]: 6).

For many contemporary African-American intellectuals, racial slavery is one of the most important historically defining moments of African-American culture and life. For example, in Black Theology, Black Literature, Africana Philosophy, Black Historiography, Black Dramatic Arts, and Black Musicology, slave culture has been important for interpreting fundamental questions about the historical particularity of the human condition for African Americans.[2] With some few exceptions, this has not been the case for contemporary African-American educational thought. Its tendency has been to ignore the ontological, teleological, and existential concerns of African-American slave culture and how those concerns may contribute to the development of a radical humanism in African-American educational thought. The reason is that the pedagogical has been conceptualized in a very restrictive way, meaning that pedagogy or education within African-American educational thought has tended to be reduced to issues of teaching literacy. What is neglected is how slave culture functioned pedagogically—that is, how it implicitly transmitted values and understandings that taught African slaves how to live a human existence that was more than simply surviving but also thriving despite the stresses of chattel slavery.

But choosing to continue to live on in spite of enslavement is fundamentally an existential question that is associated with the slave's consciousness of his or her value or worth as a human being. The only published work that explicitly addresses the problem of the slave's worth as a pedagogical concern of African-American slave culture is *Deep Like the River: Education in the Slave Quarter Community* (1978), written by Thomas Webber. There are other well-known books that do not directly address this issue, although they provide important insight into the pedagogical function and organization of African-American slave culture.[3] However, these books, including *Deep Like the River,* are generally historical studies of slavery, and do not make theoretically explicit the existential, ontological and teleological, and therefore philosophical dimensions of pedagogy within African-American slave culture. In addition to this work, there are studies in which slave education is reduced to literate culture. The focus of this research is on the role of slave literacy in religious instruction, as well as early initiatives by slaves and ex-slaves to establish black schools for the purpose of developing a modern black political culture in the postslavery South.

The two most well known and respected published works to address this view are Janet Duitsman Cornelius's *When I Can Read My Title Clear: Literacy, Slavery, and Religion in the Antebellum South* and James D. Anderson's *The Education of Blacks in the South, 1860–1935.* The central thesis of each author is that slaves and ex-slaves had fundamental beliefs in the value of literate culture. Anderson and Cornelius develop separate arguments about how this belief was based on the idea that literacy was a condition for establishing self-worth, self-determination, and a liberating consciousness in the slave and ex-slave communities. While this may be true, the unintended consequence of both authors' overdetermination regarding literacy is that self-dignity, self-determination, and the development of a liberating consciousness appear to be only a function of literate culture. The issue raised here is not whether slave culture was a literate or nonliterate culture, for it was both. And as Cornelius shows clearly, approximately 30 percent of the slave population was literate. But I would add that both literate and nonliterate are situated within a lived context that also had pedagogical significance. It was slave culture that taught the slaves how to live a human life in a system that attempted to "tame" them as if they were wild animals.

In fact, as a pedagogical force, slave culture was existentially preoccupied with the slaves' conflicts over responsibility and anxiety, over life affirmation. Suicidal nihilism was articulated not through argument and reason but through stories—in narrative, music, and craft—that went right to the hearts of the enslaved.[4] With slave pedagogy, there is "an ontological value on the spoken word, [which] was not principally intended to transmit information but to produce a certain psychic effect in the listener" (Hadot 1995: 19). The purpose was not simply to develop the intelligence of a person but also to transform all aspects of his or her being—intellect, imagination, sensibility, and will. The goal of slave pedagogy as a philosophical stance was to orient the slave toward choosing a way of life that affirmed his or her existence as a human being. In the *Souls of Black Folk,* W. E. B. Du Bois says: "[Slave songs] are the music of an unhappy people, of the children of disappointment, they tell of death and suffering and unvoiced longing toward a truer world, of misty wanderings and hidden ways" (Du Bois 1999 [1903]: 156-157). This meant that to affirm the slave's worth, slave songs had to articulate a purpose for slaves; in other words, these songs functioned as an act of remembering that fed their dreams of a future-world. Slave songs gave rise to a mode of consciousness that was creative and transformative because it was prophetic in its vision.

The focus of this chapter is not on slave pedagogy as a teaching moment; nor is it a historical study of slave education or pedagogy. Rather, the intention is to address more broadly the philosophical problem of pedagogy in relation to concerns about ontology as an existential problem in African-American slave culture. Also addressed is the nature of black dehumanization under racial slavery. Doing so can better help us understand how the lived experience of being a "black slave" gave impetus to a particular existential orientation in relation to slave pedagogy. Supported in this discussion is the view that questions about the nature of being human were of profound philosophical concern for African-American slaves and that such concerns determined the pedagogical intentions within the larger African-American slave quarters and community (Webber 1978: 156-245, 249-250). In other words, because slaves were preoccupied with the question of their being, the aims of slave pedagogy were presupposed by a philosophy of existence that was grounded in the slaves' lived experience of race and racism as blacks. This was a philosophy of existence that addressed, to paraphrase Alain Locke, the "lived reality of value" of being black, a philosophical standpoint that had as its priority the inner life of black people (e.g., Gordon 2000b: 4; Locke 1983: 242-251). One consideration here is that the slave's consciousness of his or her existence as a black, and therefore its meaning, was hermeneutically encountered; another is that the existential reality of this encounter was the impetus behind slave pedagogy redressing the problem of black dehumanization and, thus, black suffering under racial slavery. It is because of this concern that slaves were engaged, if we use Karl Jaspers's definition, in philosophizing (cf. Jaspers 1954 [1995]). Before turning to these issues, I will develop a context for understanding why the pedagogical concerns of African-American slave culture were deeply shaped by the slaves' preoccupation with their humanity.

The Existential Problem of Ontology in African-American Slave Culture

Slave consciousness, which shaped the pedagogical aims of slave culture, was marked by an existential ontology that emerged from the slaves' lived experience with the dehumanizing project of American slavery. For example, between 1935 and 1939 the Works Project Administration's (WPA's) Federal Writers' Project collected the oral testimonies of ex-slaves.[5] A central theme running throughout the former slaves' testimonies was a defense of their humanity as black people. This is captured, for instance, in the testimony of Tom Windham, an ex-slave from Arkansas, when he proclaims: "I think we should have our liberty cause us ain't hogs or horses—us is human flesh" (Windham 1972: 211). Throughout their oral testimonies, however, ex-slaves constantly compared their dehumanized status to the condition of domestic animals, drawing parallels between themselves and the subordination of domestic animals.

The identifying of similarity between the condition of slaves and domestic animals was a tradition that long predated the popularity of this analogy in the Antebellum South. For example, Herodutus when referring to slaves uses the Greek term "andraphon," meaning a man-footed creature—"an unpleasant word formed on the analogy of 'four-footed creature, i.e., cattle'" (Jacoby 1994: 90). The enslavement of human beings emerged along with the domestication of animals as human communities shifted from hunting and gathering to agricultural societies (*ibid.:* 90–91). In fact, "all the practices used to domesticate animals—such as whipping, chaining, branding, castration, cropping ears—were ones that humans also applied to human slaves" (*ibid.:* 90). What is so similar is that the drive for control, whether of a slave or a domestic animal, overwhelms most distinctions. Slavery, in other words, can be interpreted as the domestication of human beings because, as with domestic animals, masters sought to direct or control the breeding, behavior, and movement of their slaves (*ibid.:* 91).

Yet if slavery was an institution that treated human beings like domestic animals, how did it make human beings appear to be the same as livestock? In addition to inventing "a lesser category of human that differed little from a brute beast," slaves were generally foreign captives and not members of one's own society. And the most commonly used distinction for categorizing foreign captives deemed animals and justifiably enslaved—"strangers," as they were termed—was linguistic dissimilarity. From the perspective of the slaveholders, the unintelligible speech of the foreign captives implied a lack of rationality, making them appear less than fully human, to be treated as though they resembled animals. In the case of African slaves it was not only their "unintelligible speech" but, more significantly, their dark skin that gave others permission to treat them as if they were animals (*ibid.:* 94-95).

In *White over Black,* Winthrop Jordan maintains that the African's "blackness" signified for the European the beastly nature of the "Negro" (Jordan 1968: 216-259). In fact, travel accounts by European explorers in West Africa suggested that the beast most resembling man was the ape, and that because of geographical proximity there was suspicion of copulation between the two. These travel accounts gave rise to a popular sentiment that the Negro and the ape were closer in kin than the Negro and the European. This sentiment was discursively conditioned by the idea amongst eighteenth-century Europeans of a "Great Chain of Being," which suggested that there was continuity between man and beast, but that the Negro was the link connecting them (*ibid.:* 482-505). Since a clear line was not drawn between man and animal in the "Great Chain of Being," the Negro, though related to the human family, was deemed a lower species of human because the "Negro was closer to the ape than other men" (*ibid.:* 230). This raised the possibility of hybridization between the two species, meaning that they "could be crossed to produce a third which in turn would be fertile" (*ibid.:* 235-236). The suggestion is that the "Negro was able to breed with the ape or that the Negro sprung from some mixture with that animal" (*ibid.:* 235). The association of the Negro's "blackness" with the Negro being a cross between man and beast—an indication of Negros' subhuman status, operated as the rationale for enslavement. St. Clair Drake in *Black Folk Here and There* maintains that racial slavery was a form of bondage that "differed profoundly from systems of slavery prevalent in the Old World" (Drake 1991: 24). He goes on to say that "in the new system the slave owner was expected to differ in physical type from the enslaved. The existence of a few exceptional cases of slaveholders who were allowed to rise from the 'inferior black race' was considered an anomaly and no whites could ever 'fall' into a state of slavery" (*ibid.*).

The WPA oral testimonies were informed by the ex-slaves' lived experience of race and racism under American slavery. The ex-slaves' memory of their bondage was shaped by their consciousness of themselves as enslaved "black people." Hence, their understanding of race and racism emerged out of their prior condition of enslavement along with their everyday encounters with whites and white institutions of the Antebellum South. In particular, the oral testimonies show that the slaves' lived experience—or rather their consciousness of themselves as a race, or more exactly as "black"—was bound up with their fear of being taken for animals. As noted earlier, ex-slaves complained that under racial slavery whites hardly distinguished between black people and domestic animals. In fact, all through their oral testimony, ex-slaves likened their situation as slaves to the condition of livestock (Bay 2000).

Interpreting their condition in this way contradicted the idea that American slavery was a paternalistic institution. The animal metaphors used by ex-slaves to describe their condition of enslavement disrupted the view that slavery was a humane institution because it was premised on the ideology of paternalism, on the obligation and duty of the slave-master to care for his slaves as a father would care for his dependent children. From the perspective of the slave-master, slaves were to be treated as childlike because it was believed that their moral and intellectual capacities made them incapable of taking care of themselves. In *American Negro Slavery,* the Southern historian Ulrich B. Phillips supported this proslavery apologist position of the planter class before the Civil War. Phillips utilized the plantation diaries and records of slave-masters as well as the travel journals of foreign visitors to the Antebellum South to substantiate his argument that American slavery was not a harsh institution in its treatment of slaves. Says Phillips, "In short, their despotism, so far as it might properly be so called, was benevolent in intent and on the whole beneficial in effect" (Phillips 1966: 328).

According to Phillips, a spirit of paternalism that Laurence Thomas says characterized the slave as a "moral simpleton" (Thomas 1993: 119) dominated the slave-master's patriarchal rule of the plantation. In the following passage Phillips retells the travel account of a British visitor in his conversation with a planter: "I respect them as my children, and they look on me as their friend and father. Were they to be taken from me it would be the most unhappy event of their lives" (Phillips 1966: 308). Phillips also found support for this conclusion in a planter's last will and testament, where the planter indicated that "the liberation of ... his slaves was prevented by a belief that the care of generous and humane masters would be much better for them than a state freedom" (*ibid.:* 329). The attitudes of planters toward their slaves, Phillips claims, contributed to a regime of slavery in the American South that was moderate in its system of control. Thus, Phillips writes, "[s]laves must be impelled as little as possible by fear, and as much as might be by loyalty, pride and the prospect of reward" (*ibid.:* 294). Phillips cites this entry from the diary of a planter as an example of moderation in slave management: "I never interfered in their connubial concerns nor domestic affairs, but let them regulate these after their own manner.... My object was to excite their ambition and attachment by kindness, not to depress their spirits by fear and punishment" (*ibid.*).

In their oral testimonies ex-slaves countered this paternalistic view of American slavery, arguing instead that the relationship between masters and slaves was not a familial one, not a relationship between parents and their dependent children, but more analogous to a relationship between masters and their domesticated animals. For example, former slaves in their testimonies drew comparisons between how they were fed and lived as slaves with the feeding and caring of farm animals (Carter 1972: 356; Johnson 1972: 2049; Peters 1972: 326; Williams 1973: 235).

As for those ex-slaves whose food provisions were plentiful and of good quality during their enslavement, they testified that being well fed must not be confused with being treated humanely because wealthy slaveholders also indulgently cared for their livestock (Milling 1972: 194). On the other hand, former slaves who were not well fed during their bondage complained that their masters' animals ate better than they did (Cole 1972: 225). And again, because slaves could be whipped, bred, or sold, ex-slaves likened themselves during slavery to livestock (Jones 1972: 2146; Watson 1999: 451).

Orlando Patterson, in *Slavery and Social Death,* maintains that slavery shaped the existential and historical predicament of black slaves in the Americas: The slaves not only doubted their humanity but found themselves in the absurd position of having to defend it. For slavery to function in this manner, human bondage cannot be merely reduced to "a mode of production in which labor is the most important social relation" (Aronowitz 1994: 210, 212).[6] This is the case because "in slavery," says Patterson, "wealth confronts direct forced labor not as capital, but rather as a relation of domination" (Patterson 1982: 2). Patterson argues that slavery is a distinct form of social domination whose features are distinguishable from capitalist relations of economic exploitation. In a system of slavery, he adds, economic exploitation is presupposed by the creation of an elaborate symbolic order that erases through "symbolic instruments" the slave's status as a person, rendering the slave a "socially dead person" (Patterson 1982: 37).

In this case Patterson rejects, in his words, "the simplistic materialist view," which he says "fails to take account of this problem" (Patterson 1982: 38). He goes on to describe slavery as "a process involving several transitional phases" (*ibid.*). Initially, "the slave is violently uprooted from his milieu. He is de-socialized and depersonalized. This process of social negation constitutes the first, essentially external, phase of enslavement" (*ibid.*). The second phase "involves the introduction of the slave into the community of the master, but it involves the paradox of introducing him as a nonbeing. This explains the importance of law, custom, and ideology in the representation of the slave relation" (*ibid.*). Symbolic instruments are therefore the cultural counterpart to the physical instruments used to dominate the slave's body. But the "symbolic whips" woven from many areas of culture were fashioned from different materials than the "literal whips" (*ibid.: 37*). Patterson states: "Masters used special rituals of enslavement upon first acquiring slaves: the symbolism of naming, of clothing, of hairstyling, of language, and of body marks. And they used, especially in the more advanced slave systems, the sacred symbol of religion" (*ibid.: 37–38*).

In this connection Patterson maintains that although slavery entailed the inflicting of severe bodily pain, physical brutalization was not the worst element of slavery. Instead, Patterson contends, it was moral brutalization—the ability of the slave-master to render the slave nameless and invisible as a human being through the use of symbolic instruments that caused the slave to become what Patterson calls "socially dead"—that was the most degrading.[7] But as long as the slave came to terms with being made into a nonperson with no socially recognized existence outside of being a slave, he or she was spared a violent fate. It is in this context that Patterson explains that slavery was "one of the most extreme forms of domination, approaching the limits of total power from the viewpoint of the master, and of total powerlessness from the viewpoint of the slave" (Patterson 1982: 2).

The focus up to this point has been to illustrate that during slavery, former slaves were anxiously preoccupied with not being taken for domestic animals. Patterson describes the historical reality that led to this fear amongst slaves through his concept of "social death," a term that highlights how the processes of enslavement attempted to end a person's claim to life as a human being. Patterson thus anticipated the existential predicament created by human bondage, which is also complicated by the fact that the physical characteristics of African-American slaves—in particular, their "blackness"—functioned ideologically as a rationale for slaveholders to enslave and treat them as livestock.

The absurdity of the African-American slaves' existential predicament was that they had to prove not only to others but also to themselves that they were human beings. This suggests that "racism is not simply about racist epistemologies and beliefs, but about their ontological content, about what people are, that is, the whole question of the being of that group" (Gordon 1999f: 108).[8] Slaves were therefore compelled to respond to ontological questions regarding their existence as human beings. In fact, the choice to continue to live on for slaves was essentially an ontological problem that was associated with the slaves' feelings and thoughts about their own value and worth. Alain Locke's conception of the "lived reality of values" proposes that values "function as imperatives of action and as norms of preference and choice" (Locke 1989: 35). The values and understandings transmitted by slave culture regarding the slaves' ontological status, as blacks, was not only pedagogical but also philosophical in nature.

For Locke, then, philosophy cannot be value-neutral because values are central to human life. In short, philosophy is a subjective activity; or, as Locke says, "it is merely the lineaments of a personality, its temperaments and dispositional attitude" (*ibid.:* 36). And because "values are rooted in attitude, not in [absolute objective] reality, and pertain to ourselves, not to the world" (*ibid.*), doing philosophy or philosophizing is bound up with the value choices we make about how to live. Locke writes: "[A]ll philosophies are in ultimate derivation philosophies of life and not of abstract, disembodied 'objective' reality; products of time, place and situation, and thus systems of timed history rather than timeless eternity" (*ibid.:* 34).[9] In general agreement with this perspective, Edmund Husserl argues that philosophical reflection is distinct from the "positivistic thinking" of the natural sciences in that it considers issues related to the human condition—issues that, in light of human tragedy and upheaval, have as their focus the meaning and meaninglessness of the whole of human existence (Husserl 1995: 318). Karl Jaspers similarly explains that "philosophy deals with the whole of being" (Jaspers 1954 [1995]: 8) and that "philosophizing is stimulated by so-called ultimate situations" (*ibid.:* 1-2; see also Wallraff 1970: 141-166). These are, says Jaspers, "situations of profound import" that cause us to call into question the whole of our being. He concludes: "It is when doubt erodes the values and principles by which people regulate their lives that philosophizing is called for" (Wallraff 1970: 141). Doing philosophy, or what Jaspers calls "philosophizing," is therefore attentive to the paradoxes or contradictions of our being. The source of philosophizing then lies with the situation of our existence, a situation that is characterized by freedom, but a freedom that confronts us with constant uncertainty. This assumes an understanding of ontology that is coterminous with being as becoming. For example, Jaspers maintains that because being is encompassed or constituted by existence, being is always in the process of becoming. However, Jaspers uses the term "Existenz" in the place of "existence" to illuminate this point. The latter, existence, is empirical existence, and the former, Existenz, is our consciousness of being free. This presupposes that we, as human beings, have the potential to transcend or surpass what we are as natural beings (see Jaspers 1954 [1995], 1971, 1997). The equating of being with freedom means that being escapes or recedes into our consciousness and can be grasped only existentially—that is, grasped in relation to our lived situation. Consciousness of being is bound up with the consciousness we have of our situation in the world. Thus, the source of the question of being begins with the situation of the questioner (Kruks 1990: 11–13). In other words, because the slave is a situated and therefore embodied being, the slave is not only a thinking, knowing, and self-conscious subject but a self that is conscious of being alive. Subjectivity, in this case, is broadened to acknowledge that the "'self' is irreducibly sentient" (*ibid.:* 12). Hence, the subjectivity of the slave and the surrounding social world in which the slave lives are mutually permeable. The slave comes to discover him- or herself as possessing a particular physique, race, and gender, and as having been born into a unique human situation—with a particular spatial and temporal location, personal history, and cultural and economic context (*ibid.*). For example, the slave is born and constructs a personal history out of the context of slavery in which racial domination is an essential feature that marks the slave's existential situation. That is to say, individual slaves confront the meaning of their existence as a slave, but also must confront the meaning of their violent transfiguration into "blacks" so as to signify simultaneously their subhuman status and natural condition as slaves. The lived-context or situation of existence for the slave, therefore, is about existing not simply as a slave but as a "black" slave. And in an antiblack world such as that constructed by racial slavery, to be rendered a "black" slave is to be rendered a nonbeing and to create doubt in the subjectivity of the slave about his or her humanity as a black. Gabriel Marcel maintains that "the domain of [being] is that in which our own situation, the situation of the questioner, is called into question, and becomes the object of our scrutiny" (quoted in Wahl 1969: 55). But for the black slave, it is his or her being as human that is called into question and scrutinized. In other words, the particular situation of questioning of the black is one in which what is asked is "What am I?" rather than "Who am I?" (Gordon 1998f: 104). In the latter case, one's humanity and uniqueness are a given. In the former, one's humanity is interrogated and negated. Thus, what is denied is the legitimacy of the slave's black existence (cf. Fanon 1963: 47).

Furthermore, the preoccupation of slave culture with the question of the slave's "blackness" is coterminous with the rise of Western modernity. The characteristic feature of Western modernity, which was complicit with the development of European colonialism, conquest, and enslavement of non-European peoples, was the violent transformation of African peoples in Africa, the Americas, and Europe into "blacks." In fact, black people are a modern people because their preoccupation with the question of their "blackness" is an essential feature or phenomenon of the "underside" of modernity (Dussel 1998). In *Black Skin, White Masks,* Frantz Fanon notes: "White Civilization and European culture have forced an existential deviation on the Negro. What is often called the black soul is a white artifact" (Fanon 1967a: 110). Consequently, Fanon observed, in an antiblack world the Negro "[is driven to struggle desperately] to discover the meaning of black identity" (*ibid.*).

Nonetheless, it is from this underside or periphery that slaves reconstituted "blackness" into forms of black consciousness that affirmed their humanity and ability. Slave culture, along with its pedagogical concerns, was grounded in a black philosophy of existence, which for clear reasons raised existential questions about the nature of being by virtue of the lived-context of the slave as a black. This is the context in which Gordon noted that

> [a] centering of what is often known as the situation of questioning or inquiry itself marks philosophies of existence. Another term for situation is the lived context of concern. Implicit is the existential demand for recognizing the situation or lived context of Africana peoples who live in that situation. A slave's situation can only be understood, for instance, through recognizing the fact that a slave experiences it; it is to regard the slave as a perspective in the world. (2000b: 10)

Slave Pedagogy and the Affirmation of "Black" Humanity

The slaves' philosophy of existence was not a philosophy that rose above the "determinations of history and everyday life" (Henry 2000a: 1). It was a philosophy that was "intertextually embedded in discursive practice," (*ibid.:* 2) and therefore bound up with what Thomas Webber calls the "educational instruments" of slave institutions, which he identifies as the family, peer groups, clandestine congregations, songs and stories, and the larger slave quarter community (Webber 1978: 156–250).

The slave quarter community functioned pedagogically to counter slaveholders' attempts to teach slaves the values, attitudes, and understandings of the obedient and trustworthy servant (Webber 1978: 26). The nature of what was taught by slaveholders, says Webber, "saw blacks as savages to be civilized; as children at best and animals at worst" (ibid.: 249). He goes on to note: "[The] content of white teaching directly contradicted understandings, attitudes, values, and feelings which slaves had learned from birth in an educational process created and controlled by slaves themselves" (ibid.: 249–250). And through slave institutions, members of the slave quarter community were "able to sustain and transmit values and understandings despite a slave system which deliberately limited their self-expression and outlawed any formalized, slave controlled, educational practices" (ibid.: x).

The slave quarter community's philosophy of education was implicitly rather than explicitly "referenced or engaged in the production of answers to everyday questions and problems that were framed in non-philosophical discourse" (Henry 2000a: 2). Put another way, the slave quarter community's educational philosophy was embedded in its expressive culture and patterns of slave life. It was expressed, therefore, in the symbolic creativity of their culture, not only as text and artifacts but also in the aesthetics of language, the body, music, and dramatic forms (e.g., gestures, dress, and movement) as well as in religious myths and symbols. The kinds of questions that African-American slave culture posed were philosophical in nature because the questions asked tended to be those regarding the origins, ends, and truth value of the slave's everyday activities (e.g., Levine 1978; Raboteau 1978; Stuckey 1987). Paget Henry maintains that the discursive practices of slave cultures throughout the Americas were grounded in foundational and teleological concerns that were mediated by inherited traditional African worldviews, reconfigured by Africana slaves to deal with the life challenges they would face as "black people" in the Americas. It is from this perspective that Henry wrote:

> Philosophy's primary concerns tend to be foundational, teleological, and discursive in nature. Foundational concerns include the

bases of all discursive practices we employ in grasping self and world, as well as questions such as the origin of life and creation. Teleological concerns include the ends of many of our social activities, the fate of the individual, and the ends of creation. Consequently, whenever we write or attempt to answer a significant problem we necessarily raise philosophical issues, which may or may not be addressed explicitly. (Henry 2000a: 2)

The foregoing indirectly suggests that culture is, first and foremost, about the intentional and therefore rational planning of social life around foundational and teleological concerns that have to do with human existence (Outlaw 1996; Schutz and Luckman 1995). It is in this context that slave pedagogy functioned to support a social life that affirmed the slave's humanity as a black (Levine 1978; Webber 1978). At a more general level, then, the question of pedagogy is ultimately interwoven with questions concerning the nature of being human. This is indicated by Maxine Greene's statement that "[w]e all learn to become human within a community of some kind or by means of a social medium" (Greene 1978: 11). So, invariably, pedagogy is situated within the uneasy relationship between what a person is and what a person ought to become. And as Lewis Gordon notes, these two questions—what is and what ought to be—are fundamentally philosophical questions about identity and action. "They are questions of ontological and teleological significance, for the former," says Gordon, "addresses being and the latter addresses what to become—in a word, purpose" (2000a: 7).

In Western philosophy of education, the question of pedagogy has been linked with the notion of education as a humanizing project. Also, from this perspective, to be fully human is to be a "knowing" subject. And to be a knowing subject is to reduce knowing simply to a function of "reasonable arguments." Here, reason is equated with the capacity to think systematically, abstractly, or logically so as to be able to "discover," with the human mind or language, "real" knowledge. Humanization, in this case, is rooted in a mode of knowing that is identical to the natural sciences. At issue is how this view results in the naturalizing of consciousness. Edmund Husserl has criticized this idea of consciousness understood as a function of what happens in the brain, proposing instead a phenomenological interpretation of consciousness that maintains that the essential character of consciousness, as the bearer of perceptual reality, is located in its structure and not in its neurological aspect. And by "structure," Husserl means that every act of thinking implies an object thought of, so that "thinking" is necessarily "thinking about." Thus, all acts of perception such as remembering, imagining, and willing have a directional force or intend some object; the nature of consciousness is that it is always consciousness *of* something (Natanson 1973: 12-13).

In *Cartesian Mediations,* Husserl directs his critique first at René Descartes, who develops a "method of doubt" to demonstrate the existence of his subjectivity by doubting provisionally the reality of the senses. Husserl's disagreement with Descartes has to do, in part, with his argument that the "ego" is a "mental substance"—that because the ego is capable of doubting, and doubting is a "mode of thinking," Descartes exists as "cogitating ego" or, in Descartes's words, as "a thing that thinks." Husserl describes Descartes's association of the ego with a "substance" or "thing" as "naïve objectivism." Descartes's argument fails, according to Husserl, because he has formulated a manner of philosophizing that seeks its ultimate foundation in the subjective—that is, in spite of its subjective grounding, Descartes's manner of philosophizing persists in pure objectivism.[10] The problem, in other words, is that the ego for Descartes is experienced as something independent of our conscious acts of thinking, remembering, willing, valuing, judging, expecting, and hoping. Husserl, on the other hand, believed that conscious acts can reflect upon or describe the world without assuming the existence of the world, which also means that the *meaning* of the world's existence and the entities or things that exist in it must be dependent upon our conscious acts. Thus, for Husserl, it is the ego as consciousness and not as a "mental substance" or "thinking thing" that establishes the ego and its conscious acts as a "transcendental ego." The ego is described as transcendental because of the presuppositional relationship it has to the world; the ego provides the world with its meaningful and existential status, yet its own existence cannot be said to have the same character of the world. "Transcendental" suggests, then, that "the ego goes beyond the experienced world in that it is necessary for, and thus not itself a part of, that world" (Hammond et al. 1991: 34).

The transcendental character of consciousness that Husserl describes is exemplified by the modes of thinking that constitute the forms of remembering, imagining, willing, hoping, and so on, that were integral to the expressive culture of African-American slaves. Paget Henry argues that the Africans' inherited religious myths, rituals, songs, folktales, and dance that make up their expressive culture allowed African-American slaves a "phenomenological bracketing" of the world, providing them with the existential space to create a new self-world. That is, it allowed them to engage in conscious acts that permitted them to transcend the narrow confines of the world in which they were forced to live. They enlarged the "boundaries of their restrictive universe backward until it fused with the world of the Old Testament, and upward until it became one with the world beyond" (Levine 1978: 33). In short, the African-American slaves sought to bring the spirit tangibly into this world, so that they might be transformed, healed, and made whole. Through their religious myths, rituals, and songs, they "found the status, the harmony, the values, the order they needed to survive by internally creating an expanded universe, by literally willing themselves to be reborn" (*ibid.*). In *Landscapes of Learning,* Maxine Greene, as previously mentioned, argues that "we learn to become human within a community of some kind ... "; she goes on to say that "learning is stimulated by a sense of future possibility and by a sense of what we might be" (Greene 1978: 11). It is in this context that African-American slave culture contributes to defining what ought to be the humanizing aims of an education for a suffering people that have experienced the underside of European and European-American modernity. But first, what does it mean to become human? Perhaps initially Hegel's approach is useful in terms of elaborating on Greene's statement that the function of education is about learning to become human within a community. Hegel equates "becoming" not with animal desire but, instead, with the human desire for recognition, and therefore for self-consciousness, both of which are necessary for a "sense of what we might be."

Animal desire, on the other hand, is restricted to only biological or material preservation, and is dependent upon negating nature—that is, on transforming nature for its sustenance. In short, it is incapable of self-consciousness because it "does not transcend itself as given, as body; it does not rise above itself in order to come back toward itself; it has no distance with respect to itself in order to contemplate itself." According to Hegel, human desire, then, is directed not toward a given being but toward nonbeing; it is associated, like animal desire, not with natural reality and immediacy but with becoming, which is the negation of the givenness of being. Human reality, for Hegel, is a reality in which one's desire is imposed on another so as to get recognition, directing one to go beyond one's immediacy in order to become self-conscious. Hence, recognition is fundamental to learning to become human within a community. Inasmuch as learning goes on in a community, becoming human is mediated by an individual's heritage. Tsenay Serequeberhan's understanding of heritage as lived existence is useful for discerning the particular meaning of becoming human within various pedagogical communities. He writes:

> Existence is always actualized in a specific and concrete heritage. Existence? The word derives from the Latin *exsistere: ex-*, out, plus *-sistere,* to cause to stand, set, place, to come forth, stand forth. Based on this we can say that that which exists is that which stands forth. A heritage, then, is the sedimented layering over time—that is, the life of a community—of the actuality of existence, which in "standing forth" does so necessarily in specific and determined ways and thus constitutes a heritage, a certain way of being-in-the world. (Serequeberhan 2000: ix)

The heritage that informed the pedagogical concerns of early modern Western philosophy is distinguishable from the one that informed enslaved African Americans. For the former, the existential concerns of education with becoming human gave rise to human anxieties that were the result of an obsession with wanting to be perfect, and hence god-like. The etymology of the word "education" in Western thought is derived from the Latin word "erudire" which is "taking someone or something out of a rude or crude condition" (Rorty 1998: 11). Thus, Kant says, without education, "the uncultivated man is crude, the undisciplined is unruly" (Kant 1960: 7), meaning for him that "[m]an can only become man by education" (*ibid.:* 6). This understanding of education is foregrounded by a pre-ancient Greek mythical worldview that posited that the human and animal worlds overlapped. In *The Philosophy of Symbolic Forms,* Ernst Cassirer, for example, maintains that in the mythical consciousness there is not a firm separation of the species human from other creatures and plants (Cassirer 1955: 179).

Modern Western philosophy of education could be said to be adverse to a mythical worldview or consciousness. Kant's insight, in his book *Education,* is relevant here: "[M]an is the only being who needs education," because education "changes animal nature into human nature" and "prevents man from being turned aside by his animal impulses from humanity, his appointed end" (Kant 1960: 1-3). He concludes that "education bring[s] ... our nature one step nearer to perfection.... [For] with education is involved the great secret of the perfection of human nature" (*ibid.:* 7).

The human anxieties, which preoccupied the pedagogy of slave culture, emerged out of a specific historical reality in which the slave's humanity as a black was denied. Prompted by these anxieties, the slave culture's existential concerns struggled to affirm or assert the slave's recognition of his or her humanity, which was learned within the slave quarter community. However, in contrast to Western philosophy of education, it understood that being human is not something one becomes through education but, rather, is what one already is. Serequeberhan's reading of heritage as lived existence allows for a fuller appreciation and understanding that slave pedagogy functioned to create and reproduce a way of "being in the world" through the slave community's expressive culture.

The pedagogical-existential concerns of slave culture are therefore bound up and responsive to a heritage that had as its purpose the slaves' recognition of their being in the world as freedom. "Freedom" here is taken to mean existential freedom. This freedom is a function of a situated and embodied consciousness that is for-it-self—that is incomplete, lacking, unfulfilled, and full of possibilities to choose, to act and represent itself both individually or collectively as a "self."

The slave's recognition of his or her freedom is the result of slave culture's pedagogical privileging of the spiritual domain of human existence, which it inherited from its African past. Similarly—yet distinct from existential phenomenology, which rejects the naturalizing of subjectivity and sees the significance of consciousness in transcending the world of things—the spiritual domain, as articulated by African-American slave culture, recognizes that as human beings we are more than solely physical entities or objects of the empirical world. Spirituality is a mode of being that involves an intentional act of reflective consciousness in which there is an awareness of one's being as a "being-for-itself" (to use a phrase from Sartre); this is a mode of being that is directed outward and, therefore, points beyond itself to objects. It is a being with a point or purpose in the world. In this sense, spirituality is a reality that is potentially transforming.

Pedagogically, in African-American slave culture spirituality was given cultural-expressive form through religious myths. Mircea Eliade maintains that "[myth] narrates a sacred history; it relates an event that took place in primordial Time, the fabled time of the 'beginnings'" (Eliade 1963: 5). Eliade also argues that the function of myth in religion is to demarcate the worlds of the profane and the sacred. The profane is the world of the ordinary, of everyday mundane things, contrasted with the sacred, the world of the extraordinary. And when myths manifest something as sacred, that something, whether an object or an act, becomes saturated with Being, acquiring value, and in doing so becomes real. However, it is real not in the literal sense but in the implicit meanings of myths. That is, myths become perceived as real either by inspiring people to change the way things are or by enabling people to project their view of reality over the world, even when that world remains the same (Eliade 1963; Cave 1993: 68). Myths do this, particularly religious myths, by privileging spirit, in which case ordinary things become sacred and thus extraordinary by subjecting the economic, political, cultural, and biological dimensions of everyday life to the spiritual domain. As Paget Henry contends, the African diaspora inherited from its African past a conception of spirituality that is consistent with the idea of force or agency rather than as personal qualities. Myth is perceived, he argues, in relation to its enabling capabilities, its creative intelligence and drives. It is this creative energy that makes spirit capable of realizing the nonspiritual world and of shaping events in it. The ontological significance of this observation is that for African-American slave culture, being or existence is constructed as force, in which case force is being and being is force (cf. Henry 2000a: 26).

The pedagogical-existential significance of the religious myths of African-American slaves, as expressed in their spirituals or songs of God and mythic heroes, is that the sacred functioned as a process of incorporating this world within the domain of the spiritual world. African-American slaves created a new self-world by transcending the narrow confines of the one in which they were forced to live.

To understand fully the pedagogical significance of African-American slave culture's preoccupation with the spiritual dimensions of human existence, and thus with its bracketing of the ordinary world, we need to consider the nature of the slaves' suffering given the historically peculiar system of bondage under which they labored.

Slave Pedagogy and Black Suffering as Affliction

Slave pedagogy's purpose within African-American slave culture was to redress the problem of black suffering within the day-to-day life of the slave. The pedagogical challenge of slave culture was to prevent the slave's painful existence from turning into despair and, thus, giving up to the point of indifference to life itself. This purpose is linked to the fact that the slave's existence as a black was conditioned by a dehumanizing project that was unique to American slavery. Put differently, American slavery was the only form of human bondage that used the slave's racial membership—in this case, the enslaved person's black body—ideologically to rationalize the domesticating of human beings, as if they were wild animals that could be turned into livestock. The slave's lived experience of racism was one in which the line between human and beast was blurred—an experience of particular significance in a racialized system of slavery where all slaves were black and most blacks were slaves.

Again, to suffer as a black slave is to have one's black body seen by others and possibly oneself as a thing that is an absence of human presence. It is to be forced into the realm of property, whereby the slave's cries for recognition go unheard because "he or she falls below the category of otherness, for an Other is another human being" (Gordon 2000a: 223). Treated as an animal, the slave is presumed to be without human consciousness. Like an animal, the slave is treated as if he or she has no self-consciousness, henceforth possessing no possibilities of the freedom to choose, to act, and to define oneself.

To be without human consciousness is to be incapable of bodily self-awareness and, therefore, to be incapable of experiencing pain as a person who is conscious of being alive. Put another way, to experience pain as an absence of human presence in the world is to be indifferent to life and its possibilities. In *On the Genealogy of Morals,*

Friedrich Nietzsche maintains that suffering is the ground of moral life in that it draws our reflective attention upon the problems of living and, henceforth, on our human presence in the world. But, he says, "[n]egroes ... taken as representatives of prehistoric man" (Nietzsche 1967: 67–68) are, in contrast to Europeans, not able to suffer because their constitution is such that Negroes are supposedly not capable of experiencing bodily pain (see also Preston 1997 and Kant as quoted in Eze 1997: 116).

The question of bodily pain raises the distinction between corporeality and the lived body. A physical body is a body that is in-itself, a body that is a "thing," in which case it is perceived as complete and fulfilled, and thus has no possibilities in that it is incapable of exercising freedom. Conversely, a lived body is a body for-itself; it has possibilities and is therefore a body with intentionality. Which is to say that the lived body is bound up with, and directed toward, an experienced world (see Leder 1990: 75).

In an antiblack world the lived experience of the black is such that the black slave is conscious of his or her body through the perspective of the white world. Fanon notes, "In the white world the [black] encounters difficulties in the development of his bodily schema. Consciousness of the body is solely a negating activity" (Fanon 1967b: 110). This is a perspective that degrades the slave's black body to that of a nonhuman animal and, therefore, to a mere physical existence. The perspective of the white world is a negation of the black body as a lived body. Hence, the pained body of the black slave is reduced merely to a physiological sensation or to physical pain, making the painful existence of the slave qualitatively no different from the pain experienced by a nonhuman animal. This is in contrast to the fact that the human experience of pain is intricately bound up with the quest for meaning, legitimacy, and understanding. Human pain, in other words, is not simply suffered; we are always compelled to make sense of it, in which case human pain is also a subjective experience. Howard Thurman once wrote:

> Because man has a mind and is in a very profound sense an
> experiencer of life, pain is something that is seen as happening
> to him. He is aware that it is happening to him. He knows that
> he hurts—it is a very local experience. Thus for man suffering is
> possible. For him the physical pain is interpreted; it is at this point
> that the crucial issue of all suffering arises. What does the pain
> mean? (Thurman 1998: 43)

But to understand what pain meant to the slaves, we must understand how pain functions in relation to the lived body. For one thing, because pain hurts, it seizes our attention and forces a reorientation of our whole being; hence, pain, according to Drew Leder, is a "manner of being-in-the-world" (Leder 1990: 73). By this Leder means that pain disrupts the body's relationship with the world; it forcibly "reorganizes our lived space and time, our relations with others and with ourselves" (*ibid.*). In short, pain disrupts the body's processes of perception and, therefore, the body's intentional movement toward an experienced world. The reason is that pain is experienced in the confines of one's flesh and thus is marked by an interiority that another cannot share. Elaine Scarry notes that "when one speaks about 'one's own physical pain' and about 'another person's physical pain,' one might appear to be speaking about two wholly distinct orders of events. For the person whose pain it is, it is effortlessly grasped while for persons outside the sufferer's body, what is effortless is not grasping it" (Scarry 1985: 4).

Because pain is confined to the flesh, it calls us to the here-and-now, to the present. Yet to escape our pain we are forced to establish a future goal, to be free of pain. Therefore, it is in the context of focusing "outward upon the world, or dwelling in our past or a hoped-future" that human subjectivity—and its processes of remembering, willing, hoping, valuing, expecting—is integral to redressing the hold that pain has on the lived body. Sartre wrote: "[P]ain consciousness is a project toward a future consciousness which would be empty of all pain; that is, to a consciousness whose contexture, whose being-there would not be painful" (Sartre 1956: 438). Human pain is a living pain; it cannot be reduced to neural impulses for the reason that pain always contains at its heart the human encounter with meaning.

It is in this context that pain gives rise to a hermeneutical moment—that is, to a quest for interpretation, legitimacy, and understanding that, in itself, is bound up with the pragmatic goal of getting rid of or mastering pain. David Morris points out that "the culture we live in and our deepest personal beliefs subtly or massively recast our experience of pain" (Morris 1991: 2). Hence, culture can be a significant force in redressing the problem of human suffering. The reason is that culture potentially can "affirm a human being's capacity to move out beyond the boundaries of our own body into the external, shareable world"—in which case culture gives the sufferer the capacity to reverse what Scarry calls the "'de-objectifying' work of pain by forcing pain itself into avenues of objectification" (Scarry 1985: 5). She maintains that this "enables pain to enter a realm of shared discourse that is wider, more social," and that this "is a necessary prelude to the collective task of diminishing pain" (*ibid.:* 9).

Finally, in making "pain more social," its interpretation, legitimacy, and understanding as well as the pragmatic goal of eliminating pain become a site of social and political appropriation and conflict. The concern at this point is with the way in which the pain of the oppressed is appropriated and conflated with debased forms of oppressive power. For example, the logic of social domination under racial slavery was to disavow black pain by appropriating the felt pain of the slave away from his or her body and presenting it as the attributes of something else.

That something else was the fact that the bodily pain of the slave was reduced to a mere physical pain, in which case the slave's suffering was disavowed as a living pain; and the black body, as a living body. Disavowed was the belief that the pained body of the black slave was conscious of being alive and that the slave's embodied existence contained a point of view that had a moral intent.

The suffering of the slave should be understood as a problem of "extreme suffering," which Simone Weil refers to as "affliction." Oppression for Weil is not merely bound up with social conflict but is rooted "in a state of extreme and total humiliation" that "corrodes the human soul"—a mark of what she calls affliction (Weil 1999: 332; see also Bell 1998: 45). The concept of affliction is useful for understanding the character of the suffering experienced by black slaves. Interestingly, in Weil's conception of oppression she equates the existential situation of those individuals who are oppressed with that of the slave; thus, to be oppressed is to "receive," in Weil's words, "the mark of the slave" (Weil 1999: 439).

These are situations of oppression that involve the employment of forms of systematic cruelty that undermine the human soul and lead to affliction (Finch 1999: 65–66). Weil maintains that the suffering of affliction is like that of the suffering slave; in her words, "it takes possession of the soul with its own mark and marks it through and through with its own particular mark—"the mark of a slave" (Weil 1999: 439). But to receive "the mark of a slave" is not only to be totally at the command of other human beings, and to have no control over your situation, but also to have no attention given to your condition; it is to have no one hear your cries of pain (Bell 1998: 27). Says Weil, "The afflicted are not listened to. They are like someone whose tongue has been cut out. When they move their lips no ear perceives any sound. And they themselves soon sink into impotence in the use of language, because of the certainty of not being heard" (Weil 1999: 332–333). And to have no attention given to your pain is to be deprived of all human relationships, and thus to have your life uprooted and your existence as a human being made insignificant by others and even yourself.

Weil's conception of affliction allows for a more subtle approach to understanding the human toll of oppression. It shifts attention away from what Vivian Patraka (1999: 88) calls "spectacular suffering" by illuminating the mundane and quotidian but pernicious forms of cruelty and terror that inflict hurt and humiliation. Spectacular suffering, on the other hand, reduces the attention given to the pain of the sufferer to that of displays of graphic physical violence, including elaborate acts of atrocity that violate, damage, and disintegrate the sufferer's body. This raises some potentially important concerns about the nature of the attention that has been given to black suffering within slavery. The character of that attention is such that it obscures and evades the suffering of the slave, inasmuch as the slave's suffering is reduced to bodily experiences of physical pain that are the result of violent beatings consummate of the master's brutal authority.

It cannot be denied that physical violence and acts of atrocity were central to the making of the slave, particularly the making of the slave into an object. But also central were those forms of violence and domination perpetuated by what Saidiya Hartman and Laurence Thomas respectively describe as *terror* and *cruelty,* which operated perniciously within the moral tissue of everyday benign relationships between slave and master. These so-called benign relationships were a function of the paradoxical character of black enslavement that constructed the slave as an object, while at the same time enabling recognition of the slave's humanity. This was specifically the case in regard to the Slave Codes and Christianity—the former enabling the slave's recognition as having the status of a person; and the latter, as having a soul, while simultaneously constructing the slave as a brute, rationalizing the slave's status as property.[11]

According to some commentators, because the slave's humanity was defined as property, even if this definition did not put an end to the slave's construction as a thing, it at least curbed the physical brutality of slavery and transformed slavery into a benign institution (Genovese 1974; Phillips 1966). This position mistakenly assumes that the pain of the slave is given attention and that the master (and the abolitionist) hears the cries of the slave. The focus of attention here is on spectacular suffering, on the horrific physical violence inflicted on the slave's black body. It is this kind of attention that arouses for whites, both master and abolitionist, what Saidiya Hartman calls "empathetic identification," which is encouraged by humanism's empathetic feelings that identify with the other by making their suffering one's own (Hartman 1997: 17–22). The humanity of the slave, says Hartman, "is recognized so that the slave's suffering, and therefore black body, can serve as a conduit through which whites can get in touch with their own painful thoughts and feelings" (*ibid.:* 21). Even though emphatic identification establishes "the brute materiality of existence [it] evades the materiality of black suffering" (*ibid.*); that is to say, the pained existence of the black is intelligible only in the most hideous and grotesque examples and not in the everyday routines of life. This is the kind of attention that reduces the slave to a physical existence. Thus, what is obscured is how the slave's day-to-day relationships with other human beings presuppose a moral existence, and therefore situations, in which the slave confronts the paradoxes of human freedom.

The point here is that the fundamental basis of moral existence is human freedom. Freedom is not something that we possess, as if it were a human quality or property; rather, freedom is what we are as human beings. Freedom is the stuff of human existence. But what is freedom as human existence? It is choice; and it is the reality of choice that is disclosed in the very structure of what a human being is, therefore choice is what constitutes us as finite freedom. Also, our awareness of our limited freedom confronts us with decisions of whether to strive beyond what we are. This is why, for Kierkegaard, human existence is a continuous task (Wahl 1969: 31). To then exist as freedom is to always be in the process of becoming. Kierkegaard regards becoming as the ethical sphere of moral existence because it is the sphere of decision and resolute choice. Thus, to exist ethically is to be fully aware of our freedom and to choose ourselves within the conditions of freedom. As choice, freedom liberates us from the now, from just living in the moment—meaning that our existence is one of striving toward and fulfilling ends.

When attention to black pain is minimized to "spectacular suffering" (to displays of horrific physical violence inflicted on the pained black body), the day-to-day strivings of slaves—and therefore the paradoxes of choice, decision, freedom, and responsibility that constitute the slave's moral existence—are obscured. Hence, the slave's suffering is not recognized, nor are his cries of pain heard. It is in this context that Laurence Thomas explains, "[T]he cruelty of slavery was far more mental than physical. This is not to 'discount in any way' the murders, beatings, and lynching that blacks endured," but "considerations of these physical harms do not fully capture the brutality of American Slavery" (Thomas 1993: 135).[12]

According to Thomas, whites sought to establish relationships of trust with blacks; whites wanted blacks to believe that if blacks did their part, whites would freely do right by blacks as slaves. Thomas's definition of trust is similar to that of Simone Weil's: It denotes an expectation that another will not harm us. An aspect of this expectation of trust, of not being harmed by another, is that our pain is recognized and heard by others. Thomas goes on to argue that one of the ways in which our "humanity is revealed" is by "unequivocally meeting the complex conditions of trust and gratitude called for by social interaction" (Thomas 1993: 137). But the cruelty of American slavery is that even when slaves trusted whites, by "doing their part," the slaves continued to be harmed and degraded by whites. This is because trusting relationships are presupposed by acts of good will that call for gratitude. But gratitude can be felt toward other human beings only if there is first an acknowledgment of their full humanity—that is, recognition of their freedom, striving, and suffering, all of which constitute not only what human beings are but also their moral existence (cf. Thomas 1993: 137; see also Douglass 1988).

As mentioned above, Thomas describes this cruelty as "mental cruelty." I, however, prefer Weil's conception of the cruelty of oppression as the destroying of the soul, which allows us to understand black suffering within slavery as extreme suffering, or what Weil calls affliction. She also maintains that affliction is the combination of physical pain, distress of the soul, and social degradation. Affliction is the complete negation of another's existence—that is, the negation of his or her freedom and all those things that are determined by it—one's strivings and sufferings. To be afflicted is to be deprived of all human attention as if one were a nonentity, an object in the natural world with a mere physical existence. In such cases, life is reduced to just being alive, to just surviving.

The pedagogical relevance of the concept of affliction, then, is that it situates the aim of slave pedagogy in relation to the redress of the slaves' distressed soul. Slave pedagogy was conditioned by the slaves' existential freedom—that is, by their choice as human beings to strive toward something more than just being alive. More directly, the major intention of slave pedagogy was to console, to inspirit, and to animate the distressed soul of slaves. The fundamental significance of religion in most aspects of slave life was a major influence on the orientation of slave pedagogy toward the slave's soul.

Charles Long, in his discussion of slave religion, maintains that "religion is not a cultural system, much less rituals or performance, nor a theological language, but an orientation, a basic turning of the soul toward another defining reality" (Long 1999: 14). He describes the soul as that which is sacred in the human—that which is composed of a basic material or substance he calls "soul stuff." Long explains that it is "soul stuff" that allows human beings to transcend and to be more than solely physical entities or objects of the natural world. It is therefore "soul stuff" (or the slave's existence as freedom) that makes human beings more than just mere existence. In this context, Long argues that the slaves' resistance to their enslavement was more than the simple desire to survive because their very being expressed "soul stuff"—that is, the conviction that "life is more than being alive."

It is this enthusiasm that oriented slave pedagogy toward mitigating the slave's affliction by resisting efforts to render him or her a social nonperson. Because black affliction within slavery consisted of stripping the slave of ancestry and family tradition, of uprooting life, pedagogical resistance consisted of the slave's desperate effort to remember, to reclaim heritage, through story, song, and rituals of confirmation and self-naming. The pedagogical expectation of slave culture was to create a community of belonging so as to "redress the condition of the enslaved and restore the disrupted affiliation of the socially dead" (Hartman 1997: 51). Slave culture operated pedagogically to create a context in which slaves collectively attended to their pain. And black enjoyment was fundamental to mitigating black pain under the pressure of domination and the utter lack of autonomy. As Hartman notes, black "pleasure was central to the mechanisms of identification and recognition that discredit the claims of pain but also to those that produce a sense of possibility" (*ibid.:* 58). The possibilities that black pleasure produces consist in its redressing of black affliction by facilitating a sense of belonging (*ibid.:* 61).

The pedagogical expectations of slave culture therefore sought to forge a sense of belonging that affirmed the slaves' existence as human freedom. This occurred under oppressive conditions that denied them liberty and constituted slaves as nonautonomous subjects. Accordingly, the forms of resistance of slave pedagogy attempted to make something out of nothing, to give life purpose, by adopting, manipulating, or using imposed systems. Therefore, it strove to make do with what one had by creating a space where slaves could find ways of establishing a degree of plurality and creativity in a situation where there was no choice but to live. This is suggestive of the fact that slaves did not have the capacity to "secure a territory outside the space of domination nor the power to keep what was won in incomplete victories" (*ibid.*). However, the significance of slave culture was that it provided slave pedagogy with an orientation toward resistance that allowed slaves to refashion pleasure so as to affirm their existential freedom. But the limitation of this resistance—and, hence, of black enjoyment—is that it allowed whites to disavow black pain, to believe that blacks were incapable of feeling pain (*ibid.:* 19–23).

Nevertheless, because slave pedagogy was ultimately concerned with asserting the existential freedom of slaves, it was presupposed by hope, and thus by possibility. Ernst Bloch (1996) argues that hope is distinct from wishful dreams. He points out that wishing accomplishes nothing because there is not yet the dimension of activity and, therefore, for possibility of action. Wishful dreaming functions as a release from routine and is therefore inconsequential to disrupting the natural attitude of the life-world (Schutz 1970). This is an attitude that takes the world for granted and perceives it as self-evidently "real." The result is that wishing never threatens to unravel the everydayness of the world.

On the other hand, hope affirms openness in everyday life where it is not easily revealed by the natural attitude of everydayness. In so doing, hope is open to possibilities for human attachment, expression, and assertions of human freedom. The slaves as hopeful people acted upon possibilities by loosening and refusing the hold that taken-for-granted realities and routines had over the imagination. It was this pedagogical imagination that allowed them to redress and resist the soul-destroying capacities of affliction. Through symbolic work—that is, through their songs, stories, and rituals of confirmation, for instance—slaves taught each other the moral and ethical significance of creating a sense of community belonging. It was in forging a community of belonging that slave culture functioned pedagogically to humanize slaves by redressing their suffering—and in the process it remade blackness, a Western European white supremacist invention, into a standpoint of historical consciousness and leverage for change (e.g., Levine 1978).

Notes

1. See, for example, Levine (1978).

2. See, for example, Cone (1991); Connor (2000); Goatley (1996); Hopkins (2000); Thurman (1975); Du Bois (1999a [1903]); Gordon (1997a); McGary and Lawson (1998); Lott (1998); Lawson and Kirkland (1998); Davis and Gates (1985); and Hazzard-Gordon (1990).

3. See, for example, Gutman (1976) and Levine (1978).

4. Connor (2000: 2). See also Gordon (2000b: 6–7). Gordon argues that existential philosophy is not unique to Europeans. He writes: "The body of literature that constitutes European existentialism is but one continent's response to a set of problems that date from the moment human beings faced problems of anguish and despair. That conflicts over responsibility and anxiety, over life affirmation and suicidal nihilism, preceded Kierkegaardian formulations of fear and trembling raised questions beyond Eurocentric attachment to a narrow body of literature. Existential philosophy addresses problems of freedom, anguish, dread.... [I]t addresses these problems through a focus on the human condition." This view causes Gordon to ask skeptics "if slaves did not wonder about freedom, suffer anguish; notice paradoxes of responsibility; have concerns of agency, tremors of broken sociality, or a burning desire for liberation. Do we not find struggles with these matters in the traditional African proverbs and folktales that the slaves brought with them to the New World?"

5. Throughout the mid- to late 1930s the Works Project Administration Federal Writers Project interviewed ex-slaves. These oral testimonies were compiled and edited by Rawick (1972) into a forty-one volume series.

6. Stanley Aronowitz (1994) argues that for Patterson "to call slavery a relation of domination disputes one major claim of most recent theorists—that the slave system is defined as a mode of production in which labor is the most important social relations." Aronowitz concludes that Patterson's bold thesis—that slavery is, first and foremost, social domination—is a "step toward a radical redefinition of slavery." For a similar analysis, see David Brion Davis (1983b).

7. Patterson also writes: "If the slave no longer belongs to a community, if he had no social existence outside of this master, then what was he? The initial response in almost all slaveholding societies was to define the slave as a socially dead person" (1982: 38).

8. Gordon also writes that "race has to be understood through ontology, that is, existential ontology, not epistemology" (1998c: 108).

9. Hadot writes: "Philosophies of life ... represent a choice of life, a wish to live in such and such a way, with all the concrete consequences that implies in everyday life" (1995: 27).

10. Husserl argues that philosophy is not a natural science but rather, in his words, "a humanistic science, it is the science of the world as the surrounding world of persons, or as the world appearing to them, having validity for them" (1999: 318).

11. For further discussion on the Slave Codes, see, for example, Stampp (1956: 192-193); and on Christianity, see Raboteau (1978: 100).

12. Hartman agrees with this same point when she states that "the most invasive forms of slavery's violence lie not in these extreme exhibitions of extreme suffering or in what we see but in what we don't see. Shocking displays easily obfuscate the more mundane and socially endurable forms of terror" (1997: 42).

6
Double Consciousness and the Problem of Political Legitimacy

Jane Anna Gordon

◆

W. E. B. Du Bois offers an insightful response to a problem of political legitimacy raised by Jean-Jacques Rousseau. In both the *Discourse on the Origins of Inequality* and the *Social Contract,* Rousseau asked: Can politics and political institutions do more than rationalize the exploitation of existing natural, social, and economic inequalities? Is it possible for there to be political right? Can there be political legitimacy? Rousseau's tentative answer, that legitimate governance was republican governance, people living under laws of their own making—that political right could emerge out of the displacement of the absurd social convention of the "right" of the strongest by political bodies seeking their general will—was embedded in a larger philosophical anthropology. People could will the conditions for their ongoing shared life and, in so doing, become autonomous and self-governing. But they face an indispensable problem: They have to be able to grasp or be inspired to embrace the requirements for their own enlightenment without yet being enlightened. They would have to see with the kind of eyes that would be the fruit of their transformation. Crucially, their doing this would have to go on within and itself constitute a unit that was "general." Rousseau's efforts to bring the notion of the general will, an idea from French theology, into secular political thought, has fundamentally shaped the terrain of participatory democratic thought. Yet for all of the insight it continues to offer, its interpretation has borne the mark of its origins. Discussion of it has been locked in a theodician grammar that an engagement with double consciousness will help us to shed.

I

Theodicy is the effort to understand how God could be both benevolent and all-powerful in a world replete with undeserved suffering, unpunished injustice, and incorrigible stupidity. Even if the legitimacy of God had become irrelevant in modern life, Lewis Gordon argues, the grammar of legitimating practices has not changed. There is always something "to fill the vacuum of a lost god even if that something is the system itself" (Gordon 2003: 3).

Consider lines in Rousseau of the following type: "This is irrefutable proof that the most general will is also the most just, and that the voice of the populace is, in effect, the voice of God" (Rousseau 1987: 115). Or, "This difficulty, which must have seemed insurmountable, was removed with the first inspiration which taught man to imitate here below the immutable decrees of the divinity" (p. 117).

These claims and arguments turned scholars like Patrick Riley (1986) to the resources of intellectual history—more precisely, to documenting the origins of Rousseau's general will in French theological debates concerning the will of God to save all men. Rousseau's hope that people might "'save' the polity" by placing the common good of the city above the private interests of the particular self echoed Pascal's urging that people will with the generality he identified in God. Generality and general lawfulness, Helena Rosenblatt (1997) explains, were the way of salvation and wisdom, in contrast with the particular that was depraved, corrupt, and selfish. Mark Cladis's response is of a more sociological nature. He frames Rousseau as knowing from the history of bloodshed in the name of religion that anomie combined with clashing moral claims was dangerous. Similarly dangerous was not to attend to the need for both common faith and inwardness in the project of public life. Cladis writes, "[Rousseau] held that if a society had any shared life at all, any shared understanding and ideals and practices, then it assumes some religious form of life, even if a secular, democratic one ... [even if] the sacred emerges in the creative process of forging a common life" (2003: 212).

Carl Schmitt, the influential twentieth-century German jurist and political theorist, has combined these kinds of responses into a more searching unifying question about what it is about the very nature of politics that makes religious metaphors and grammar the most apt means through which to capture what we in the modern world seek to name and understand. He claimed that the structure of political organization that seems appropriate to a given epoch mirrors the metaphysical image that it forges of the world. In Rousseau's period, Schmitt claims, this was a sole sovereign, architect, and master builder of the world, simultaneously the creator and legislator. He could will anything but evil. The general will, then, was identical with the will of the sovereign people whose will as a citizenry was always good.

But what is the status of the "general" in the general will? For Rousseau generality is godly. It has a fixed, clear, pure quality that is evaded or ignored but never completely eradicated. The aim is for us to perceive it, grasp it, institutionalize it, knowing all the time that we are intensely limited. If we see as we must, as the Legislator can, we see with an unqualified concern and love, as if we and everyone else were transparent to us, as if we could hear their inner thoughts, longings, and rationalizations. And to hear these is to be moved by and to have responded to them. And yet, Rousseau insists, politics would cease to exist if people were godly.

It is frequently assumed that processes of secularization ease the challenges of developing a viable account of political legitimacy. Indeed, secularization and legitimization are often treated synonymously, as if the one is a clear index of the other. Actually, processes of secularization only bring to the surface a complex of issues described powerfully by Max Weber. He wrote:

> Indeed anyone living in the "world" (in the Christian sense of the word) can only feel himself subject to the struggle between multiple sets of values, each of which, viewed separately, seems to impose an obligation on him. He has to choose which of these gods he will and should serve, or when he should serve the one and when the other. But at all times he will find himself engaged in a fight against one or other of the gods of this world, and above all he will always find that he is far from the God of Christianity—or at least from the God proclaimed in the Sermon on the Mount. (Weber 1994: 78-79)

As modern human beings, a comprehensive sense of substantive right is not available to us. We cannot retreat into an absolute religious view that appears confirmed at every turn. We do not feel that the weather, the faces of others, and the fate that awaits them affirm the rightness of the view that we uphold. Even if we try, through persistent and determined assertion; to choose one god or set of values as absolute, we confront the different accounts of value in the choices of everyone else. Each such position vies for attention. The modern world suffers from an overpopulation of competing "gods." Weber continues: "As Hellenic man at times sacrificed to Aphrodite and at other times to Apollo, and, above all, as everybody sacrificed to the gods of his city, so do we still nowadays, only the bearing of man has been disenchanted and denuded of its mystical but inwardly genuine plasticity" (Weber 1946: 148). There is no overarching and unifying structure to our activity. We cannot forge one out of the splinters. We understand these gods spatially—which belongs to each domain that we must negotiate or avoid. We nervously hope that we have accounted for all of them: "What is hard for modern man, and especially for the younger generation, is to measure up to *workaday* existence" (Weber 1946: 149). We face life that can only be interpreted in its own terms. None of the many ultimately possible attitudes and values rest on secure foundations. We live with a sense that if there ever was an age of certainty, it was an interlude between more uncertain eras (Scaff 2000: 97-98). Sublime values retreat from public life, living reclusively within the mystical life and in personal brotherly relations. We struggle to imagine the possibility of really bringing together instrumental with substantive considerations.

What is more, these urgent questions—of which gods deserve praise and devotion and why they require mutually exclusive praise when their own domains are each limited—are not the kinds that modern science or any other ascendant *technique* seeks to answer. Modern science does not ask with Tolstoy: What shall we do and how shall we live? What science, soberly understood, can offer are methods for self-clarification. It can help us to give an account of the "inconvenient facts" of all of our commitments, values, or political positions. It may, in other words, be linked to developing a sense of mature limitation.

Hans Blumenberg (1983), the existential historian, defends both the project of modern life and our ability to be the source of its legitimacy. He urges that the avowed efforts in modernity to conform to the requirements of reason is not an aggression which it does not understand as such against a theology from which it actually, though in a hidden way, derived everything that belongs to it. No, insists Blumenberg, reason posited radical requirements for itself, including a self-foundation that emerges from nothing.

But, warns Ernst Cassirer, we must be alert to the extremes of rationality. We must understand human culture in humble terms and face the reality that "our science, our poetry, our art, and our religion are only the upper layer of a much older stratum that reaches down to a great depth" (Cassirer 1946: 297). This means that "we must always be prepared for violent concussions that may shake our cultural world and our social order to its very foundations" (Cassirer 1946: 297). Cassirer illustrates this point with the Babylonian creation myth of Marduk, the highest god, who must vanquish the serpent Tiamat and other dragons of darkness before he can begin his other foundational work. Marduk, as do the heroes in many other such myths, slays the serpent and binds the dragons. Having done this, he shapes the world out of their subordinated limbs. With them, he makes heaven, earth, constellations, and planets. He carefully arranges the movements of each and then, finally, he makes man (Cassirer 1946: 297; Cassirer 1955: 113-114).

We can easily become carried away in our own efforts to make the world completely rational, Cassirer cautioned, and think of the living domain of reason only in terms of rationality. We could mistake the growing rigidity of the relationship between reason and myth, on the one hand, and rationality, on the other, as a trajectory inborn in their respective lives.

Our own inability to reconcile the many domains of our lives within ourselves is mirrored in the gods that we project onto the world, gods that occupy domains that multiply in narrower and narrower forms, each promising a tiny purity, a retreat from the ever more ambiguous task of integration. We link legitimacy nostalgically to transcendent gods that no longer really live for us, that seem to have been above the challenge of instrumental reason. Such gods could carry out their intended aims with perfect knowledge. But human beings face moments when we must stand apart and constitute ourselves and our shared lives with fear and dread. Those moments promise to make us naked in our fallibility, in a skin only of weakness, before our own eyes and those of others.

But we do still make decisions and we must still act, even if we do so through indecision and inaction. A well-tried alternative is to cover ourselves in a shroud of narcissism, hoping that with time and some effort, it and we may become what we prefer.

Indeed the narcissism of modern life is literally one of mythical proportions. It is both theodician and Manichean in its form. We turn to it here, for it brings together an account of the relationship between rationality and reason with the parallel relationship of whiteness or the white to the black. In each, legitimacy is sought by asserting rationality or the white as the rightful occupant of a vacated divine domain. The recalcitrance of the world, then, is not explained by the failures of the occupant, but by the very existence of the others, the damned.

II

Consider this reflection of Lewis Gordon on what he calls "'God' in an antiblack world":

> The black is always too black. The white, on the other hand, is never white enough—except from the standpoint of the black. For the black, to be white enough is to be a human being and hence one step closer to God. But since such a goal is out of his reach, he might as well regard whiteness as divine. If the black is human, and whiteness is above blackness, then to be white is tantamount to being a god. The white is aware of this ideal. But every white is simultaneously aware of not being this ideal. To be white requires the choice of whiteness as a project. (Gordon 1995a/1999: 147)

The process of asserting the absolute status of gods that are no longer structurally absolute is also frequently to assert one's kinship to them. To be genuinely divine is to be at an unsurpassable distance from everything earthly. To make comparisons of oneself or one's race with such a God is at the least unthinkable; at worst, blasphemous hubris. But God, like whiteness, turns out to be a project. In its transcendent version, it will always be out of reach. But as soon as it becomes teleological, we may measure the relative proximities of different people and different groups to this ideal. Proximity for both whiteness and rationality is evaluated in terms of their purity, their distance from things mythic and black.

All that is not pure white is tinted black. Similarly, to be rational is to be shorn of all orienting commitments, experiences, and metaphors that might cling to one. Like whiteness, rationality is rational enough only from the perspective of reason and myth. In its own eyes, it is never sufficiently rational. Its own rationality becomes its project.

Myth, then, is, like the black, always too mythical. It no longer gives an account of making order of primeval chaos. Myth and its insights have themselves, along with the black, become the primeval chaos, the antistructure that must be eradicated for the sake of order. But there is a problem: One cannot eradicate these. In mythic terms, they are the nothingness out of which all meaning is shaped. Primeval chaos and civilization, myth and rationality, the black and the white are constituted together.

There is, however, an alternative to eradication, and that is subordination.

Paget Henry explores one dimension of such processes of subordination in his critical engagement of the formulation of reason in Jürgen Habermas's second volume of *The Theory of Communicative Action* (1984). Habermas began with concerns, shared by Edmund Husserl (1970), Max Horkheimer, and Theodor Adorno (2002), with the eclipse of self-reflective philosophical reflection by scientific rationality and sought to defend subject-centered reason against its othering by techno-scientific rationality. Habermas claims that these practices of epistemological exclusion were linked to the attempts of scientific and technocratic discourses to be self-legitimating. Everything that could not be easily absorbed had to be systematically devalued. This, in turn, necessitated the

> concealing of the shared transcendental domain within which the categories, schemas, and presuppositions of both scientific and nonscientific discourses arose. These knowledge-constitutive activities and their independence of scientific knowledge production were ignored in favor of a strong emphasis on superiority, if not universality, of the scientific method of knowing. (Henry 2000b: 92)

The difficulty, however, is that although Habermas's account of rationality has changed continuously, it has mirrored these kinds of devaluation. It has consistently been inscribed in a binary opposition, against a conceptual other, myth, with all of its attendant discursive and institutional practices. Habermas at once defined rationality in terms of structures of argumentation and as the negation of myth, distorting myth in such a way that not only contradicted the ideals of communicative action but also resulted in both an overinvestment in "the explanatory and behavior-coordinating power of language" and the devaluing of the explanatory and behavior-coordinating power of the ego/spirit that are elucidated in myth. The devaluations of both technocratic and Habermasian reason were excessive, observes Henry. What is more, he suggests, borrowing from Sylvia Wynter (1984), these processes of othering are liminal; they attempt to suppress what embody chaos or antistructure from the point of view of hegemonic discourses (Henry 2000b: 129–136).

To move beyond this compromised state of reason, Henry argues, requires perceiving and engaging the distinctive rationality of myth. What might emerge from the reinscription of myth, he suggests, is an additional set of knowledge-constitutive interests, a set concerned with "reconciliation between ego-unified worlds and the larger cosmic order ... whose rationality was being eclipsed in the modern period" (Henry 2000a: 108). By way of example, Henry suggests that what emerges from the perspective of African myths is a Western discursive economy that is

> accelerating out of control in search of a unifying center and epistemic guarantees that it rejected with its extreme othering of myth.... At the same time, there are no mythic discourses to facilitate rebalancing and the restoration of equilibrium. Many contenders have arisen to take this place left by the decline of myth in the modern West. Levi-Strauss saw politics as taking the place of myth; for Habermas, it is language, and for others it is science or art. However, ... the cultural rationalization of the West ... points to the inability of these alternatives to substitute for the unifying, grounding, and integrating powers of myth. As the West continues to ride this train and to globalize its tracks, it will continue to make great scientific discoveries and unprecedented conquests. However, these will continue to be haunted by that shadow of which Adorno and Horkheimer wrote, and with which Habermas is still wrestling. (Henry 2000a: 109)

Genuine reason would require a humbled rationality, an honest account of it as able to produce countless fractured and fragmented insights that it is unable to integrate, and it is myth, more accurately understood, that can assist in the undertaking of such unifying work.

Let us examine the similar structure of the position of the black in modernity. Think, in particular, of the practice of lynching. During the Revolutionary War in the United States, the lynched included Loyalists and British sympathizers who were tarred and feathered (first made black and then into animals associated with Native Americans).[1] In the nineteenth century mob violence in the North targeted blacks, immigrants, Mormons, and Catholics; in the South, abolitionists and rebellious slaves. Vigilante justice was the norm in Western cities and mining camps. In the "lynching era," the 1890s, the lynched also included trade unionists, immigrants, German-Americans, and Mexicans, but the vast majority of the murdered were black. The practice of lynching predated the Civil War: Beginning in the 1830s it was used to forestall rebellion and is listed in records as punishments for slaves who killed masters. Nevertheless, with the defeat of the Confederacy, Southern racial violence became more systematic. Freed people hoped to cease being chattel, to be free *de facto* instead of only *de jure*. For many others, rather than black freedom, what remained was the perception of blacks as the answer to white labor problems. Writes Anne Rice, "Many whites thus viewed as tantamount to insurrection any effort by blacks to assert their rights or improve their situation. From the earliest days of freedom, then, whites used organized violence to destroy African-American autonomy" (Rice 2003: 4).

Consider the activity that surrounded planned lynchings. People would take out ads in newspapers and circulate flyers announcing an upcoming murder. Trains were chartered to bring countless spectators and reporters:

> At some lynchings, broadsheets were sold of ballads that had been composed in advance to celebrate the event. Photographers did a brisk business selling postcards and snapshots of the torture in progress and of carefully posed portraits of the lynch party with the charred and dismembered remains. They ignored with impunity the ban on sending violent material by mail, and their products crisscrossed the nation. Although concentrated in the South, racial violence took place throughout the country. Descriptions of lynchings were standard fare in nearly every newspaper in the United States. Lynchings sold papers. (Rice 2003: 5)

Ida B. Wells-Barnett, who in her earlier days had seen lynching as a regrettable punishment for the crime of rape, quickly revised her position as she learned that many cases of "rape" were consensual relationships between white women and black men that had accidentally become public and that much more lynching was "[a]n excuse to get rid of Negroes who were acquiring wealth and property and thus [to] keep the race terrorized and 'keep the nigger down'" (quoted in Rice 2003: 6). In addition to accusations of rape and murdering whites, blacks were lynched for trying to vote, for being acquitted by a jury, for being prosperous or related to people who were such, for appearing in the "wrong places," for being "uppity," or without any offense so as to terrorize other blacks. Sutton Griggs summed this up as follows: "[T]he real 'one crime' that paves the way for a lynching whenever we have the notion, is the crime of being black" (quoted in Rice 2003: 110).

Why was it insufficient for black men, women, and children to be hanged with a noose in the town square for their "crimes" as white families picnicked and sang and took photographs? Why were the black men so frequently castrated? Why were the tongues of both lynched men and women so frequently removed? Why were the fetuses in hanging pregnant women also gruesomely extracted? Although the grammar most immediately available in this period was of a God in the shape of a white supremacist master and in black communities of Christ's crucifixion, the constituting of identity and order through dismemberment mirrors the logic of the Babylonian creation myth, which predated the work of Mani and Manicheanism that was formalized in Christian theology. The act of lynching reopened the role of Marduk, allowing ordinary white men and women to play the role of foundational heroes, who urgently created light from darkness. It is no accident that the limbs to which so much attention were paid were the tongue and the penis. Primeval chaos, after all, had to be subdued. In several instances blacks were lynched by mobs that included their own white relatives (Rice 2003: 16).

Think as well of how little black political activity is required to foster white fears of "volcanic eruptions." The intensity of violent reaction in the Reconstruction era is the first example, but another emerges in the brief period of forced school desegregation in the 1950s and the activities of the Black Power movement that signaled their failure in the late 1960s. These events led not only to the development of an independent surveillance wing in the federal government but also to the rise of the religious right, who trace their own resurgence to what they explain as the threat to U.S. culture embodied particularly in the concluding years of that 1960s decade. The activism of this period is described by its critics as if it intended the skewering of the very project of modern civilization, the protection of which, in turn, required the mobilization of all of the resources of the white world in defense of white humankind. Efforts of black people to run their own countries, or to attend schools that their tax dollars suffused, were seen by many white-dominated nations as attacks on the very notions of sovereignty, politics, education, rationality, and morality (Feagin 2000; Feagin, Vera, and Imani 1996). These tentative entrances, always brutally circumscribed, were perceived to have had the effect of "closing the American mind."

But if the myth of rationality and whiteness is that they have eradicated myth, how can we expect anything else to emerge? The epistemological limitations, the elaborate fictions, required to sustain these projects should be of concern to our efforts to articulate a viable contemporary account of political legitimacy. From where and how are reality, evidence, a commitment to communicable truth to rear their submerged heads?

Both myth and blackness, embodiments of the contradictions of the formal projects of modernity, might offer some insight. I do not want to suggest that lying within these, waiting dormant, are the answers to all of the dilemmas of the modern age. Instead what I do wish to claim is that the subordination of myth by those in search of the project of rationality and of the black by those seeking whiteness necessarily leads them to a less rigorous grasp of the reality of the modern world than might emerge from an attempt to understand the coexistent reality of all four. Rationality and whiteness are domains defined by purity, with the consequence that all that they are not is relegated to the myth and the black. The effect is that the latter two must incorporate more. The variability contained within them presents more with which to grapple—a more complex reality—than the aim, purity, allows. What is more, myth and blackness have not run from the illegitimacy ascribed to them as successfully as rationality and whiteness have from the occasional charge of that kind hurled their way.

III

Primeval chaos may be expected to roar. It is certainly not expected to generate prose. But let us consider reflection that explicitly emerges from blackness. It is here that the notion of double vision, or double consciousness, described by Du Bois, is so useful. He does not describe these as assets, as I will. They are, for him, a source of agony. He writes:

> And yet, being a problem is a strange experience,—peculiar even for one who has never been anything else, save perhaps in baby-hood and in Europe.... [T]he Negro is a sort of seventh son, born with a veil, and gifted with second-sight in this American world,— a world which yields him no true self-consciousness, but only lets him see himself through the revelation of the other world. It is a peculiar sensation, this double-consciousness, this sense of always looking at one's self through the eyes of others, of measur-ing one's soul by the tape of a world that looks on in amused contempt and pity. One ever feels this twoness,—an American, a Negro; two souls, two thoughts, two unreconciled strivings; two warring ideals in one dark body, whose dogged strength alone keeps it from being torn asunder." (Du Bois 1982: 45)

To be a problem is strange, even for those for whom it is a familiar and only "normal" condition. Veiled and gifted, those with double consciousness live in an American world that sees them as possess-ing no "true self-consciousness," as unable to perceive themselves through their own eyes, unable to measure their own value. Double consciousness in such a context is an experience of irreconcilable twoness with no horizon of integration. Du Bois continues:

> The history of the American Negro is the history of this strife,— this longing to attain self-conscious manhood, to merge his double self into a better and truer self. In this merging he wishes neither of the older selves to be lost. He would not Africanize America, for America has too much to teach the world and Africa. He would not bleach his Negro soul in a flood of white Americanism, for he knows that Negro blood has a message for the world. (Du Bois 1982: 46)

The maturity that Weber so strongly endorsed, that he described so many of his contemporaries as using all of their resources to escape or shun, is the project of the black American in Du Bois's account. In the absence of such reconciliation, what emerges is waste, from the waste of the powers of body and mind—"the powers of single black men flash here and there like falling stars, and die sometimes before the world has rightly gauged their brightness" (Du Bois 1982: 46)—to the waste of double aims and of a black message to the world that meaningful history is far from complete.[2] Du Bois elaborates:

> No Negro who has given earnest thought to the situation of his people in America has failed, at some time in life, to find himself at these cross-roads; has failed to ask himself at some time: What, after all, am I? Am I an American or am I a Negro? Can I be both? ... [S]uch incessant self-questioning and the hesitation that arises from it ... is making the present period a time of vacillation and contradiction. (Du Bois 1998: 272)

Du Bois argued that although "the children of Emancipation" had sensed their own powers and mission, that to affirm their place in the world they would need to be themselves, they felt helpless before the ideals of civilization that they were ready also to revere. They encountered the humiliation that came of a readiness to ignore the best of everything black while embracing the worst. They inculcated this disdain that led quickly to a self-disparaging lowering of expectations and aspirations. Du Bois's own response was to call for the development of race organizations, designed at every step to wed the projects of study, education, and political and economic progress together with the charge that U.S. institutions hire and reward on the basis of merit. When doing this work, the double consciousness that seemed a liability emerges, however tentatively, as a strength. In both *Darkwater* and "The Study of Negro Problems," where he does not refer explicitly to double consciousness, he exemplifies what a twoness reveals when it looks back. Take, for example, his *Darkwater* essay "The Souls of White Folk." He writes:

> Not as a foreigner do I come, for I am native, not foreign, bone of their thought and flesh of their language. Mine is not the knowledge of the traveler or the colonial composite of dear memories, words and wonder. Nor yet is my knowledge that which servants have of masters, or mass of class, or capitalist of artisan. Rather I see these souls undressed and from the back and side. I see the

working of their entrails. I know their thoughts and they know
that I know. This knowledge makes them now embarrassed, now
furious. They deny my right to live and be and call me misbirth!
My word is to them mere bitterness and my soul, pessimism. And
yet as they preach and strut and shout and threaten, crouching
as they clutch at rags of facts and fancies to hide their naked-
ness, they go twisting, flying by my tired eyes and I see them ever
stripped—ugly, human. (Du Bois 1999/1920: 17)

White folks appear transparent to the onlooker with double consciousness. For those who are most likely to possess it, blacks, are born as
black people of the thought and language of the project of white
modernity. Most significant, the eyes that see in two are felt by whites.
They attempt to put off this penetrating and solid gaze through denial,
framing it only as the eyes of resentment and resignation. The unaffected
look is not that. While caught in resentment and resignation it is not
double consciousness that emerges, but an envy that desperately affirms
a desire for whiteness. Double vision sees through the shrouds of the
narcissistic whiteness that aggressive "speech" attempts to buttress.

Du Bois continues that "personal whiteness" is a "very modern
thing,—a nineteenth and twentieth century matter," one that the ancient world would have mocked. But suddenly, whiteness is serious
and wonderful. When, or if ever, asked why whiteness is so desirable,
it is because "whiteness is the ownership of the earth forever and
ever, Amen!" (Du Bois 1999/1920: 18). For Du Bois, his own suffering
is outweighed by a pity for people so enthralled and imprisoned by
their own fantasies. He mocks the idea of a nation like the United
States, for which "I am white" seems the one fundamental tenet of
practical morality, trying to make the world safe for democracy:

Murder may swagger, theft may rule and prostitution may flourish
and the nation gives but spasmodic, intermittent and lukewarm
attention. But let the murderer be black or the thief brown or
the violator of womanhood have a drop of Negro blood, and the
righteousness of the indignation sweeps the world. Nor would this
fact make the indignation less justifiable did not we all know that
it was blackness that was condemned and not crime. (Du Bois
1999/1920: 20)

Not everyone is taken in by this white seriousness. Some see with eyes
able to be made old by experience of the world. Du Bois continues:

We whose shame, humiliation, and deep insult his aggrandizement so often involved were never deceived. We looked at him clearly, with world-old eyes, and saw simply a human thing, weak and pitiable and cruel, even as we are and were. These super-men and world-mastering demi-gods listened, however, to no low tongues of ours, even when we pointed silently to their feet of clay. (Du Bois 1999/1920: 20)

It is not that there are black Americans who are not weak, pitiable, and cruel. Du Bois is fully aware that black people are, after all, human beings. What is different and significant is that blacks do not frame their failings as the height to which humanity itself might soar in emulation. But then there is nothing that makes people cling more to their claims to being human than the experience of this being actively and consistently denied. The honest mirror offered in the reflection of black eyes was, and is, ignored. But what is the actual content of these low tones? Du Bois writes:

But may not the world cry back at us and ask: "What better thing have you to show? What have you done or would do better than this if you had today the world rule? Paint with all riot of hateful colors the thin skin of European culture,—is it not better than any culture that arose in Africa or Asia?"

Du Bois gives a resounding "no" and continues:

Why, then, is Europe great? Because of the foundations which the mighty past have furnished her to build upon: the iron trade of ancient black Africa, the religion and empire-building of yellow Asia, the art and science of the "dago" Mediterranean shore, east, south, and west, as well as north. And where she has builded securely upon this great past and learned from it she has gone forward to greater and more splendid human triumph; but where she has ignored this past and forgotten and sneered at it, she has shown the cloven hoof of poor, crucified humanity,—she has played, like other empires gone, the world fool! (Du Bois 1999/1920: 23)

Blumenberg's identification of the desire to create modernity *ex nihilo* reads with a different ring here. What is being erased is a history of human achievement upon which Europe was able to build. Her greatness emerges in moments where she is a culmination of human struggle. Her actual attempts at rootless creation reveal her feet of clay, a distorted and gruesome self-image.

The degrading of men by men is not new; neither is the using of men by other men who call themselves masters. What is unique to the project of white Europe is the scale and elaborateness; the culminating "width of the thing,—the heaven-defying audacity—makes its modern newness" (Du Bois 1999/1920: 24). And more:

> But what of the darker world that watches? Most men belong to this world. A belief in humanity is a belief in colored men. If the uplift of mankind must be done by men, then the destinies of this world will rest ultimately in the hands of darker nations. (p. 27)

Most of the world is dark. To speak of humanity, then, is to insist on the humanity of darkness. This problem of mankind can be formulated only by human beings. Its fate will lie in dark hands.

From Du Bois's perspective, the aspiration to freedom is never a search for unbridled license. He tries to imagine what a political economy in which people were not wasted would be like. This is linked as well to the conclusion of his essay concerning studying black problems. There he frames both the study and the uplifting of black people as more than a private community's aims, eventual accomplishment as more than the triumph of one minority group. For Du Bois, then, blacks must not seek whiteness, not only because it is not available to them—there may be an individual white black, but "white blacks"?—but because everyone, white and black, should aim higher. To do this requires seeking something other than an idealized image of oneself or one's race. In a poem entitled "The Riddle of the Sphinx" that appears in *Darkwater,* he sees our burden as adulthood (Du Bois 1999/1920: 31). In *The Souls of Black Folk,* the aspiration is always the freedom to realize individual and collective potential in work, reflection, love, and politics. The project of the human being then emerges as teleological.

Du Bois rejects identities that pose as universal. And he does so as he opts for identities defined fundamentally by the limitations of social stigmatization. Recall how rationality and whiteness were posited as divine and pure, as ultimate projects. A universal status was claimed for both. They were right, for everyone and everything, for all times—even those preexisting them. Their own efforts to be universal and absolute, however, required the ongoing and radically violent suppression of all that was different. What is more, their own efforts at self-definition and self-legitimation were possible only through the caricature of the alternatives.

To be particular is to be linked to the small and the local, to the details of mundane life. Those seeking particularity often valorize being parochial, for being so is associated with living authentically, immediately, intensely, without the kind of distance required to translate the significance of one's efforts to others. It would seem, then, that one cannot be both particular and historic, for as soon as something is historic, it would, by definition, have broader scope and significance. In the modern world, myth and blackness have been characterized as the embodiments of particularity, the antitheses of universal whiteness that is not only historic but the ultimate culmination, the completion, of historicity as such.

But there is an ironic dimension to the conclusion of black particularity. How can something be *the* embodiment of the particular and not itself be historic? A particular town, tribe, or tune may have meaning that is only local, but once one has become a prototype of the particular, the meaning of one's existence has become emblematic, useful analogically and metaphorically, to make sense of conditions beyond one's time and place. But is the historic significance of blackness and myth accidental? Are these simply the product of the quest of whiteness for the status of what Lewis Gordon (1995a/1999: Part IV) has called *Absolute Being*?

Blackness and the mythic demotion of myth are both linked to the very meaning of modernity in the West. They are its contradictions, and significantly for our purposes, in reminding us of submerged, coextensive realities, they point to the possible meaning and significance of generality.

Generality or the general is always limited. For it is with a sense of its limits that self-definition, responsibility, and maturity can emerge. The opposite, supposed limitlessness, is linked to the project of universality. To be without limits is never to face the task of integration, for one can simply continue to seek out open terrain. Collective limitlessness is not possible. But if generality is to be general, the limits that centrally define it must also be permeable and shifting. Generality is never too neat. It coexists with other generalities, with differences that it need not obliterate for its self-constitution. Double consciousness is a model of epistemological generality, of what comes of the project of mature reconciliation in the face of limitations. It suggests how we should read "the general" in the general will.

IV

Returning to our initial Rousseauian formulations, we are now compelled to ask: Is the consequence of Rousseau's claims about what is necessary to legitimate politics—cosmopolitanism? For although the units for which the general will may be general may be limited and local, these units need to relate to one another in a way that is also political and legitimate.

The answer must be "no." Cosmopolitanism is a "politics" articulated against writers like Schmitt who have suggested that identities must be developed in antagonism, through an identification of extreme and threatening difference. My use of "cosmopolitanism" here is based in its Greek etymology, "kosmopolitês" or citizen of the world. Cosmopolitans, who draw their position from this classic notion, seek to inhabit the world as a city, emphasizing what is shared in our various local conditions, elucidating what links each to all (Held 1995). The major difficulties with this position are two: The first, as so many writers have pointed out, is that this may be a rational solution, but it underestimates how we actually feel affective connections (Smith 2003). This is not to say that intimacy is linked only to physical proximity. As Anne Norton (2004) has observed about contemporary life, the model of associations is the web or network of people who cohere around increasingly specific concerns and identities. If physical proximity is not the only criterion for intimacy, it is still the opposite of what is suggested by generic relations. One cannot feel universally. There is, as well, a greater problem for us. Cosmopolitanism downplays the extent to which international relations and mobility are premised upon genuine, precarious, and very incomplete political achievements. Its advocates seek a final triumph of rationality that might work if we were only like the gods.

Generality does not emerge easily, however. Consider the concluding lamentation of Sheldon Wolin's *Politics and Vision: Continuity and Innovation in Western Political Thought* (1960):

> From an examination of recent theorizing, it is fairly clear that a
> reaction against some of the major categories of political thought

has occurred.... Expressed in a somewhat awkward way, it is a
reaction against the general nature of traditional political theory
and, along with this, against the claims of the political to a scope
as wide as society itself. (p. 429)

He explains further that for most of the history of Western thought,
what is "political" is what is general to a society, general responsibili-
ties, broader than the parochial units of family, class, or sect. Against
this history, recent social and political theory has turned to smaller
groupings and local associations, adamantly arguing that there are
no general human needs beyond peace and defense that require the
integrative forms of political life. What is relegated to the political
order are largely administrative functions. He writes:

In this way, the political order comes to occupy the status of
residuary legatee, shouldering those tasks which other groups or
organizations are unwilling or unable to perform. But always there
is the hope of steadily reducing the number of political functions
and always the attempt to add one more political function to the
groups. (p. 431)

The political order is a vestige of a legacy in decline and thus unable
to make constructive demands. It takes on tasks that are unwanted
by other, still vibrant, spheres of life. If it is only administrative and
technical, it is no longer politics. For politics and political theory to
continue requires a return to questions of what is general to and
of what integrates human beings.

Is generality itself in shorter supply or only the willingness to
pursue it? Does the denial of its reality have the effect of eliminating what of it may actually remain?

At the level of descriptive life, generality does appear to be in
danger. The language used to describe what people are seems to
narrow against the reality of our multiple and sloppily unified selves.
Fixing these appears as an attempt to mobilize fighting words, a
will to power in a context of seemingly perpetual war. Indeed, one
might wonder whether collective identities can still be formulated
without military conflict. But then, it is not clear that identities
formed for war are general, particularly if wars are sought out to
sustain the very meaning of sovereign identity in crisis. Does this
suggest less that grounds for generality are gone than that they are

actively suppressed? That the antagonism toward generality that Wolin described is an indication that it does still have life? That there are meaningful ways in which differences continue to have things in common?

The mass quality of contemporary democracies does appear to pose fundamental problems for the generality that politics requires. There is not only an antagonism toward genuinely standing out, there is a sense that when individuals do "stand out" they cease to be part of "the people" who collectively are the source of legitimacy.[3] Generality requires genuine diversity, whereas the desire to be a source of legitimacy without individual responsibility would seem to make inevitable a "politics" that is actually perpetual war. For in war, strategy requires the fixing of identities of "we" and "them" in a state of emergency that erases distinction and ambiguity.[4]

Conclusion

We have considered some of the ways in which we attempt to wriggle out of the responsibility for the legitimacy of the modern age that rests firmly in our laps and the mythic forms that our avoidance takes on. From Du Bois there is more than the world that the absolute projects of modernity seek. Indeed, from these historic experiences of particularity emerged a vision of the generality to which Rousseau referred. Rooted in time and place, the general is fundamentally defined by an embrace of limitations through which the project of integration and maturity might emerge. These limitations, because shared and social, are necessarily permeable. If a project were made of their rigidity we would be stuck again. But we may already be, for there is a deep suspicion of the very notion of generality, of claims as broad as societies themselves. This antagonism may ironically be reassuring. It can be read as an instance of a consolation offered by Cassirer that the social world, like the natural world, has a logic with rules that cannot be violated without impunity.

There is a final ironic dimension. It is when we seek projects in the world, for the world, rather than idealized narratives of ourselves, that we most manifest attributes that are uniquely human, those invoked by the idea of legitimate self-governance. Our efforts to be God are profane. Our efforts to be human, to make a purpose of understanding our own and our community's role in a world replete with powers beyond our control, may actually point toward unities that are not violent. They may, in a word, be mythic.

Notes

1. The term "lynching" is reputed to have its namesake in Colonel Charles Lynch of Virginia, a brutal vigilante in the Revolutionary period who was known for executing his victims without putting them to trial.

2. By contrast, for all of Du Bois's criticisms of Booker T. Washington, he writes of him: "this very singleness of vision and thorough oneness with his age is a mark of the successful man" (p. 81).

3. This is one of the central reasons why representation posed such a problem for Rousseau. Democratic participation required everyone or no one. Individuals with responsibility for representing the collective will quickly became representatives, a class of people with their own interests and their own status-specific, epistemological commitments.

4. A striking feature of contemporary war is that it is war without individual men and women who are heroes. The only individuals who seem to emerge alone are those who become icons of victimization—who, like the American soldier Jessica Lynch, point at the nastiness of the antagonist rather than at any legitimate cause of "our" own.

7
On the Possibilities of Posthumanism, or How to Think Queerly in an Antiblack World

David Ross Fryer

⊸

The Problem

We live in an antiblack world.[1] We live in an antiqueer world. An antipoor world, an antiwoman world, an anti-Semitic world,[2] an anticommunity world.

An antiblack world takes blackness as inferior; and an antiblack world takes all things it stands against as black and takes blackness as including all things it stands against.

The black man is effeminate. The black man is poor. The black man is a criminal. The black man is infiltrating our community. The black man is taking the white man's job. The black woman is a welfare mother. The black woman is a crack addict. Addiction is a black problem. Poverty is a black problem. Crime happens only in the black ghetto. The gay man is spreading AIDS, which is the gay man's disease. AIDS comes from Africa. AIDS is an African disease. AIDS is a black disease. The gay man isn't a real man. Neither is the black man. The lesbian hates men. The black lesbian hates them even more than the white lesbian. No one is lower than the black whore.

In an antiblack world, anything that stands in opposition to the norm is feared, denigrated, held down, cast out. In an antiblack world, slavery is not a distant memory; rather, it haunts us as the very notion of freedom comes under attack in our day.

Our world hates Jews; Muslims; women; queers; criminals; the poor; and blacks.

We live in an antiblack world.

The Preliminaries

I am an ethicist. This means that I explore how we, as human beings, ought to act in the world—this world. The overarching issues that we ethicists explore in our work can be summed up in the single question: What are the ethical imperatives of being human? Changing (healing, *mending*) the world is, as I see it, *the* ethical imperative. Among the particulars that concern me in this regard are questions such as: What is the value of identity, and how should we comport ourselves to identities in the world? How do cultural and linguistic norms shape and constrain us in our efforts to engage in meaningful living? What does the fulfillment of one's possibilities entail? Issues of racial, gender, and sexual identity and their origins, meanings, and usefulness are central for me in studying these questions and thus for the project of ethics itself. This chapter attempts to weave together these themes in a new way. It begins with a series of questions and unfolds in an attempt to provide answers.

Contrary to how most academics go about studying ethics in the predominantly analytical world of philosophy and religious studies, I argue from the perspective that questions of the *ought* are fundamentally bound up with questions of the *is*. In fact, I would say that it is precisely in the *is* that we find the *ought;* that is, it is precisely in describing actual human reality, as we live it, that we not only see the origin of the ethical imperative but also learn how we ought to act in particular situations. As I argue from a phenomenological perspective, this claim is all the more potent, since, from a phenomenological perspective, every act of description is at the same time an act of constitution; that is, whenever we describe the world, we are, in a very real sense, remaking it. While I do offer answers to some of my questions, I by no means want to suggest that they are final answers. Or, at the very least, to the extent that they are, I hope that they are final in the Hegelian sense—that is, finalities that do not foreclose the task of thinking but, rather, open it up again.

We live in an antiblack world. We live in an antiqueer world. An antipoor world, an antiwoman world, an anti-Semitic world, an anticommunity world.

Some of us want to change it.

We draw upon various histories when we attempt to change things: histories of the oppressor and of the oppressed; of the self and of the other; of the good and of the bad; of universalism and of particularism; of transcendence and of immanence; and, perhaps most poignantly, of the master and of the slave. Drawing upon these histories is no simple task, for it is all too easy simply to take sides, one against the other, losing sight of the value of the other or falling prey to the myopia of the one.

Is there another way to draw upon these histories? Is there another way to answer the call of resistance and social change? Is there another way to think of the human other than through the not so useful categories of humanism and antihumanism? Is there another way to be humane? In short, what are the possibilities of *posthumanism* in an antihuman(e) world?

The Opening Gambit

Let us begin by posing a deceivingly simple question:

Is phenomenology queer?

The question is not mine. It was asked to me by another.

In June 2001, in Providence, Rhode Island, at the first meeting of the Phenomenology Roundtable,[3] in response to a presentation I had just made on gender identity and phenomenology, Lewis Gordon asked me: "Is phenomenology inherently queer?" In my presentation, I had suggested that a turn to phenomenology was the best—and indeed the only—way to theorize gender identity in nonnormative ways without falling into the trap of the positivism latent in the antinormative critiques of poststructuralism. I had discussed the early work of Judith Butler and more recent work in transgender theory (specifically, photographic work by Loren Cameron [1996] and theory by Riki Wilchins [1997]). I argued that Butler's poststructuralist account of performativity, though subversive, was ultimately inadequate for the task of thinking gender beyond a binary construction, and I found in Cameron's photography and Wilchins's thinking clear manifestations of a queerness that moved beyond the gender binary in ways foreclosed by Butler's thought. Gender theory was stuck, I argued, when it came to the issue of queer identity. I postulated that Husserlian transcendental phenomenology might be the way out of this impasse, and called for a return to it as a method (if not *the* method) of thinking gender and sexual identity beyond positivism, in both its constructive and negative forms.

Gordon's question arose out of this presentation.[4] And upon our struggling with it, an entire series of other questions arose. The reflections that follow chart this course.

The Queer Issue

The question of the human manifests itself in several regional ontologies or ways of being, the most interesting ones for me being queer, race, and feminist theory. As we explore the question of whether or not phenomenology is queer, we must first go into one of these regional ontologies and inquire into its constituting term. So we ask the question: What does it mean for something/someone to be "queer"?

"Queer" is a relatively new term in the academy. Teresa de Lauretis introduced it into academic discourse as a *technical* term in 1991 for an issue of *Differences: A Journal of Feminist Cultural Studies.* She used it as a description of gay and lesbian studies, but it has since grown to take on several different meanings. Today, "queer" tends to be used in two ways: as an umbrella term that signifies gay, lesbian, bisexual, transgender, intersexed, and questioning communities, and as a descriptive term that signifies an identity or a stance that opposes the essentialism and normativity that are implied in the terms "gay," "lesbian," and "bisexual." It is the second meaning that holds the most interest for our purposes, and it is this meaning that we need to interrogate.[5]

In this second sense of the term, "queer" is used as an adjective that describes nonnormative gendered and sexual identities, actions, stances, practices, subject-positions, linguistic operations, and theoretical stances, both within and beyond the academy. Those of us who use the term "queer" in this way, and who call ourselves "queer" in this way, are making a statement that our goal in our work and in our lives is not primarily (or perhaps even at all) to be included in the discourses and practices from which we have historically and personally been excluded, though the emancipatory goal of gay and lesbian liberation movements is still on our minds. We are not primarily seeking access to mainstream culture and acceptable society; we are not asking that the concentric circles of identity-based movements for inclusion be expanded one last time to allow us room at the table of the American dream; rather, we are taking a stance against normative thinking, against being "normalized" at the sake of our own identities and the rights of others (who have not yet gained access to the table). We are making a statement that, contrary to the commonly heard position of the gay and lesbian couples seeking the right to marry, who invariably get interviewed on the television show *20/20*, we are *not* "just like everyone else." The desire to be like everyone else, we say, is a desire to be accepted not for who we are but, rather, for whom or what others want us to be. The desire to be like everyone else is the death-knell of a radical politics, the signal of assimilation, and the end of the struggle for the true emancipation of human possibilities. No, we are not like everyone else, nor do we wish to be seen that way. Rather, we are a challenge to much of what straight society holds dear. We are, in fact, a *danger.*[6]

As I have pondered the question "Is phenomenology queer?" over the past few years, I have struggled with what I mean by "queer" when I use it as an antinormative stance. More to the point, I have struggled with how I can reconcile such an antinormative stance with my philosophical inclination toward phenomenology, whose main tenet is that we suspend all presuppositions and agendas in our search for the truth and engage in a truly critical exploration in which nothing is sacred—not the normative and not the antinormative. So I thought more about those of us who use the term "queer" in the second sense that I cited above. And I asked the following questions: In what sense are we queers *not* "just like everyone else"? In what sense are we a danger? Are all of us queers polyamorous communists engaging in sadomasochistic threesomes? Are we all tattooed, pierced, and shaven (or very hairy), decked out in leather or drag? Many of us are some or all of these things and proud of it. But we are not all of these things, and not all for quite the same reasons.

Upon further reflection, it seems to me that my second sense of the term "queer" needs to be broken down into two subcategories: (1) queer as antinormative thought and (2) queer as postnormative thinking. The desire to fight the norm manifests itself in both of these.

In the first subcategory, the norm is seen as a substantive enemy by virtue of its opposition to those of us who stand outside of it; it is a set of beliefs—thoughts—that need to be undermined by positing directly challenging beliefs. Here polyamory (loving many people) challenges monogamy, sadomasochism challenges vanilla sex (i.e, "plain" sex), threesomes challenge the couple, and polysexuality (sexual desire for many sexualities/genders) challenges monosexuality (sexual desire for one sexuality/gender). But it doesn't stop there, for being queer is about challenging more than how we have sex. It is also about how we relate to our own bodies and identities and the meanings we attach to them. So, the modified body challenges the unadorned one; the transsexual body challenges the unaltered one; and the transgendered identity (people who don't fall into transsexual or transvestite categories and also not single-gendered ones) challenges the traditional one. Genderfuck (an act of "fucking with" or playing with gender roles) challenges gender normativity. Genderqueer challenges everything.

This is a powerful stance, this sense of the term "queer." But is it phenomenologically sound? Is phenomenology, in other words, queer like that?

I am compelled to answer no to both of these questions, at least on the first go, for it seems to me that if one is queer in these ways for the reason that I suggested above—that is, for the very reason of challenging the normative status quo—then queer we are, phenomenological we are not, for we are failing to take a truly critical stance, one that interrogates all of our assumptions, not simply the ones that we associate with dominant thought. And so, in pondering Gordon's question, I wondered if there was a different sense of the term "queer" that might be compatible with phenomenology, and so I came to develop the second subcategory of this second meaning of the term "queer": queer as a postnormative stance.

In this subcategory, the norm isn't necessarily a substantive enemy, although it might turn out to be in particular cases or for particular persons. Rather, in this subcategory, the norm is a methodological enemy. What we are at odds with, what we challenge, what we reject and replace when we think in a way that is queer, is normative thinking, not normative thought.

Normative thinking is the kind of thinking where we accept the world as given to us, where we do not question the assumptions that underlie our everyday goings on, and where we do not see our role in the world as critical thinking. Normative thinking is the kind of nonthinking we engage in when we refer to an unnamed doctor as "he" or picture the president fifty years from now as white. Normative thinking is the kind of nonthinking we engage in when we ask our children if they want to have children when they get married or assume that our co-workers are straight. Normative thinking is the kind of nonthinking we engage in when we take for granted the way the world seems to be.

Queer thinking is postnormative. Postnormative thinking does not assume that all professionals are white, that all presidents will be men, or that all people are straight. Nor does it simply posit that blacks are professionals too, that someday the president will be a woman, or that some of us aren't straight. It calls into question these assumptions that normative culture has about the world and that we, when we fail to think, let structure our thoughts. To think queerly is to think, *really to think,* about gender, sex, sexuality, and indeed all forms of identity and expression as open to various instantiations, as having multiple, even infinite modalities, as never what we assume them to be from surface appearances or uninterrogated presuppositions. To think queerly, then, is to make room for the tattoos, piercings, transsexuality, genderfuck, s&m, group sex, polyamory, and intersexuality (having both female and male sex characteristics), as well as monosexuality (hetero and homo), monogamy, and vanilla sex—all as potential ways of being human. To think queerly is to recognize that most of us occupy identities in bad faith, and to choose consciously not to do so ourselves. Queer thinking is critical thinking through and through.

In these ways, queer thinking—and this second subcategory of the second meaning of the term *queer*—means refusing to be what others tell us to be simply because they tell us to be that. And since both Freud and Foucault were definitely on to something, queer thinking also means refusing to accept who we think we are without having interrogated it simply because it seems natural to us.

Queer thinking, in this sense of the term, is clearly postnormative.

Queer as Phenomenology

Now, having in large part already predetermined our answer, we can return to Gordon's question and ask it again:
Is phenomenology queer?

If phenomenology is precisely our ability to suspend the natural attitude, to call into question and put out of play the normative thinking that dominates our everyday life and to replace it with a critical eye that questions until it discovers the true and infinitely thematized possibilities of being human, and if by "queer" we mean the type of thinking that suspends compulsory heteronormative thinking in favor of exploring the possibilities that lie beyond our narrow lenses of straightness without either falling into a mere reification of its assumptions (what I call "straight-gay") or simply setting itself up as an oppositional paradigm (what I call "anti-straight-gay"), then the answer is, quite simply, yes. If phenomenology and queer thinking are both forms of postnormative thinking, then they very clearly converge.

The Question of the Human

Queer theory is but one regional ontology in the human sciences, of course, and now knowing that phenomenology is queer, we wonder what this tells us about phenomenology, queer thinking, and human studies more broadly. For being queer is but one modality of being human, and thinking queerly is but one modality of human thinking. And so, compelled to discover the implications of our inquiry and looking toward the larger issues that they entail, we ask the broader question so that we can explore these larger issues and ultimately come back to our initial questions of ethics. To get there, we now ask this:

What is it to be human?

This is the question of the human sciences—the overarching question for which each branch seeks an answer from the perspective of its ontological presuppositions. For instance, at the most basic level, biology can answer the question in terms of life, reproduction, or evolution, while psychology can answer at the level of psyche, cognition, behavior, or neuronal activity, while religious studies can answer in terms of faith, awe, and ritual, while sociology can answer in terms of sociality, membership, and demographics. The question of what it means to be a human being is at the heart of all the fields and disciplines of human studies; indeed, it is the question that constitutes the category itself. Nowhere is it more important a question than in the discipline that we might broadly construe as "philosophy."

Elsewhere I have argued that in the history of our addressing the question of the human in the modern West, there are three basic approaches that we have taken—the humanist, the antihumanist, and the posthumanist. I associated the humanist vision both with the self-defining subjects of (for instance) Husserl (1970) and Sartre (1984) and with the essences of the human put forth by (for instance) Descartes (1999), Rawls (1971), and Habermas (1985). I associated the antihumanist vision with both the social constructionist claims of (for instance) Berger and Luckmann (1967), the communitarian claims of (for instance) MacIntyre (1981), and the poststructuralist claims of (for instance) Foucault (1970) and Lacan (1981). I then made the claim that the humanist vision was fundamentally naive and could not withstand the antihumanist critique, and that philosophy now finds itself in what I called a posthumanist landscape—that is, one in which humanism has had to reformulate itself, absorb the antihumanist critique, and emerge in a new form. I labeled this new form "posthumanism" and associated the posthumanist vision with Emmanuel Levinas's (1991) philosophy of the other. What bound together each of these three approaches was its subject matter—the human—and its question—What is it to be human? I still find this approach a useful one. However, in pondering the question of the queerness of phenomenology, two things happened. First, I found myself returning to this heuristic and, while finding it adequate for the task for which I formulated it (an analysis of the ideas of Emmanuel Levinas and Jacques Lacan), I found it inadequate for the task of thinking the question of queerness, for queerness doesn't easily fit into any of these three schema. Second, I found myself returning to both Husserl and Sartre (especially Husserl) and reconsidering the naiveté that I had previously ascribed to them. So, I now return to this threefold categorization to see if there is another way of thinking—one that might be helpful here and now.[7]

Let me now put forth a new historico-theoretical schema for how philosophy has attempted to approach the question of the human by redefining these three theoretical stances: humanism, antihumanism, and posthumanism.

Humanism: The attempt to think human history has been dominated by attempts to answer the question, What is the essence of the human person? "Humanism" is a slippery term that denotes many things to many people, but at its base humanism is a theoretical stance, a statement that there is something universal to the human that we can ascertain and that we ought to champion in the face of all attempts at dehumanization. What I would call "humanisms" attempt to define the essence(s) of the human person, and do so by identifying what they believe to be the foundational qualities that all human beings have.[8] This is a noble cause and a noble stance. Unfortunately, the history of humanism has long suffered from myopia—a shortsightedness to its presumptions and overgeneralizations. Historically, humanism, in its various instantiations, has most often put forth positions that reflect the basic cultural-philosophical meanings that are already dominant in a particular society or culture. Hence, humanism has rarely moved beyond the uninterrogated belief systems of society.[9] It is, in other words, normative.

Antihumanism: If humanism's question concerns the essence of the human person, antihumanism challenges the idea of essentialism and claims that the human person is fundamentally a contingent construction. Specifically, antihumanism emerges in opposition to the very center of humanism itself by undermining the very idea of an essence by, for instance, showing how specific claims to essence(s) have been particular, not universal, or by showing how such posited essences are fictive, further offering an explanation as to how such fictions have come to be seen as real. Antihumanism, then, is a theoretical position that criticizes humanism's myopic universalism by calling our attention to the social, cultural, and linguistic constitution of the human being. However, like humanism, antihumanism has its shortcomings; for it, too, has its presuppositions that it fails to call into question and, in so doing, remains primarily a reactionary position. In this respect it fails to undermine, in any meaningful way, the dominant thought paradigm that it challenges. As Derrida (1972, 1988) has rightly shown us time and again, oppositional thinking remains caught up in the very system it claims to challenge. This suggests that humanism and antihumanism are two sides of the same coin. Is there a way out of this bind?

Posthumanism: Posthumanism, I believe, is the way out. Posthumanism takes humanism's desire to battle dehumanization and antihumanism's suspicion of too-easily-found universals and steps back in its attempt to understand the human. Posthumanist theorists engage in a historically informed search for the transcendental, the realm in which all humanity takes part but that which is beyond any singular manifestation or understanding of the human. Posthumanism instead defines the human person through the possible modalities of being human as such, and recognizes that these modalities are subject to historical forces that might not only occlude them but also make them inaccessible at any moment in time. In this way, posthumanism hears the warnings of antihumanism without giving up the hope of humanism. Posthumanism may still search for essences, but these are phenomenological, not substantive essences. That is, they are not qualities we as human beings possess but are possibilities of being and acting in which we as human beings may take part. In this way, they are "open" essences, not "closed" ones.[10]

Phenomenology and the Question of the Human

Where does this lead us?

Back to phenomenology.

For now we want to know how this question of the human and these theoretical schools that ask it line up with the method that we have been endorsing since the beginning of this chapter. And so we now ask the question:

Is phenomenology posthumanist?

To begin, most work that I would place in the category of humanism turns out to be complicit with the natural attitude. This is both a historical and a theoretical claim. Foucault (1990) and Sylvia Wynter (in this volume) provide excellent historical analyses of humanisms that are shown to be founded on basic uninterrogated presuppositions.[11] From a theoretical standpoint, attempts at discovering the substantive essence(s) of the human begin from a prejudiced belief about the nature of the human that is not supported by phenomenological investigations.

Further, it should be clear that most work that I would place in the category of antihumanism could also be shown to be complicit with the natural attitude, albeit from a position in direct contrast to the humanist one. For instance, in *Gender Trouble,* Judith Butler (1999) offers an antihumanist critique of gender identity. Her critique, while claiming to undermine the positivism of both antifeminist biological accounts of the essence of sex and second-wave feminist accounts of the essence of woman, turns out to rely (unaware that it is doing so, I claim) on the very positivist assumptions of its target. Specifically, Butler offers a strong criticism of so-called objective biology in which she shows that some of the scientists working on sex and gender (she cites the work of David Page, in particular) presuppose the very categories of male and female that they are trying to explain. In doing so, Butler cites the work of feminist scientist Anne Fausto-Sterling. Butler's criticism is out of place in the book, and one wonders what role she intended the criticism to play. I claim that Butler's project relies on an appeal to natural science precisely because her project fails to go beyond the positivist assumptions that inform the positions that she is herself opposing. If what the scientists are saying is true, then she is wrong and her argument stops. However, if what they are saying can be shown to be unreliable because it rests upon unproven premises—in other words, if what they are saying is false—then Butler's argument can proceed apace. Either way, Butler has failed to move beyond the positivist assumption that (hard, objective, and natural) science deserves its status as the final court of appeals. Instead of showing how the very concept of rooting a study of gender in science necessarily fails on theoretical grounds, Butler takes on the particular scientists of gender to expose their work as problematically unscientific. Put crudely, instead of arguing that science is bad, Butler exposes bad science, thereby failing to challenge the status of positivist science itself, and thereby reinscribing the very positivism that underlies the work she is challenging.[12]

This leaves open the possibility, then, that in the category of posthumanism we can place the type of philosophical work that is rooted in the phenomenological attitude and is, as such, postnormative. Posthumanisms are the kind of discourses that attempt to define the human person by identifying the possible modalities of being human as such. In other words, posthumanisms do not seek to locate and explicate particular substantive qualities that are essential to humans. They do not argue for a core concept that all humans must possess or embody in order to be considered human; to do so is already to presuppose an idea about the nature of being human that one ought to have put out of play upon setting out on the philosophical journey itself. To the extent that a theory starts out by calling into question those very assumptions that we bring to the table—that is, to the extent that it steps out of the natural attitude into a state in which we keep our assumptions suspended and inquire to the very root of the question—it is in the phenomenological attitude. We can see how this becomes a criterion of posthumanist work, for only by being in the phenomenological attitude can we transcend the natural attitude that dominates humanist and antihumanist thinking.

Under this schema, Husserl's, Sartre's, Fanon's, Gordon's, Wilchins's, and my theories, then, are rightly posthumanist. While each of these theories ends up positing the human as constitutive of her world, none of them does so by positing a substantive essence to the human because of the remnant assumptions that humans have qualities in much the same way that objects have essential qualities. If one fails sufficiently to suspend the natural attitude, assumptions such as this remain, and the inquiry remains naïve and misguided. If one successfully suspends the natural attitude and enters into a phenomenological mode of inquiry, one sees that consciousness does, in fact, have a history in the life-world (that is, it is in great measure constituted through layers of positivistic assumptions that have sedimented)—in other words, it takes the insights of antihumanism seriously—but it finds that the intentional consciousness is still the center of all experience, and thus finds the transcendental ego at the root of the life-world.

Posthumanism clearly emerges as the preferred philosophical approach—the favorite child, if you will, and it does so in part because it falls firmly within the phenomenological framework, while humanism and antihumanism have failed to do so. But the question of the human takes full form only when we inquire into specific modalities of being human and explore the range of possibilities that lie within them. In other words, the transcendental ego is a realm of infinite abstract possibility that becomes all the more meaningful when we begin to explore some concrete (and yet perhaps still infinite) possibilities that lie within a particular regional ontology such as the study of race, gender, or sexuality. And so, having broadened our inquiry from the meaning of "queer" to the question of the human, we are led back to the particulars. Only now, those particulars take on new meaning.

The Promise

Queer Thinking is postnormative; phenomenology is posthumanist; phenomenology is queer. What follows from all of this? Putting together these three schema, we see that a pattern emerges, and this allows us to extend that pattern a bit further.

According to this new, integrated schema, the identity "straight" can be read as an instance of normative humanism that emerges from within the natural attitude, while the identity "gay" can be read as an instance of normative antihumanism that emerges within the natural attitude. The identity "queer" can be read as an instance of a postnormative posthumanism that emerges from within the phenomenological attitude. We can extend this thinking further to other paradigms such as race theory. Frantz Fanon's new humanism stands as an instance of a postnormative posthumanism that emerges from within the phenomenological attitude (see Fanon 1967b; Gordon 1997b). We can further extend this to gender identity, class, ethnicity—the possibilities are endless. In each case, where we end up is not a stable identity, either normative or antinormative (black, white, straight, gay, man, woman, rich, poor), nor a rejection of identity as constructed and therefore replaceable, but a position of possibilities in which identity is open, fluid, lived. Moreover, when we extend this thinking, we connect struggles against racism with struggles against heteronormativity, and with all struggles for human freedom, and we do so without sacrificing the specificity of any of them, for each is a valid instantiation of the wider project; and making these connections is essential, for antiblackness is not simply the hatred of the black by the white but is also the hatred of the gay by the white, the poor by the white, and the woman by the white, for normative whiteness excludes all others, and does so under the category of black. Posthumanist thought allows us to confront antiblackness, then, in a holistic way. This is its promise.

Thinking Queerly in an Antiblack World

What is it, then, to think queerly in an antiblack world?[13] It is to think postnormatively about our sex, our gender, our race, our ethnicity, our very selves. It is to theorize postnormatively when we theorize the infinite possibilities of being human. It is not only to transcend normative thinking but also to change the very terrain upon which thinking occurs.

Thinking queerly in an antiblack world takes many forms. Taste This (1998), a performance collective out of Canada, thinks queerly when it shatters our conceptions of gender and sexuality in exploring new possibilities of embodiment and expression. Robert Reid-Pharr (2001) does so when he lays a claim to his lesbian identity. C. Jacob Hale (1997) does so when he talks about leather daddy and boy as new ways of thinking our gender and sexual identities. Cherrie Moraga (2000: 82) does so when she writes the words that still shatter our thinking: "My brother's sex was white. Mine, brown." And these are but a few examples."[14]

What is it to think queerly in an antiblack world?

It is to think the human beyond humanism and antihumanism. It is to challenge not the normative but normativity itself.

It is to refuse to be silenced by, defined by, and denounced by the other.

It is the possibility of ethical thought in an unethical world.

It is the ethical imperative in action.

Notes

1. There are many "we's" in the world. My "we" here refers to the dominant paradigm of the modern West—in particular, the social milieu of the United States fifty years ago, though these conditions have their roots and reach much further back and much farther away than that.

2. I am using this term to signify its etymological meaning, not simply its popular meaning. Our world is anti-Semitic in that it is biased against all Semitic peoples, Jews and Arabs alike.

3. The Phenomenology Roundtable is a group of scholars working on practico-theoretical philosophical issues from the Husserlian perspective who meet yearly to discuss our work. For more on the Roundtable, see our website: http://web.ics. purdue.edu/~mmichau/roundtable.html.

4. While I was suggesting that phenomenology might help us think gender beyond normative conceptions (that is, queerly), Gordon asked me if I thought phenomenology was itself inherently queer. In other words, while I was taking up what I saw as a "practical" issue (Q: How do we move gender theory forward? A: Through a return to phenomenology), Gordon pushed me to take up a "theoretical" issue (What is the nature of phenomenology itself?).

5. In Fryer (2005) I lay out three meanings of the term "queer." I am here engaged in a slightly different discussion and so, for the sake of focus, I am putting aside the second definition from that other piece, but more fully exploring the meaning of the third.

6. As should be clear by now, the term "queer," in this second sense of the term, is not the same "queer" of popular culture's current love affair with gay male culture. For instance, in this sense of the term, there is nothing "queer" about the popular television show *Queer Eye for the Straight Guy.*

7. For a brief, but fuller, explanation of the original schema, see Fryer (2001). For a more detailed explanation, see Fryer (2004).

8. I think this stands as a good description of the work of Descartes (1999) and Habermas (1985).

9. Sylvia Wynter offers a penetrating analysis of this phenomenon in Chapter 4 of this volume, "On How We Mistook the Map for the Territory, and Re-Imprisoned Ourselves in Our Unbearable Wrongness of Being, of *Désêtre.*"

10. I think this stands as a good description of the work of Husserl (1970), Fanon (1967a), and Gordon (1997b, 1995a/1999). While each, in some form or another, adopts the term *humanism*, I would place their work in the category of posthumanism.

11. Sylvia Wynter explains this as being more a product of a kind of blindness to or a forgetting of the origins of these claims as claims putting forth a historical understanding of "man." Again, see her chapter in this volume.

12. For her critique, see Butler (1999). For a fuller account of my argument, see Fryer (2003).

13. Thinking queerly in an antiblack world is but one model for the kind of postnormative thinking I am advocating. Other models can be found quite nearby. Nelson Maldonado-Torres suggests one such model when he argues that we need to look past continentality in conceiving the terrain of philosophy and critical thought today, and Kenneth Knies suggests another when he advocates a turn to what he calls the post-European sciences. I see these three statements as all part of the same struggle for full human recognition. See their chapters in this volume.

14. Cameron (1996) and Wilchins (1997) are two other excellent examples.

8

Philosophy in the African Tradition of Resistance

Issues of Human Freedom and Human Flourishing

Maulana Karenga

⊹

The question of the nature and function of a philosophy of struggle and the subsidiary questions of the purpose, means, and imperatives of struggle, of necessity, take on an added urgency at this critical juncture in our history and the history of the world. Likewise, the allied concern of how do Africana philosophers who are cultivated in and committed to a *philosophy born of struggle* live a *tradition of resistance* is informed and inspired by this same sense of urgency. For we are clearly in the midst of world-shattering changes, many of which go against our ancient and ongoing notions of the right, the just, and the good, and we understandably feel a need for critical and effective intervention to address them.

Surely, we are at a moment of history fraught with new and old forms of anxiety, alienation, and antagonism; deepening poverty in the midst of increasing wealth; proposals and practices of ethnic cleansing and genocide; pandemic diseases; increased plunder; pollution and depletion of the environment; constant conflicts, large and small; and world-threatening delusions on the part of a superpower aspiring to a return to empire, with spurious claims of the right to preemptive aggression, to openly attack and overthrow nonfavored and fragile governments openly, and to seize the lands and resources of vulnerable peoples and establish "democracy" through military dictatorship abroad, all the while suppressing political dissent at home (Chang 2002;

Cole et al. 2002). These anxieties are undergirded by racist and religious chauvinism, by the self-righteous and veiled references of these rulers to themselves as a kind of terrible and terrorizing hand of God, appointed to rid the world of evil (Ahmad 2002; Amin 2001; Blum 1995). At the same time, in this context of turmoil and terror and the use and threatened use of catastrophic weapons, there is the irrational and arrogant expectation that the oppressed will acquiesce, abandon resistance, and accept the disruptive and devastating consequences of globalization, along with the global hegemony it implies (Martin and Schumann 1997). There is great alarm among the white-supremicist rulers of these globalizing nations, given the radical resistance rising up against them, even as globalization's technological, organizational, and economic capacity continues to expand (Barber 1996; Karenga 2002c, 2003a; Lusane 1997). There is great alarm when people who should "know" when they are defeated ridicule the assessment, refuse to be defeated or dispirited, and, on the contrary, intensify and diversify their struggles (Zepezauer 2002).

Certainly the battlefields of Palestine, Venezuela, long-suffering Haiti, and Chiapas, Mexico, along with other continuing emancipatory struggles everywhere, reaffirm the indomitable character of the human spirit and the durability and adaptive vitality of a people determined to be free, regardless of the odds and assessments against them. Indeed, they remind us that the motive force of history is struggle, informed by the ongoing quest for freedom, justice, power of the masses, and peace in the world. Despite "end of history" claims and single-super-power resolve and resolutions, these struggles continue. *For still the oppressed want freedom, the wronged and injured want justice, the people want power over their destiny and daily lives, and the world wants peace.* And all over the world—especially in this U.S. citadel of aging capitalism with its archaic dreams of empire—clarity in the analysis of issues, and in the critical determination of tasks and prospects, requires the deep and disciplined reflection characteristic of the personal and social practice we call philosophy.

But this sense of added urgency for effective intervention is prompted not only by the critical juncture at which we stand but also by an awareness of our long history of resistance as a people, because in our collective strivings and social struggles we seek a new future for our people, our descendants, and the world. Joined also to these conditions and considerations is the compelling character of our self-understanding as a people, as a moral vanguard in this country and the world. For we have launched, fought, and won with our allies struggles that not only have expanded the realm of freedom in this country and the world but also have served as an ongoing inspiration and a model of liberation struggles for other marginalized and oppressed peoples and groups throughout the world. Indeed, they have borrowed from and built on our moral vocabulary and moral vision, sung our songs of freedom, and held up our struggle for liberation as a model to emulate. Now, self-understanding and self-assertion are dialectically linked. In other words, how we understand ourselves in the world determines how we assert ourselves in the world. Thus, an expansive concept of ourselves as Africans—continental and diasporan—and as Africana philosophers forms an essential component of our sense of mission and the urgency with which we approach it.

The Kawaida Philosophical Framework

It is important to note that I have conceived and written this chapter within the framework of *Kawaida* philosophy (Karenga 1978, 1980, 1997). Kawaida is a philosophic initiative that was forged in the crucible of ideological and practical struggles around issues of freedom, justice, equality, self-determination, communal power, self-defense, pan-Africanism, coalition and alliance, Black Studies, intellectual emancipation, and cultural recovery and reconstruction. It continued to develop in the midst of these ongoing *struggles within the life of the mind* and *struggles within the life of the people,* as well as within the context of the conditions of the world. Kawaida is defined as *an ongoing synthesis of the best of African thought and practice in constant exchange with the world.* It characterizes culture as a unique, instructive, and valuable way of being human in the world—as a foundation and framework for self-understanding and self-assertion.

As a philosophy of culture and struggle, Kawaida maintains that our intellectual and social practice as Africana activist scholars must be undergirded and informed by ongoing efforts to (1) ground ourselves in our own culture; (2) constantly recover, reconstruct, and bring forth from our culture the best of what it means to be African and human in the fullest sense; (3) speak this special cultural truth to the world; and (4) use our culture to constantly make our own unique contribution to the reconception and reconstruction of this country, and to the forward flow of human history.

To achieve these aims, according to Kawaida, African persons in general and African intellectuals in particular must constantly dialog with African culture—continental and diasporan, ancient and modern. To dialog with African culture is to ask constant questions and seek from it answers to the fundamental questions of human life. In short, it is to use African culture as a rich and instructive resource for addressing enduring issues as well as the fundamental challenges of our time. These issues involve questions of how to create the just and good society and the good and sustainable world; how to build strong male-female relations, raise children, and honor our elders and ancestors; how to treat the vulnerable people and strangers among us; how to establish a right relationship with the environment; how to discover the mission and meaning in human life as well as the ground for defining humans as bearers of divinity and dignity and for arguing the sanctity of life; and, finally, how to achieve and sustain an ever-expanding realm of human freedom and human flourishing.

To dialog with African culture, we must therefore ask at every critical junction of thought and practice, research and reflection, initiative and experience: What do Africa—its peoples, its culture—have to offer to the ongoing historical project of improving the human condition and enhancing the human future? Answering this question requires that we constantly engage African texts—continental and diasporan, ancient and modern, oral, written, and living-practice texts. That is, we must connect with the lived and living initiatives and experiences of African persons and peoples. This means using our culture as a resource rather than as a reference. Here one engages in subject-centered and agency-oriented interpretive practices that find below-the-surface meanings and paradigms of human excellence and human possibility in the lived life of African people in all its rich variety and multidimensionality.

In this process, one does not simply make a historical reference to Harriet Tubman as a major leader of the Underground Railroad. Rather, one stands at the crossroads of history with her, at the moment of her self-liberation, when she moves from elation over being free to sadness at having left all those she loved in the Holocaust of enslavement. It is when she decides that freedom is a shared good, that the profound happiness in freedom she first felt should be shared by all, and then chooses to return and free others that offers such a fruitful field for philosophic engagement. For in that moment, she redefines freedom from individual and individualistic escape to the collective practice of self-determination in community. Now, the importance of such an interpretive approach is that it goes beyond simple reference to a lived-experience and engages Tubman's experience and initiative as a site and resource for reflective problematics. Indeed, despite claims of multiculturalism and respect for one's culture, if one's culture is never or insufficiently used as a source of reflective problematics—the hub around which both the philosophical and educational enterprises revolve—the claims have little or no validity.

Kawaida recognizes the rich, ancient, and varied character of African culture and sees in it shared orientations that give it fundamental contours and content. As Kwame Gyekye notes, "[I]t is the underlying cultural unity or identity ... that justifies references to varieties of thought as a whole"—varieties such as African, Native American, Latino, Asian, and European thought (1987 [1995]: x). Thus, despite the diversity of African culture, its shared orientations give it enough identity and integrity to provide us with a particularly African way of being human in the world, which in turn provides a pathway to the universal in which Africans speak their own special cultural truth and make their own unique contribution to the forward flow of human history. As Sékou Touré states, "Black culture, free from profound changes which violate its independence and integrity, emerges on the universal path, not as an antagonistic element but with cautious care to be a factor of equilibrium, a power for peace and a force of solidarity supportive of a new civilization which projects itself towards the great hopes of humankind and fashions itself in contact with combined currents of thought" in Africa and the world (1959: 112–113). Although the stress here is on African culture and the African community, similar observations can be made concerning the particularity and universality of all cultures and the capacity to contribute in their own unique way to the human project. For it is a central Kawaida contention that *each people or culture is a unique and equally valuable way of being human in the world,* and that each people has both the right and the responsibility to speak their own special cultural truth and make their own unique contribution to the forward flow of human history.

And concerning the cultural resources we bring to the human project of repairing and improving the world, no culture is as ancient as African culture; none is richer in resources or reflective of greater concern for creating the just and good society and the good and sustainable world. In other words, no other people's history and struggle for good in the world is as long as ours or more significant than ours. It is Africans who stood up at the dawn of human history and spoke the first human truth, searching intently for the meaning and motion of things. It is they, too, who in the quest to understand what it is to be human first defined humans as bearers of divinity and dignity. Moreover, it is Africans who first insisted on the interrelatedness and oneness of being, the sacredness of life, and the integrity of the environment. It is Africans who first advocated freedom for the oppressed, justice for the wronged and injured, and cooperative harvesting and sharing of the world's good for everyone. Indeed, as our foremother Mary McLeod Bethune taught us, "we are heirs and custodians of a great legacy," and we must bear the burden and glory of this legacy with strength, dignity, and determination. The core of this legacy, Kawaida holds, is our *ethical tradition,* which is the oldest in the world and serves as a resource and reference for some of humanity's most cherished moral and spiritual principles. As argued above, it is a tradition rooted in our ancient and ongoing concern for the world and in the rich and instructive lessons born of our life and struggle as African people.

This ancient tradition of the search and struggle for the good evolved in the Nile Valley amidst an unsurpassed level of human achievement and excellence in the basic disciplines of human knowledge, which has been shared with neighboring people. It was tested and tempered in the Holocaust of enslavement, as we struggled to free ourselves, radically transform society, and hold steadfastly to our humanity in the most inhuman and barbaric situation—a morally monstrous genocide in both the physical and the cultural sense. This lived and living tradition was reinforced during the Reaffirmation of the 1960s, when we reaffirmed our Africanness and social justice tradition and, in the process, struggled to return to our history and culture, expand the realm of freedom in the United

States and the world, and contribute meaningfully to building the good society we all want and deserve to live in. It is in the ancient, rich, and varied resources of this history and culture that Kawaida roots itself and seeks to constantly discover and bring forth what it means to be African and human in the fullest sense.

The Classical African Philosophical Initiative

Kawaida, in its commitment to dialoging with African culture, embraces the Akan concept of *sankofa*, which literally means "return and retrieve it." Represented by an ideogram of a bird reaching back into its feathers with its beak, sankofa, G. Niangoran-Bouah tells us, is "a quest for knowledge and the return to the source" (1984: 210). Furthermore, it implies that the resulting knowledge "is the outcome of research, of an intelligent and patient investigation." In short, it is for Kawaida a call for a kind of intellectual archeology that seeks to recover and reconstruct classical African civilizations' most useful and fruitful paradigms and to place them in the service of the present and future.

Certainly critical study of the philosophical initiative in ancient Egypt (Diop 1991; Karenga 2004; Obenga 1990) and ancient Yorubaland offers an abundance of resources and possibilities of immense value for Africana philosophy. And this is true not only in exploring the original meaning and mission of African philosophy, and in seeking to reaffirm the enduring relevance of this original meaning and mission, but also in offering concepts, ideas, and paradigms that expand the range and kinds of philosophic discourse and discussion. It is Cheikh Anta Diop who argued that "a look toward Egypt is the best way of conceiving and building our cultural future" (1991: 12). For him, critical study of ancient Egypt or Kemet provides us with the necessary conditions "to reconcile African civilization with history, to build a body of modern human sciences and renew African culture." It is in this context that Africana Studies scholars have undertaken the critical study for which Diop called (Asante 1990; Bilolo 1995; Karenga 2004; Obenga 1990). Although ancient Egypt remains the major African classical civilization used as a resource for such work, it is important to note that ancient Yorubaland also figures prominently in the areas of art and literature (Abimbola 1975; Abiodun et al. 1994; Lawal 1996) as well as in ethical philosophy, an area of particular relevance to the present chapter (Hallen 2000; Karenga 1999; Oluwole 1999).

At the dawn of the African philosophical enterprise in ancient Egypt, it was the responsibility of the intellectual to think deeply about life and the world, as well as about the problematics and possibilities inherent in them. This moral and intellectual responsibility was reaffirmed in the moral and professional claims found in the autobiographies of the sSw (*seshu*), Kemet's civil servants and intellectuals (Jansen-Wilkeln 1985; Lichtheim 1988, 1992; Otto 1954). However, philosophical activity was also engaged in by the sage rx (*rekh*), the priest wab (*wab*), and the moral teacher sbaw (*sebau*), who left a legacy of instructions (Sebait) and advice for well-being and flourishing in life (Brunner 1991). These seshu, like the later Mandarins of ancient China, understood themselves in moral, intellectual, and professional terms. They began their autobiographies by locating themselves in the communal context of their professional practice and then declared virtues and attendant practices that, for them, were defining sources of an expansive self-concept (Karenga 1993b).

Typical of these declarations of virtue or moral and professional self-presentations is the one found in the autobiography of the priest Wer-Khuu. He says, "I have come from my town. I have descended from my district. I spoke truth [Maat] there. I did justice [Maat] there." This self-location and moral self-presentation speak to both a situated and a self-conscious practice. Doing Maat is concrete and contextual. One acts in a definite community and it is here, as the text goes on to suggest, that one proves one's excellence iqr (*iqer*). Iqr here has the same meaning as the later Greek term "arête" and may refer to intellectual, moral, or social excellence.

In Kemet, philosophy as a quest for wisdom requiring deep and disciplined thought was understood as a constant, careful, and critical activity of the heart/mind. Thus, for example, the High Priest, Somtutefnakht, says in his autobiography, "my heart/mind sought HHy [hehy] Maat [truth] in your temple, day and night" (Karenga 2004: 119). And the sage Khakheperrasoneb, confronted by the challenge of interpreting the turmoil and changing times sweeping through Egypt, speaks of "probing deep Dar [*djar*] into a matter by searching [Hhy] the heart/mind" (Karenga 2004: 72).

Now, the Kemetic word "ib" or "Haty" (haty) means both heart and mind and speaks to the ancient Egyptians' interest in linking "cognition" and "conscience." This is related to the purpose of the philosophical enterprise, which was to pursue Maat as a moral, epistemological, and social project. "Maat" is a polysemic word and thus has an extensive range of meanings, but essentially it refers to "the right" or "rightness"—or, in a larger sense, an interrelated order of rightness in the realm of the Divine, the natural, and the social (Assmann 1990; Karenga 2004).

Most often "Maat" is translated as truth, justice, righteousness, and order. Most meaningful for us here is its connotation of truth and justice, for it points again to issues of cognition and conscience, knowledge and moral sensitivity, and their meaning and use in the quest for a good life and a good world. In fact, there are texts in which one may translate "Maat" simultaneously as truth and justice. For example, the sesh Ineni says, "I searched after Maat [truth, justice] without being biased—literally, without leaning to one side." Thus, it may be unbiased truth or unbiased justice that Ineni is searching for everywhere. Again, this linking of cognition—whose metaphor is truth—and conscience—whose metaphor is justice—speaks to the Kemetic interest in a knowledge informed and engaged by a profound moral sensitivity essential to the practice of Maat and the creation and maintenance of moral community in and for the world.

In the philosophy or quest for wisdom in ancient Egypt, the definition of the philosophical enterprise revolves around four basic and interrelated kinds of practice and/or requirements. The first is *to seek the truth constantly*—pXr m-sA MAat (pekher m-sa Maat). Now, the verb "pXr" means to turn around, go around, move about, travel about, and perambulate (Faulkner 1976: 93–94). Used in the phrase "pekher m-sa Maat," it has the essential meaning of perambulating in search of—walking around, through and over, to inspect and investigate. In the sense in which I am using it, then, it means moving about, investigating, examining in order to find truth—in other words, *searching diligently after truth everywhere*. This is the meaning of Seba Ankhsheshonqi's instruction in the *Husia,* the sacred text of ancient Egypt, which says, "Examine every matter that you may understand it. Do not say I am learned, but rather set yourself to become wise.... Study the structure and functioning of the heavens. Study the structure and functioning of the earth" (Karenga 1984: 64). In addition to the verb "pekher," ancient-Egyptian deep thinkers had access to several other verbs used in defining and pursuing the philosophical project. These included swAswA (suasua), ponder; nkA (neka), meditate; HHy (hehy), seek, search for; and Dar, which has the widest range of meaning, including search out, investigate, seek, probe, plan, and take thought for the future (Faulkner 1976: 141, 176, 216, 320). In fact, when used in medical diagnosis, "Dar" suggests a careful and focused probing.

A second pillar of the ancient-Egyptian philosophical enterprise is *to bear witness to truth*—smtr MAat (semeter Maat). Now, the word "smtr" means not only to bear witness (to truth) but also to examine, to make inquiry (Faulkner 1976: 229). Thus, one can argue that inherent in the concept and practice of bearing witness to truth is the correlative moral and intellectual obligation to ex- amine thoroughly and make critical inquiry into a matter so that one can bear real and responsible witness to truth. In any case, the requirement here is not simply to discover truth and contemplate it but, on the contrary, to share, raise up, defend, and use truth in the service of the right and the good.

A third pillar of the ancient-Egyptian philosophical project is *the obligation to do justice.* Often, bearing witness to or speaking truth and doing justice are seen and spoken of as a joint project. Thus, in the *Book of Coming Forth by Day,* we find the obligation "to bear witness to truth and set the scales of justice in their proper place—smtr MAat rdit iwsu r ahaw.f" (Karenga 1990b: 78, 77). And in numerous autobiographies, the claim is made as part of one's moral and professional self-presentation that "I spoke truth and did justice—Dd.n.i MAat irn.n.i MAat." Inherent, then, in the obligation to seek and speak the truth is the correlative responsibility to do justice or, more expansively, to "set the scales in their proper place"—that is, to do, establish, and restore justice so that there is balance in the world. In the paradigmatic Maatian text, the *Book of Khunanpu,* Khunanpu says "The balancing of the land, lies in Maat [truth, justice, righteousness]." Thus, he tells the High Steward and Judge Rensi, "Do not speak falsely for you are great; do not act lightly for you have weight; do not be untrue for you are the balance; and do not swerve for you are the standard" (Karenga 1984: 32).

A fourth pillar in the Maatian philosophical enterprise is *the ob- ligation to seek after the good for humans and the world.* Thus, Ineni says, "I sought out [Dar] the good [Axt] and I was vigilant in seeking [HHy] the beneficial (Sethe 1906-1958: vol. 57: 6, 8). This seeking the good through searching the heart and mind is expressed in varied ways with terms such as Dar, seeking out; mAA n, looking toward; kAi m, thinking of; and HHy n, searching for. It is important also to note the strong emphasis placed on seeking good for the future—that is, future generations and the world they will live in. Thus, for example, Ineni says, "I search out [what was good] for future generations [imyw-xt]." And Queen Hatshepsut, as part of her moral self-presentation, describes as a central aspect of her responsibility as ruler her "divine heart/mind searching out that which is good for the future" (*ibid.:* 384, 12).

It is important to note here that that the rx or sAA (saa) (wise person) or Seba Maat (moral teacher) is concerned with truth and justice not as abstracts but, rather, as kinds of practice—as indispensable elements in the just and good society and world, and the good life, and as formative factors in the grounding of human flourishing. Here we find an important difference between Kemetic and Hellenistic philosophy. As George Kerford (1990: 326) points out, Greek philosophy has a tradition of the wise man as both a knower of practical knowledge (*ho phronimos*) and a knower of theoretical knowledge (*ho sophos*). But the tendency, except perhaps with the Stoics, was to privilege the latter. Furthermore, he states that "Plato in his *Republic* developed the concept of the wise man as a philosopher in a highly technical sense, that is, as someone possessing a knowledge of truth" as an abstraction (*ibid.:* 320). Thus, it differs from the truth sought after and possessed by the Kemetic wise person. For the truth sought was a concrete knowledge of reality and its possibilities for human relations and human actions and good in the world.

Therefore, in the Sebaitic tradition, the Seba teaches Maat not as an abstract but as an obligatory practice. Thus, one is instructed to "speak truth, do justice." And when the sesh Intef says, "I am a listener who listens to Maat and ponders [swAswA] it in his heart," he is indeed contemplating Maat, thinking in a deep and disciplined way about it (Sethe 1906-1958: 81). But he is contemplating it not as an abstract truth or idea but as a compelling and valuable moral practice. Even if we translate "Maat" here as "justice," it remains a focus of contemplation not as an abstract but as a moral and social aim and practice.

Moreover, the ancient writer, meditating on the meaning of creation and being in the *Book of Knowing the Creations,* is certainly concerned with a high level of metaphysics and abstraction, when he records or writes that Ra, the Creator, says: "When I came into being, being itself came into being. All beings came into being after I came into being." But these ontological assertions about the Creator, creation, and being are ultimately transformed into ethical lessons about self-, social, and world transformation—in other words, lessons about the concept and practice of becoming xprt (*khepert*) and its human possibility and the cooperative creation of good in and of the world. In conclusion, then, the ideas of truth and justice always have practical meanings and applications within the context of lived experience.

Even Maat itself, the overarching and grounding principle of existence and the world, is essentially geared toward providing foundation and framework to practices that involve bringing good into the world and sustaining it. If one were to create a word for philosophy in ancient Egypt, one might first call it HHy n rx, "a quest for wisdom." But although this is a legitimate understanding of Kemetic philosophy and reminds us of the Greek concept of philosophy as the "love of wisdom," such a definition is only partially correct, for it leaves open the question, Wisdom for what? And as in other African cultures, knowledge (or wisdom) is never simply knowledge for knowledge's sake, but always knowledge for humans' sake and the sake of the world (English and Kalumba 1996; Eze 1997, 1998; Gordon 1997a: intro.; Harris 1983 [2000]). Thus, a more appropriate term in ancient Egyptian would be HHy-n-MAat, "a quest for Maat"—that is, a quest for truth and justice, a term that defines the project as having both intellectual and practical tasks.

Thus, ancient Egypt offers us an added vantage point for understanding and pursuing the philosophical enterprise, especially from an Afrocentric perspective, in terms of both vision and vocabulary. The Afrocentric initiative put forth by Molefi Asante (1990, 1998, 1999) rightfully insists on placing Africans at the center of any studies of Africa and Africans, engaging them as subjects rather than as objects and stressing their agency and initiative in history and life rather than describing a mute and victimized experience. Concurring with this understanding, I have defined "Afrocentricity" as "a methodology, orientation or quality of thought and practice rooted in the cultural image and human interests of African people" (Karenga 1995a: 45). Moreover, "to be rooted in the cultural image of African people is to be anchored in the views, values and practices of African people." And "to be rooted in the human interests of African people is to be informed of and attentive to the just claims on life and society we share with other peoples, such as respect and concern for truth, justice, freedom and the dignity of the human person."

Therefore, as an Africana Studies scholar and ethical philosopher, I have chosen to use the varied and fruitful resources of Kemet, as well as other ancient African sources, as a foundation and framework for the philosophical enterprise. As I have noted elsewhere (Karenga 2003b: 4), it should be understood that my intention is not to construct or suggest a direct causal relationship between ancient-Egyptian and African-American philosophic practice. Rather, it is to build self-consciously on this African legacy and resource by identifying shared insights and shared orientations in a larger African tradition of philosophic practice, as well as by recovering and employing these classical African understandings to expand the range of useful concepts and approaches in defining and explicating the philosophical enterprise in general and the Africana philosophical project in particular.

This practice parallels European scholars' use of classical Greek philosophical insights to develop and explicate philosophical initiatives, as well as the embrace of Greek philosophy by various European cultural groups, without needing to show direct causal links between Greek and every other form of European thought. Certainly, with appropriate modifications, this position holds true for African-American philosophers who use Greek or other forms of European philosophy—in this case, too, without needing to show direct causal links between their philosophical initiative and the European cultures and forms of thought that inform their initiatives. Again, the point here is to root ourselves in African tradition and to recover and engage useful views, concepts, and concerns that expand the range of philosophic concepts, understandings, and initiatives open to us. In this way, we enrich and expand the philosophic enterprise and create an indispensable comparative and complex exchange concerning the enduring and current issues confronting us.

Excursus

In this regard, I am reminded of a particular claim Cornel West made during our dialog on Christianity as a liberational or emancipatory project and the comparative merits and meanings of ancient Egyptian and ancient Jewish ethical traditions.[1] Responding in part to my making a necessary distinction between emancipatory forms of nationalism and Christianity and the debased forms they each can take, on the one hand, and my stress on African cultural grounding, on the other, he reaffirmed his commitment to prophetic Christianity and appreciation for its Jewish roots. He said that the ancient Hebrews made three unique contributions—(1) the concept of *imago dei,* image of God; (2) the concept of covenant; and (3) the use of ordinary people for their narratives—and that they were unlike what he called "the narratives, myths and legends of other earlier peoples."

Now, the importance of both a multicultural grounding and the expanded range of concepts and insights generated by West's observation is clear here. West is following standard Eurocentric approaches to the genealogy of human ethics when he makes this claim. For most of these religious and ethical accounts assert that the Hebrews introduced the concept of humans as the image of God (Frankena 1983; Sidgwick 1931: 122ff). However, the evidence does not support this assumption (Karenga 2004: 317-325; Ockinga, 1984). In fact, the concept of humans as the image of God is attested in ancient Egypt in the *Book of Kheti* as early as 2140 b.c.e. Kheti says "humans are the images of God, snn nTr [*senen netjer*], and came from his very person." And it is from this concept of *senen netjer,* humans as the image of God, that the concept of human dignity, Spsw [*shepesu*] in ancient Egyptian, is derived and developed. Thus, in the "Narrative of the Sage Djedi," Djedi tells King Khufu that he can neither kill nor experiment on a nameless prisoner. For even he is a noble image of God. Thus, it is in ancient Africa, in ancient Egypt, not ancient Israel, that humans are first defined as the image of God and possessors of dignity—in short, as *bearers of divinity and dignity.*

On the second point, the covenant idea, which leads to the concept of one chosen people and one chosen people alone, or an elect or specially favored people, is clearly problematic in a world where human equality and multicultural respect represent the best of our moral thinking and where the notion of specialness and the conversations and behavior that evolve from it can lead to the devaluing of others, justification for wars and occupation, and other oppressive and destructive practices (Bowser et al. 1995; Reed 1997; Taylor 1992). It is interesting to note that in ancient Egypt the chosen-people concept did not exist. Indeed, the *Husia,* the sacred text of ancient Egypt, teaches that rmT (*remetj*), all men and women, are in the image and care of the Divine and all are obligated constantly to repair and restore srD tA (*serudj ta*), the world, making it more beautiful and beneficial than it was when they inherited it (Karenga 1984; Karenga 2004: 397–402). Perhaps the Kemetic concept closest to that of "the chosen of God" is the concept of the appointed, rdiw nTr (*rediu netjer*), whose range of meaning could be extended to "chosen" in the sense of "selected," although "stp" is the word most often used to mean "chosen" (Sánchez Rodríguez 2001: 405). This use of "rdiw," in its most ethical and instructive sense and for our purposes here, can be found in the *Book of Ptahhotep.* Ptahhotep says iw wr-ib rdiw NTr, "those great of heart wr-ib [wer-ib] are the appointed"—that is, the chosen of God (Dévaud 1916: 29.247). Here it is a moral quality—*greatness of heart* in all its varied moral meanings—that merits divine appointment. And this appointment is not over or against anyone, but ostensibly to the good of everyone. For surely this virtue and the appointment are for doing Maat—that is, right and good in the world.

Moreover, the sacred text of ancient Yorubaland, the *Odu Ifa* (78: 1), offers the concept of *chosenness,* which is unique among the spiritual traditions of the world. It says that *all humans are divinely chosen.* Furthermore, they are chosen not to the exclusion of anyone or over and against anyone, but *with everyone.* And they are chosen not by or for ethnicity or for any attribute or promise, but for a lifetime task—that is, to bring good into the world. The text says, "*Dandan èniyàn ni a yàn kí wón mú're l s'áyé*—Surely humans are divinely chosen to bring good into the world," and this, the *Odu* teaches, is the fundamental meaning and mission in human life. Indeed, the Yoruba word for human being is "èniyàn," meaning "chosen one," reaffirming in daily speech the status of all humans as special, equally valued, and equally valuable—in short, as bearers of divinity and dignity, as in ancient Egypt.

Finally, West asserts that the Hebrew narratives were about ordinary people transforming and being transformed, and that this was not so with other narratives. However, evidence does not support such a claim about either the Hebrew narratives or the others. The biblical narratives, like other peoples' narratives, are about royal, noble, and ordinary people. Obviously the kings, prophets, and nobles of various houses were not ordinary people. On the contrary, they were privileged in various ways. Moreover, poor ordinary people did not write these narratives. In terms of ancient Egypt, and beyond the biblical mythology about this region as the land of bondage, the intellectuals, seshu, came from all classes. And in fact, the most definitive text on Maat, the moral ideal in ancient Egypt, is the *Book of Khunanpu*. Khunanpu, as we saw earlier, is a peasant who speaks truth to power, lecturing nobles and kings on the meaning and requirements for *justice* in society and the world (Assmann 1990: 58ff; Karenga 2004: 69-71, 365-371).

It is in light of this rich moral, spiritual, and philosophical legacy of ancient Egypt or Kemet that I have engaged in this intellectual archeology of recovery and reconstruction of the ancient texts under discussion, exploring and testing the conceptual elasticity of their fundamental insights and using them to engage in modern moral and philosophic reflection and discourse. Certainly the comprehensive Kemetic conception of philosophy as a constant, profound, disciplined, and morally sensitive search for truth—bearing witness to truth, doing and seeking justice, and doing good for the world and future generations—as well as the language and concepts that inform it, have proven useful in our quest to ground our philosophical project, understand it as an ancient African tradition, and bring it forth as a fruitful field and space for an expanded and enriched philosophical discourse.

A Tradition of Resistance

The question of resistance as a lived and living tradition is at the heart of the Africana philosophical enterprise. In this connection Lewis Gordon makes two important points (1997a: 3, 4). The first is that a defining feature of Africana philosophy is its existential initiative, which he calls a philosophy of existence or existential philosophy—namely, "philosophical questions premised upon concerns of freedom, anguish, responsibility, embodied agency, sociality and liberation." Second, he notes that "[t]he reflective dimension of situated life always brings in an element of concrete embodiment of relevance." Continuing, he says that "[w]hat this means is that theory, any theory, gains its sustenance from that which it offers *for* and *through* the lived-reality of those who are expected to formulate it." Africana philosophy, then, is necessarily shaped by the legacy of our past, the urgency of our present, and the requirements of our future, a future of maximum human freedom and human flourishing. Moreover, such a tradition of resistance calls for all to participate—workers, peasants, athletes, artists, intellectuals, teachers, students, writers, and philosophers, among others. In this context of the struggle for freedom, justice, and liberation, Paul Robeson addresses the issue of the role of the artist and intellectual in his "Manifesto Against Fascism." He says:

> Every artist, every scientist must decide, now, where he stands. He has no alternative. There are no impartial observers.
>
> Through the destruction, in certain countries, of man's literary heritage, through the propagation of false ideas of national and racial superiority, the artist, the scientist, the writer is challenged. This struggle invades the former cloistered halls of our universities and all her seats of learning.
>
> The battlefront is everywhere. There is no sheltered rear. The artist elects to fight for freedom or slavery.
>
> I have made my choice! I had no alternative! (*Paul Robeson: The Great Forerunner* 1965: 192)

To understand this issue of living the tradition of resistance in our time, we must begin with a definition of the terms "tradition" and "resistance." A central philosophical problem is how to deal with the concept of the African-American tradition. First, there is a tendency to deny, diminish, or devalue the African aspect of the African-American tradition and pay exclusive homage to the American (essentially European) aspect. Second, there is a deconstructionist tendency to make inherited tradition irrelevant or restrictive and to suggest an unlimited and transcendent capacity to reinvent self—that is, to escape history. And thirdly, there is the bad-faith position, bordering on hypocrisy, that although one can reinvent oneself, she or he may choose any identity but African.

Such facile and deficient notions of tradition are at best unin-
formed, at worst intellectually dishonest and invidious, and, in any
case, clearly not useful. One is compelled by reason to recognize
the problematic possibilities inherent not only in tradition but
also in modernity—with which tradition is so often contrasted, as
Gyekye argues (1997: xi, chapter 4). Indeed, modernity contains
within itself traditional elements, which it inherited, cherishes, and
maintains. Moreover, modernity is often equated with Europe and
Europeanization and thus requires embracing European culture,
which, of necessity, contains and maintains its own traditions. But
as Asante says, "[O]ne steps outside one's history (only) with great
difficulty.... In fact, the act itself is highly improbable from true historical consciousness" (Asante 1990: 5). Therefore, one seeks place
and centers oneself in the midst of one's own history and culture.
This idea Asante calls "the groundness of observation and behavior
in one's own historical experiences" (*ibid.:* 12), which, of course,
speaks to the question of tradition.

Finally, genuine moral and philosophic inquiry requires and reflects membership in a particular kind of moral community. Thus,
as Alasdair MacIntyre states, "The enquiries of the individual moral
life are continuous with those of past tradition and the rationality of that life is the rationality both embodied in and transmitted
through tradition" (1990: 142). Alan Chan (1984: 424ff) further
notes that although "tradition as a form of authority is seen to be
diametrically opposed to freedom and reason," in fact "there is no
intrinsic opposition between reason and tradition," for "tradition
serves to provide a horizon from which we may view the world."
In tradition, "the past and present are constantly merged in the
experience of understanding."

The ancient Egyptians put great emphasis on grounding oneself
in tradition, in the ways of the ancestors, sxrw imyw-hAt [*sekheru
imyu-hat*]. Indeed, Seba Kheti says, regarding the wise person [rx],
"Maat comes to him distilled and shaped in the tradition of the discourse of the ancestors." Therefore, he continues, "[f]ollow in the
footsteps of your foreparents, your ancestors. For work is carried
out through knowledge. See, their words endure in books. Open
and read them and emulate [seni] their wisdom (Karenga 1984:
50). Here the verb "seni" means to emulate, in the sense of emu-
lating with the intention to *equal* or *surpass.* Moreover, the sage

Khakheperrasoneb, in his dealing with the social crisis confronting him, is described as engaging in "the gathering together of sayings (concepts, ideas), the culling of phrases, the search for words by an inquisitive mind" (Simpson 1972: 231). Khakheperrasoneb goes on to say, "Would that I had unknown speeches, erudite phrases in a new language which have not been used before, not phrases of past speeches which [our] forefathers spoke." Again, one seeks not simply to imitate but to *emulate,* and not simply to receive and repeat tradition but to receive it, reinterpret it, and transform it in the process and in the interest of its ongoing relevance and vitality. In this sense, as Antonio Loprieno points out, Khakheperrasoneb's discourse and other Kemetic literature reflect the presence of a context "in which ideas are philosophically debated," not simply received and accepted (1996: 46).

Lucius Outlaw provides us with a comprehensive and useful definition of Africana philosophy as "a gathering notion under which to situate the articulations (writings, speeches, etc.) and traditions of Africa and peoples of African descent collectively, as well as the subdiscipline—or field-forming, tradition-defining or tradition-organizing reconstructive efforts which are to be regarded as philosophy" (1992-1993: 64). The interest here revolves around delineated practices that bring the field into being and develop it. Africana philosophy, Outlaw tells us, is "a field-forming, tradition-defining and organizing and reconstructive" practice. Here, for Kawaida, the reconstructive efforts—or, more precisely, the recovery *and* reconstructive efforts—of Africana philosophy are a priority practice. For without such a recovery and reconstructive initiative, one cannot define the tradition based on definitive elements or even call the tradition African—that is, grounded in African culture.

To talk of a *tradition,* then, is to speak of a distinct and persistent pattern of practice within a larger culture that carries with it an authority and precedent, a foundation and framework, for both its embrace and continuance, on the one hand, and its maintenance and change, on the other. Within this understanding, there are great traditions and small traditions. The great traditions can be a dominant tradition within the culture, or they can be the culture itself as when we refer to, say, the African, Native American, Latino, Asian, or European tradition. The small traditions are characteristic patterns of practice that inform and are constitutive of the larger tradition. Thus, for example, the tradition of resistance is part and parcel of the African tradition—indeed, a defining and constitutive element of it. In fact, African culture is shaped by four basic factors: (1) our history; (2) our oppression; (3) our resistance; and (4) our ongoing internal creative capacity—that is, our enduring ability to create meaning, beauty, good, and free space, despite the unfree and oppressive context in which we might find ourselves. Surely among our most defining characteristics as a people is our adaptive vitality, human durability, and creative capacity to make place out of no place, to make way out of no way, and to continue to create the new out of the old in our ongoing struggle to bring good into the world.

Resistance is any and all efforts to deny, diminish, and destroy the oppressive and unjust hold of the established order (Karenga 2002b: 145ff). Forms of resistance are thus varied and numerous, ranging from day-to-day resistance, holding on to one's humanity in an inhuman situation, teaching, writing, organizing, boycotting, and striking to confrontation and armed struggle. Resistance means rejecting and refusing to accept both the *rightfulness* and the *rationality* of the existence and function of the established order. To deny its rightfulness is to deny its legitimacy, its claims to being a just and good society, whether in actuality, in process, or in promise. And to deny its rationality is to deny its claims of reasonableness in structure and functioning. Consider, in this light, the irrationality of the established order, with its racist, classist, and sexist practices, its instrumental reasoning for profit and control at the expense of human freedom and human flourishing, and its contribution to environmental degradation and, ultimately, societal, world, and species destruction.

Surely it is the case that knowingly degrading the environment and causing needless suffering, deprivation, and death—contrary to the potential good for which science and technology could be used—is irrational in any moral or meaningful sense. Indeed, although the established order is rational in instrumental calculation, it is irrational in its functioning and its effects on the world (Borgman 1984; Heidegger 1977; Marcuse 1964). Here we must make a distinction between instrumental reasoning—a detached internally coherent and consistent mode of reasoning that may be used for any purpose—and a systematic and morally grounded mode of reasoning—whose purpose informs both the process and the practice itself, both of which are self-consciously directed toward constantly improving the human condition and enhancing the human prospect. The former reasoning is the business of the capitalist market; the latter reasoning is the business or, rather, work of the Africana philosopher.

Clearly, resistance is an ancient and ongoing African tradition. Our tradition of resistance extends back to ancient Egypt's liberation struggle against the Hyksos, the first liberation struggle recorded in history, and it includes the continuous labor strikes by workers for just pay and work conditions, also the first recorded in history. This most ancient of resistance traditions also includes Continental and Diasporan Africans' struggles against imperialism, colonialism, and the Holocaust of enslavement, that morally monstrous act of genocide which was not only a grievous crime against the African people but also a crime against humanity. And, finally, it includes our ancient and ongoing struggle for social justice in the United States and elsewhere.

The concept and practice of resistance as an intellectual and practical project take on added meaning in connection with Europe during its period of imperialism, colonization, and the Holocaust of enslavement. It is here that we encounter racism in its violent impositional, ideological, and institutional forms; and we are challenged to defend ourselves, our humanity, and our right to freedom both intellectually and practically. Frederick Douglass's defense of our humanity, Sojourner Truth's and Anna J. Cooper's definition and defense of black womanhood, Henry Highland Garnet's and Ida B. Wells-Barnett's defense of our right to rebel in self-defense and self-determination, Maria Stewart's and Martin Delaney's quest for a return to the source of paradigms and possibilities, and W. E. B. Du Bois's defense of our right to live free and full lives without the problematization of race and racism imposed on us, as well as other contemporary activist-intellectuals—all offer core elements in our current conception and tradition of resistance as an intellectual and practical project (Bracey et al., 1970; Cooper 1988; Douglass 1950; Du Bois 1969; Garnet 1951; Gordon 2000b: ch. 4; Hamlet 1998; Logan 1999; Niles 1995; Stewart 1987; Wells-Barnett 1970).

Likewise, Continental and Caribbean activist-intellectuals such as Frantz Fanon (1952, 1963, 1967a, 1967b, 1967c), Sékou Touré

(1959b), Aimé Césaire (1972), Marcus Garvey (1977), Amilcar Cabral (1979), and Julius Nyerere (1968) not only form a vital part of the Africana philosophical project of resistance but also expand the range and quality of exchange and contestation that sustains and invigorates the tradition (Eze 1998; Gordon 1995b; Karenga 1997). And finally, the Black Freedom Movement—both its civil rights and Black Power periods and tendencies—serves as a direct source of concepts, ideas, and philosophical initiatives from such activist-intellectuals as Malcolm X (1965a, 1965b), Ella Baker (Ransby 2003), Martin Luther King, Jr. (1958), James Washington (1986), Robert Williams (1973), Timothy Tyson (1999), Harold Cruse (1967), Kwame Ture (1994), and Maulana Karenga (1978, 1980, 1997). Indeed, the Black Power Movement provides the philosophical framework in which I write this paper. Current Africana philosophy borrows from and builds on, as well as contests and counters, these initiatives in a process of ongoing reflexivity, retrieval, reconstruction, and refinement (Boxill 1992; Gordon 1995c, 1997a, 2000b; Harris 1983 [2000]; Outlaw 1996).

Political Engagement

A *philosophy born of struggle* must at some point and in a meaningful way become and understand itself as a *philosophy of struggle*. What this means is that it must move from a simple concern with explaining reality to a focus on crafting ideas and plans of action to change it. In the final analysis, such a philosophy of struggle must also evolve from the philosopher participating in the struggle out of which his or her philosophy evolves.

The Africana philosophic project of resistance, as argued above, is both an intellectual and a practical project. Never simply a process isolated in the life of the mind, it is a practice which requires that one search the heart and mind (HHy ib) for ways to bring and sustain good in the world, thus improving the human condition and enhancing the human project. It is at this juncture that the Africana philosopher, the intellectual who thinks and cares deeply about the human condition and human prospect, is especially called upon to engage the major issues of our times and to bring to bear, as best she or he can, the rich and ancient resources of African culture as a lived and living tradition (Fanon 1967c; Karenga 1997). For who is more able than the Africana philosopher, dedicated to deep and disciplined thought, to reach below the surface and reveal a portrait of things more complex and reliable than the portrait provided by the established order in the academy or media? Who is better equipped to deconstruct and dissolve would-be herrenvolk nations' specious claims of the right of conquest, the right of occupation, and the establishment of democracy through military dictatorship? And who can better draw the distinction between a people's right and responsibility of resistance against occupation and other forms of oppression and an aggressor's spurious claim to preemptive aggression and occupation as a form of self-defense?

Clearly, if the Africana philosopher is to live a tradition of resistance and constantly enrich and expand a philosophy born of struggle, she or he must deal with issues of struggle, of war and peace, of occupation and oppression; of group and state terrorism, and of ethnic cleansing, genocide, and reparations. And she or he must reject hegemonic powers' attempt to outlaw resistance and to redefine guerillas as gunmen, freedom fighters as terrorists, and state-terrorism as self-defense with collateral damage. Indeed, it is the Africana philosopher who must reveal the moral absurdity of giving equal moral status to the oppressed and the oppressor or to an occupied country and an occupying country—or, more egregious still, of giving a superior moral status to the oppressor as a victim of resistance by the oppressed.

Further, it is the Africana philosopher who should explain patiently and respectfully that reparations—repair of the Holocaust of enslavement and subsequent gross injuries—are not simply about money or about what the oppressor gives the oppressed and injured; indeed, reparations are about what the injured and oppressed get from the struggle for justice itself (Munford 1996; Robinson 2000, 2002). And that struggle, in its most expansive sense, must be a struggle that seeks a national dialogue on reparations; a national admission of the Holocaust of enslavement as the root injury; a national apology for the Holocaust of enslavement; a national recognition of its horror and root meaning for Africans and humanity through monuments, the media, and the educational system; various forms of compensation; and, ultimately, corrective measures that require a radical restructuring of U.S. society to prevent its reoccurrence (Karenga 2002b: 393–399). For surely it is in the process of such a struggle that a grossly injured people will truly heal and repair themselves and contribute to the healing and repairing of the country and world.

The Africana philosopher as an activist intellectual is among those whom Fanon called on to imagine and propose a path and practice that contribute to the "upward thrust of the masses." We must, he states, imagine a new world, start a new history of humankind, and set in motion a new man and woman to accomplish these tasks (Fanon 1963: 311ff). This requires that we "reconsider the question of mankind ... reconsider the question of cerebral reality and of the cerebral mass of all humanity, whose connections must be increased, whose channels must be diversified and whose messages must be rehumanized." So, it is in this context that we ask ourselves, both as activist scholars and as philosophers, *What are we to do?* In the struggle for answers to this question, we need to become engaged intellectually and practically. And it is out of this struggle over the question of what to do, and the conditions that gave rise to it, that our philosophy of struggle is born and developed in an ongoing and meaningful way.

Moreover, Sékou Touré (1959a) and Frantz Fanon (1967c) tell us that, regardless of the intellectual offering we make on the altar of resistance, eventually we must throw ourselves into the practical struggle to bring into being the good society and world we all want and deserve to live in. As Touré says, "Thus, the true political leaders of Africa whose thought and attitude are directed toward the national liberation of their people can only be *engaged persons (hommes engagés), fundamentally* engaged against all the forms and forces of dehumanization of African culture." Indeed, "they represent, by the anti-colonial nature and national content of their struggle, the cultural values of their society mobilized against colonialism" (1959a: 105; emphasis added).

Touré realizes that oppression is not only physical and structural but also psychological, and thus he argues that African intellectuals and leaders must decolonize both the structures and the minds and hearts of themselves and the people. This *mutatis mutandis* refers also to the struggle against racism, which entails violent imposition and institutional arrangements as well as an ideology that seeks to justify and ennoble itself by savaging, dehumanizing, and devaluing the oppressed and their culture. Therefore, Touré says, "decoloniza-tion consists not only of liberating oneself from the *colonial presence* (*la présence coloniale*), it, of necessity, must be achieved through the total liberation of the spirit of the 'colonized,' that is to say, all the negative consequences—moral, intellectual and cultural of the colonial regime" (1959a).

Having freed themselves from colonial and racist complexes and the resultant dislocations, intellectuals can fully root themselves in the struggle of the people and, as Fanon says, "put at the people's disposal the intellectual and technical capital [they have] snatched" from the dominant society (Fanon 1967c: 150). Here, too, the intellectuals will necessarily have to deal with Almicar Cabral's challenge to them to commit class suicide and identify with the struggle and aspiration of the people (Cabral 1979: 110; Karenga 1990a). Concerning the intellectuals, Fanon (1963: 234) notes that "the problem is to get to know the place these men mean to give their people, the kind of social relations that they decide to set up and the conception they have of the future of humanity. It is this that counts; all else is mystification, signifying nothing."

Finally, both Fanon and Touré provide excellent discussions of the need for practical engagement in the struggle. In fact, in "On National Culture," a chapter in his classic work *Wretched of the Earth*, Fanon quotes from Touré's seminal and much-quoted lecture at the Second Congress of Black Writers and Artists held in 1959, titled "The Political Leader Considered as Representative of a Culture." Stressing the value of political engagement as both an aid to the people's and humanity's liberation struggle and to the quality and value of one's own intellectual and creative work, Touré says that:

> To take part in the African revolution, it is not enough to write a revolutionary song; you must make the revolution with the people and if you make the revolution with the people, the songs will come of themselves.
>
> In order to achieve real action, you must, yourself, be a living part of Africa and of its thought, an element of that popular energy totally mobilized for the liberation, progress and happiness of Africa. There is no place outside this single struggle for the artist or the intellectual who is not himself engaged and totally mobilized with the people in that great struggle of Africa and of suffering humanity. (Touré 1959a: 111)

Here, then, is the task and mission of the African philosopher whose philosophy is born of and rooted in a tradition of struggle.

It is to overturn oneself first, decolonizing one's heart and mind; to root oneself in one's culture; to bring forth the best of what it means to be African and human in the world; to speak one's own special cultural truth to the world and use it to resist and affirm; to deconstruct and reconstruct both the realm of human knowledge and human society, and, as Fanon says, dare to contribute to the project, setting in motion a new history of humankind (Gordon 2000a, 2000b).

What I want to do now by way of conclusion is to retrieve and reconstruct some of the ancient and modern concepts and ideas from these philosophical initiatives and use them to frame and give foundation to a public policy and public philosophy initiative called the *ethics of sharing*. It is a Kawaida project and thus seeks a useful and ongoing synthesis of African thought and practice—ancient and modern—in constant exchange with the world. Thus, I want to sketch the outline of a public policy that is self-consciously ethical, uniting reflection, care, and resultant practice in the ancient Egyptian tradition of defining the Maatian way (see also Karenga 1995b).

Conclusion: Toward an Ethics of Sharing

In reaffirming and constantly developing the original meaning of African philosophy as a deep and disciplined thought directed toward what is good for the people and the world, we have an excellent point of departure for developing a policy initiative with national and international applications. This meets the classical African requirement that philosophy be a practice-oriented and practice-grounded intellectual initiative that self-consciously seeks to bring good into the world, drawing from the lived experience of the people. In short, philosophy becomes a personal task and a social responsibility in terms of communication and cooperation with one's community and culture and then with society and the world.

The *Odu Ifa* (78: 1) says that the first requirement for realizing good in the world is "wisdom adequate to govern the world." Now, in classical African philosophy, wisdom, regardless of its varied forms—philosophic, technical, political, social, and so on—must always be undergirded and informed by a moral reasoning and sensitivity. Indeed, the Yoruba word for "govern," as used in the quote above, is "àkóso," which literally means "gathering people together for good purposes." In addition to wisdom, The *Odu* lists "the virtue of sacrifice, character, the love of doing good, especially for the needy and those who ask for our assistance and the eagerness and struggle to increase good in the world and not let any good be lost." Thus, we begin with a reflective and morally grounded *wisdom* and then move toward a deepening of our understanding, realizing our goals through *struggle*—both an internal and a social process.

It is in the quest for wisdom, born of deep and disciplined thought and infused with a profound sense of the moral and oriented toward practice, that Africana philosophers can live a tradition of resistance—specifically, by crafting and conducting a national and international conversation, a public philosophy and policy initiative around an ethics of sharing for the country and the world. Calvin Schrag, referring to the Socratic model, has rightly noted that the "definition of the philosophical task, along the lines of a rhetoric of inquiry directed *to* the public and drafted *for* the public, should not be taken as an invitation to popularize by leveling thought to its lowest. It does, however, provide a motivation to communicate what one considers to be of philosophic importance and interest to a general audience and wide readership" (Schrag 1997: x). For the Africana philosopher, the ancient model is both ancient Egyptian and ancient Yoruba, given these traditions' emphasis on the essentiality of wisdom for good in the world. In fact, according to the *Odu Ifa* (78: 1), the first criterion for creating a good world is "full knowledge of things" and the first requirement for realizing good in the world, as noted above, is "wisdom adequate to govern the world." Both of these criteria require an informed people and public, and both speak to the need not only to speak truth to power but also to speak truth to the people and mobilize and organize them so that they will become self-conscious agents of their own lives and liberation.

Now, this initiative for an ethics of sharing is informed by the classical African ethical understanding that the greatest good is shared good, the good that is planted, cultivated, harvested, and shared together. As stated in the *Odu* (202: 1), "Indeed, all goodness took the form of coming together in harmony" since the dawn of creation. Therefore, the great goods of freedom, justice, love, family, friendship, sisterhood, brotherhood, a life of peace, a life of dignity and decency, and the world itself, are all shared goods. And they are not real if only some people are deemed worthy of them or worthier than others. Indeed, the problems of the world revolve around the denial of these and other similar goods essential to human freedom and human flourishing. It is an ethics of sharing that offers promising possibilities of addressing this unjust and unacceptable state of affairs.

This ethics of sharing (Karenga 2002a) requires sharing on a minimum of seven basic levels: shared status, shared knowledge, shared space, shared wealth, shared power, shared interests, and shared responsibility for building the world we all want and deserve to live in. The principle of *shared status* speaks to the mutual commitment to the dignity of the human person-in-community, not as an abstraction but in and from the cultural context to which the individual owes his or her existence. It requires mutual respect and recognition, rejects all concepts of superior and inferior persons and peoples, and upholds the equal status, rights, dignity, and opportunities of all as human beings and citizens both in theory and in practice.

The principle of *shared knowledge* reaffirms the human and social need for and right to knowledge essential for human development and human flourishing. The ancient Egyptians called humans rxyt (*rekhit*), which literally means "knowing beings." This indicates the emphasis they placed on knowledge and knowing in defining our humanity, but also in realizing our humanity. The stress in the Du Boisian sense is on a knowledge of the highest quality, which is designed not only for "making a living" but for conceiving and living a good life.

The principle of *shared space* speaks to our need to share the country and the world in equitable and ethical ways; the development of immigration policies untainted by race, class, religion, and other irrational and unethical considerations; and respect for the integrity of the environment—especially in terms of protecting it against the ravages of privatization and globalization, which so often means plunder, pollution, and depletion. The principle of *shared wealth* speaks to the issue of equitable distribution of wealth in society and the world, and of shared use of resources throughout the world, in order to deal with global problems such as poverty, homelessness, poor or nonexistent health care, lack of education, and other deficient conditions. It speaks to the necessity of caring for the vulnerable and aiding the poor in their struggle to reduce and ultimately end poverty. It links the right to a life in dignity with the right to a life of decency—that is, a life in which the basic necessities of food, clothing, shelter, health care, education, and physical and economic security are ensured. And it upholds the right of the worker to fair wages, safe working conditions, just treatment while working and at the end of work, unionization, and shared decision making.

The principle of *shared power* speaks to the central concern of self-determination, the principle and practice of self-governance, and the right to participate in every decision that affects our destiny and daily lives. It encourages coalitions and alliances and other cooperative practices of mutual benefit and common good. And it calls for actual rather than symbolic representation of groups and peoples in the central institutions of community, society, and the world.

The principle of *shared interests* is rooted in four pillars of African ethics, which entail respect for and commitment to (1) the dignity and rights of the human person; (2) the well-being and flourishing of family and community, (3) the integrity and value of the environment, and (4) the reciprocal solidarity and cooperation of humanity for mutual benefit. This principle, too, is informed by the ancient African ethical teaching that the greatest good is always a shared good and that each person and people should share in the good of and in the world.

The last principle of the ethics of sharing is *shared responsibility,* which calls for an active commitment to building the communities, society, and world we all want and deserve to live in. It requires us constantly to reflect, discuss, and practice that which transforms the "ideal life of the mind" into the improvement and enhancement of the actual lives of people and the conditions in which they live. It encourages personal and collective responsibility for the constant moral assessment of policies and practices in terms of the problems and possibilities they pose for the world. And it urges us constantly to repair and restore the world and leave a legacy rooted in and reflective of the best of African and human thought and practice. We are to recognize and respect the meaning and ongoing urgency of our shared active responsibility. And we do this knowing that, as Seba Kheti teaches, "every day is a donation to eternity and every hour is a contribution to the future."

Notes

1. This dialog occurred during the question and answer session following his keynote address at the 10th Annual Philosophy Born of Struggle Conference on October 24, 2003.

References

꙰

Abelove, Henry, Michèle Aina Barale, and David M. Halperin, eds. 1993. *The Lesbian and Gay Studies Reader*. New York: Routledge.

Abimbola, Wande, ed. 1975. *Yoruba Oral Tradition: Poetry in Music, Dance and Drama*. Ilè Ifé, Nigeria: Department of African Language and Literature, University of Ifé.

Abiodun, Rowland, H. J. Drewal, and J. Pemberton, eds. 1994. *The Yoruba Artist: New Theoretical Perspectives on African Arts*. Washington, DC/London: Smithsonian Institution Press.

Abukhalil, As'ad. 2002. *Bin Laden, Islam and America's New "War on Terrorism."* New York: Seven Stories Press.

"A Case for Continental Philosophy." 1966. *American Philosophical Quarterly* 33, no. 1: 131.

Adell, Sandra. 1994. *Double Consciousness/Double Bind: Theoretical Issues in Twentieth-Century Black Literature*. Urbana: University of Illinois Press.

Africana Philosophy. 1992-1994. Special issue of *Philosophical Forum* 24, nos. 1-3 (Fall-Spring).

Ahmad, Nadia Batool, et al., eds. 2002. *Unveiling the Real Terrorist Mind*. New York: Students for International Peace and Justice.

Alarcón, Norma, Caren Kaplan, and Minoo Moallem. 1999. "Introduction: Between Woman and Nation." In *Between Woman and Nation: Nationalisms, Transnational Feminisms, and the State* (pp. 1-16), edited by Caren Kaplan, Norma Alarcón, and Minoo Moallem. Durham, NC/London: Duke University Press.

Allen, Ernest, Jr. 1997. "On the Reading of Riddles: Rethinking Du Boisian 'Double Consciousness.'" In *Existence in Black* (pp. 49-68), edited and with an introduction by Lewis Gordon. New York/London: Routledge.

Allen, James. 1988. *Genesis in Egypt: The Philosophy of Ancient Egyptian Creation Accounts*, Yale Egyptological Studies, Vol. 2. New Haven: Yale Egyptological Seminar.

Amin, Samir. 2001. "U.S. Hegemony and the Response to Terror," *Monthly Review* 53, no. 6 (November).

Anderson, James D. 1988. *The Education of Blacks in the South, 1860-1935*. Chapel Hill: University of North Carolina Press.

Antonello, Gerbi. 1944. *Viejas polémicas sobre el nuevo mundo (comentarios a una tésis de Hegel)*. Lima, Peru: Banco de crédito del Perú.

Anzaldúa, Gloria. 1999. *Borderlands/La Frontera: The New Mestiza*, 2nd ed. San Francisco: Aunt Lute.

Appiah, K. Anthony. 1992. *In My Father's House: Africa in the Philosophy of Culture*. New York: Oxford University Press.

Aptheker, Herbert. 1963. *American Negro Slave Revolts*. New York: International Publishers.

Arendt, Hannah. 1958. *The Human Condition*. Chicago: University of Chicago Press.

Aronowitz, Stanley. 1994. *Dead Artists, Live Theories, and Other Cultural Problems*. New York: Routledge.

Asante, Molefi Kete. 1988. *Afrocentricity*. Trenton: Africa World Press.

———. 1990. *Kemet, Afrocentricity and Knowledge*. Trenton, NJ: Africa World Press.

———. 1997. "Afrocentricity and the Quest for Method." In *Africana Studies: A Disciplinary Quest for Both Theory and Method* (pp. 69–90), edited by James L. Conyers, Jr. Jefferson, NC/London: McFarland.

———. 1998. *The Afrocentric Idea*, rev. ed. Philadelphia: Temple University Press.

———. 1999. *The Painful Demise of Eurocentricism: An Afrocentric Response to Critics*. Trenton, NJ: Africa World Press.

———. 2000. *The Egyptian Philosophers: Ancient African Voices from Imhotep to Akhenaten*. Chicago: African American Images.

Asante, Molefi Kete, and Abu Abarry. 1996. *The African Intellectual Heritage*. Philadelphia: Temple University Press.

Assmann, Jan. 1990. *Màat, Gerechtigkeit und Unsterblichkeit im Alten Egypten*. Munche: Verlag C. H. Beck.

Austin, Allan D. 1997. *African Muslims in Antebellum America: Transatlantic Stories and Spiritual Struggles*. New York: Routledge.

Axelson, Sigbert. 1970. *Culture Confrontation in the Lower Congo, Etc.* Stockholm: Gummeson.

Baldwin, James. 1992. *Another Country*. New York: Vintage.

Bales, Kevin. 1999. *Disposable People: New Slavery in the Global Economy*. Berkeley: University of California Press.

Balibar, Etienne. 1991. "The Nation Form: History and Ideology." In *Race, Nation, Class: Ambiguous Identities*, edited by Etienne Balibar and Immanuel Wallerstein. London: Verso.

Baraka, Amiri. 1963. *Blues People: Negro Music in White America*. New York: William and Morrow.

———. 1997. *The Autobiography of LeRoi Jones/Amiri Baraka*. New York: Lawrence Hill Books.

Barber, Benjamin R. 1996. *Jihad vs. McWorld*, New York: Ballantine.

Barthes, Roland. 1972. *Mythologies*, translated by Annette Lavers. New York: Hill and Wang.

———. 1975. *The Pleasure of the Text*, translated by Richard Miller. New York: Hill and Wang.

References

Batstone, David, Eduardo Mendieta, Lois Ann Lorentzen, and Dwight N. Hopkins, eds. 1997. *Liberation Theologies, Postmodernity, and the Americas*. London: Routledge.

Bay, Mia. 2000. *The White Image in the Black Mind*. New York: Oxford University Press.

Bell, Richard H. 1998. *Simone Weil: The Way of Justice as Compassion*. Lanham, MD: Rowman and Littlefield.

Berger, P., and T. Luckmann. 1967. *The Social Construction of Reality*. New York: Anchor Books.

Bernal, Martin. 1987. *Black Athena: The Afroasiatic Roots of Classical Civilization*, vols. I and II. New Brunswick: Rutgers University Press.

Bernasconi, Robert. 1997. "African Philosophy's Challenge to Continental Philosophy." In *Postcolonial African Philosophy* (pp. 183–196), edited by Emmanuel Chukwudi Eze. Malden, MA: Blackwell.

Bernasconi, Robert, and Tommy Lott, eds. 2000. *The Idea of Race*. Indianapolis: Hackett Publishers.

Bilolo, Mubabinge. 1995. *Meta-Ontologie pharonique IIIe millénaire* av. J-C. Munish/Kinshasa: Academy of African Thought and Cheikh Anta Diop Center for Egyptological Studies—INADEP, Sec. I, Vol. 5, African University Studies.

Birt, Robert, ed. *The Quest of Community and Identity: Critical Essays in Africana and Social Philosophy*. Lanham, MD: Rowman and Littlefield.

Blackburn, Robin. 1988. *The Overthrow of Colonial Slavery*. London/New York: Verso.

———. 1997. The Making of New World Slavery: From the Baroque to the Modern 1492–1800. London/New York: Verso.

Bloch, Ernest. 1996. *The Principle of Hope*, translated by Neville Plaice, Stephen Plaice, and Paul Knight. Cambridge, MA: MIT Press.

Blum, William. 1995. *Killing Hope: U.S. Military and CIA Intervention Since World War II*. Monroe, ME: Common Courage Press.

Blumenberg, Hans. 1983. *The Legitimacy of the Modern Age*, translated by Robert M. Wallace. Cambridge, MA: MIT Press.

———. 1985. *Work on Myth*, translated by Robert M. Wallace. Cambridge, MA: MIT Press.

———. 1997. *Shipwrecked with Spectator: Paradigm of a Metaphor for Existence*, translated by Steven Rendall. Cambridge, MA: MIT Press.

Blyden, Edward. 1908. *African Life and Customs*. London: C. M. Phillips.

Borgman, Albert. 1984. *Technology and Character of Contemporary Life*. Chicago: University of Chicago Press.

Bourdieu, Pierre. 1984. *Distinction:A Social Critique of the Judgement of Taste*, translated by Richard Nice. Cambridge, MA: Harvard University Press.

———. 1998. *Acts of Resistance: Against the New Myths of Our Time*. Cambridge, UK: Polity Press.

———. 1999. "On the Cunning of Imperialist Reason," *Theory, Culture and Society* 16, no. 1: 41–58.

References

Bowser, Benjamin P., Terry Jones, and Gale Auletta Yong, eds., 1995. *Toward the Multicultural University*. Westport, CT: Praeger.

Boxill, Bernard. 1992. *Blacks and Social Justice*, rev. ed. Lanham, MD: Rowman and Littlefield.

Bracey, John, Jr., August Meier, and Elliot Rudwick, eds. 1970. *Black Nationalism in America*. Indianapolis: Bobbs-Merrill.

Bradley, Patricia. 1998. *Slavery, Propaganda and the American Revolution*. Jackson: University of Mississippi Press.

Brunner, Helmut. 1991. *Die Weisheitsbücher der Ägypter: Lehren für das Leben*. Zürich: Artemis.

Budge, E. A. Wallis. 1904. *Gods of the Egyptians* (2 vols.). London: Methuen.

———. 1934. *From Fetish to God in Ancient Egypt*. London: Oxford University Press.

Butler, Johnnella E. 2001. "Ethnic Studies as a Matrix for the Humanities, Social Sciences, and the Common Good." *In Color-Line to Borderlands: The Matrix of American Ethnic Studies*, edited by Johnnella E. Butler. Seattle: University of Washington Press.

Butler, Judith. 1993. *Bodies That Matter: On the Discursive Limits of "Sex."* New York: Routledge.

———. 1999. *Gender Trouble: Feminism and the Subversion of Identity*. New York: Routledge.

Cabral, Amilcar. 1970. *Revolution in Guinea*. New York: Monthly Review Press.

———. 1979. *Return to the Source: Selected Speeches*. New York: Monthly Review Press.

Cameron, L. 1996. *Body Alchemy: Transsexual Portraits*. San Francisco: Cleis Press.

Carter, Aaron. 1972. *The American Slave: A Composite, Arkansas Narratives,* edited by George R. Rawick. Westport, CT: Greenwood.

Casalla, Mario. 1992. América en el pensamiento de Hegel: admiración y rechazo. Buenos Aires: Catálogos.

Cassirer, Ernst. 1946. *The Myth of the State*. New Haven: Yale University Press.

———. 1955. *The Philosophy of Symbolic Forms: Mythical Thought*. New Haven: Yale University Press.

Cavalli-Sforza, L. Luca, Paolo Menozzi, and Alberto Piazza. 1994. *The History and Geography of Human Genes*. Princeton: Princeton University Press.

Cave, David. 1993. *Mircea Eliade's Vision for a New Humanism*. New York: Oxford University Press.

Caws, Peter. 1965. *The Philosophy of Science: A Systematic Account*. Princeton, NJ: Van Nostrand.

———. 1967. *Science and the Theory of Value*. New York: Random House.

———. 1993. *Yorick's World: Science and the Knowing Subject.* Berkeley: University of California Press.

———. 1996. *Ethics from Experience.* Boston: Jones and Bartlett.

Césaire, Aimé. 1956. *Letter to Maurice Thorez/Lettre à Maurice Thorez,* 3rd ed. Paris: Présence Africaine.

———. 1972. *Discourse on Colonialism.* New York: Monthly Review Press.

———. 1992. "Interview with Aimé Césaire," by Mybe Cham. In *Ex-iles: Essays on Caribbean Cinema* (pp. 367–368). Trenton, NJ: Africa World Press.

———. 2000/1972. *Discourse on Colonialism,* translated by Joan Pinkham. New York: Monthly Review Press.

Chan, Alan. 1984. "Philosophical Hermeneutics and the Analects: The Paradigm of 'Tradition,'" *Philosophy East and West* 34, no. 4 (October): 421–436.

Chang, Nancy. 2002. *Silencing Political Dissent.* New York: Seven Stories Press.

Chavolla, Arturo. 1993. *La idea de América en el pensamiento europeo de Fernández de Oviedo a Hegel.* Guadalajara, México: Universidad de Guadalajara.

Churchill, Ward, and Jim Vander Wall. 2002. *The Cointelpro Papers: Documents from the FBI's Secret Wars Against Dissent in the United States,* 2nd ed. Boston: South End Press.

Cladis, Mark S. 2003. *Public Vision, Private Lives: Rousseau, Religion, and 21st-century Democracy.* New York: Oxford University Press.

Clarke, Cheryl. 1983. "Lesbianism: An Act of Resistance." In *This Bridge Called My Back: Writings by Radical Women of Color.* New York: Kitchen Table: Women of Color Press.

Clarke, John Henrik, Esther Jackson, Ernest Kaiser, and J. H. O'Dell, eds. 1970. *Black Titan: W. E. B. Du Bois.* Boston: Beacon Press.

Cleaver, Eldridge. 1968. *Soul on Ice.* New York: Dell Books.

Cole, David, James X. Dempsey, and Carol E. Goldberg. 2002. *Terrorism and the Constitution: Sacrificing Civil Liberties in the Name of National Security.* New York: The New Press.

Cole, Thomas. 1972. *The American Slave. A Composite, Texas Narratives* (Vol. 4, Pt. 1), edited by George P. Rawick. Westport, CT: Greenwood Publishing.

Coles, Romand. 2003. "Contesting Cosmopolitan Currencies: The Nepantlist Rose in the Cross(ing) of the Present," *Nepantla: Views from South* 4, no. 1: 5–40.

Collins, Patricia Hill. 2000. *Black Feminist Thought: Knowledge, Consciousness, and the Politics of Empowerment,* rev. ed. New York: Routledge.

Comaroff, John L., and Jean Comaroff. 1997. *Of Revelation and Revolution,* Vol. 2: *The Dialectics of Modernity on a South African Frontier.* Chicago: University of Chicago Press.

Cone, James H. 1991. *The Spiritual and the Blues*. Maryknoll: Orbis Books.

Conerly, Gregory. 1996. "Black Lesbian, Gay, and Bisexual Identity." In *Queer Studies* (pp. 133-145). The Politics of New York: New York University Press.

Connor, Kimberly Rae. 2000. *Imagining Grace: Liberating Theologies in the Slave Narrative Tradition*. Urbana: University of Illinois Press.

Conyers, James L., Jr., ed. 1997. *Africana Studies: A Disciplinary Quest for Both Theory and Method*. Jefferson, NC/London: McFarland.

———. 2003. *Afrocentricity and the Academy: Essays on Theory and Practice*. Jefferson, NC: McFarland.

Cooper, Anna Julia. 1988. *A Voice from the South*. Oxford: Oxford University Press.

———. 1998. *The Voice of Anna Julia Cooper, Including "A Voice from the South" and Other Important Essays, Papers and Letters*, edited by Charles Lemert and Esme Bhan. Lanham, MD: Rowman and Littlefield.

Cornelius, Janet Duitsman. 1991. *When I Can Read My Title Clear: Literacy, Slavery, and Religion in the Antebellum South*. Charleston: University of South Carolina Press.

Cotkin, George. 2003. *Existential America*. Baltimore: Johns Hopkins Press.

Cox, Oliver C. 2000. *Race: A Study in Social Dynamics—50th Anniversary Edition of Caste, Class and Race: A Study in Social Dynamics*. New York: Monthly Review Press.

Critchley, Simon. 1998. "Introduction: What Is Continental Philosophy?" In *A Companion to Continental Philosophy* (pp. 1-17), edited by Simon Critchley and William R. Schroeder. Malden, MA: Blackwell.

Cruse, Harold. 1967. *The Crisis of the Negro Intellectual: A Historical Analysis of the Failure of Black Leadership*. New York: William Morrow.

Darwin, Charles. 1981 [1871]. *The Descent of Man and Selection in Relation to Sex*, introduction by J. T. Bonner and Robert M. May. Princeton: Princeton University Press.

Davis, Angela Y. 1983. *Women, Race, and Class*. New York: Vintage.

Davis, Carole Boyce, and Elaine Savory-Fido. 1990. *Out of Kumbla: Caribbean Women and Literature*. Trenton, NJ: Africa World Press.

Davis, Charles T., and Henry Louis Gates, Jr., eds. 1985. *The Slave's Narrative*. New York: Oxford University Press.

Davis, David Brion. 1983. *The Emancipation Moment*. Gettysburg, PA: Gettysburg College.

———. 1984. *Slavery and Human Progress*. New York: Oxford University Press.

———. 1999. *The Problem of Slavery in the Age of Revolution 1770-1823*. New York: Oxford University Press.

Dayan, Joan. 1998. *Haiti, History, and the Gods*. Berkeley: University of California Press.

de Costa, Miriam, ed. 1977. *Blacks in Hispanic Literature: Critical Essays*. Port Washington, NY: Kennikat Press.

de Lauretis, T. 1991. "Queer Theory, Lesbian and Gay Studies: An Introduction." *Differences: A Journal of Feminist Cultural Studies* 3, no. 2 (Summer): iii–xviii.

Derrida, Jacques. 1972. *Margins of Philosophy*. Chicago: University of Chicago Press.

———. 1988. *Limited Inc*. Evanston, IL: Northwestern University Press.

Descartes, René. 1985. *Meditations on First Philosophy*. Cambridge: Cambridge University Press.

———. 1999. *"Discourse on Method" and "Meditations on First Philosophy,"* with an introduction by Donald A. Cress. Indianapolis: Hackett Publishing Company.

Dévaud, Eugene. 1916. *Lex Maximes de Ptahhotep*. Fribourg: University of Fribourg.

Dickstein, Morris. 1998. "Introduction: Pragmatism Then and Now." In *The Revival of Pragmatism: New Essays on Social Thought, Law, and Culture* (pp. 1–18), edited by Morris Dickstein. Durham, NC/London: Duke University Press.

Diop, Cheikh Anta. 1981. *Civilisation ou Barbarie: Anthropologie Sans Complaisance*. Paris: Présence Africaine.

———. 1974. *The African Origin of Civilization: Myth or Reality*, translated by Mercer Cook. New York: Lawrence Hill Books.

———. 1977. *Parenté Génétique de L'Égyptien Pharaonique et des Langues Negro-Africaines*. Ifan-Dakar: Nouvelles Éditions Africaines.

———. 1987. *Precolonial Black Africa*, translated by H. J. Salemson. Westport, CT: Lawrence Hill Books.

———. 1991. *Civilization or Barbarism: An Authentic Anthropology*, translated by Yaa-Lengi Meema Ngemi, edited by Harold J. Salemson and Marjolijn de Jager. New York: Lawrence Hill Books.

———. 2003. *Cheikh Anta Diop: L'homme et l'oeuvres*. Paris: Présence Africaine.

Douglass, Frederick. 1950. *The Life and Writings of Frederick Douglass*, Vols. 1–5, edited by Philip Foner. New York: International Publishers.

Drake, St. Clare. 1991. *Black Folk Here and There: An Essay in History and Anthropology*. Los Angeles: Center for Afro-American Studies, University of California Press.

Dubey, Madhu. 1994. *Black Women Novelists and the Nationalist Aesthetic*. Bloomington: Indiana University Press.

Du Bois, W. E. B. 1903. *The Souls of Black Folk: Essays and Sketches*. Chicago: A. C. McClurg.

———. 1938. *Black Reconstruction in America, 1860–1880*. New York: Harcourt, Brace.

———. 1968. *The Autobiography of W. E. B. Du Bois: A Soliloquy on Viewing My Life from the Last Decade of Its First Century*. New York: International Publishers.

———. 1969. *The Souls of Black Folk*. New York: Signet Classics.

References

————. 1982. *The Souls of Black Folk,* with introductions by Dr. Nathan Harre and Alvin Poussaint, M.D., and with a revised and updated bibliography. New York: New American Library.

————. 1996 [1897]. *The Philadelphia Negro,* with an introduction by Elijah Anderson. Philadelphia: University of Pennsylvania Press.

————. 1998. "On the Conservation of Races." In Emmanuel Chukwudi Eze, *African Philosophy: An Anthology* (pp. 269–274). Malden, MA: Blackwell.

————. 1999a. [1903]. *The Souls of Black Folk: Authoritative Text, Contexts, and Criticism.* New York: W. W. Norton.

————. 1999b [1920]. *Darkwater: Voices from Within the Veil,* with an introduction by Manning Marable. Mineola: Dover Publications.

————. March 2000a. "The Study of the Negro Problems," *The Annals of the American Academy of Political and Social Science* 56: 13–27. (Originally published in the same journal in 1898.)

————. 2000b. "Sociology Hesitant." *Boundary 2* 27, no. 3 (Fall): 37–44.

————. 2000c [1897]. "On the Conservation of the Races." In *The Idea of Race,* edited by Robert Bernasconi and Tommy Lott. Indianpolis: Hackett Publishers.

Dussel, Enrique. 1996. *The Underside of Modernity: Apel, Ricoeur, Rorty, Taylor, and the Philosophy of Liberatsion,* translated and edited by Eduardo Mendieta. Atlantic Highlands, NJ: Humanities Press.

————. 1999. *Posmodernidad y transmodernidad: Diálogos con la filosofía de Gianni Vattimo.* Puebla, Mexico: Universidad Iberoamericana, Golfo Centro; Instituto Tecnológico y de Estudios Superiores de Occidente; Universidad Iberoamericana, Plantel Laguna.

Eddins, Berkley B., and Essie A. Eddins. 1983. "Liberalism and Liberation." In *Philosophy Born of Struggle: Anthology of Afro-American Philosophy from 1917* (pp. 159—173), edited by Leonard Harris. Dubuque, IA: Kendall/Hunt.

Eliade, Mircea. 1963. Myth and Reality. Illinois: Waveland Press.

Ellison, Ralph. 1986. *Going to the Territory.* New York: Random House.

————. 1995. *Invisible Man.* New York: Vintage International.

English, Parker, and Kibujjo M. Kalumba. 1996. *African Philosophy: A Classical Approach.* Upper Saddle River, NJ: Prentice-Hall.

Eze, Emmanuel Chukwudi, ed. 1997. *Post-Colonial African Philosophy,* Cambridge/Oxford: Blackwell.

————. 1998. *African Philosophy: An Anthology,* Malden, MA: Blackwell.

Fanon, Frantz. 1952. *Peau noire, masques blancs.* Paris: Éditions du Seuil.

————. 1961/1991. *Les Damnés de la terre,* préface de Jean-Paul Sartre. Paris: François Maspero éditeur S.A.R.L./Éditions Gallimard.

————. 1963. *The Wretched of the Earth,* translated by Constance Farrington, with an introduction by Jean-Paul Sartre. New York: Grove Press.

————. 1967a. *A Dying Colonialism,* translated by Haakon Chevalier, with an introduction by Adolfo Gilly. New York: Grove Weidenfeld.

————. 1967b. *Black Skin, White Masks*, translated by Charles Lamm Markman. New York: Grove Press.

————. 1967c. *Toward the African Revolution*, translated by Haakon Chevalier. New York: Grove Press.

————. 1975 /1968 [1959]. *Sociologie d'une révolution: l'an V de la révolution algérienne*, 2me ed. Paris: François Maspero.

Faulkner, Raymond O. 1976. *A Concise Dictionary of Middle Egyptian*. Oxford: Griffith Institute.

Feagin, Joe R. 2000. *Racist America: Roots, Current Realities, and Future Reparations*. New York: Routledge.

Feagin, Joe R., Hernán Vera, and Imani. 1996. *White Racism: The Basics*. New York: Routledge.

Fernández-Armesto, Felipe. 1987. *Before Columbus: Exploration and Colonization from the Mediterranean to the Atlantic, 1229-1492*. Philadelphia: University of Pennsylvania Press.

Ferry, Luc, and Alain Renaut. 1990. *French Philosophy of the Sixties: An Essay on Antihumanism*, translated by Mary H. S. Cattani. Amherst: University of Massachusetts Press.

Finch, Charles S., III. 1991. *Echoes of the Old Darkland: Themes from the African Eden*. Decatur, GA: Khenti.

Finch, Henry Leroy. 1999. *Simone Weil and the Intellect of Grace*. New York; Continuum.

Fink, Eugen, and Edmund Husserl. 1988. *Sixth Cartesian Meditation: The Idea of a Transcendental Theory,* translated by Ronald Brnzina. Bloominton: Indiana University Press.

Fischer, Sibylle. 2004. *Modernity Disavowed: Haiti and Cultures of Slavery in the Age of Revolution*. Durham, NC: Duke University Press.

Forster, Michael N. 1998. *Hegel's Idea of a Phenomenology of Spirit*. Chicago: University of Chicago Press.

Foucault, Michel. 1970. *The Order of Things: An Archaeology of the Human Sciences,* translated by A. M. Sheridan Smith. New York: Random House.

————. 1980. *Power/Knowledge: Selected Interviews and Other Writings, 1972-1977,* translated and edited by Colin Gordon. New York: Pantheon Books.

————. 1990. *The History of Sexuality: An Introduction*. New York: Vintage Books.

————. 1995. *Discipline and Punish: Birth of the Prison,* translated by Alan Sheridan. New York: Vintage.

————. 1997. *The Politics of Truth*, edited by Sylvére Lotringer and Lysa Hochroth. New York: Semiotext(e).

————. 2003. *"Society Must Be Defended": Lectures at the College de France, 1975-1976,* translated by David Macey. New York: Picador/St. Martin's Press.

Frankena, William. 1983. "The Ethics of Respect for Life." In *Ethical Principles for Social Policy* (pp. 1-35), edited by John Howie. Carbondale: Southern Illinois University Press.

References

Franklin, John Hope. 1988. *From Slavery to Freedom: A History of American Negroes*. New York: Knopf.

Freire, Paulo. 1970a/1988. *Cultural Action for Freedom*. Cambridge, MA: Harvard Educational Review, Monograph Series No. 1.

———. 1970b/1981. *Pedagogy of the Oppressed*, translated by Myra Bergman Ramos. New York: Continuum.

———. 1973. *Education for Critical Consciousness*. New York: Seabury Press.

French, Peter A., Jr., Theodore E. Uehling, and Howard K. Wettstein, eds. 1981. *The Foundations of Analytic Philosophy*. Minneapolis: University of Minnesota Press.

Freud, Sigmund. 1949. "Mourning and Melancholia," in *Collected Papers*, Vol. 4. London: Hogarth.

Fryer, David. 2001. "Post-Humanism and Contemporary Philosophy." *Radical Philosophy Review* 4, nos. 1 and 2: 247–262.

———. 2003. "Toward a Phenomenology of Gender Identity: Butler, Husserl, and the Problem of Experience," *Listening: A Journal of Religion and Culture* 37, no. 2 (Spring): 135–162.

———. 2004. *The Intervention of the Other*. New York: Other Press.

———. 2006. "African-American Queer Studies." In *A Companion to African-American Studies*, edited by Lewis R. Gordon and Jane Anna Gordon. Malden, MA: Blackwell.

Fuller, Hoyt. 1971. "Introduction: Towards a Black Aesthetic." In *The Black Aesthetic* (pp. 3–12), edited by Addison Gayle. Garden City, NY: Doubleday.

Gallop, Jane. 1982. *The Daughter's Seduction: Feminism and Psychoanalysis*. Ithaca, NY: Cornell University Press.

———. 1985. *Reading Lacan*. Ithaca, NY: Cornell University Press.

Gans, Herbert. 1999. "The Possibility of a New Racial Hierarchy in the 21st Century United States." In *The Cultural Territories of Race: Black and White Boundaries* (pp. 371–390), edited by Michéle Lamont. Chicago: University of Chicago Press.

Garnet, Henry Highland. 1951. "An Address to the Slaves of the United States of America," in *A Documentary History of Negro People in the United States*, edited by Herbert Aptheker. New York: Citadel Press.

García, Alma M., ed. 1997. *Chicana Feminist Thought: The Basic Historical Writings*. New York/London: Routledge.

Garcia, Jorge J. E. 1999. "Ethnic Labels and Philosophy," *Philosophy Today* 43, no. 4: 42–49.

Garvey, Marcus. 1977. *Philosophy and Opinions of Marcus Garvey* (Vols. I and II), edited by Amy Jacques Garvey. New York: Atheneum.

Gates, Henry Louis, Jr., ed. 1990. *Reading Black, Reading Feminist: A Critical Anthology*, edited by Henry Louis Gates, Jr. New York: Meridian-Penguin.

Gates, Henry Louis, Jr., and Cornel West. 2000. *The African-American Century: How Black Americans Have Shaped Our Country*. New York: Free Press.

Gayle, Addison, ed. 1971. *The Black Aesthetic*. Garden City, NY: Doubleday.

Geertz, Clifford. 1973. *The Interpretation of Cultures: Selected Essays*. New York: Basic Books.

———. 1983. *Local Knowledge: Further Essays in Interpretive Anthropology*. New York: Basic Books.

———. 2000. *The Interpretation of Cultures*. New York: Basic Books.

Genovese, Eugene. 1974. *Roll Jordan Roll: The World the Slaves Made*. New York: Vintage Books.

Gerald, Carolyn. 1971. "The Black Writer and His Role." In *The Black Aesthetic* (pp. 370–378), edited by Addison Gayle. Garden City, NY: Doubleday.

Gilroy, Paul. 2000. *Against Race: Imagining Political Culture Beyond the Color Line*. Cambridge, MA: Harvard University Press.

Goatley, David Emmanuel. 1996. *Were You There? Godforsakenness in Slave Religion*. Maryknoll: Orbis Books.

Godelier, Maurice. 1999. *The Enigma of the Gift*. Chicago: University of Chicago Press.

Godzich, Wlad. 1986. Foreword to *Heterologies: Discourses on the Other*, by Michel de Certeau. Translated by Brian Massumi. Minneapolis: University of Minnesota Press.

———. 1987. Afterword to *Institution and Interpretation*, by Samuel Weber. Minneapolis: University of Minnesota Press.

Goldfarb, Jeffrey C. 1991. *The Cynical Society: The Culture of Politics and the Politics of Culture in American Life*. Chicago: University of Chicago Press.

———. 1998. *Civility and Subversion: The Intellectual in Democratic Society*. Cambridge/New York: Cambridge University Press.

Gordon, Jane Anna. 2001. *Why They Couldn't Wait: A Critique of the Black-Jewish Conflict over Community Control in Ocean Hill–Brownsville, 1967–1971*. New York: Routledge/Falmer.

———. 2005. "The General Will and Political Legitimacy: Secularization, Double Consciousness, and Force in Modern Democratic Theory." Doctoral dissertation in Political Science: The University of Pennsylvania.

Gordon, Lewis R. 1995a/1999. *Bad Faith and Antiblack Racism*. Amherst, NY: Humanity/Prometheus Books. (Originally published in Atlantic Highlands, NJ, by Humanities International Press.)

———. 1995b. *Fanon and the Crisis of European Man: An Essay on Philosophy and the Human Sciences*. New York: Routledge.

———. 1995c. "Sartrean Bad Faith and Antiblack Racism." In *The Prism of the Self: Essays in Honor of Maurice Natanson* (pp. 107–129), edited by Steven Crowell. Dordrecht, Netherlands: Kluwer Academic Publishers.

———. 1996. Introduction to *Fanon: A Critical Reader*, translated and edited by Lewis R. Gordon, T. Denean Sharpley-Whiting, and Renée T. White. Oxford, UK: Blackwell.

————. 1997a. *Existence in Black: An Anthology of Black Existential Philosophy*, edited and with an introduction by Lewis R. Gordon. New York/London: Routledge.

————. 1997b. *Her Majesty's Other Children: Sketches of Racism from a Neocolonial Age*, with a foreword by Renée T. White. Lanham, MD: Rowman and Littlefield.

————. 1999. "Frederick Douglass as an Existentialist." In *Frederick Douglass: A Critical Reader*, edited by Bill E. Lawson and Frank M. Kirkland. Malden, MA: Blackwell.

————. 2000a. "Africana Thought and African Diasporic Studies," *The Black Scholar* 30, nos. 3-4 (Fall-Winter): 25-30.

————. 2000b. *Existentia Africana: Understanding Africana Existential Thought*. New York/London: Routledge.

————. 2001a. "Introduction: The Call in Africana Religion and Philosophy," *Listening: A Journal of Religion and Culture* 36, no. 1 (Winter 2001): 3-13.

————. 2001b. "The Unacknowledged Fourth Tradition: An Essay on Nihilism, Decadence, and the Black Intellectual Tradition in the Existential Pragmatic Thought of Cornel West." In *Cornel West: A Critical Reader* (pp. 38-58), edited by George Yancy. Malden, MA: Blackwell.

————. 2002a. "A Philosophical Account of Africana Studies: An Interview with Lewis Ricardo Gordon," interviewed by Linda Martín Alcoff, *APA Newsletter on Hispanic/Latino Issues in Philosophy* 1, no. 2 (Spring): 92-101.

————. 2002b. "A Questioning Body of Laughter and Tears: Reading *Black Skin, White Masks* Through the Cat and Mouse of Reason and a Misguided Theodicy," *Parallax* 8, no. 2: 10-29.

————. 2002c. "Making Science Reasonable: Peter Caws on Science Both Human and 'Natural,'" *Janus Head: An Interdisciplinary Journal of Literature, Continental Philosophy, Phenomenological Psychology, and the Arts* 5, no. 1 (Spring):14-38.

————. 2003. "Some Thoughts on Philosophy and Scripture in an Age of Secularism," *Journal of Philosophy and Scripture* 1, no. 1 (2003). Available online at http://www.webmail.brown.edu/agent/mobmain?mobmain=1. www.philosophyandscripture.org.

————. 2004. "Critical Reflections on Three Popular Tropes in the Study of Whiteness." In *What White Looks Like: African-American Philosophers on the Whiteness Question* (pp. 173-193), edited by George Yancy. New York: Routledge.

————. 2005. "Black Latin@s and Blacks in Latin America: Some Philosophical Considerations." In *Latin@s in the World-System: Decolonization Struggles in the 21st Century U.S. Empire* (pp. 89-103), edited by Ramón Grosfoguel, Nelson Maldonado-Torres, and José David Saldívar. Boulder, CO: Paradigm Publishers.

————. Forthcoming (in 2006). *Disciplinary Decadence: Living Thought in Trying Times*. Boulder, CO: Paradigm Publishers.

References

Gordon, Lewis R., and Jane Anna Gordon, eds. 2006. *A Companion to African-American Studies*. Malden, MA: Blackwell.

Gordon, Lewis R., T. Denean Sharpley-Whiting, and Renée T. White, eds. 1996. *Fanon: A Critical Reader*, with an introduction and translations by Lewis R. Gordon, T. Denean Sharpley-Whiting, and Renée T. White; a foreword by Leonard Harris and Carolyn Johnson; and an afterword by Joy Ann James. Malden, MA: Blackwell.

Gottlieb, Anthony. 2000. *The Dream of Reason: A History of Western Philosophy from the Greeks to the Renaissance*. New York: W. W. Norton.

Goveia, Elsa V. 1965. *Slave Society in the British Leeward Islands at the End of the Eighteenth Century to the End of the Nineteenth Century*. Washington, DC: Howard University Press.

———. 1981. *Study on the Historiography of the British West Indies*.

Grassi, Ernesto. 1980. *Rhetoric as Philosophy: The Humanist Tradition*. University Park: Pennsylvania State University Press.

Greene, Maxine. 1978. *Landscapes of Learning*. New York: Columbia University Teachers College Press.

Gutman, Herbert G. 1976. *The Black Family in Slavery and Freedom: 1750-1925*. New York: Pantheon Books.

Gutting, Gary. 1989. *Michel Foucault's Archaeology of Scientific Reason*. Cambridge/New York: Cambridge University Press.

Gyekye, Kwame. 1987 [1995]. *An Essay on African Philosophical Thought: The Akan Conceptual Scheme*, rev. ed. Philadelphia: Temple University Press.

———. 1997. *Tradition and Modernity: Philosophical Reflections on the African Experience*. New York/Oxford: Oxford University Press.

Habermas, Jürgen. 1973. *Legitimation Crisis*, translated by Thomas McCarthy. Boston: Beacon Press.

———. 1984. *The Theory of Communicative Action* (Vols. I and II), translated by Thomas McCarthy. Boston: Beacon Press.

———. 1985. *The Philosophical Discourse of Modernity*. Cambridge, MA: MIT Press.

———. 1987. *The Theory of Communicative Action*, Vol. II. Boston: Beacon Press.

Hacker, Andrew. 1992. *Two Nations, Black and White: Separate, Hostile, Unequal*. New York: Scribner's.

Hadot, Pierre. 1995. *Philosophy as a Way of Life: Spiritual Exercises from Socrates to Foucault*, edited and with an introduction by Arnold I. Davidson, translated by Michael Chase. Malden, MA: Blackwell.

Hale, C. J. 1997. "Leatherdyke Boys and Their Daddies: How to Have Sex Without Women or Men." *Social Text* 15, nos. 3 and 4 (Fall/Winter): 223-226.

Hallen, Barry. 2000. *The Good, the Bad and the Beautiful: Discourse About Values in Yoruba Culture*. Bloomington/Indianapolis: Indiana University Press.

Hallyn, Fernand. 1990. *The Poetic Structure of the World: Copernicus and Kepler*, translated by Donald M. Leslie. New York: Zone Books.

Hamlet, J., ed. 1998. *Afrocentric Visions: Studies in Culture and Communications*. Newbury Park, CA: Sage Publications.

Hammond, Michael, Jane Howarth, and Russell Keat. 1991. *Understanding Phenomenology*. Malden, MA: Blackwell.

Harris, Leonard, ed. 1983 [2000]. *Philosophy Born of Struggle: Anthology of Afro-American Philosophy from 1917*. Dubuque, IA: Kendall/Hunt.

———. 1999. *Critical Pragmatism of Alain Locke: A Reader on Value Theory, Aesthetics, Community, Culture, Race and Education*. Lanham, MD: Rowman and Littlefield.

Harrison, Lawrence E., and Samuel P. Huntington, eds. 2000. *Culture Matters: How Values Shape Human Progress*. New York: Basic Books.

Hartman, Saidiya V. 1997. *Scenes of Subjection: Terror, Slavery, and Self-Making in Nineteenth-Century America*. New York: Oxford University Press.

Harvey, David. 1989. *The Condition of Postmodernity: An Enquiry into the Origins of Cultural Change*. Malden, MA: Blackwell.

Hazzard-Gordon, Katrina. 1990. *Jookin': The Rise of Social Dance Formations in African-American Culture*. Philadelphia: Temple University Press.

Hegel, Georg Wilhelm Friederich. 1979 [1807]. *Phenomenology of Spirit*, translated by A. V. Miller. Oxford: Oxford University Press.

———. 1989. *Hegel's Science of Logic*, translated by A. V. Miller. Amherst, NY: Humanity/Prometheus Books.

Heidegger, Martin. 1977. *The Question of Technology and Other Essays*, translated by William Lovitt. New York: Garland Publishers.

Henry, Paget. 1997a. "African and Afro-Caribbean Existential Philosophies." In *Existence in Black: An Anthology of Black Existential Philosophy* (pp. 11–36), edited and with an introduction by Lewis R. Gordon. New York/London: Routledge.

———. 1997b. "Rastafarianism and the Reality of Dread." In *Existence in Black: An Anthology of Black Existential Philosophy* (pp. 157–164), edited and with an introduction by Lewis R. Gordon. New York/London: Routledge.

———. 2000a. *Caliban's Reason: Introducing Afro-Caribbean Philosophy*. New York: Routledge.

———. 2000b. "Myth, Language, and Habermasian Rationality: Another Africana Contribution." In *Perspectives on Habermas* (pp. 89–112), edited by Lewis Edwin Hahn. Chicago: Open Court.

———. 2005. *After Man, the Human: Critical Essays on the Thought of Sylvia Wynter*, edited by Anthony Bogues et al. Kingston, Jamaica: Ian Randle.

Hershel, Helena Jia. 1995. "Therapeutic Perspectives on Biracial Identity Formation and Internalized Oppression." In *American Mixed Race*, edited by Naomi Zack. Lanham, MD: Rowman and Littlefield.

Hick, John. 1978. *Evil and the God of Love*, rev. ed. San Francisco: Harper San Francisco.

Hine, Darlene C. 1997. "Black Studies: An Overview." In *Africana Studies: A Disciplinary Quest for Both Theory and Method* (pp. 7–15), edited by James L. Conyers, Jr. Jefferson, NC/London: McFarland.

Hochschild, Adam. 1998. *King Leopold's Ghost: A Story of Greed, Terror and Heroism in Colonial Africa.* Boston: Houghton Mifflin.

hooks, bell. 1981. *Ain't I a Woman.* Boston: South End Press.

———. 1984. *Feminist Theory from Margin to Center.* Boston: South End Press.

Hopkins, Dwight N. 2000. *Down, Up, and Over: Slave Religion and Black Theology.* Philadelphia: Fortress Press.

Hübner, Kurt. 1983. *Critique of Scientific Reason,* translated by Paul R. Dixon and Hollis M. Dixon. Chicago: University of Chicago Press.

Humphries, Ralph. 1999. "Analytic and Continental: The Division in Philosophy," *The Monist* 82, no. 2 (April). Database online, cited August 20, 2002: Available from Academic Search Elite.

Huntington, Samuel P. 1996. *The Clash of Civilizations and the Remaking of World Order.* New York: Simon and Schuster.

———. 2004. *Who Are We? The Challenges to America's National Identity.* New York: Simon and Schuster.

Husserl, Edmund. 1960. *Cartesian Mediations: An Introduction to Phenomenology,* translated by Dorion Cairns. The Hague: M. Nijhoff.

———. 1965. "Philosophy as Rigorous Science." In *Phenomenology and the Crisis of Philosophy: Philosophy as Rigorous Science, and Philosophy and the Crisis of European Man,* translated and with an introduction by Quentin Lauer. New York: Harper and Row.

———. 1970. *The Crisis of European Sciences and Transcendental Phenomenology: An Introduction to Phenomenological Philosophy,* translated and with an introduction by David Carr. Evanston, IL: Northwestern University Press.

———. 1997. *Experience and Judgment.* Evanston, IL: Northwestern University Press.

———. 2001. *The Shorter Logical Investigations,* translated by J. N. Findlay. New York: Routledge.

Hyppolite, Jean. 1974. *Genesis and Structure of Hegel's Phenomenology of the Spirit,* translated by Samuel Cherniak and John Heckman. Evanston, IL: Northwestern University Press.

Ifekwunigwe, Jayne O. 2004. *"Mixed Race" Studies: A Reader.* London: Routledge.

Jacoby, Karl. 1994. "Slaves by Nature? Domestic Animals and Human Slaves," *Slavery and Abolition* 15, no. 1 (April): 89–99.

James, C. L. R. 1938/1989. *The Black Jacobins: Toussaint L'Ouverture and the San Domingo Revolution.* New York: Vintage.

James, Joy. 1997. *Transcending the Talented Tenth: Black Leaders and American Intellectuals,* with a foreword by Lewis R. Gordon. New York: Routledge.

Jansen-Wilkeln, K. 1985. *Ägyptische Biographien der 22. und 23. Dynastie* (2 vols.). Wiesbaden, Germany: Otto Harrasowitz.

Jaspers, Karl. 1954 [1995]. *Way to Wisdom: An Introduction to Philosophy*, translated by Ralph Manheim. New Haven: Yale University Press.

———. 1971. *Philosophy of Existence*, translated and with an introduction by Richard F. Grabau. Philadelphia: University of Pennsylvania.

Johnson, Sallie. 1972. In *The American Slave: A Composite—Texas Narratives*, edited by George R. Rawick. Westport, CT: Greenwood, Vol. 6, pt. 5.

Jones, Leroi. 1963. *The Blues People: Negro Music in America.* New York: William Morrow.

Jones, Leroi (Amari Baraka), and Larry Neal, eds. 1968. *Black Fire: An Anthology of Afro-American Writings.* New York: William Morrow.

Jones, Toby. 1972. *The American Slave: A Composite, Texas Narratives Supplement Series II*, Vol. 6, Pt. 5, edited by George R. Rawick. Westport, CT: Greenwood Publishing.

Jordan, Winthrop. 1968. *White over Black.* Durham: University of North Carolina Press.

Joseph, Peniel, ed. 2001. "Black Power Studies: A New Scholarship," special issue of *The Black Scholar* 31, nos. 3–4 (Fall/Winter).

Kant, Immanuel. 1960. *Education*, translated by Annette Churton. Ann Arbor: University of Michigan Press.

Karenga, Maulana [Ron]. 1968. "Black Cultural Nationalism," *Negro Digest* 13, no. 3: 5–9. (Reprinted in 1971 in *The Black Aesthetic*. Garden City, NY: Doubleday.)

———. 1978. *Essays on Struggle: Position and Analysis.* San Diego: Kawaida Publications.

———. 1979. *Introduction to Black Studies.* Los Angeles: University of Sankore Press.

———. 1980. *Kawaida: An Introductory Outline.* Inglewood, CA: Kawaida Publications.

———. 1984. *Selections from the Husia: Sacred Wisdom of Ancient Egypt.* Los Angeles: University of Sankore Press.

———. 1990a. "The African Intellectual and the Problem of Class Suicide: Ideological and Political Dimensions." In *African Culture: The Rhythms of Unity* (pp. 91–106), edited by Molefik Asante et al. Westport, CT: Greenwood.

———. 1990b. *The Book of Coming Forth by Day: The Ethics of the Declarations of Innocence.* Los Angeles: University of Sankore Press.

———. 1993a. *Introduction to Black Studies.* Los Angeles: University of Sankore Press.

———. 1993b. "Sources of Self in Ancient Egyptian Autobiographies." In *Black American Intellectualism and Culture: A Social Study of African American Social and Political Thought* (pp. 37–56), edited by James Conyers. Stamford, CT: JAI Press.

———. 1995a. "Afrocentricity and Multicultural Education: Concept, Challenge, and Contribution." In *Toward the Multicultural University* (pp.

46-61), edited by Benjamin P. Bowser, Terry Jones, and Gale Auletta Yong, Westport, CT: Praeger.

———. 1995b. *The Million Man March/Day of Absence Mission Statement*. Los Angeles, CA: University of Sankore Press.

———. 1997. *Kawaida: A Communitarian African Philosophy*. Los Angeles: University of Sankore Press.

———. 1999. *Odu Ifa: The Ethical Teachings*. Los Angeles: University of Sankore Press.

———. 2002a. *The Ethics of Sharing: Towards a New Collective Vocation and Public Philosophy*. Los Angeles, CA: University of Sankore Press.

———. 2002b. *Introduction to Black Studies*, 3rd ed. Los Angeles: University of Sankore Press.

———. 2002c. "9/11, Liberation Struggles and International Relations: Sharing the Burden and Possibilities of the Crisis." In *Unveiling the Real Terrorist Mind* (pp. 229-235), edited by Nadia Batool Ahmad et al. New York: Students for International Peace and Justice.

———. 2003a. "Du Bois and the Question of the Color Line: Race and Class in the Age of Globalization," *Socialism and Democracy* 17, no. 2 (Winter-Spring): 141-160.

———. 2003b. "Nommo, Kawaida and Communicative Practice: Bringing Good into the World." In *Understanding African American Rhetoric: Classical Origins to Contemporary Innovations* (pp. 3-22), edited by Ronald L. Jackson and Elaine B. Richardson. New York: Routledge.

———. 2004. *Maat, the Moral Ideal in Ancient Egypt: A Study in Classical African Ethics*. New York/London: Routledge.

Katz, William Loren. 1986. *Black Indians: A Hidden Heritage*. New York: Atheneum.

Kearny, Richard, ed. 1994. *Twentieth-Century Continental Philosophy*. London/New York: Routledge.

Kennedy, Ellen. 2004. *Constitutional Failure: Carl Schmitt in Weimar*. Durham, NC: Duke University Press.

Kerford, George B. 1990. "The Sage in Philosophical Literature (399 B.C.E.-199 C.E.)." In *The Sage in Israel and the Ancient Near East* (pp. 319-328), edited by John G. Gammie and Leo G. Perdue. Winona Lake: Einsenbraus.

King, Martin Luther, Jr. 1958. *Stride Toward Freedom*. New York: Harper and Row.

Kojeve, Alexandre. 1980 [1947]. *Introduction to the Reading of Hegel: Lectures on the Phenomenology of the Spirit*, edited by Allan Bloom, translated by James H. Nichols. Ithaca: Cornell University Press.

Lacan, Jacques. 1981. *The Four Fundamental Concepts of Psychoanalysis*. New York: W. W. Norton.

Lakatos, Imre. 1978. *The Methodology of Scientific Research Programmes: Philosophical Papers* (Vol. 1), edited by John Worrall and Gregory Currie. Cambridge: Cambridge University Press.

Lamming, George. 1984. "Introduction to 1984 Edition." In *The Pleasures of Exile*. London: Allison and Busby, Ltd.

———. 1970 [1953]. *In the Castle of My Skin* (reprint), with an introduction by Richard Wright. New York: Collier Books.

La Rue, Loyal. 2000. *Everybody's Story: Wising Up to the Epic of Evolution*. Albany: State University of New York Press.

Lawal, Babatunde. 1996. *The Gèlèlé Spectacle: Art, Gender and Social Harmony in an African Culture*. Seattle: University of Washington Press.

Lawson, Bill, and Frank M. Kirkland, eds. 1998. *Frederick Douglass: A Critical Reader*. Malden, MA: Blackwell.

Leder, Drew. 1990. *The Absent Body*. Chicago: University of Chicago Press.

Legesse, Asmarom. 1973. *Gada: Three Approaches to the Study of an African Society*. New York: Free Press.

Le Goff, Jacques. 1992. *The Medieval Imagination*, translated by Arthur Goldhammer. Chicago: University of Chicago Press.

Levinas, Emmanuel. 1991. *Otherwise Than Being, or Beyond Essence*, translated by Alphonso Lingis. Boston: Kluwer Academic Publishers.

Levine, Lawrence. 1978. *Black Culture and Black Consciousness: Afro-American Folk Thought from Slavery to Freedom*. New York: Oxford University Press.

Lewis-Williams, David. 2002. *The Mind in the Cave: Consciousness and the Origins of Art*. London/New York: Thames and Hudson.

Lichtheim, Miriam. 1988. *Ancient Egyptian Autobiographies Chiefly of the Middle Kingdom*. Fribourg, Switzerland: Biblical Institute, University of Fribourg.

———. 1992. *Maat in Egyptian Autobiographies and Related Studies*, OBO 120. Frieburg, Göttingen: Universitäts-verlag.

Locke, Alain. 1989. *The Philosophy of Alain Locke: Harlem Renaissance and Beyond*, edited by Leonard Harris. Philadelphia: Temple University Press.

———. 1989. "Values and Imperatives." In *The Philosophy of Alain Locke: Harlem Renaissance and Beyond*, edited by Leonard Harris. Philadelphia: Temple University Press.

Logan, Shirley W. 1999. *We Are Coming: The Persuasive Discourse of Nineteenth-Century Black Women*, Carbondale: Southern Illinois University Press.

Long, Charles H. 1999. "Passage and Prayer: The Origins of Religion in the Atlantic World." In *The Courage to Hope: From Black Suffering to Human Redemption*, edited by Quinton Hosford Dixie and Cornel West. Boston: Beacon Press.

Loprieno, Antonio. 1996. "Defining Egyptian Literature: Ancient Texts and Modern Theories." In *Ancient Egyptian Literature: History and Forms* (pp. 197–312), edited by Antonio Loprieno. Leiden: E. J. Brill.

Lorde, Audre. 1984. *Sister Outsider: Essays and Outsiders*. Trumansburg, NY: The Crossing Press, 1984.

References

Lott, Tommy. 1998. *Subjugation and Bondage: Critical Essays on Slavery and Social Philosophy*. Lanham, MD: Rowman and Littlefield.

Love, Monifa. 1998. *Freedom in the Dismal*. Chicago: Chicago Academy Publishers.

Lusane, Clarence. 1997. *Race in the Global Era: African Americans at the Millennium*. Boston: South End Press.

Lyotard, Jean-François. 1984. *The Postmodern Condition: A Report on Knowledge*, translated by Geoff Bennington and Brian Massumi. Minneapolis: University of Minnesota Press.

———. 1990. *Heidegger and "the Jews,"* translated by Andreas Michel and Mark S. Roberts, with a foreword by David Carroll. Minneapolis: University of Minnesota Press.

MacIntyre, Alasdair. 1990. *Three Rival Versions of Moral Enquiry: Encyclopedia, Genealogy and Tradition*. Notre Dame, IN: University of Notre Dame Press.

Malcolm X. 1965a. *The Autobiography of Malcolm X*. New York: Grove Press.

———. 1965b. *Malcolm X Speaks*. New York: Merit Publishers.

Maldonado-Torres, Nelson. 2001. "The 'Cry' of the Self as a Call from the Other: The Paradoxical Loving Subjectivity of Frantz Fanon." *Listening* 36, no 1 (Winter): 46–60.

———. 2002. "Post-imperial Reflections on Crisis, Knowledge, and Utopia: Transgresstopic Critical Hermeneutics and the 'Death of European Man,'" *Review: A Journal of the Fernand Braudel Center for the Study of Economies, Historical Systems, and Civilizations* 25, no. 3: 277–315.

———. 2004a. "Hispanics: A Challenge to America? A Critique of Samuel Huntington's *Who Are We?*" *Enfoque de CLPR* 5, no. 1 (Fall): 1, 3.

———. 2004b. "Searching for Caliban in the Hispanic Caribbean." *C.L.R. James Journal* 10, no. 1: 106–122.

———. 2005. "Decolonization and the New Identitarian Logics after September 11: Eurocentrism and Americanism against the Barbarian Threats." *Radical Philosophy Review* 8, no. 1 (2005): 35–67.

———. Forthcoming (a). *Against War: Views from the Underside of Modernity*. Durham, NC: Duke University Press.

———. Forthcoming (b). "Decolonization and the New Identitarian Logics After September 11: Eurocentrism and Americanism Against the Barbarian Threats," *Radical Philosophy Review.*

———. Forthcoming (c). "Intervenciones filosóficas al proyecto inacabado de la descolonizacion." In *Filosofía y liberación. Homenaje a Enrique Dussel*, edited by Juan Manuel Contreras Colín and Mario Rojas. México, D.F.: Universidad de la Ciudad de México.

———. Forthcoming (d). "Reconciliation as a Contested Future: Decolonization as Project or Beyond the Paradigm of War." In *Reconciliation: Nations and Churches in Latin America*, edited by Iain S. Maclean. Aldershot, England: Ashgate.

Marcuse, Herbert. 1964. *One-Dimensional Man*. Boston: Beacon Press.

Marquínez Argote, Germán, Luis José González Alvarez, and Francisco Beltrán Peña, eds. 1979. *Latinoamérica se rebela: contestación al discurso de Hegel sobre América*, 2nd ed. Bogotá, Colombia: Nueva América.

Martin, Hans-Peter, and Harold Schumann. 1997. *The Global Trap: Globalization and the Assault on Prosperity and Democracy*. New York: St. Martin's Press.

Martin, Reginald. 1988. *Ishmael Reed and the New Black Aesthetic Critics*. New York: St. Martin's.

Martinich, A. P., and David Sosa, eds. 2001. *A Companion to Analytic Philosophy*. Malden, MA: Blackwell.

Maturana, Humberto, and Francisco Varela. 1980. *Autopoesis and Cognition: The Realization of the Living*, with a preface by Sir Stafford Beer. Dordrecht, Holland; Boston: D. Reidel.

McCumber, John. 2001. *Time in the Ditch: American Philosophy and the McCarthy Era*. Evanston, IL.: Northwestern University Press.

McCutcheon, Russell T. 2000. *The Imperial Dynamic in the Study of Religion: Neocolonial Practices in an American Discipline. In Postcolonial America* (pp. 275–302), edited by C. Richard King. Urbana: University of Illinois Press.

McGary, Howard, and Bill E. Lawson. 1998. *Between Slavery and Freedom: Philosophy and American Slavery*. Bloomington: Indiana University Press.

McKay, Nellie Y. 1998. "Naming the Problem That Led to the Question 'Who Shall Teach African American Literature?', or Are We Ready to Disband the Wheatley Court?," *PMLA* 113, no. 3: 359–369.

McKenzie, Renee Eugenia. 2005. "A Womanist Social Ontology: An Exploration of the Self/Other Relationship in Womanist Religious Scholarship," dissertation, Temple University, Department of Religion.

McWhorter, Gerald. 1969. "Deck the Ivy Racist Walls: The Case of Black Studies." In *Black Studies and the University*, edited by Armstead Robinson, Craig Foster, and Donald Ogilvie. New Haven: Yale University Press.

———. 1982. "Academic Excellence and Social Responsibility: Notes on a Theory of Black Studies," *Minority Voices* 5 (Spring): 51.

McWhorter, John. 2001. *Losing the Race: Self-Sabotage in Black America*. New York: Harper Perennial.

Mendieta, Eduardo. 1999. "Is There a Latin American Philosophy?" *Philosophy Today*, SPEP Supplement 43, no. 4: 50–61.

———. 2001a. "Chronotopology: Critique of Spatiotemporal Regimes." In *New Critical Theory: Essays on Liberation* (pp. 175–197), edited by William S. Wilkerson and Jeffrey Paris. Lanham, MD: Rowman and Littlefield.

———. 2001b. "Which Pragmatism? Whose America?" In *Cornel West: A Critical Reader* (pp. 83–102), edited by George Yancy. Malden, MA: Blackwell.

References

Mendieta, Eduardo, and Pedro Lange-Churión. 2001. *Latin America and Post-modernity: A Contemporary Reader*. Amherst, NY: Humanity Books.

Merleau-Ponty, Maurice. 1964a/1989. "*The Primacy of Perception*," and *Other Essays on Phenomenological Psychology, the Philosophy of Art, History, and Politics*, edited and with an introduction by James M. Edie. Evanston, IL: Northwestern University Press.

———. 1964b/1998. *Signs*, translated by Richard McCleary. Evanston, IL: Northwestern University Press.

———. 2002. *Phenomenology of Perception*, translated by Colin Smith. London: Routledge and Kegan Paul.

Mignolo, Walter. 1995/1999. "Philosophy and the Colonial Difference." *Philosophy Today*, SPEP Supplement 43, no. 4: 36–41.

———. 2000a. *Local Histories/Global Designs: Coloniality, Subaltern Knowledges, and Border Thinking*. Princeton: Princeton University Press.

———. 2000b. "The Larger Picture: Hispanics/Latinos (and Latino Studies) in the Colonial Horizon of Modernity." In *Hispanics/Latinos in the United States* (pp. 99–124), edited by Jorge J. E. Garcia and Pablo de Greiff. New York/London: Routledge.

———. 2000c. "The Many Faces of Cosmo-polis: Border Thinking and Critical Cosmopolitanism," *Public Culture* 12, no. 3 (Fall): 721–748.

———. 2000d. "The Role of the Humanities in the Corporate University, "*PMLA* 115, no. 5: 1238–1245.

———. 2000e. "(Post)Iccudebtakusnm (Post)Coloniality, and (Post)Subaltern Rationality." In *The Pre-Occupation of Postcolonial Studies* (pp. 86–118), edited by Fawzia Afzal Khan and Kalpana Seshadri-Crooks. Durham, NC: Duke University Press.

———. 2003a. "Globalization and the Geopolitics of Knowledge: The Role of the Humanities in the Corporate University," *Nepantla* 4, no. 1 (Spring): 97–120.

———. 2003b. "Las humanidades y los estudios culturales: proyectos intelectuales y exigencias institucioneles." In *Estudios culturales latinoamericanos retos desde y sobre la región andina* (pp. 31–57), edited by Catherine Walsh. Quito: Universidad Andina Simón Bolívar and Abya Yala.

———. 2003c. "Os esplendores e as misérias da sciência: colonialidade, geopolitica do conhecimento e pluriversalidade epistémica." In *Conheciento Prudente pra uma Vida Decente; Um Discurso sobre as Ci*ências'revistado. Edited by Boaventura de Sousa Santos (Edições Afrontamento.): 631–671.

———. 2005. *The Idea of Latin America*. Malden, MA: Blackwell.

Milling, Cureton. 1972. In *The American Slave: A Composite—Texas Narratives*, edited by George R. Rawick. Westport, CT: Greenwood, Vol. 4, pt. 1.

Mills, Charles. *The Racial Contract*. Ithaca: Cornell University Press.

Monges, Miriam Maat. 1997. *Kush: The Jewel of Nubia, Reconnecting the Root System of African Civilization.* Trenton: Africa World Press.

Moosa, Ebrahim. 2001. Moosa: "Humanity Is Global and Not Continental," June 20 (cited August 11, 2002). Available online at http://news-service.stanford.edu/news/june20/moosatext-620.html.

Moraga, Cherrie. 2000. *Loving in the War Years.* Cambridge, MA: South End Press.

Moraga, Cherrie, and Gloria Anzaldúa, eds. 1983. *This Bridge Called My Back: Writings by Radical Women of Color,* 2nd ed. New York: Kitchen Table: Women of Color Press.

Mordekhai, Laurence Thomas. 1993. *Vessels of Evil: American Slavery and the Holocaust.* Philadelphia: Temple University Press.

Morris, David. 1991. The Culture of Pain. Berkeley: University of California Press.

Morrison, Toni. 1994. "Unspeakable Things Unspoken: The Afro-American Presence in American Literature." In *Within the Circle: An Anthology of African-American Literary Criticism from the Harlem Renaissance to the Present* (pp. 368–401), edited by Angelyn Mitchell. Durham, NC: Duke University Press.

———. 2000. *The Bluest Eye.* New York: Plume.

Mosse, George L. 1978/1985. *Toward the Final Solution: A History of European Racism.* Madison: University of Wisconsin Press.

Moya, Paula M. L. 2000a. "Postmodernism, 'Realism,' and the Politics of Identity: Cherríe Moraga and Chicana Feminism." In *Reclaiming Identity: Realist Theory and the Predicament of Postmodernism* (pp. 67–101), edited by Paula M. L. Moya and Michael R. Hames Garcia. Berkeley: University of California Press.

Mudimbe, Valentin Y. 1988. *The Invention of Africa: Gnosis, Philosophy, and the Order of Knowledge.* Bloomington: Indiana University Press.

———. 1995. "Romanus Pontifex (1454) and the Expansion of Europe." In *Race, Discourse, and the Origins of the Americas* (pp. 58–65), edited by Vera Lawrence Hyatt and Rex Nettleford. Washington, DC: Smithsonian Institution Press.

Muhammad, Elijah. 1973. *The Fall of America.* Chicago: Muhammad's Temple of Islam No. 2.

———. 1965. *Message to the Black Man in America.* Chicago: Muhammad's Temple of Islam No. 2.

Munford, Clarence J. 1996. *Race and Reparations: A Black Perspective for the 21st Century.* Trenton, NJ: Africa World Press.

Munitz, Milton K. 1981. *Contemporary Analytic Philosophy.* New York: Macmillan.

Nascimento, Abdias do, and Elisa Larkin Nascimento. 1992. *Africans in Brazil: A Pan-African Perspective.* Trenton, NJ: Africa World Press.

Nascimento, Elisa Larkin. 1980. *Pan Africanism and South America: Emergence of a Black Rebellion.* Buffalo, NY: Afrodiaspora.

Natanson, Maurice. 1973. *Edmund Husserl: Philosopher of Infinite Tasks.* Evanston, IL: Northwestern University Press.

Neal, Larry. 1971. "The Black Arts Movement." In *The Black Aesthetic* (pp. 370–338), edited by Addison Gayle, Jr. Garden City, NJ: Double Day.

Neves, Walter A., and Hector Pucciarelli. 1998. "The Zhoukoudian Upper Cave Skull 101 as Seen from the Americas." *Journal of Human Evolution* 34, no. 2 (February): 219–222.

Neves, Walter A., André Prous, Rolando González-José, Renato Kipnis, and Joseph Powell. 2003. "Early Holocene Human Skeletal Remains from Santana do Riacho, Brazil: Implications for the Settlement of the New World." *Journal of Human Evolution* 45, no. 1 (July): 759–782.

Neves, Walter A., Joseph F. Powell, and Erik G. Ozolins. 1999. "Modern Human Origins as Seen from the Peripheries." *Journal of Human Evolution* 37, no. 1 (July): 129–133.

Niangoran-Bouah, G. 1984. *The Akan World of Gold Weights: Abstract Design Weights,* Vol. I. Abijan, Ivory Coast: Les Nouvelles Editions Africaines.

Niles, L. A. 1995. *African American Rhetoric: A Reader.* Dubuque, IA: Kendall/Hunt.

Nishitani, Keiji. 1983. *Religion and Nothingness.* Berkeley: University of California Press.

Norton, Anne. 2004. *Leo Strauss and the Politics of Empire.* New Haven: Yale University Press.

Nussbaum, Martha C. 1996. "Patriotism and Cosmopolitanism." In *For Love of Country: Debating the Limits of Patriotism* (pp. 2–17), edited by Joshua Cohen. Boston: Beacon Press.

Nyerere, Julius. 1968. *Freedom and Socialism: Uhuru na Ujamaa.* Dar-es-Salaam, Nairobi/London: Oxford University Press.

Oakes, James. 1990. *Slavery and Freedom: An Interpretation of the Old South.* New York: Knopf.

Obenga, Théophile. 1990. *La Philosphie africaine de la période pharaonique, 2780-330 avant notre ère.* Paris: Éditions L'Harmattan.

Ockinga, Boyo G. 1984. *Die Gottenbildlichkeit im Alten Ägypten und im Alten Testament,* Wiesbaden: Otto Harrasowitz.

O'Gorman, Edmundo. 1941. *Do the Americas Have a Common History?* translated by Angel Flores. Washington, DC: Division of Intellectual Cooperation, Pan American Union.

Okafor, Victor Oguejiofor. 2002. *Towards an Understanding of Africology.* Dubuque, IA: Kendall/Hunt.

Oliver, Kelly. 2004. *The Colonization of Psychic Space.* Minneapolis: University of Minnesota Press.

Olson, Gary A., and Lynn Worsham, eds. 1999. *Race, Rhetoric, and the Postcolonial.* Albany: State University of New York Press.

Oluwole, Sophie B. 1999. *Philosophy and Oral Tradition.* Ikeja, Nigeria: ARK Publishers.

References

Omi, Michael, and Howard Winant. 1994. *Racial Formation in the United States: From the 1960s to the 1990s*. 2nd ed. New York: Routledge.

Ortner, Sherry B. 1974. "Is Female to Male as Nature Is to Culture?" In *Woman, Culture and Society*, edited by M. Z. Rosaldo and Louise Lamphere. Stanford, CA: Stanford University Press.

Otto, Edel. 1954. *Die biographische Inschriften de ägyptischen Spatzeit* Leiden: E. J. Brill.

Outlaw, Lucius T., Jr. 1992-1993. "African, African American, Africana Philosophy," *The Philosophical Forum*, 24, no. 103: 63-93.

———. 1996. *On Race and Philosophy*. New York: Routledge.

Pagden, Anthony. 1982. *The Fall of Natural Man: The American Indian and the Origins of Comparative Ethnology*. Cambridge: Cambridge University Press.

Pandian, Jacob. 1985. *Anthropology and the Western Tradition: Toward an Authentic Anthropology*. Prospect Heights, IL: Waveland Press.

Pappas, Gregory F. 1998. "The Latino Character of American Pragmatism," *Transactions of the Charles S. Peirce Society* 34, no. 1: 93-112.

Patraka, Vivian. 1999. *Spectacular Suffering: Theatre, Facism and the Holocaust*. Bloomington: Indiana University Press.

Patterson, Orlando. 1982. *Slavery and Social Death: A Comparative Study*. Cambridge, MA: Harvard University Press.

"Paul Robeson: The Great Forerunner." 1965. In *Freedom Ways*. New York: International Publishers.

Pérez, Emma. 1999. *The Decolonial Imaginary: Writing Chicanas into History.* Bloomington/Indianapolis: Indiana University Press.

Peters, Sallie. 1972. *The American Slave: A Composite, Texas Narratives Supplement* (Series II, Vol. 6, Pt. 5), edited by Geroge P. Rawick. Westport, CT: Greenwood.

Phillips, Ulrich B. 1966. *American Negro Slavery: A Survey of the Supply, Employment and Control of Negro Labor as Determined by the Plantation Regime*. Baton Rouge: Louisiana State University Press.

Pinkard, Terry. 1999. "Analytics, Continentals, and Modern Skepticism." *The Monist* 82, no. 2 (April): 189-218. Database online, cited August 20, 2002: Available from Academic Search Elite.

Pittman, John, ed. 1997. *African-American Perspectives and Philosophical Traditions*. New York: Routledge.

Poussaint, Alvin, and Amy Alexander. 2001. *Lay My Burden Down: Suicide and the Mental Health Crisis Among African-Americans*. Boston: Beacon Press.

Preston, William A. 1997. "Nietzche on Blacks." In *Existence in Black* (pp.165-172), edited with an introduction by Lewis R. Gordon. New York: Routledge.

Putnam, Hilary. 1997. "A Half Century of Philosophy, Viewed from Within," *Daedalus* 126, no. 1: 175-208.

Quijano, Anibal. 1995. "Modernity, Identity, and Utopia in Latin America." In *The Postmodernism Debate in Latin America* (pp. 201-216), edited by Michael Arona, John Beverly, and José Oviedo. Durham, NC: Duke University Press.

———. 2000. "Coloniality of Power, Eurocentrism, and Latin America." *Nepantla: Views from South* 1, no. 3: 533–580.

———. 2001. "Globalización, colonialidad y democracia." In *Tendencias básicas de nuestra época: globalización y democracia* (pp. 25–61). Caracas, Venezuela: Instituto de Altos Estudios Diplomáticos "Pedro Gual."

Rajchman, John, and Cornel West, eds. 1985. *Post-Analytic Philosophy.* New York: Columbia University Press.

Ransby, Barbara. 2003. *Ella Baker and the Black Freedom Movement: A Radical Democratic Vision.* Chapel Hill/London: University of North Carolina Press.

Rawick, George P., ed. 1972. *The American Slave: A Composite Autobiography.* Westport, CT: Greenwood.

Rawls, John. 1971. *A Theory of Justice.* Cambridge, MA: Harvard University Press.

Reed, Ishmael, ed. 1997. *MultiAmerica: Essays on Cultural Wars and Cultural Peace.* New York: Viking Penguin.

Reid-Pharr, R. 2001. *Black Gay Man.* New York: New York University Press.

Rice, Anne, ed. 2003. *Witnessing Lynching: American Writers Respond.* New Brunswick, NJ: Rutgers University Press.

Ricouer, Paul. 1979. "Ideology and Utopia as Cultural Imagination." In *Being Human in a Technological Age*, edited by D. M. Borchert and D. Stewart. Athens: Ohio University Press.

Riley, Patrick. 1986. *The General Will Before Rousseau: The Transformation of the Divine into the Civic.* Princeton: Princeton University Press.

Robinson, Armstead, Craig Foster, and Donald Ogilvie, eds. 1969. *Black Studies in the University.* New Haven: Yale University Press.

———. 1990. *Paradigms in Black Studies.* Chicago: Twenty First Century Press.

Robinson, Randall. 2000. *The Debt: What America Owes to Blacks.* New York: Dutton.

———. 2002. *The Reckoning: What Blacks Owe to Each Other.* New York: Dutton.

Rorty, Richard. 1998. *Achieving Our Country: Leftist Thought in Twentieth-Century America.* Cambridge, MA: Harvard University Press.

———. 2002. "Analytic Philosophy and Transformative Philosophy," cited September 22, 2002. Available online at www.stanford.edu/~rrorty/analytictrans.htm.

Rosenblatt, Helena. 1997. *Rousseau and Geneva.* New York: Cambridge University Press.

Rousseau, Jean-Jacques. 1987. *The Basic Political Writings*, translated by Donald A. Cress, with an introduction by Peter Gay. Indianapolis: Hackett Publishing Company.

————. 1988. *Rousseau's Political Writings*, translated by Julia Conaway Bondanella, edited by Allan Ritter and Julia Conaway Bondanella. New York: W. W. Norton.

Royce, Josiah. 1958. *Religious Aspects of Philosophy.* New York: Harper Collins.

Said, Edward W. 1994. *Representations of the Intellectual: The 1993 Reith Lectures.* New York: Pantheon Books.

Saldívar, José David. 1991. *Dialectics of Our America: Genealogy, Cultural Critique, and Literary History.* Durham, NC: Duke University Press.

————. 1997. *Border Matters: Remapping American Cultural Studies.* Berkeley: University of California Press.

Sánchez Rodríguez, Ángel. 2001. *Diccionario Jeroglíficos Egipsios.* Madrid: Alderabán Ediciones.

Sartre, Jean-Paul. 1956. *Being and Nothingness*, translated by Hazel E. Barnes. New York: Washington Square Press.

————. 1963. "Preface," translated by Constance Farrington. In *Les Damnés de la Terre/The Wretched of the Earth*, préface de Jean-Paul Sartre. Paris: François Maspero éditeur S.A.R.L./Éditions Gallimard.

————. 1970. "Intentionality: A Fundamental Idea of Husserl's Phenomenology." In *Journal of the British Society of Phenomenology*, 1, no. 2 (May): 4–5.

————. 1995 [1948]. *Anti-Semite and Jew*, translated by George J. Becker; preface by Michael Walzer. New York: Schocken Books.

Scaff, Lawrence. 2000. "Weber on the Cultural Situation of the Modern Age." In *Cambridge Companion to Weber.* New York: Cambridge University Press.

Scarry, Elaine. 1985. *The Body in Pain: The Making and Unmaking of the World.* New York: Oxford University Press.

Schmidt, James, ed. 1996. *What Is Enlightenment? Eighteenth-Century Answers and Twentieth-Century Questions.* Berkeley: University of California Press.

Schmitt, Carl. 1985. *Political Theology: Four Chapters on the Concept of Sovereignty*, translated by George Schwab. Cambridge, MA: MIT Press.

————. 1923/1988. The Crisis of Parliamentary Democracy, translated by Ellen Kennedy. Cambridge, MA: MIT Press.

————. 2004. *Legality and Legitimacy*, translated and edited by Jeffrey Seitzer, with an introduction by John P. McCormick. Durham, NC: Duke University Press.

Schneewind, J. B. 1983. "Moral Knowledge and Moral Principles." In *Revisions: Changing Perspectives in Moral Philosophy* (pp. 113–126), edited by Stanley Hauerwas and Alasdair MacIntyre. Notre Dame, IN: University of Notre Dame.

Schrag, Calvin O. 1997. *The Self After Postmodernity.* New Haven/London: Yale University Press.

Schütz, Alfred. 1970. "The Life World," in *Alfred Schütz on Phenomenology and Social Relations*, edited by Helmut R. Wagner. Evanston: Northwestern University.

Schutz, Alfred, and Luckman, Thomas. 1995. *The Structure of the Life-World*. Evanston: Northwestern University Press.

Schwartz, Gary. 1997. "Toni Morrison at the Movies: Theorizing Race through *Imitation of Life*." In *Existence in Black: An Anthology of Black Existential Philosophy* (pp. 111-128), edited by Lewis R. Gordon. New York: Routledge.

Serequeberhan, Tsenay. 2000. *Our Heritage: The Past in the Present of African-American and African Existence*. Lanham, MD: Rowman and Littlefield.

Sethe, Kurt, ed. 1906-1958a. *Aegyptische Lesestücke zum Gebrauch im akademischen Unterricht*, Leipzig: J. C. Hinrichs'sche Buchhandlung.

———. 1906-1958b. *Urkunden des ägyptischen Altertums, Abteilung IV, Urkunden der 18.Dynastie Fasc. 1-22*. Leipzig: J. C. Hinrichs'sche Buchhandlung.

Shakespeare, William. 1964. *The Tempest*, edited by Robert Langbaum. New York: New American Library, Signet Classic.

Shepherd, Verene A., and Hilary Beckles, eds. 2000. *Caribbean Slavery in the Atlantic World: A Student Reader*. Kingston, Jamaica: Ian Randle.

Sidgwick, Henry. 1931. *Outlines of the History of Ethics*. London: Macmillan Publishing.

Silverman, Hugh J., John Sallis, and Thomas M. Seebohm, eds. 1983. *Continental Philosophy in America*. Pittsburgh: Duquesne University Press.

Simpson, William Kelly. 1972. *The Literature of Ancient Egypt*. New Haven/London: Yale University Press.

Smith, Rogers M. 1997. *Civic Ideals: Conflicting Visions of Citizenship in U.S. History*. New Haven, CT: Yale University Press.

———. 2003. *Stories of Peoplehood: The Politics and Morals of Political Membership*. New York: Cambridge University Press.

Solomon, Robert C. 1988. *Continental Philosophy Since 1750: The Rise and Fall of the Self*. Oxford/New York: Oxford University Press.

Spencer, Jon Michael. 1993. *Blues and Evil*. Knoxville: University of Tennessee Press.

Stampp, Kenneth. 1956. *The Peculiar Institution: Slavery in the Ante-Bellum South*. New York: Vintage Books.

Steele, Shelby. 1990. *The Content of Our Character*. New York: St. Martins.

Stewart, James B. 1997. "Reaching for Higher Ground: Toward an Understanding of Black/Africana Studies." In *Africana Studies: A Disciplinary Quest for Both Theory and Method* (pp. 108-129), edited by James L. Conyers, Jr. Jefferson, NC/London: McFarland.

Stewart, Maria W. 1987. *The Political Speeches of Maria Stewart*, edited by M. Richardson. Bloomington/Indianapolis: Indiana University Press.

Stroll, Avrum. 2000. *Twentieth-Century Analytic Philosophy*. New York: Columbia University Press.

Stuckey, Sterling. 1987. *Slave Culture: Nationalist Theory and the Foundations of Black America*. New York: Oxford University Press.

Tannenbaum, Frank. 1946. *Slave and Citizen*. New York: Alfred A. Knopf.

"Taste This." 1998. *Boys Like Her: Transfictions*. Vancouver: Press Gang Publishers.

Tate, Claudia, ed. 1983. *Black Women Writers at Work*. New York: Continuum.

Taylor, Charles. 1992. *Multiculturalism and the "Politics of Recognition": An Essay by Charles Taylor*. Princeton, NJ: Princeton University Press.

Taylor, Clyde. 1988. "We Don't Need Another Hero: Anti-Theses on Aesthetics." In *Blackframes: Critical Perspectives on Black Independent Cinema* (pp. 80–85), edited by Mbye B. Cham and Claire Andrade-Watkins. Cambridge, MA: Massachusetts Institute of Technology Press.

———. 1989. "Black Cinema in the Post-Aesthetic Era." In *Questions of Third Cinema*, (pp. 90–110), edited by Jim Pines and Paul Willemen. London: British Film Institute.

Thurman, Howard. 1956. *The Growing Edge*. New York: Harper.

———. 1975. *Deep River and the Negro Spiritual Speaks of Life and Death*. Richmond, VA: Friends United Press.

———. 1998. "Suffering." In *A Strange Freedom: The Best of Howard Thurman on Religious Experience and Public Life* (pp. 35–54), edited by Walter Earl Fluker and Catherine Tumber. Boston: Beacon Press.

Tobin, Diane Kaufmann, Gary A. Tobin, and Scott Rubin. 2005. *In Every Tongue: The Racial and Ethnic Diversity of the Jewish People*, with a foreword by Lewis R. Gordon. San Francisco: Institute for Jewish and Community Research.

Todorov, Tzvetan. 1984. *The Conquest of America: The Question of the Other*, translated by Richard Howard. New York: Harper and Row.

Touré, Sékou. 1959a. "Le leader politque considéré comme le représentant d'une culture," *Présence Africaine*, nos. 24-25 (February-March): 104-115.

———. 1959b. *Towards Full Reafricanization*. Paris: Présence Africaine.

Ture, Kwame. 2003. *Ready for Revolution: The Life and Struggles of Stokely Carmichael (Kwame Ture)*. New York: Scribner.

Ture, Kwame, and Charles V. Hamilton. 1994 [1967, 1971]. *Black Power: The Politics of Liberation in America*. New York: Vintage Books.

Turner, James E. 1997. "Africana Studies and Epistemology: A Discourse in the Sociology of Knowledge." In *Africana Studies: A Disciplinary Quest for Both Theory and Method* (pp. 91-107), edited by James L. Conyers, Jr. Jefferson, NC/London: McFarland.

Turner, William. 2000. *A Genealogy of Queer Theory*. Philadelphia: Temple University Press.

Tyson, Timothy B. 1999. *Radio-Free Dixie, Robert Williams and the Roots of Black Power*. Chapel Hill: University of North Carolina Press.

Van Deburg, William L. 1992. *New Day in Babylon: The Black Power Movement and American Culture 1965-1975*. Chicago: University of Chicago Press.

Van Deburg, William L., ed. 1997. *Modern Black Nationalism*. New York: New York University Press.

Vasconcelos, José. 1997. *The Cosmic Race/La raza cósmica*, translated and edited by Didier T. Jaén. Baltimore: Johns Hopkins University Press.

Veyne, Paul. 1988. *Did the Greeks Believe in Their Myths? An Essay on the Constitutive Imagination*, translated by Paula Wissing. Chicago: University of Chicago Press.

Von Eschen, Penny. 1957. *Race Against Empire: Black Americans and Anticolonialism, 1937–1957*. Ithaca: Cornell University Press.

Wahl, Jean. 1969. *Philosophy of Existence: An Introduction to the Basic Thought of Kierkegaard, Heidegger, Jaspers, Marcel, Sartre,* translated by F. M. Lory. New York: Schocken.

Wallerstein, Immanuel. 1979. *The Capitalist World-Economy: Essays*. Cambridge: Cambridge University Press.

———. 1991. "The Inventions of TimeSpace Realities: Towards an Understanding of Our Historical Systems." In *Unthinking Social Science: The Limits of Nineteenth-Century Paradigms* (pp. 135–148). Cambridge, MA: Polity Press.

———. 1996. "Neither Patriotism nor Cosmopolitanism." In *For Love of Country: Debating the Limits of Patriotism* (pp. 122–124), edited by Joshua Cohen. Boston: Beacon Press.

Wallraff, Charles T. 1970. *Karl Jaspers: An Introduction to His Philosophy*. Princeton: Princeton University Press.

Washington, James, ed. 1986. *A Testament of Hope: The Essential Writings of Martin Luther King, Jr.* San Francisco: Harper and Row.

Watson, James R., ed. 1999. *Portraits of American Continental Philosophers*. Bloomington/Indianapolis: Indiana University Press.

Watson, Mollie. 1996. *The WPA Oklahoma Slave Narratives*, edited by T. Lindsay Baker and Julie P. Baker. Norman: University of Oklahoma Press.

Webber, Thomas. 1978. *Deep Like the Rivers: Education in the Slave Quarter Community.* New York: W. W. Norton.

Weber, Max. 1948. *From Max Weber: Essays in Sociology*, translated and edited and with an introduction by H. H. Gerth and C. Wright Mills. New York: Oxford University Press.

———. 1958. *The Protestant Ethic and the Spirit of Capitalism*, translated by Talcott Parsons, with an introduction by R. H. Tawney. New York: Scribner.

———. 1994a. "The Profession and Vocation of Politics." In *Political Writings*, translated and edited by Peter Lassman and Ronald Speirs. New York: Cambridge University Press.

———. 1994b. "Science as a Vocation." In *Political Writings*, translated and edited by Peter Lassman and Ronald Speirs. New York: Cambridge University Press.

Weil, Simone. 1986. *The Self*. In *Simone Weil: An Anthology*, edited and with an introduction by Sian Miles. New York: Weidenfeld and Nicolson.

———. 1999. *The Love of God and Affliction*. In *The Simone Weil Reader*, edited by George A. Panichas. Wakefield: Moyer Bell.

———. 1999. *Human Personality*. In *The Simone Weil Reader*, edited by George A. Panichas. Wakefield: Moyer Bell.

Wells-Barnett, Ida B. 1970. *Crusade for Justice: The Autobiography of Ida B. Wells*, edited by A. Barnett Duster. Chicago: University of Chicago Press.

Welton, Donn, ed. 1999. *The Essential Husserl: Basic Writings in Transcendental Phenomenology*. Bloomington: Indiana University Press.

West, Cornel. 1982. *Prophesy! Deliverance: An Afro-American Revolutionary Christianity*. Philadelphia: Westminster Press.

———. 1989. *The American Evasion of Philosophy: A Geneology of Pragmatism*. Madison: University of Wisconsin Press.

———. 1993. *Keeping Faith: Philosophy and Race in America*. New York: Routledge.

———. 1993. *Race Matters*. Boston: Beacon Press.

———. 1996. "American Radicalism." Interview. In *A Critical Sense: Interviews with Intellectuals* (pp.127-144). London: New York: Routledge.

———. 1999. "Introduction: To Be Human, Modern and American." In *The Cornel West Reader* (pp. xv-xx). New York: Basic Civitas Books.

———. 2001. "Afterword: Philosophy and the Funk of Life." In *Cornel West: A Critical Reader* (pp. 346-362), edited by George Yancy. Malden, MA: Blackwell.

———. 2004. *Democracy Matters: Winning the Fight Against Imperialism*. New York: Penguin.

Wilchins, R. 1997. *Read My Lips: Sexual Subversion and the End of Gender*. Ithaca: Firebrand Books.

Williams, Robert. 1973. *Negroes with Guns*. Chicago: Third World Press.

Wills, George. 2003. "Race-norming in Michigan," *Newsweek*, June 23: 74.

Winch, Peter. 1964. "Understanding a Primitive Society." *American Philosophical Quarterly* 7: 307-324.

Windam, Tom. 1972. *The American Slave: A Composite—Arkansas Narratives* (Vol. 11, Pt. 7), edited by George P. Rawick. Westport, CT: Greenwood Publishing.

Wolin, Sheldon. 1960. *Politics and Vision: Continuity and Innovation in Western Political Thought*. Boston: Little, Brown.

Wood, Mark D. 2000. *Cornel West and the Politics of Prophetic Pragmatism*. Urbana: University of Illinois Press.

Woodson, Carter G. 1972. *The Mis-education of the Negro*. Washington: A.M.S. Press.

Wright, Richard. 1940. *Native Son*. New York/London: Harper and Brothers.

———. 1953. *The Outsider*, unabridged ed. New York: Harper and Row.

Wynter, Sylvia. 1984. "The Ceremony Must Be Found: After Humanism," *Boundary 2* 12, no. 3 (Spring–Autumn): 19-70.

———. 1989. "Beyond the Word of Man: Glissant and the New Discourse of the Antilles." *World Literature Today*: 637-647.

References

————. 1990. "On Disenchanting Discourse: 'Minority' Literary Criticism and Beyond." In *The Nature and Context of Minority Discourse*, edited by David Lloyd. New York: Oxford University Press.

————. 1991. "Columbus and the Poetics of the *Propter Nos*," *Discovering Columbus*, edited by Djela Kadir. *Annals of Scholarship* 8: 251-286.

————. 1992. "Rethinking 'Aesthetics': Notes Towards a Deciphering Practice." In *Ex-iles: Essays on Caribbean Cinema* (pp. 237-279), edited by Mybe Cham. Trenton, NJ: Africa World Press.

————. 1995. "1492: A New World View." In *Race, Discourse, and the Origin of the Americas: A New World View* (pp. 5-57), edited by Vera Lawrence Hyatt and Rex Nettleford. Washington, DC: Smithsonian Institution Press.

————. 2000. "Africa, the West, and the Analogy of Culture: The Cinematic Text After Man." In *Symbolic Narratives/African Cinema* (pp. 25-76), edited by June Givanni. London: British Film Institute.

————. 2001. "Towards the Sociogenic Principle: Fanon, Identity, the Puzzle of Conscious Experience and What It Is Like to Be 'Black.'" In *Natural Identities and Sociopolitical Changes in Latin America* (pp. 30-66), edited by Mercedes F. Durán-Cogan and Antonio Gómez-Monaria. New York: Routledge.

————. 2006. "On How We Mistook the Map for the Territory, and Re-Imprisoned Ourselves in Our Unbearable Wrongness of Being, of *Désêtre:* Black Studies Toward the Human Project." In *A Companion to African-American Studies*, edited by Lewis R. Gordon and Jane Anna Gordon. Malden, MA: Blackwell.

Yancy, George, ed. 1998. *African-American Philosophers: 17 Conversations*. New York: Routledge.

————. 2001. *Cornel West: A Critical Reader*. Malden, MA: Blackwell.

————. 2004. *What White Looks Like: African-American Philosophers on the Whiteness Question*. New York: Routledge.

Zack, Naomi. 1994. *Race and Mixed Race*. Philadelphia: Temple University Press.

————. 1995. *American Mixed Race*. Lanham, MD: Rowman and Littlefield.

————. 2001. *Rethinking Mixed Race*.

Zepezauer, Mark. 2002. *Boomerang: How Our Covert Wars Have Created Enemies Across the Middle East and Brought Terror to America*. Monroe, ME: Common Courage Press.

Žižek, Slavoj. 1997a. "Multiculturalism, or the Cultural Logic of Multinational Capitalism," *New Left Review*, no. 225 (September/October): 28-51.

————. 1998. "A Leftist Plea for 'Eurocentrism,'" *Critical Inquiry* 24, no. 4 (Summer): 988-1009.

Žižek, Slavoj, and F.W.J. von Schelling. 1997b. *The Abyss of Freedom/Ages of the World*, translated by Judith Norman. Ann Arbor: University of Michigan Press.

Zuberi, Tukufu, and Elijah Anderson, eds. 2000. Special Commemoration Issue of W. E. B. Du Bois's "The Study of the Negro Problems," *Annals of the American Academy of Social and Political Science* 568, no. 1 (March): 7-316.

Zunes, Stephen. 2002. *Tinderbox: U.S. Middle East Policy and the Roots of Terrorism*. Monroe, ME: Common Courage Press.

Index

Index

Index

Index

Index

About the Editors and Contributors

⊹

David Ross Fryer teaches contemporary religious thought, Continental philosophy, and race, gender, and queer theory at Illinois Wesleyan University. He is the author of *The Intervention of the Other: Levinas and Lacan on Ethical Subjectivity* (Other Press, 2004) and the forthcoming *Thinking Queerly: Essays on Race, Sex, Gender, and the Ethics of Identity* (Paradigm Publishers).

Jane Anna Gordon teaches in the Department of Political Science at Temple University, where she is Associate Director of the Institute for the Study of Race and Social Thought and the Center for Afro-Jewish Studies. She is the author of *Why They Couldn't Wait: A Critique of the Black-Jewish Conflict over Community Control in Ocean-Hill Brownsville, 1967–1971* (Routledge, 2001), which was listed by the *Gotham Gazette* as one of the four best books recently published on Civil Rights, and editor of "Radical Philosophies of Education," a special issue of *Radical Philosophy Review.* She also is co-editor, with Lewis R. Gordon, of *A Companion to African-American Studies* (Blackwell's, 2006).

Lewis R. Gordon is a Laura H. Carnell University Professor of Philosophy and Religion and Director of the Institute for the Study of Race and Social Thought and the Center for Afro-Jewish Studies at Temple University and Ongoing Visiting Professor of Government and Philosophy at the University of the West Indies at Mona, Jamaica. He is the author of several books, including *Her Majesty's Other Children* (Rowman & Littlefield, 1997), which won the Gustavus Myers Award for Outstanding Book on Human Rights, and *Existentia Africana: Understanding Africana Existential Thought* (Routledge,

2000), as well as many articles in Africana studies, philosophy, political theory, religious thought, and literature. He is editor of *Existence in Black: An Anthology of Black Existential Philosophy* (Routledge 1997) and, with Jane Anna Gordon, *A Companion to African-American Studies* (Blackwell's, 2006). He is also President of the Carribean Philosophical Association. He was most recently chairperson of Africana Studies (1999–2003) at Brown University, and he has taught in African-American Studies at Purdue University and Yale University.

Stephen Haymes teaches philosophy of education and sociology of education at DePaul University. From 1999 to 2001 he was a Ford Fellow and visiting scholar at Brown University. Currently, he is working on three manuscripts. The first focuses on the philosophical anthropology of African-American slave culture; the second, on eighteenth-century Africana educational thought; and the third, on African-American collective memory. His book *Race, Culture and the City* was named Outstanding Book on the Subject of Human Rights in North America by the Gustavus Myers Center, Boston University.

Maulana Karenga is Professor of Black Studies at California State University, Long Beach. An activist-scholar, he is Chair of the Organization Us, National Association of Kawaida Organizations and Executive Director of the Kawaida Institute of Pan-African Studies. He is also creator of the pan-African holiday Kwanzaa and author of numerous scholarly articles and books, including *Introduction to Black Studies, Kwanzaa: A Celebration of Family, Community and Culture; Kawaida: A Communitarian African Philosophy; Odu Ifa: The Ethical Teachings; Selections from the Husia: Sacred Wisdom of Ancient Egypt;* and *Maat, The Moral Ideal in Ancient Egypt: A Study in Classical African Ethics.* His fields of teaching and research within Black Studies are Black Studies theory and history, Africana (Continental and Diasporan) philosophy; ancient Egyptian (Maatian) ethics; ancient Yoruba (Ifa) ethics; African-American intellectual history; ethnic relations and the socio-ethical thought of Malcolm X. He is currently writing a book entitled *Malcolm X and the Critique of Domination: An Ethics of Liberation.*

Kenneth Danziger Knies holds the Graduate Council and Presidential fellowships in Philosophy at the State University of New York at

Stony Brook. His areas of focus are phenomenology, philosophy of existence, social and political thought, and Africana studies. His current projects include developing the idea of post-European science as a way into phenomenology and elaborating a descriptive theory of political expression. He has previously taught African-American Studies at the Rhode Island School of Design, and his writings include articles for *The C.L.R. James Journal* and *Radical Philosophy Review.*

Nelson Maldonado-Torres is Assistant Professor of Comparative Ethnic Studies in the Department of Ethnic Studies at the University of California–Berkeley and former Ford Foundation Postdoctoral Fellow in the Center for Global Studies and the Humanities at Duke University. He specializes in Latin American, Latina/o and Africana philosophy, critical theory, theories of religion, and modern religious thought. He works on theories of decolonization as they emerge in different contexts and from different points of view in the Americas. His first book, *Against War: Views from the Underside of Modernity,* is being published by Duke University Press, and, with Ramón Grosfoguel and José David Saldívar, the anthology *Latin@s in the World-System: Decolonization Struggles in the 21st Century U.S. Empire* (Paradigm Publishers, 2005).

Sylvia Wynter is Professor Emerita of Black Studies and Spanish and Portuguese Studies at Stanford University. She also taught at the University of the West Indies at Mona, Jamaica. Wynter is an internationally acclaimed literary theorist, novelist, playwright, and performing artist, and she is known as one of the Caribbean's most prized women of letters. Her writings include several plays and a novel, *The Hills of Hebron* (J. Cape, 1962) and, forthcoming, *The Sylvia Wynter Reader.*